INDIA'S CLAIM FOR HOME RULE

INDIA'S CLAIM FOR HOME RULE

GYAN

Published by

Gyan Publishing House
5, Ansari Road
Daryaganj, New Delhi-110002
Phone: 011-47034999, 9811692060
E-mail: books@gyanbooks.com

Distribution Network
gyanbooks.com
India, USA, Canada, UK, Australia, France

ISBN: 978-81212-8750-0 (PB)
First Published, 1917

2nd Impression 2023

Printed at: Gyan Press, Delhi.

INDIA'S CLAIM FOR HOME RULE

INDIA'S CLAIM FOR HOME RULE

INDIA'S CLAIM FOR HOME RULE

GANESH & CO., MADRAS

"*Has God given to me a greater destiny than this that I become the standard-bearer of my country's honour, that I become the soldier of her cause, the champion of her work, the defender of her glory, the creator of her regenerated power among the Nations of the world:*"

—Mrs. Sarojini Naidu.

PUBLISHERS' NOTE

Herein are collected the speeches and writings of most of the eminent men both Indian and European, expounding with sound arguments "India's Claim for Home Rule."

In the Appendix are given the authoritative pronouncements of persons of high culture and reputation.

An index is added to facilitate reference.

The publishers note with satisfaction that their labours have already been rewarded in the appreciation of their work by no less a person than Dr. Sir S. Subramanya Aiyar, Honorary President, "Home Rule League," to whom they feel grateful.

Their hearty thanks are due to Mr. K. Vyasa Rao for his able introduction.

OLD MAN'S HOPE

Sons of Ind, why sit ye idle,
Wait ye for some Deva's aid?
Buckle to, be up and doing!
Nations by themselves are made!

Yours the land, lives, all, at stake, tho'
Not by you the cards are played;
Are ye dumb? Speak up and claim them!
By themselves are nations made!

What avail your wealth, your learning,
Empty titles, sordid trade?
True self-rule were worth them all!
Nations by themselves are made!

Whispered murmurs darkly creeping,
Hidden worms beneath the glade,
Not by such shall wrong be righted!
Nations by themselves are made!

Sons of Ind, be up and doing,
Let your course by none be stayed;
Lo! the Dawn is in the East;
By themselves are nations made!

A. O. HUME.

INDIA

Robed in mourning crowned with ashes,
Night enshrouded India weeps;
Rolls the storm the lightning flashes,
Still the Nation heedless sleeps.
" Hath," she cries, " this bitter tempest,
Hath this cruel night no end ?
Must pain ever rack this sad breast ?
Will none save me, none befriend ?
Once I reigned the Orient's Empress;
Oh, the glory of that past
Crowned with learning, science, gladness,
Woe is me, too bright to last.
And around me heaven aspiring
Myriad brave sons dauntless trod,
Bowing heart and head to nothing
But their country and their God.
Crownless now, forlorn, I'm weeping,
Dust and ashes all my meed,
Sluggish sons ignobly sleeping,
In a slough of a sluggish greed."
Weep no more, a star is gleaming
In the pearling Eastern skies,
And see thy children long spell-bound dreaming
Hear at last thy call arise.
Weep no more, my love, my glory,
Weep no more, dear Motherland,
See thy children rally round thee
Heart to Heart and hand to hand.

A. O. HUME.

AN APPRECIATION

BY

Dr. SIR S. SUBRAMANYA IYER

Two topics which are uppermost in men's minds at the present time are 'Home Rule' and 'Mr. Montagu's Visit.'

Messrs. Ganesh & Co. have acted most timely in bringing out a volume with the above title which supplies in an eminent degree the sources from which a really adequate knowledge of Home Rule for our country can be easily gathered, by those interested in the subject who are, of course, a vast majority.. These sources include explicit and unmistakable declarations on the subject by leading Indians, Anglo-Indians and British politicians for over thirty years with Dadabhai Naoroji at their head and among others with such well-known names as W. C. Bonerjee, Dr. Sir Rash Behari Ghose, Mr. B. G. Tilak, Khan Bahadur Sarfaraz Hussain Khan, Sir Rabindranath Tagore and Mr. V. P. Madhava Rao among Indians and the late Mr. George Yule and Messrs. Ramsay MacDonald, Wilfrid Blunt, Bernard Shaw, Andrew Carnegie, Sidney Webb, and the Lord Bishop of Calcutta among British leaders of opinion and friends of India.

The unquestionable conclusion that emerges out of the pronouncements thus made at different times by such highly competent authorities points alike to the justice and expediency, nay, the inevitable necessity of granting Home Rule to the Indian people without further lapse of time.

My object however in writing these lines is generally to draw attention to the very valuable collection of the opinions of such eminent authorities, which cannot but be of the utmost interest to every student of Indian politics at the present moment and specially to the full and striking introduction to the volume contributed by Mr. K. Vyasa Rao. The importance of this introduction to my mind consists in the effectual refutation of the prevalent mischievous view now so assiduously sought to be spread that the demand for Home Rule is solely due to a foreign intruder and intrepid agitator, Mrs. Besant without any background whatever in the past history of indegenous politics. The introduction falls under three heads, *viz*:—

1. A new name for an old Demand
2. The authorities and the Demand
3. For and Against.

That even the term Home Rule with reference to India did not originate with Mrs. Besant but with a well-known Indian Mr. Shyamji Krishna Varma who was working for his country long before Mrs. Besant made her appearance on the scene is shown conclusively by the writer in the first section. He proceeds to point out further in the course of this section that the highest credit due to Mrs. Besant—this true friend of India to whom no sacrifice in the interest of her adopted country has been too great—is her having made "Home Rule" a household word throughout the country and the watchword of the Nation within the short period of less than 3 years pursuing all the time absolutely constitutional means and none other. In thus tracing the true history of the word "Home Rule" the author has done real service to our countrymen in enabling them to disprove the false suggestion by the opponents of Home Rule whose sole object is to mislead those in whose hands lie the destinies of India at this critical juncture. Under the second head will be found a most instructive account of the trials aud difficulties which prominent Home Rule leaders like Mr. B. G. Tilak and Mrs. Besant have had to overcome to establish the entire legality and constitutionality of their demand for the Indian people. In the third and the last section the *pros and cons* in regard to the demand for Home Rule are summarised so as to enable the reader to judge for himself as to the preponderance of the authorities on the question.

My sole reason for drawing pointed attention to this volume and the introduction is that the salient point brought out therein should be at the fingers' end of every Home Ruler in order that he may be ready to remove misconception which he may have to encounter in the course of his work as a member of the league and an active worker especially now that Mr. Montagu is in our midst and whom it is so necessary for us to convince of the justice of our demand.

I write these lines as in my judgment as the Honorary President of the League this volume and the introduction in particular are calculated to be helpful to every member of the league in the discharge of his self-imposed task for the Motherland.

CONTENTS

APPENDIX

INTRODUCTION

Sec. I. A NEW NAME FOR AN OLD DEMAND

In bringing out the present publication it is necessary to explain the underlying unity of its contents which otherwise might appear as a disjointed collection of speeches and writings of men of mark in the political world within the British Empire. Self-government for India is no longer a question of speculative politics, but has come within the domain of necessary legislation. Many are the causes that have contributed to this result, but among them the most potent is of course the position of India as revealed by the War that has now entered upon its fourth year. British merits as well as bureaucratic defects have had their share in forcing upon Indians the conviction that nothing can be set right without a substantial and radical change in the principles of Indian Government. This conviction has been arrived at in the course of several years not by a few stray individuals here and there, not by men unknown to British reputation or unhonored by the Bureaucracy; it has grown, on the other hand, with the growth of British Administration in India and has come to embrace the entire area of the mental and moral aspiration of the best sections and classes of the country. Nothing can be a greater mistake than to look upon it as the offspring of a phantasy, as an artificial craving created by the meretricious eloquence of an enchantress, by the siren voice of a gifted self-seeking demogogue, of a seasoned and vainglorious adventurer, as some have sought to convey it, identifying the demand for Home Rule with Mrs. Besant and describing her as an enchantress, demogogue and adventurer. At the outset one may admit that the systematic and determined application of the term "Home Rule" we owe to Mrs. Besant conspicuously more than to anybody else. But that in no way means that the problem of Home Rule for India is not older than about twenty-four months. Mr. Shyamji Krishna Varma fourteen years back chalked out a plan of "Home Rule" which soon became however, a movement for Indian Independence. Political terms may vary, political ideals may also vary, while political facts more or less remain the same. This great truth, great not in being too complex for understanding, but great in its bearings and consequences, should not be ignored by those who look upon Mrs. Besant's Home Rule propaganda as the importation of an attractive foreign luxury to the pretentions of which Indians have succumbed without so much as a passing thought. They seem to think that but for the term Home Rule, Indians would have been fast asleep and would have made no demand for a radical change in the present system of Government in India. How untenable, how utterly false this is, will become evident by a perusal of the contents of this volume.

As we said, political terms vary, party nomenclature and party denominations vary almost without an intelligible explanation therefor, while political facts may remain the same. When Mrs. Besant took to Indian politics, she saw that "Self-government within the Empire," or "Colonial Self-government" as a political party word was too cumbrous and without sufficient rallying power. She saw that what was wanted was a word with vitality; a word that could convey the character of the party and the nature of the demand by it. Mr. Shyamji Krishna Varma, who had used it, crossed the boundary line and made his movement a movement for Indian Independence. "Colonial Self-government" that became so prominent as an outcome of the Surat split a few years later was too flabby as a political expression and not quite accurate either. For one thing, there is no such thing as Colonial Self-government in general, each colony having its particular form and each form still being in a process of development. Then again, there is no merit in making much of the fact that while the Colonies have Self-government, not so India. The Colonies, except South Africa, are in fact a part of the United Kingdom for all practical purposes; they are all peopled by Britishers who have settled down in the Colonies and who in doing so may be considered as having taken their political instincts with them. Indians may well ask to be treated on the footing of colonials, if the latter are a race foreign to Great Britain as Indians are. What we therefore really want is a form of Self-government, suited to our own conditions and capable of expansion as these conditions change and not colonial government which in fact means nothing definite. The term colonial Self-government came into use at a time when Indian politicians were anxious to convey that they did not want separation from England, but union with England on the footing of the Colonies. Not that they wanted to escape a prosecution for sedition, but they wanted to be clear beyond mistake in the eyes of their political critics and opponents.

"Swaraj" had come into existence no doubt some time previously and had been upheld by judicial pronouncement and sanctified by the Patriarch of Indian politics Dadabhai Naoroji. But "Swaraj" born at a time of national upheavel, as a repelling force against a particularly offensive exercise of the autocratic powers vested in the Governors-General in Council, having a historic background in the national hymns and songs of the country, and sinking deep in the national mind as an aspiration, instead of acting as the mustercall of a party of politicians, is fit more for appeal than for party nomenclature. Mrs. Besant, with her quick perception of the need for party names and watchwords, knew that to an Englishman "Swaraj" would necessarily take a lot of explaining. She knew that in spite of judicial pronouncements and in spite of its adoption by Dadabhai Naoroji, "Swaraj" as an active *propagandic* party-word would lend itself to misinterpretations by unscrupulous opponents in power. "Home Rule," on the other hand, has a historical record as a political expression; it cannot be twisted to mean "separation," "Independence" or Freedom from ulterior control; its history is still a current and unconcluded chapter of British politics; its use cannot be dispensed with in spite of the War and the problem of Home Rule for Ireland is being attempted to be solved even as the War is going on. The only objection that could be taken to its use in connection with India now is that what might become inevitable in regard to Ireland at this moment may be deferred for consideration to a more convenient time in regard to India. But if the whole Empire has undergone a great change in its outlook and if British statesmen have been the foremost factor of influence in anticipating post-War changes and reforms in a variety of Imperial concerns of vast import to the future of the Empire, it is carrying punctiliousness to an insufferable degree of absurdity to say that the people of India alone must place themselves under a self-denying ordinance and ought to scrupulously refrain from adverting to their status in the Empire. That status has reference to the position of the people of India firstly in their own country and secondly outside the limits of India but within the limits of the Empire. To connote that status by a political term, incapable of being mistaken or distorted, Mrs. Besant had to fall back upon so-well understood a party word and political expression as "Home Rule" and founded the Home Rule League with the assent of a large section of Hindu and Moslem politicians of note and this section since her internment has become co-terminous with Political India, excluding a small section of protogonists of the Bureaucracy, completely out of touch with and discredited by their countrymen. Had the Home Rule propaganda been a matter of yesterday's origin, not simply in its name, but in its substance as well, it would have been impossible for it to become a factor of such consequence in the politics of the country as it has become.

We have referred to the circumstances under which the term Home Rule has come into use to correct the wrong impression that, but for Mrs. Besant, the demand for post-War reforms would have been scarcely heard of or quite languidly pursued, so that Anglo-India would not have been hustled out of its bed until the last shot on all the frontiers had been discharged and the era of lasting peace ushered in. There need be no hesitation, however, in all India gratefully acknowledging the ardent and unsparing devotion, the intense application and zeal with which Mrs. Besant has worked for the cause of Indian political advancement at a critical period in its history. And this acknowledgment need not be made in a halting spirit or in a half-hearted manner, lest we should deprive the long course of Indian agitation for Self-government of its inherent merit and independent value. The acknowledgment of what the country owes to Mrs. Besant for her labours during the last two years particularly, need not amount to an indirect depreciation of what the country has laboured for the last thirty years directly for representative institutions in India. These labours she has herself amply and in her own splendid way portrayed in her book "How India wrought for Freedom." But for these years of labour by Indians, with the assistance, every now and then, of large hearted, true-spirited British men and women, it would have been impossible even for Mrs. Besant to cross the path of the Bureaucracy. Without her aid, —although she was even then a great organising force in India and had a considerable following of wealth, culture, and enthusiasm,—crucial questions of great moment, test questions of the rights of the Indian Nation as against the arbitrariness of the Bureaucracy had been fought and won. In the withdrawal, at the last resort, of the Punjab Colonisation Bill at the insistence of Lord Kitchener,—that man of unerring prescience, as firm footed in statesmanship as he was great in Military organisation,—in the annulling of the partition of Bengal at the instance of one of the greatest Trustees of British interests sent out to India, in the modification of the oppressive and unholy ordinances of the South African States against Indian subjects of the Crown, not to go back to earlier episodes as the revocation of the plague policy of the Bombay Government, where was the help of Mrs. Besant's powers of agitation and organisation? To go back even to much earlier events, was not Indian power of organization up to the required standard to impel Lord Salisbury to recognise the justice and policy of the Rendition of Mysore to its rightful sovereign? And was it done without Indians urging their case for justice and the vested official and non-official European interests opposing the step with all the weapons of offence and defence which they know so well to use and have never flinched to use? To attribute to Mrs. Besant the output of the demand for post-War Reforms is to ignore that just before the War broke out, and particularly after the Delhi announcements in 1911 December, Indian opinion was concentrating on the promised grant of Provincial Autonomy from which there was a clear attempt to back out a process that was accomplished thereafter, by a tacit understanding among the Party leaders in England. The British wheel easily lends itself to spokes being put as a matter of mere party pastime, party prestige and party pleasure. The promise of Provincial Autonomy was caught in this wheel and Indian opinion was anxiously concerned in rescuing the promise from a noiseless end, amidst the distractions of the South African Imbroglio, the Mahomedan preoccupation on account of the Balkhan War, the inexpiable outrage on Lord Hardinge and the gloom that it cast all over the country, followed sometime after by the death of his noble lady to whom India will always cherish a respectful affection as it does to the heroines of her Pantheon like Sita and Savitri. When the War broke out, to add to all other anxieties, Indian representatives in the Imperial and Provincial Councils begged the Government to make the fullest and freest use of India's resources in the conduct of the War, so that it might be terminated as quickly as possible and with victory to the allies. Numerous public meetings were held spontaneously and contributions to War Funds poured in. Voluntarily, princes and peoples, provinces and states vied with one another in sharing what India could do in the hour of peril to England and the Empire. All these do not show that Indians wanted to embarrass the Government. But when it became known that the Government of India was sending despatches behind the back of the public so to say on the post-War schemes it was found necessary that the public should place their side of the case. It was soon after this that active support had to be canvassed for the popular view and a conflict between the Bureaucracy and the public became inevitable as the latter could not become a different body simply on account of the War. The angle of vision of England may change, but not that of the Bureaucracy. It did not give up for these three years its exodus, it asked for and obtained after the outbreak of the War compensation in money for lack of promotion, because European officials could not go on leave. It heard with concern the encomiums of the Prime Minister promising a new dawn even for India; it followed one policy of "business as usual" in regard to one set of matters, as in the case of the exodus; it followed the policy of "not until the end of the War" in regard to others; but it followed neither maxim if it was a matter of compensation for the service or of creating costly special appointments for lucky Europeans. How can one possibly have confidence in such a body to obtain for this country its due after the War? Is it meant to be implied that a country which so well knows the Bureaucracy and has obtained whatever modicum of British justice it has over the head of the Bureaucracy, with the evidence of the Civil Service before the Public Services Commission as an eye opener, that such a country can go into a mesmeric trance, leaving its destiny into the hands of the Bureaucracy? It is therefore unspeakably absurd from every point of view to attribute the output of the agitation to Mrs. Besant, while we do not deny that she has entitled herself to the gratitude of the country by her strenuous labours on our behalf during the last two years.

One point alone is enough to bring out our position here; whatever may be attributed to Mrs. Besant's activities, the moment she was interned and rendered tongueless and penless, the Home Rule propaganda must have been scotched if not killed were the contention and the reading of the authorities correct. On the other hand it was no European that came forward to administer artificial respiration to a dying cause; it was no one from another part of the country that rushed to the first aid of the patient; it was a man of the Presidency itself, Dr. Sir Subramanya Iyer, full of years and honors, five years older than the Bibilical three score and ten, who had served Queen Victoria, King Edward and King George as one of their judges; an ardent Congressman who had been present as a delegate at its very first session and taken prominent part in its conduct; who, when Lord Ripon's scheme of Municipal expansion was promulgated for adoption, had incurred the displeasure of the local executive for not consenting to repudiate its desirability or need, but had the disconcerting candour to welcome it with open arms and waxed eloquent over its liberal and far sighted character; who should have adorned the Presidential chair of the Congress long ago but for his official robes as a judge, and for his growing age and physical weakness after retirement from office; who, after the outbreak of the War in the Congress Session of 1914, acted as the spokesman of South India in welcoming the delegates and opening its proceedings as the chairman of the Reception Committee; it was he, with a frail body, a lustrous expression, and a refulgent impulse that lit up the country with a single ray of light that beamed right across a thick, moist atmosphere of gloom, doubt and vacillation. He stood out against the action of the local Government as an embodied spiritual belief in the ultimate vindication of the higher justice of the British Sovereign and the British Nation. He did so in his capacity as President of the Home Rule League. His letter which rivetted the nation, as though by a moral spell, to its duty as against all extraneous authority ran as follows :—

"To my countrymen! We have all read the speech of H.E. the Governorof Madras to his Legislative Council, in which he foreshadows measures for the suppression of the Home Rule Propaganda, and asks for the support, in the measures taken, of all who have personal or hereditary influence. I answer that appeal, being a responsible public man, having held high judicial office in the State, having been recognised and rewarded by the Crown and honoured by my University, and being an old man, of trained caution in coming to a decision, and of mature judgment. I therefore think that it is my duty to the Government to state my position. Before I was raised to the Bench, I was a Congressman, and to me, Self-Government or Home Rule is no new thing. I believe and have long believed, that its early establishment is vital for the welfare of the country and the stability of the Empire, and that it is therefore necessary to carry on a constitutional and educative agitation for it, as ordered by the Congress at its last session. Believing thus I gladly accepted the Honorary Presidentship of the Home Rule for India League, Honorary only because my health forbids active and strenuous work. I cannot retrace my steps; I will not resign my office even if the League be declared unlawful. I am ready to face any penalties which may follow on my decision, for I believe that the time has come when God, in whose hands are all earthly Governments calls on India to assert that right to Freedom which He has given, and to claim Self-Rule in the words of the Congress—in the reconstruction of the Empire after the War. To defend Home Rule is to me a religious as well as a civic duty and this duty I will discharge. I call on you, my countrymen to do the same."

But for the stand he then took, at a time when no one anticipated the appointment of Mr. Montagu as Secretary for India, on the rights of a British subject, the feeling of disgust and disaffection created by the application of a War measure to a woman, and to a woman who had ardently supported the Government in all its measures for the prosecution of the War and which came as a blow against constitutional agitation, would have found vent in some cases at least in the adoption of counsels born of despair. The lead that so spontaneously emanated from Sir Subramanya Iyer as a reflex action in the body politic would have proved, however, of little consequence had there not been a volume of public feeling which responded to the lead in the same spirit, prepared openly to take all risks involved in doing so. But for these two factors the triumph of the party of constitutional agitation as against the unconstitutional action of the Bureaucracy in this respect would have been difficult of attainment, in spite of the fact that Mrs. Besant is a British woman with a reputation on both sides of the Atlantic. To look upon the Home Rule movement as a mere creation of a restless spirit which suddenly took to political turmoil and agitation is to seek to wipe off in fact the political history of India, if not from the time of Raja Ram Mohun Roy, from the time of Dadabhai Naoroji at any rate ; and to deny

India's Claim to Self-government because of the word Home Rule, or because of Mrs. Besant's entry into Indian politics, is to dispose of the destiny of India in a supremely easy and affable way indeed.

Sec. II. THE AUTHORITIES AND THE DEMAND

We have shown that the demand for Home Rule is not a two-year old baby born of the travail of a restless ambition and sprung into the political world with the deliberate malignant purpose of embarrassing the authorities. A Government that feels unequal to be embarrassed with a problem that has been before it for over a generation and especially at a time when the entire imperial structure is under a survey for better adaptation to present-day conditions may as well complain of the legitimate demands made upon it, if not in the way of constructive effort, at least in regard to a policy of patience and non-interference. This accusation of embarrassing, brought against the leaders of political thought and public movements after the whole country had shown how impossible it was to make any distinction between England and India on the score of loyalty, is an apt exhibition of the attitude of the Bureaucracy towards constitutional expansion. Nor was it simply a mere exhibition, stopping short of an actual attempt to arrest the march of progress by construing the demand for a change in the form of Government as an act of disloyalty. The District Magistrate of Poona, acting on behalf of the Government of Bombay, took proceedings against Mr. Tilak on the express ground that his speeches advocating Home Rule amounted to sedition against Government established by law in India. In finally ordering him to enter into a bond the Magistrate observed that "Mr. Tilak should consider himself very fortunate that the Government did not intend to proceed against him under the substantive section 124-A. Indian Penal Code." Mr. Tilak's speeches delivered in Marathi and reported in English attracted at the time attention mainly on the ground that he drew a most scrupulous distinction between Government established by law and the machinery of administration which was sought to be reformed. He showed at every step how the form of Government might and has to change from time to time, the sovereignty of Great Britain over India remaining the same. His penetrating and masterly analysis, then and there in the course of his speeches, of the law of sedition as applicable to the demand he was making showed how cautious and wary he had determined to be in handling a subject so risky for one who had become the pet solicitude of the local Government. He asked if it was sedition to demand that the District Magistrate should not also be the head of the police or that the legislature must have an elected majority of the representatives of the people or that the executive should become responsible to it? In all these where is it sought to take away the power of the Crown or to create disaffection against Government established by law? Nevertheless, the perpetual plan of a dominant section of the Bureaucracy has been to identify the bureaucratic form with Government established by law. Is Government established by law once for all and for eternity established? If so, it must be no more than an axis for varying forms of administration. Yet, soon after the high-minded influence of Lord Hardinge was withdrawn from the country, the Government of Bombay sought to penalise by the application of the provisions of the Code of Criminal Procedure a demand for a form of Government that will no longer be the present bureaucratic form. Mr. Tilak appealed to the High Court of Bombay against the order of the Government. The judgment of the Bombay High Court once again showed where Great Britain's constitutional safeguard lies in India. The conviction was quashed and Mr. Tilak's position was upheld in the decision of the Court. This judgment is of course not a new charter; but, on account of the clearness of the issues raised and definitely and unmistakably decided, it is as good as an additional charter to the expanding liberties of India. One should rather be glad than sorry that the Bombay Government chose to give battle in a way worthy of the better traditions, as they go, of the Indian Bureaucracy, and in a manner in this respect at least worthy of its foeman's steel. It is a great relief to know the boundaries that divide permissible from illegal agitation, the demarkation between a demand that the strictest interpretation of the law will countenance and the widest benefit of the doubt to the accused cannot condone. For one thing it was a legal process that the Government of Bombay preferred to resort to. Had it, on the other hand, taken any other course of action outside the pale of the law, or had the High Court of Judicature, like the subordinate branch of the judiciary, been a part and parcel of the executive, or had it chosen to forget its role as an arbitrator between the people and those in authority over them, the result might have been disastrous for the prestige of British Rule and for the peace and tranquillity in Western India. The result of the decision has only shown that after all there is room enough for the aspirations of the people and the necessary powers of the executive to co-exist in a British province.

In the Southern Presidency, on the other hand, the Government, having had the benefit of what took place in Bombay and in view of its own admission in regard to the legitimacy of the demand for Home Rule, gave a wide berth to the test of law courts in seeking to give effect to its repressive attitude. When it took action under the Press Act against Mrs. Besant as keeper of "New India" Press in 1916, it had necessarily to admit that to Home Rule, *per se*, there was no objection. The Hon. the Advocate General, under instruction from the Government, made a formal declaration that he did not object "to any Home Rule propaganda as such." His Lordship the Acting Chief Justice who was one of the Special Bench that heard the petition of Mrs. Besant went further in accepting the admission of the Advocate General and laid down :—

" It is difficult to see how any such movement " (for Home Rule) " can be regarded as illegal *per se*. It lies entirely with the Sovereign, that is in the compendious phrase of Dr. Dicey, the King in Parliament, to establish any Government he chooses for India or any other part of the British Empire. There can be nothing wrong, therefore, in a subject of the Crown urging the desirability of a change in the machinery of the Government of India. Changes in the constitution of the Government do take place from time to time with the consent of the sanction of the Sovereign. In certain stages of the society reforms in the constitution of the Government are a bilogical, political necessity. To say that such questions are not open to public discussion, supposing the law is not violated in the manner and method adopted in such discussion, would be opposed to all sound maxims of constitutional law."

The Madras Government, therefore, both by its admission and the enunciation of the law which it elicited from the Hon. the Chief Justice was precluded from questioning the legality of the Home Rule demand at a later period. But it failed to see what this executive admission and the judicial enunciation alike clearly lead to. In the first place, if Home Rule is a legitimate and lawful demand, it cannot be made without assigning reasons for advocating the desired change in the constitution. These reasons must perforce have reference to the defects and drawbacks of the form of Government which a Home Rule form is to displace. When however, such drawbacks and defects are pointed out it is strange consistency indeed for the executive to turn round and say " you are depriving us of our escutcheon, robbing us of our character and creating disaffection against us in the public mind." Lord Hardinge who realised that no ideal can be brought to fruition except by effort and agitation spoke of the "*National*" ideal of Self-government for India as "*a perfectly legitimate agitation* having the warm sympathy of all moderate men." No one would advocate that if these defects and drawbacks are pointed out in a manner that will endanger public peace, the authorities should sit quite and tolerate such an abuse of the liberty of criticism. Instead of alleging that the leaders of the Home Rule party were guilty of such conduct either on the platform or in the public press and taking steps under the law for obtaining a legal conviction, the Madras Government threw from the top of the blue hills a veritable bolt, that produced panic and dismay thoughout the presidency, adjuring the country "to put out of thought" all ideas of self-Government in the post-War constitutional changes.* This warning was a fortnight later, followed by the application of the Defence of

* At a meeting of the Legislative Council held at Ootacamund, on the 22nd May, Lord Pentland made a most unexpected pronouncement on the dangers of an agitation for Self-government and said "All thoughts of the early grant of responsible Self-government should be put entirely out of mind and all violence of language should be condemned. * * On behalf of my Government, I call upon all who hear me or read these words for their support in any action which the Government may be forced to take to discourage these unwise and dangerous methods and the extravagant aims which they are designed to further."

India Act to Mrs. Besant and two of her associates. One need not be concerned here with all that followed the speech of Lord Pentland on the 22nd May 1917 and the order of internment issued on the 16th June following. The attempts made by some of the authorities to canvas support for the success of the repressive policy by trying to secure silent acquiescence in quarters from which initial opposition was anticipated; the declarations and manifestoes in its favour which found their way into the Press from others which had remained absolutely apathetic in matters political till then and from persons who had not raised their little finger till then in the redress of a single wrong, in the reform of a single abuse, in the removal of a single anomaly; the demoralization that followed this singularly instructive and amusing outturn and the widening of the clevages of caste and racial distinctions that it led to, are matters over which one may well afford to draw a veil. Nor need we recall the white heat of public excitement that went up steadily in temperature week by week and month by month, until at last the country, led by men of no insignificant status, was openly prepared to embark upon a course of lawful resistance to a situation to which there was no other remedy. What is pregnant with meaning to British statesmen in this connection, however, is the restoration of absolute tranquillity that immediately succeeded the cancellation of the arbitrary orders of internment. The allegation made by the supporters of the action of the executive, was that Mrs. Besant's release would be a blow to public peace; but not even a child can make any mistake now after the annulment of the order whether the blow to public peace was the internment or the release. The country now seems to have gone back to rest on the lap of peace, amity and goodwill to work waking up in a sweetened temper of restored confidence and refilled trust. In fact it has fallen, as has been observed, to the most prosaic work of collecting signatures to monster memorials. The magnificient ovation that greeted Mrs. Besant and Messrs. Wadia and Arundale on their return to Madras could not have been organised by any number of political associations or Theosophical bodies. It was indeed an outburst of national sentiment transcending the barriers of race and colour, of religion and alien birth. Without any attempt whatsoever to organise a demonstration, there was such a stupendous wave of enthusiasm among all classes, and castes impelled by the one desire of showing the identity of public feeling with the cause for which they had suffered executive displeasure. It was an unprecedented reception that so spontaneously awaited them and it was repeated beyond all anticipation in far off Calcutta, Allahabad and Bombay. The public feeling, especially in Madras, which had become so alienated from the executive, partly on account of the arbitrary nature of its action, and partly on account of the ways and means by which some men in power had sought support in favour of that action at the expense of long-standing social amity and harmony between persons and castes, wanted by one supreme, splendid and spontaneous testimony to furnish an unforgettable record of its conclusive judgment in regard to the policy and action of the Government. Mrs. Besant's unanimous election to the presidentship of the Congress session of 1917, was another immediate result of the blunder of the executive. Although, after the close identity which Mrs. Besant had established between her vast resources, mental, moral and financial and the political good of India, her election would have been certain sooner or later, her choice to the Congress presidency of the session immediately following the internment was the direct outcome of Anglo-Indian statemanship, inspired on one side by the Anglo-Indian press and counselled on the other side by a few exponents of caste and race antoganism. In fact, if the Madras Government in its unmatched wisdom, wanted to make her an irresistable power with the people, and hers a name venerated by men and women of all grades and ranks, a triumphant war cry with the populace, a guarantee of sterling worth and value with the substantial monied and middle classes and the educated community in general, a name held dear by Indian women and lovingly lisped by many a child,—the Government of Madras could have scarcely done better. Those who differed from her in honest difference and hesitated not to avow that difference and who resented the reference that they had become converts to Home Rule were the first and foremost to recognize that Mrs. Besant's position had passed from leadership the authorities disliked to established ascendency over the public mind. Not to have anticipated all these results, shows a melancholy lack of foresight even of an inferior order, such as one has a right to expect, even of a Provincial Indian Bureaucracy. The mistake of the Government might have been a bona fide mistake according to a generous view of the matter; but the support assiduously stimulated for its action to make it appear that it was supposed to represent public feeling could by no means be bona fide, since it has proved an abject failure, or at any rate a lamentable miscarriage of expectations and an egregious misreading of the public mind.

We have only to imagine the effect that would have been produced, had the statement by His Majesty's ministers in Parliament been made without the strain on the public mind brought about by Lord Pentland's speech, the order of internment, and all the events that in natural sequence followed it. That speech, however, was not an isolated factor in creating the impression that there was a deliberate attempt to stifle the demand for post-War reforms of a substantial nature. Almost every provincial head of Government thought it necessary and becoming to appropriate to himself a part of the function that belonged only to His Majesty and his ministers; and subordinate officials, high and low, Indian and European, here and there began to take and exercise the powers of a miniature local Government. All these unprovoked, uncalled for and out of the way declarations of policy and exercise of authority, bearing a very close resemblance in their objective, having for their common concern the Home Rule propaganda, and following a Circular on the subject issued by the Government of India left no doubt that there was a systematic attempt to thwart the voice of the Nation being heard by the King in Parliament. The Government of India admitted in August 1917 in answer to an interpellation subsequent to Mr. Montagu's statement in the House of Commons that they had issued a Circular on the subject of Home Rule to local Governments about April 1917. They, however, refused to disclose its terms. Nevertheless, seeing what every provincial head from about that period to Mr. Montagu's assumption of office as Secretary of State for India had to say on the subject, there is no way of failing to know what the Circular should have been in the main.

The whole country was ablaze with a feeling of chagrin at what was taking place and when these declarations of policy terminated in muzzling Mrs. Besant, there was created a situation which would have been dangerous at any time but which at the present period would have been positively a misfortune. Had not Providence, which has always been for strengthening the bonds between England and India, brought about the Mesopotamian muddle for affording a most timely solution of a particularly difficult situation in the Indian Empire, the history of events in recent months would have thrown no little concern on British statesmen. If, on the other hand, all these had been avoided, and if the Government of India had not taken the initiative in the policy of blunder which was so faithfully followed by the provincial authorities subsequently; and if, through their instrumentality, before the Mesopotomian debate lifted the veil over the wooden anachronism, the Government of India had caused the enunciation of such a policy as fell from Mr. Montagu,—what a state of happy family relationship would not have been disclosed between the authorities and the people! They, in a fit of short-sightedness, however, did all that ought not to have been done, did it all in a way the public suspected but had no authentic knowledge of, left it to each local Government to come out with its story and issue a most arbitrary mandate under the cover of a War measure, and were silent expectators of an epidemic of caste and race antagonism, and when after all the inevitable consequences of such a thoughtless, and repressive attitude had made themselves abundantly manifest, the task was left for the higher insight of the custodians of imperial interests to rectify a whole chapter of blunders in as dignified a manner as might be possible!

Our main purpose, however, is to note that after the outbreak of the War, firstly the decision of the Bombay High Court, secondly the observations, of the Madras High Court and thirdly the declaration by His Majesty's Government through the Secretary of State in Parliament followed by the Governor-General's notification in India, taken together in conjunction with the attended circumstances in each case, constitute the emergence of the old demand of Self-government for India under a new name into the region of practical politics, triumphing over the barricades of the executive and the entanglements put up by its co-adjutors bound only by ties of race contempt and caste feeling.

Sec. III. FOR AND AGAINST

Among those who have laboured in the cause of a united political India, under the ægis of Great Britain, managing its own resources and rendering unto Cæsar what is Cæsar's, the name of Dadhabhai Naoroji will stand foremost. Beginning his association with the affairs of the country when the East India Company was the ruling power, he lived through all the intervening period working for this cause, and died a few months before the declaration made in the House of Commons by Mr. Montagu as Secretary of State. He arrived at the conclusion that the only solution alike for the poverty of India and for evolving a lasting connection between England and India would be the grant of internal autonomy for this country. Had such a step been taken even about the time of Lord Ripon's Viceroyalty, there would have been to-day, after three decades of Indian Home Rule, not a mere dependency, not either a colonial sapling or a mere offshoot of the parent stock, but a great continent peopled by a sixth of the human race as an integral part of the Empire of Great Britain, acting as a full-grown ally, not as America at so late an hour, nor as Japan in so necessarily an inadequate a measure, but from the very commencement of the War as a belligerant whose integrity and independence were as much in danger of violation as England's. However, what should have been granted during Lord Ripon's Viceroyalty came to be demanded from that period and that demand has not yet got over the initial opposition of the executive in India! In 1906, after Lord Curzon had left India as the victim of the wildest pretensions of bureaucratic governance, Mr. Dadhabhai Naoroji gave vent to his feeling in regard to England's irresponsibility towards India in these words ;—

"Since my early efforts I must say that I have felt so many disappointments as would be sufficient to break any heart and lead on to despair, and even, I am afraid, to rebel."

He reiterated his political conviction that had become a religious creed with him as his abiding admonition to England and India in these three paragraphs of crystal clearness :—

(1) "Instead of going into further divisions of details of our rights as British citizens, the whole matter can be comprised in one word 'Self-government' or 'Swaraj' like that of the United Kingdom or the Colonies."

(2) "In the short life that may yet be vouchsafed to me I hope to see a loyal, honest, honourable and conscientious adoption of the policy of Self-government for India and a beginning made at once towards that end."

(3) "If India is allowed to be prosperous by Self-government, what a vista of glory and benefits opens up

for the citizens of the British Empire and for mankind as an example and proof of supremacy of the moral law."

From 1906 to the hour of his death in 1917, he lived in constant hopes of such a declaration being made, especially after the outbreak of the War in 1914. But Mr. Montagu's statement was made only a few months after the great patriarch of a Self-governing India under British paramountcy had gone to his eternal rest, or rather to begin a new cycle of enduring benevolence to humanity.

It is not only Dadabhai Naoroji who amongst the first batch of modern Indians found the solution of India's political future under a system of Self-government. Mr. W. C. Bonnerjee, who was 19 years younger than Naoroji but who unfortunately died a few months before the Congress Session of 1906, said in one pregnant sentence so early as 1885 :—

"All we ask is that the basis of the Government shall be widened and that the people shall have their proper legitimate share in it."

Later in 1892, he made himself clear in as simple a language as possible by defining the national ambition of India as a desire for "the same facilities of national life that exist in Great Britain itself."

Those were days when the expression Colonial-government had not come into use and Mr. Bonnerjee's dictum better expresses, in fact, our need than anything that has been stated since then. Facilities of national life as existing in Great Britain are to-day insisted upon as the minimum ideal of political existence by British statesmen for *foreign* countries under autocracy, and they cannot exclude India from the benefit of such an insistence.

Another great man, one too old to be disposed of as an impatient idealist, who is now fully three score and ten in age, by no means an agitator even of an occasional type, but one of the most profound and best equipped jurists in the British Empire, Dr. Sir Rash Behari Ghose has stated India's claim as follows:—

"We want in reality and not in mere name to be sons of the Empire. Our ambition is to draw closer to England and to be absorbed in that Greater Britain in which we have now no place. The ideal after which we are striving is autonomy within the Empire and not absolute independence."

It is to this drawing closer, this absorption in Greater Britain which can only become possible by India securing complete internal autonomy that the executive as a matter of sheer self-interest has been strenuously opposed at every era of reform and reconstruction.

The late Mr. G. Subramanya Iyer, who died in his 63rd year, after having laboured for four continuous decades in building up the power of the press and of public opinion in Southern India, to whose early training several Indian journals at the present day owe their talented and tenacious editors, was guided during his 40 years of public and journalistic life by these political postulates:—

(1) That India should never think of separation from England;

(2) That we must make the British Parliament commit themselves to an open declaration that India will be made a self-governing part of the Empire within a definite time, followed by an initial instalment of reforms towards such an end.

(3) That in trying to obtain such a declaration and an initial instalment of reforms we should be prepared for the hand of the Civil Service with all its resources to be raised against us at every step throughout the period of our constitutional fight. .

He was of the deep-rooted conviction that our work must be carried on with our own masses and the British people in their own country. Trusting to the Civil Service you will get nothing but the prolongation of the *status quo*. So late as 1916 just a few weeks before his lamented death when the present writer asked him what we should concentrate upon as our post-War reform, he said raising his short thick finger with a vivacity that came as a great surprise in his touching condition of health "They must fix a time and say we will make India a Self-governing country before that time—and they must proceed to formulate their first plan of reform. Our salvation is only in such a course—and they should have no peace from our agitation until they do it." This was his last will and testament, not signed and delivered into the keeping of official and semi-official personages, but orally delivered in the spirit of *a message to his own country-*

men. He laid the utmost stress on the object of British Rule being formally and statutorily declared as that of raising India to the footing of a self-governing country. He attached far greater importance to such a formal declaration than to any scheme of reforms, however liberal, which avoided it. His object was that not until it became plain to the Civil Service that they have to give up governing India within a particular period would they ever care to co-operate in the formulation of future schemes of reform as the country becomes fit for them, or to work any scheme honestly to our best advantage. He looked to the purpose of British Rule being unmistakably expressed as a binding statutory provision—so that the authorities here will prepare themselves for handing over their responsibilities, retaining such control as may be necessary in imperial interests and in all cases of mismanagement or misdirection. He lived his life to instil this lesson into the minds of his countrymen and had to pay the penalty of transgressing the law of sedition as demanded by the authorities. His whole life stands before the writer as an example of the three political postulates given above.

Many more equally worthy Indian names, which would easily occur to the reader from the rank of non-officials, may be quoted, but for want of space we find room here for a few statements from men who have been all their lives burdened with official responsibility and who have risen to official and administrative eminence in Native States or British India. Among such the name of Mr. V. P. Madhava Row, C. I. E., who is past sixty five and who shares with his illustrious predecessor Rajah Sir. T. Madhava Row the distinction of having administered three Native States, is pre-eminent.

Presiding over the Madras Provincial Conference in May 1917, just a few weeks before Mrs. Besant's internment he stated categorically :—

(1) " The Bureaucracy has been tried and been found wanting. We must now ask to be brought face to face with the British democracy, who should take up our case and free us from the rule of the Bureaucracy. The Bureaucracy has stood between us and the British nation and should be told to step aside and allow us to place our case before the supreme authority in England."

(2) " If the Bureaucracy had discharged its trust properly and endeavoured to carry out the policy of the British nation, that India must be governed solely for the benefit of the Indians and that Indians should be trained for occupying all positions of trust and responsibility, we should have the expedition to Mesopotamia entrusted to an Indian, say a man like the Maharajah of Bikhanir, and Indians made largely responsible for the mobilization of resources in money and material which the Viceroy has so graphically described in his speech at Lahore. As it is, we have the privilege of supplying fighting men, camp followers, munitions and food-stuffs, supplies and stores, but their ordering is all in the hands of the Bureaucracy. This was not so in the times of the Indian Rajahs and Padshaws of old."

(3) "The Bureaucracy has neglected and mismanaged things so badly that when a crisis like the present war

arises India in spite of her earnest desire for giving every support to the mother country finds herself unable to do all she can in helping England in men and material. This aspect of the question has been well brought out in General Sir O'Moore Creagh's letter where he says that if the provincial autonomy recommended by Lord Hardinge in 1911 had been granted the help would have been immensely greater. The fact is, the Bureaucracy will not allow full scope being given to the schemes of Self-government even as they are. We have now arrived at a crisis when the whole question will have to be thoroughly gone into and settled once for all. Just as after the mutiny the British nation took away the Government from the hands of the Company, so now, they will have to replace the Bureaucracy by popular institutions and entrust the administration to the people themselves under the suzerainty of the British nation. How this should be done is a matter which Parliament is best qualified to decide. But this much we may safely venture to say that any reform to be made should aim at a complete change in the character of the Government and there should be no such thing as a gradual extension of Self-government."

These observations by one who has himself been looked upon as more or less a member of the Bureaucracy, must carry weight with those who may easily dismiss with a wave of the hand anything said to the prejudice of the bureaucratic form of Government as being no longer suitable to the changed condition of the country. When one remembers that Mr. Madhava Row for the first time instituted a Popular Assembly in the Native State of Travancore and established a Legislative Council with nonofficial members on it in the State of Mysore, one cannot explain away Mr. Madhava Row's courageous verdict as the outcome of a desire to embarrass the Government, after ceasing to be a bureaucrat himself.

To these pointed remarks of a distinguished Hindu statesman we may add the considered convictions of an eminent Mahomedan official, a member of the statutory Civil Service of Behar, Khan Bahadur Sarfraz Hussain Khan. Presiding at the latest Behar Provincial Conference, he made the following lucid observations:—

"For years I gave the best of what God has given me to loyal co-operation with those in whose hands Providence has placed our destinies, but I feel bound to confess that of late the conviction has been growing upon me more and more that while co-operation with the officials is good, self-dependence and self-reliance are even better and that while good Government, such as has been established in this country by our British fellow-subjects, is to be appreciated and supported, yet Self-Government for India within the Empire would be even immeasurably better and should, therefore, be sought after by every constitutional means at our disposal. It is in the fulness of this conviction that I stand before you to-day as an avowed Home Ruler so that the few years that may yet be vouchsafed to me by Providence may be devoted to the service of my Motherland. I fear I may shock the delicate sensibilities of a few friends,—for whose views I have great respect—by declaring myself at the very outset as a Home Ruler who believes that India is even to-day quite fit for enjoying a fair measure of Self-Government—popular control over her administrative and legislative machinery. But I cannot help it. Apart from the fact that the conviction I have come to entertain is now shared by the vast bulk of educated Indians throughout the length and breadth of our country, there is the additional and even more important reason for my putting it in the forefront of my address, namely, that it is the result of my life-long experience of public affairs. But when I find that the demand for Self-Government is echoed from end to end in this country, and that all classes and communities are united in its insistence as the first plank in Indian progress, I feel doubly strengthened in asking you to press it, with all the earnestness and enthusiasm you may command, on the attention of His Majesty's Government, and to strain every nerve in securing it by constitutional methods, buoyed up with the conviction that good Government can never be a proper substitute for Self-Government."

"All demonstrations of the virtues of a foreign bureaucracy, though often conclusive, are as useless as demonstrations of the superiority of artificial teeth, glass eyes, silver wind-pipes and patent wooden legs to the natural products." (Quoting from Bernard Shaw).

"And here I would like to explain that our fight is with the system and not with the holders of the office. It is a mere accident at present that by far much the larger number of the members of the Indian Civil Service are British and Irish. Yet, if the whole of the

Indian Civil Service consisted of Indians and Indians alone, our demand for Self-Government would be quite as keen and insistent, for we are against being ruled by a bureaucracy whether native or foreign, whether Indian or alien."

"As a matter of fact, the alleged unfitness of our people has no existence apart from the Anglo-Indian mind which sees what it desires to see. It is idle to attempt to argue into conviction men or classes whose judgments are warped by prejudices incidental to threatened encroachments on their vested interests."

These demands of Indian politicians, statesmen and administrators must be supplemented by the pronouncement recently made by a great Indian whose outlook has not been that of a politician. The Nobel Prize is a great distinction to Sir Rabindranath Tagore, only because he is an Indian. Otherwise, he would be considered to have honoured the distinction instead of owing honor to it. Especially as one remembers that he takes rank on account of it with Mr. Kipling, the man of letters of road side tales and of dak bungalow rhymes, who drew his inspiration from scenes in the cuisine and the gesticulations of the Bazaar, who weary of the heat of the day and of the mosquitoes of the night ran into heroics on the Whiteman's burden, and bulged out into epic narrations of Life's Handicap,—whose one unvoiced grievance seems to be that the whitemen of the Earth cannot be a race of Lotus Eaters dwelling in a land where it would always be afternoon—and who in literature is the prototype of Lord

Curzon in statesmanship and of Lord Sydenham in political philosophy—essentially men of narrow outlook and narrow inspiration and great only because of the nation to which they belong—and who when their stock is exhausted become sterile in spite of all exertions and readily available sources of easily becoming famous for a season—as one remembers Mr. Kipling as a Nobel Prize recipient, we feel positively discouraged in trying to think more highly of Rabindranath because of that prize. He is as a star of the firmament set in the clear sky of a limitless past, while men of Mr. Kipling's outlook are no more than the fire-flies of the bush. Yet, the Nobel prize has served to bring Rabindranath Tagore's name to the knowledge of Western and far-Western Nations. And what is the opinion of such a man, who sees beyond the vision of the eye and who sings in a tune which haunts the mind long, long after the tune has ceased to be heard, who is not more a Hindu, than a Moslem, Christian, Parsee or Jew—who in fact has been a personification of Harmony in the mental, moral, emotional and spiritual sides of Human Nature—the seer blest of the Age—the man of passionless passion—who has stood aloof from Politics all along ? Unfortunately the full text of his speech in English is not available; but the brief summary shows how he can make the politics of the present a thing of exquisite beauty, simple enough for the understanding of a child, beautiful enough for the appreciation of the white Hottentots of Indian politics. With the voice of one who knows all he is saying and knows what others say, he states his position in these words :—

"I do not deny that we have our weaknesses in our individual characters and in our social system. Still we want self-government. In the great democratic festival of the world no one people have all their lights burning —yet the festival goes on. If for sometime our light has gone out, may we not ask for it to be lit at the wick of England's lamp without thereby raising a howl of indignation? It will not detract from England's light but surely add to the brightness of the world's illumination."

When we turn from the testimony of official and non-official Indians of age, experience and acknowledged eminence in the public life of the country or in responsible official position, to the opinions of official and non-official Anglo-Indians and to those few British friends of India who have taken a sustained interest in its affairs, the cause of India in no way stands committed to the care and custody of the Bureaucracy. Apart from the illustrious Mr. A. O. Hume who was one of the founders of the Indian National Congress and Sir W. Wedderburn his early co-adjutor, we may quote here Mr. George Yule who was more than a British merchant in India. Presiding at the Congress session of 1888, he said referring to the bureaucratic system :—

"No rational mind can believe that the present system can go on for ever, that it is the last will and dying testament of Providence against India."

Sir Henry Cotton, who looked to the advent of the

Liberal party to power after too long a spell of conservative stagnation but who latter was mortified with the hesitency of the liberalism even of John Morley said in 1904."—

"The ideal of an Indian patriot is the establishment of a federation of free and separate states—the United States of India—placed on a fraternal footing with the self-governing colonies, each with its own local autonomy, cemented together under the ægis of Great Britain."

But seven years later, when the scheme of Provincial autonomy was mentioned in the Government of India's despatch the forces of conservatism brought about the abandonment of that policy for the time being and about six years later still Sir O'Moore Creigh's regret is alone available for our consolation.

Mr. Ramsay MacDonald is no dobut to some extent right in thinking that "whatever else this Report (Mesopotomia) may have done, it has killed the Indian Bureaucracy. It did to the prestige of the Government, what the anarchists with their picric acid failed to do to the bodies of the Governors." But he does not know in spite of all his mental grip that the Bureaucracy is not so easily killed. It has a peculiar way of rising from its own ashes confounding the best efforts of British and Indian progressive forces. Not until the Government of India is "completely changed in its character" as Dewan Madhava Row has pointed out, will there be a lack of its opportunity to keep India perpetually dwarfed. Whatever prestige the Bureaucracy may happen to lose in the estimation of the House of Commons, its prestige for practical purposes, is in its power and when that power continues even after the loss of its prestige, its tenacity seems to be all the more invulnerable. Mr. Ramsay MacDonald is however thoroughly right when he says "If we were to continue to rule India as we are now doing for a hundred decades these tales (of Indian inferiority) would not diminish but increase with time." He comes to the bed-rock of correct conclusion when he says:—

"Indeed, when the whole facts and experience are marshalled and examined, the case for the doleful prophesies of failure if India were started on the road to Self-government and full partnership in the Empire is found to rest on very slender evidence, whereas the grounds for confidence are firm and wide."

"A great part of the fears that are valid arise from the existing method and spirit of government. We shall be wise if we honestly recognize the fact and admit that a break with the part has become inevitable."

Mr. S. H. Swinny could not have expressed the case of Self-government for India better than he does when he says that "the attempt to discriminate between efficiency and popular control is idle."

Mr. Sydney Webb puts a question in a way that could hardly be improved when he asks:—

"The child is growing up; whereas it used to be only seven years old, it is now fourteen; are we to try to prevent it from attaining manhood?"

Dr. V. H. Rutherford, whose manly stand on

behalf of the victims of police oppression in India, due to the system of administration more than to anything else, this country will never forget, compresses British Political policy in a single sentence when he says "Self-Government has kept Canada, Australia, New Zealand and South Africa within the British Empire and it would do the same for India."

Mr. S. K. Ratcliffe, an honorable exception among Anglo-Indian journalists who have constituted an unconscionably favoured class of political bounders in India, and who knows the meaning of "authority" in India quite as much as any Indian, has added the prestige of his support to the claims of India in one of his most recent contribution to the *Daily News*, (London). He says:—

"The one essential principle to be established is responsibility. The one blunder that would imperil the scheme is the refusal, for any reason or through any fear, of an adequate measure of responsibility to Indian representatives and legislative bodies. Now the main and governing fact of the problem as Mr. Asquith used to say, is that in the Imperial Commonwealth of to-morrow there must be room for a self-governing and responsible India. This is the place which the greatness of India involves, which the extraordinary loyalty of India has earned."

Mr. Wilfrid Blunt, whose services as a scholar and writer have been employed in the interests of foreign Nationalities, has set forth in one sentence the nature of the change the present hour calls for in India. He writes:—

"Until it is brought home to the official understanding that the old system of administration through an alien bureaucracy is out of date, nothing will even begin to be accomplished in the direction of progressive liberty."

Mr. Andrew Carnegie is a man to whom nobody would deny dry intellectual shrewdness. His advice to his countrymen runs as follows:—

"The true policy of Britain is to say some day to India, as she said to Canada and Australia, that if she ever feels the time has arrived when she must establish government for herself, so be it. It is because this had been said to the British self-governing colonies that they remain loyal colonies to-day. Proclaim coercion and the part of America will soon be played by them again. When India is told this, the effect will be as it has been with the colonies—to bind her closer and to keep her longer than otherwise within the Empire."

A Lord Curzon may jump up and insist on the loophole furnished by the indefinite word "some." "Some day" may mean in his vocabulary "no day." But if the British Nation accepts the advice for "some" day it may accept with Mr. Ratcliffe that "the" wheel has come full circle, "that it will be to imperil the scheme of reform" if responsibility were denied to India any longer, seeing that "we stand at the threshold of momentous changes in India." If as Mr. Ramsay MacDonald has put it, "a break with the past has become inevitable," has not Mr. Carnegie's "some" day arrived?

In refreshing contrast to the thesis of the Bishop of Madras is the avowal made by the Lord Bishop of Calcutta who realising the sanctity of the place where he was speaking from, with a clear conscience in which secular considerations had no place, and elevating the duty of England by India to a stainless, sinless cause, at least from hereafter, on behalf of the higher mind of Anglo-India, laid down :—

"The first object of its rulers must be to train Indians in Self-government. If we turn away from any such application of our principles to this country, it is but hypocrisy to come before God with the plea that our cause is the cause of liberty."

Doctor J. Pollen, who although a civilian has none of the stifling bureaucratic attitude about him and whose heart has longed for increasing cordiality between India and England and whose time for years now has been cheerfully spent in working for its promotion, would advocate no half measures, and gives a straight counsel of a thoroughly honourable policy when he lays down that :—

"The right policy is to trust the Indian people all in all, for in India Faith and Unfaith could never be equal powers."

Commander J. C. Wedgewood the latest but not the least powerful accession of strength to the cause of imperial solidarity and to whose fearless services on the Mesopotomia Commission the Empire owes a debt of gratitude, has struck an imperial note that must make for higher civilization for all the world over when he assures:—

"Before this war is over we shall have more freedom, more Parliamentary Government, in British India than in the servile German Empire. That is a form of competition with Germany that involves no imitation."

At the risk of embarrassing, not the Government of India, but Mr. Montagu at whose hands we expect India would make a memorable advance, we may conclude these citations by recalling the solemn adjuration which he addressed to the House of Commons just before the mantle of Lord Morley worthily fell on him:—

"Unless you are prepared to remodel in the light of modern experience, this century old and cumbrous machine, then, I believe that you will lose your right to control the destinies of the Indian Empire."

To these testimonies we may add what the greatest soldier of the Empire, Lord Roberts, has left on record in regard to the basis of British power in India:—

"Our greatest strength" must ever rest on the firm base of a united and contented India.

A united India now asks for its contentment in the words of Mr. Montagu for "opportunity of controlling their own destinies, not merely by councils which cannot act but by control, by growing control of the executive itself."

The only outstanding question is whether this demand does or does not proceed from a United India. Such a misgiving, however, can no longer even plausibly be entertained on the ground of Moslem aloofness. So late as 1887, an influential minority of educated Mahomedans led by the late Mr. (subsequently Justice) Budruddin Tyabji, had definitely identified itself with the Congress party. During these thirty years the Aligarh Institute has materially added to the number and influence of the educated Moslem section of the country. It is a mistake to belittle the influence of the Aligarh College, founded 8 years earlier than the starting of the Indian National Congress, in the making of a modern political nationality, with tolerance to all creeds and castes under the progressive and unifying paramountcy of Great Britain and of its political institutions and liberalizing literature. The Moslem League which was in one sense an outcome of the Indian Congress as much as of the Aligarh College, has after obtaining educational facilities for the Mohomedan community joined hands with the Congress, making it truly representative of the nation. Its acknowledged spokesmen like the Hon. the Rajah of Mahmudabad, Mr. Hasan Imam who resigned a seat on the High Court Bench of Calcutta, the Hon. Messrs. Jinnah, Muzrul Haque, and the late Mr. Abdul Rasul and that hereditary Hindu-Moslem representative Nabob Syed Mahommed of Madras and Mr. Syed Wazir Hasan who represents the Congress in the Moslem League and the League in the Congress and Khan Bahadur Sarfaraz Hussain Khan all these representatives from every part of the country and drawn from every class and profession have shown unmistakably that no longer can India be held in bondage to the opinions of an uncompromising alien executive.

The royalty of India is a silent factor in the politics of the British Provinces, and has been forced to be under inevitable conditions more or less alien to the band of Indian patriots. Its members have had to remain all along as though they inhabit a different continent from their countrymen. But the War, a blessing in some respects at least, has shown the essential identities of the Indian nation from time immemorial. When the Maharajah of Bikhanir was selected to represent his brother princes and his countrymen the opportunity was thrown open for Indian Royalty to give expression to its feelings and nobody could have done it better than did His Highness the Maharajah of Alwar. In one pregnant sentence he put the question:—

"Is it possible that a nation which has drawn the sword for protecting the liberties of weaker nations such as Belgium will overlook our rights and claims to raise our heads on a footing of equality with other Dominions? When the War is successfully over and the British people extend to India their hand of comradeship, entrust us to weild the destinies of our own country, your Highness can assure them we shall be as ready to grasp their hands with feelings of warm gratitude and emotion as we have been to discharge our duties in the present crisis."

Thus in one array all India, Moslem and Hindu, royalty and commonalty and the best mind of England entitled to speak on behalf of India make a united appeal for popular autonomy subject to the suzeranity of Great Britain. Against this appeal we have firstly the attitude of descriptive non-committal as in the case of the Bishop of Madras. It is a process of vivid but endless weighing of *pros and corns,* of concluding after great labour with a word of advice to the Bureaucracy to behave better by the people and to the people to hope for better under the same Bureaucracy. It is men of his type who have to be converted by the life long convictions of Indian politicians like Naoroji and practical administrators like Mr. Madhava Rao. And being after all a public servant governed by the Service regulations, he could not have said more than he has, in his lengthy disquisition on our behalf. In the next place, we have the declarations of the accredited spokesmen of the bureaucratic system, authorised by unknown and unknowable Circulars of the Government of India, and fomented by the Anglo-Indian press. Thirdly we have to profit by the inane repetitions of these declarations by retired heads of Provincial Governments whose gratitude for the country that kept them in such regal spleandour they requite in such unbecoming, ill-informed and absolutely graspless manner as to provoke the contempt of school boys. They will perpetuate the *statusquo* with a few changes here and there and will continue to rest the centre of gravity with the Beauracracy against all reason, against all history and against the admissions of British statesmen made at the dawn of a new era when the world has sacrificed millions of lives and mints of money for divesting autocracy in any form, of any complexion and of any nationality of power to control the destinies of the people, instead of being controlled by them. And when we see that this claim of the Anglo-Indian Bureaucracy is to continue to direct, after a century of power, the life of a great continent foreign to it in almost every respect, impelled by the one consideration of self-interest as against the interests of millions, it must be a dire consequence, indeed, for the well-being of humanity if such obduracy should prevail with His Most Gracious Majesty the King-Emperor, his far seeing ministers and the British nation with whom India has become one in blood, if not in skin and colour.

As regards the steps by which the goal should be reached, we refrain from a discussion here, seeing that these have been embodied in the schemes suggested already and which will continue to be suggested upto the time of Parliamentary Legislation. Our demand however is that England must declare her intention by an express statute of making India a Self-governing part of the Empire before the lapse of a definite period to be mentioned in the statute and the first instalment of reforms should be definitely stated as being the outcome of such an object. Less than this India cannot accept and to refuse this eminently reasonable demand, after the change in the angle of vision will be little short of hypocrisy, as baneful in its effect as it will be cruel to our faith in British purpose and rectitude.

India's Claim for Home Rule

DADABHAI NAOROJI

" Good government could never be a substitute
for government by the people themselves."
(*Sir H. Campbell-Bannerman, Stirling,* 23-11-1905.)

[*The following speech was delivered by Mr. Dadabhai Naoroji in* 1904 *at the Wesley Hall, Clapham Park*]:—

British rule in India at its inception was one marked by greed, oppression, and tyranny of every kind—so much so that even the Court of Directors of the East India Company was horrified at what was going on. That was the first fact to be borne in mind. The second was that subsequent to the rise of the British Empire in India all War expenditure incurred in connection with India, and by means of which the Empire had been built up, had been paid out of Indian resources entirely, and the bloodshed which was the necessary accompaniment of War was mainly Indian. In the late Transvaal War Great Britain lost thousands of her sons and spent nearly 250 millions sterling, and the people of this country consequently had brought forcibly home to them what War meant, but in India, while the British claimed all the glory and reaped all the benefits, the burdens of War were borne by the Natives. India had, in fact, cost Great Britain nothing in money and very little in blood. But its wealth had thereby been exhausted; it had become impoverished, and it had further been subjected to a system of Government under which every Indian interest was sacrificed for the benefit of the English people. The system of corruption and oppression continued until at last the British Government was shamed by it. Anglo-Indians of high position in the service had again and again denounced the system in the most scathing terms, but it would suffice for his present purpose to remind them that Edmund Burke pointed out how every position worth having under the Government was filled by Europeans, to the absolute exclusion of Natives. The result was that there was a constant and most exhausting drain of Indian wealth. Even in those days it was estimated that the official remittances to England amounted to three millions sterling, and the capacity of the people to produce went on diminishing until it was now only about £ 2 per head, as compared with £ 40 per head in Great Britain. This country, too, enjoyed the benefit of its wealth circulating at home, while India laboured under the disadvantage that what it produced was sent to England, and it got nothing in return. She was, in fact, deprived of wealth without mercy year after year, and, in addition to the official home, remittances to which he had already referred, the servants of the Government sent home privately an almost equal sum, which they themselves obtained from the natives on their own account. In the early part of the last century there was a Government enquiry every 20 years into the administration of the East India Company, and these at last proved so effective that the statesmen of the day began to realise the responsibilities and duty of England to India, and to seriously discuss what should be Great Britain's policy. It was in 1833 that they got the first pledge and in that year a clause was inserted in the Charter of the East India Company providing that in the service of the Government there should be no distinction raised of race, creed, or colour, but that ability should be the sole qualification for employment by the State. That was the first promise made to the people of India in the name of the people of the United Kingdom, and it was embodied in an Act of Parliament. Had it been faithfully and loyally carried out, the existing state of affairs in India would have been vastly different, and it would not have been necessary for him to go about the country complaining of the dishonour and disgrace of England, and of the enormity of the evils of the British rule. The first promise was made in 1833, the period at which the British were raising to their highest glory in civilisation, an era of emancipation of all kinds, from the abolition of slavery onwards. Macaulay himself declared that he would be proud to the end of his life of having taken part in preparing that clause of the Charter, and clearly the policy of the statesmen of that day was to extend to India the freedom and the liberty which England enjoyed. But 20 years passed, and not the slightest effect was given to the clause; it remained a dead letter, as if it had never been enacted, and the policy of greed and oppression continued to obtain in the Government of India. In 1853, the East India Company's Charter was again revised, and in those days Mr. John Bright and Lord Stanley (afterwards Lord Derby) urged strongly that the service should be open to all and not reserved exclusively for Europeans for the nominees and friends of the Directors of the Company. They contended, too, for the holding of simultaneous examinations in India and England, but it was without avail. Then came the Mutiny of 1857, and after that had been suppressed, the statesmen of Great Britain were again forced to consider what should be the policy of this country in India. The administration of India was taken over from the Company, and the Proclamation which was issued was drawn up by Lord Derby, at the special request of Queen Victoria in terms of generosity, benevolence, and religious toleration, such as might well be used by a woman sovereign speaking to hundreds of millions of a people, the direct Government of whom she was assuming after a bloody civil War. Nothing could have been more satisfactory than the promise embodied in that Proclamation, and the Indian people heartily blessed the name of Queen Victoria for the sympathy she always evinced towards her Indian subjects. The Proclamation constituted the second pledge—it was a promise to extend British institutions to India too, in fact, give them Self-Government, it reaffirmed the Charter of 1833, and it declared that Her Majesty held herself bound to the natives of her Indian territories by the same obligations of duty as bound her to all other subjects. Indians were, in fact, to become true British subjects, and the Government of the country was to be administered for the benefit of all the people resident therein; for, concluded the Proclamation: "In her prosperity will be our strength, in her contentment our security, and in her gratitude our best reward." This had well been called "India's Greater Charter." It was everything they desired. But, unfortunately, it, too, had remained a dead letter up to the present time, and to the great and bitter disappointment of the people of India the promises therein contained had not been faithfully and honourably fulfilled. In defiance of the Proclamation, every obstacle had been placed in the way of the Native obtaining admission to posts under the Government; the efforts of men like Mr. John Bright, Lord Derby, and Mr. Fawcett to secure the holding of simultaneous examinations in England and India had been frustrated. In 1870, no doubt, an effort was made by Sir Stafford Northcote, and later on by the Duke of Argyll, to give effect to the promise of admission of Natives to the service, but it was defeated by the action of the Indian Government. A Native service was established, but it was made entirely distinct from European service—a distinction which was never intended—and it was so arranged that it was bound to prove a failure. Appointments to it were made by nomination, not by examination; back-door jobbery took the place of the claims of ability, and, naturally, at the end of ten years, the service was abandoned because it had never answered. In 1877, on the Proclamation of Queen Victoria as Empress of India, Lord Lytton had issued another Proclamation in the name of Queen Victoria reiterating the promises contained in her former Proclamation, but again the pledge was violated. At the Jubilee in 1887, there was a renewal of the promise, again to be followed by its being utterly ignored; while, later on, a resolution of the British House of Commons in favour of the holding of simultaneous examinations in India and England was carried by Mr. Herbert Paul, in spite of the opposition of the Government, and that, too, had been ignored. Thus, they had a long series of solemn promises made to the ear but absolutely violated in spirit and in letter, to the great dishonour and disgrace of Great Britain. Eminent statesmen and officials had frequently admitted the breaking of these pledges. A Committee appointed by the then Secretary for India unanimously reported in 1860 that the British Government had been guilty of making promises to the ear and breaking them to the hope; and that the only way in which justice could be done to Indians was by holding simultaneous examinations in England and India, of the same standard and on the same footing, instead of forcing Indians to go to London at an expense of thousands of pounds in order to secure admission to the Government service. In 1870, the Duke of Argyll declared: "We have not fulfilled our duty or the promises and engagements we have made;" later, Lord Lytton made the confession that deliberate and transparent subterfuges had been resorted to in order to reduce the promise of the Charter of 1833 to a dead letter; and that the Governments of England and India were not in a position to answer satisfactorily the charge that they had taken every means in their power to break to the heart the promises they had made to the ear. The Duke of Devonshire, in 1883, asserted that if India was to be better governed it was to be done only by the employment of the best and most intelligent of the Natives in the service; while, finally, the late Lord Salisbury described the promises and their non-fulfilment as "political hypocrisy." That was a nice description indeed of the character of the British rule in India. It was an admission that the conduct of the British Government in India had been disgraceful. But let them not forget that the promises were made by the British Sovereign, the British Parliament, and British people, of their own free will, while the disgrace for their non-fulfilment attached solely to the British Government, which by its refusal to act had sullied the honour of the British people. Two of the greatest offenders in this respect had been Lord George Hamilton and Lord Curzon, both of whom had very unpatriotically introduced most reactionary measures, and had pursued a mischievous policy which had resulted in the gravest injury to the Indian Empire and the British people. Lord George Hamilton, whose object surely should have been to make the people attached to the British people, had openly declared that it never would be popular with them; while Lord Curzon had done his very utmost to make it unpopular. He was going back to that country for a second term of office as Viceroy but the suggestion that the people would welcome his reappearance was falsified by the authoritative expression of the best Native opinion, and his continuance in the office of Viceroy could only be productive of serious injury, both to England and India. What had been the result of the non-fulfilment of this long series of promises? The system of greed and oppression still obtained in the Government of India; the country was being selfishly exploited for the sole benefit of Englishmen; it was slowly but surely being drained of its wealth, for no country in the world could possibly withstand a drain of 30 to 40 millions sterling annually, such as India was now subjected to; its power of production was diminishing, and its people were dying of hunger by the million. The responsibility for all this rested upon British rule. What was the remedy? Not the mischievous, reactionary policy now being pursued by Lord Curzon, but the taking of steps to transform and revolutionise in a peaceful manner the present evil and disastrous system of Government, so as to enable the people themselves to take their full and proper share in the administration of the affairs of their country. Lord Curzon had described India as the pivot of the British Empire. India could not be content with the present state of affairs, and he earnestly appealed to the people of Great Britain to themselves compel the Government to redeem the promises so often made, and to secure for India real Self-Government, subject, of course, to the paramountcy of Great Britain, (Cheers).

PRESIDENTIAL ADDRESS TO THE INDIAN NATIONAL CONGRESS, CALCUTTA, 1906

The work of the Congress consists of two parts:—

First and most important is the question of the policy and principles of the system of Government under which India ought to be governed in the future.

Second is to watch the operation of the administration as it now exists, to propose from time to time any reforms and changes that may be deemed necessary to be made in the various departments, till the present system of government is radically altered and based upon right principles and policy in the accomplishment of the first part mentioned above.

I desire to devote my address mainly to the first part of the work of the Congress, *viz.*, the policy and principles which ought to govern India in future.

What position do the Indians hold in the British Empire? Are they British citizens or not is my first question? I say we are British citizens, and are entitled to and claim all British citizens' rights.

I shall first lay before you my reasons for claiming that we are British citizens.

I.—The Birthright

The acknowledgment of this birthright was declared on the very first occasion when England obtained the very first territorial and sovereign possession in India. The British statesmen of the day at once acted upon the fundamental basis of the British Constitution and character that any one, howsoever and wheresoever, who came under the British flag, was a free British citizen as "if born and living in England."

The fundamental basis in the words of the present Prime Minister is:—"Freedom is the very breath of our life. . . . We stand for liberty, our policy is the policy of freedom." In the words of Mr. Morley:—"Yes, gentlemen, the sacred word "free" which represents, as Englishmen have always thought until today, the noblest aspiration that can animate the breast of man." This birthright to be "free" or to have freedom is our right from the very beginning of our connection with England when we came under the British flag.

When Bombay was acquired as the very first territorial possession, the Government of the day in the very first grant of territorial rights to the East India Company declared thus:—

Extract from the "Grant to the First East India Company of the Island of Bombay, dated 27th March, 1669."

And it is declared that all persons being His Majesty's subjects inhabiting within the said Island and their children and their posterity born within the limits thereof shall be deemed free denizens and natural subjects as if living and born in England.

And further all the terms of the first grant are extended in it to all future British territorial acquisitions. Thus is the claim of Indians to be "free" and to all the rights of British natural subjects as "if living and born in England" are distinctly acknowledged and declared from the very first political connection with England.

Having given the declaration made some two and a half centuries back in the 17th century that the moment we Indians came under the British flag we were "free" citizens, I next give you what two of the prominent statesmen of this, the 20th century, have said. When the Boers were defeated and subjugated and came under the British flag, the Present Prime Minister said (14th June, 1901) :—

This people with whom we are dealing are not only going to be our fellow-citizens, they are our fellow citizen already.

Sir William Harcourt, at the same time, said :—

This is the way in which you propose to deal with your fellow-citizens.

Thus the moment the people came under the British flag they are "free" and British "fellow-citizens." We Indians have been free British citizens as our birthright, as "if born and living in England" from the first moment we came under the British flag.

The Boer war cost Britain more than two hundred

millions and 20,000 dead and 20,000 wounded. India, on the other hand, has enriched Britain instead of costing anything—and the blood that was shed was largely Indian blood, and yet this is a strange contrast. The Boers have already obtained self-government in a few years after conquest, while India has not yet received self-government, though it is more than 200 years from the commencement of the political connection.

All honour and glory to the British instincts and principles and to the British statesmen of the 17th century. The Liberals of the present day and the Liberal Government have every right to be proud of those "old principles," and now that a happy and blessed revival of those sacred old principles has taken place, the present Government ought fairly to be expected to act upon those old principles, and to acknowledge and give effect to the birthright of Indians as "if living and born in England." England is bound to do this. Our British rights are beyond all question. Every British Indian subject has franchise in England as a matter of course, and even to become a Member of Parliament. Nobody in England dreams of objecting to it. Once in my case, from party motives, an objection was suggested to entering my name on the register as an elector, and the revising barrister at once brushed aside the objection, for that, as an Indian, I was a British citizen.

II.—Pledged Rights

The grant to the first East India Company cited in Reason I is both a declaration of the rights of Indians as British citizens as well as a pledge of those rights by that declaration.

Queen Victoria, in her letter to Lord Derby, asking him to write the Proclamation himself, said:—

> And point out the privileges which the Indians will receive in being placed on an equality with the subjects of the British Crown and prosperity flowing in the train of civilization.

Thereupon the Proclamation then declared and pledged unreservedly and most solemnly calling God to witness and bless:

> We hold ourselves bound to the Natives of our Indian territories by the same obligations of duty which binds us to our other subjects, and these obligations by the blessing of Almighty God we shall faithfully and conscientiously fulfil.

Can there be a more sacred and solemn pledge before God and Man!

On the occasion of the Proclamation of the Queen as Empress of India, she sent a telegram to Lord Lytton which he read in the open Durbar consisting of both Princes and people. In this telegram the Queen-Empress said:

> That from the highest to the humblest all may feel that under our rule, the great principles of liberty, equity and justice are secured to them, and that to promote their happiness, to add to their prosperity and advance their welfare are ever present aims and objects of our Empire.

And it is clear that this object of promoting our happiness, etc., etc., can only be attained by our enjoyment of the principles of liberty, equity and justice, *i.e.*, we must have the British liberty of governing ourselves.

On the occasion of the Jubilee of 1887 the Queen-Empress again pledged and emphasised the pledges of the Proclamation, thus:—

Allusion is made to the Proclamation issued on the occasion of my assumption of the direct government of India as the Charter of the liberties of the Princes and people of India. It has always been and will continue to be my earnest desire that the principles of that Proclamation should be unswervingly maintained.

We are now asking nothing more or less than the liberties of our Charter,—our rights of British citizenship.

The present King-Emperor has pledged:—

I shall endeavour to follow the great example of the first Queen-Empress to work for the general well-being of my Indian subjects of all ranks.

Again the King-Emperor in his speech on 19th February, 1906, said:—

It is my earnest hope that in these Colonies as elsewhere *throughout my dominions* (the italics are mine) the grant of free institutions will be followed by an increasing prosperity and loyalty to the Empire.

And the Prime Minister clinches the whole that "good government could never be a substitute for government by the people themselves."

How much less is then an economically evil government and constitutional and unconstitutional despotic government, a substitute for self-government—and how much absolutely necessary it is to produce "increasing prosperity and loyalty to the Empire," by "the grant of free institutions."

With the solemn pledges I have mentioned above, we have every right to claim an honourable fulfilment of all our British pledged rights. And so we claim all British rights as our birthright and as our solemnly pledged rights. Britain's duty, humanity, honour, instincts and traditions for freedom, solemn pledges, conscience, righteousness and civilization demand the satisfaction to us of our British rights.

III.—Reparation

All our sufferings and evils of the past centuries demand before God and Man a reparation, which we may fairly expect from the present revival of the old noble British instincts of liberty and self-government. I do not enter into our past sufferings as I have already said at the outset.

IV.—Conscience

The British people would not allow themselves to be subjected a single day to such an unnatural system of Government as the one which has been imposed upon India for nearly a century and half. Sir H. Campbell-Bannerman has made a happy quotation from Mr. Bright:—"I remember John Bright quoting in the House of Commons on one occasion two lines of a poet with reference to political matters:—

> There is on Earth a yet diviner thing,
> Veiled though it be than Parliament or King.

Then Sir Henry asks:—"What is that diviner thing? It is the human conscience inspiring human opinion and human sympathy." I ask them to extend that human conscience, "the diviner thing," to India in the words of Mr. Morley:—

It will be a bad day indeed if we have one conscience for the Mother Country and another conscience for all that vast territory over which your eye does not extend.

And now the next question is—What are the British rights which we have a right to "claim?"

This is not the occasion to enter into any details or argument. I keep to broad lines.

(1) Just as the administration of the United Kingdom in all services, departments and details is in the hands of the people themselves of that country, so should we in India claim that the administration in all services, departments and details should be in the hands of the people themselves of India.

This is not only a matter of right and matter of the aspirations of the educated—important enough as these matters are—but it is far more an absolute necessity as the only remedy for the great inevitable economic evil which Sir John Shore pointed out a hundred and twenty years ago, and which is the fundamental cause of the present drain and poverty. The remedy is absolutely necessary for the material, moral, intellectual, political, social, industrial and every possible progress and welfare of the people of India.

(2) As in the United Kingdom and the Colonies all taxation and legislation and the power of spending the

taxes are in the hands of the representatives of the people of those countries, so should also be the rights of the people of India.

(3) All financial relations between England and India must be just and on footing of equality, *i.e.*, whatever money India may find towards expenditure in any department—Civil or Military or Naval—to the extent of that share should Indians share in all the benefits of that expenditure in salaries, pensions, emoluments, etc., materials, etc., as a partner in the Empire as she is always declared to be. We do not ask any favours. We want only justice. Instead of going into any further divisions or details of our rights as British citizens, the whole matter can be comprised in one word—" Self-government " or *Swaraj* like that of the United Kingdom or the Colonies.

Mr. Morley says very truly and emphatically (Banquet, King's Hall, Holborn, 4th June, 1901):—

> But this I do say, that political principles are, after all, the root of our national greatness, strength and hope.

So for India also there can be no national greatness, strength and hope except by the right political principles of self-government.

Now the next important question is whether it is practicable to grant these rights of self-government at once or when and in what way? Nobody would, I think, say that the whole present machinery can be suddenly broken up at once, and the rights which I have defined of self-government can be at once introduced.

Taking right No. 1, of placing all administration in every department in the hands of the people of India, has the time arrived to do anything loyally, faithfully and systematically as a beginning at once, so that it may automatically develop into the full realisation of the right of self-government?

I say,—yes. Not only has the time fully arrived, but had arrived long past, to make this beginning. The statesmen of nearly three-quarters of a century ago not only considered the point of making a beginning, not merely made a pious declaration, but they actually passed an Act of Parliament for the purpose. Had that Act been honourably and faithfully fulfilled by the Governments from that time to this, both England and India would have been in the position, not of bewailing the present poverty, wretchedness and dissatisfaction of the Indian people, but of rejoicing in the prosperity of India and of the still greater prosperity of England herself.

In the thirties of the last century England achieved the highest glory of civilization by its emancipations of the body and soul of man by abolishing slavery and by freedom of conscience to enjoy all the rights of British citizenship. During those glorious days of English history, the statesmen of the time did not forget their duty to the people of India. They specially and openly considered the question of self-government of India, not only in connection with Britain, but even with the result of entire independence from Britain. When the Act of 1833 was passed, Macaulay made that memorable speech about the duty of Britain towards India of which Britain shall for ever be proud. I cannot quote that whole speech here. Every word of it is worth study and consideration from the statesmen of the day. I shall give only a few extracts. He first said: "I must say that, to the last day of my life I shall be proud of having been one of those who assisted in the framing of the Bill which contains that clause." . . . "It would be on the most selfish view of the case far better for us that the people of India were well-governed and independent of us than ill-governed and subject to us." . . . We shall never consent to administer the pousta (a preparation of opium) to a whole community—to stupefy and paralyse a great people, whom God has committed to our charge, for the wretched purpose of rendering them more amenable to our control." . . . "We are free; we are civilized, to little purpose if we grudge to any portion of the human race an equal measure of freedom and civilization." . . . "I have no fears. The path of duty is plain before us, and it is also the path of wisdom, of national prosperity, of national honour." . . . "To have found a great people sunk in the lowest depths of slavery and superstition, to have so ruled them as to have made them desirous and capable of all the privileges of citizens, would indeed be a title to glory all our own."

Such was the glorious spirit in and the auspices under which was enacted Macaulay's words "that wise, that benevolent, that noble clause":—

That no native of the said territory, nor any natural born subjects of H s Majesty resident therein, shall by reason only of his religion, place of birth, descent, colour or any of them be disabled from holding any place, office or employment under the said Company.

I would not repeat here what I have often stated about this clause. Sufficient to say that simultaneous examinations in India have been declared authoritatively as the only honourable fulfilment of the clause.

Here is then the beginning that can be made at once, not as a new thing but as one fully considered and settled by Act of Parliament 73 years ago. The power is ready in the hands of the Secretary of State for India to be put into execution at once without the necessity of any reference to Parliament or any authority.

And in connection with this step, I would earnestly urge upon the Secretary of State to retrace the pernicious step which has lately been taken in India of abolishing competition for the services to which admission is made directly in India. In England competition is the basis of all first admissions in all the services, and the same must be the basis in India as the fairest and the most in accordance with justice.

This beginning will be the key, the most effective remedy for the chief economic and basic evil of the present system.

Mr. Morley has truly said:—" But if you meddle wrongly with economic things, gentlemen, be very sure you are then going to the very life, the heart, to the core of your national existence."

And so the economic muddle of the existing policy is going to the life, to the heart, to the core of our national existence. A threefold wrong is inflicted upon us, *i.e.*, of depriving us of wealth, work and wisdom, of everything, in short, worth living for. And this beginning will begin to strike at the root of the muddle. The reform of the alteration of the services from European to Indian is the keynote of the whole.

On the score of efficiency also, foreign service can never be efficient or sufficient. Sir William Hunter has said:—"If we are to govern the Indian people efficiently and cheaply we must govern them by means of themselves." The Duke of Devonshire, as Indian Secretary, has said (23rd August, 1883): "There can, in my opinion, be very little doubt that India is insufficiently governed." In the very nature of things it cannot be otherwise.

After the simultaneous examinations are carried on for some years, it will be time to transfer the examinations altogether to India to complete the accomplishment of the rights (No. 1) of self-government without any disturbance in the smooth working of the administration.

Co-ordinately with this important beginning for Right No. 1, it is urgent to expedite this object that education must be most vigorously disseminated among the people—free and compulsory primary education, and free higher education of every kind. The Indian people will hail with the greatest satisfaction any amount of expenditure for the purpose of education. It was free education that I had at the expense of the people that made me and others of my fellow-students and subsequent fellow-workers to give their best to the service of the people for the promotion of their welfare.

Education on the one hand, and actual training in administration on the other hand, will bring the accomplishment of self-government far more speedily than many imagine.

Heavy expenditure should be no excuse. In fact, if financial justice, to which I shall refer hereafter, is done in the relations between England and India, there will be ample provision even from the poor revenues of India—and with every addition of Indians in place of Europeans, the resources of India for all necessary purposes will go on increasing.

RIGHT NO. 2—REPRESENTATION

In England itself Parliamentary government existed for some hundreds of years before even the rich and middle classes and the mass of the people had any voice or vote in it.

Macaulay pointed out in 1831 that the people living in the magnificent palaces surrounding Regent's Park and in other such places were unrepresented. It is only so late as 1832 that the middle classes obtained their votes; and it is only so late as 1885 that most of the mass of the people obtained their franchise. Women have no vote. Adult franchise is yet in struggle.

It is no use telling us, therefore, that a good beginning cannot be made now in India for what Mr. Gladstone called "living representation." The only thing needed is the willingness of the Government. The statesmen at the helm of the present government are quite competent and able to make a good beginning—such a systematic beginning as that it may naturally in no long time develop itself into full legislatures of self-government like those of the self-governing colonies. I need not go into any details here of the scope and possibilities of representation. The educated and thinking classes in India who have attended English schools and colleges are not the only people to be reckoned with. There is a large body who now are informed of the events of the world and of all British institutions by the vernacular press and literature in their own language.

The peasants of Russia are fit for and obtained the Duma from the greatest autocrat in the world, and the leading statesman, the Prime Minister of the free British Empire, proclaimed to the world "The Duma is dead! Long live the Duma"! Surely the fellow-citizens of that statesman and the free citizens of that Empire by birthright and pledged rights are far more entitled to self-government, a constitutional representative system, than the peasants of Russia. I do not despair. It is futile to tell me that we must wait till all the people are ready. The British people did not so wait for their Parliament. We are not allowed to be fit for 150 years. We can never be fit till we actually undertake the work and the responsibility. While China in the East and Persia in the West of Asia are awakening and Japan has already awakened and Russia is struggling for emancipation—and all of them despotisms—can the free citizens of the British Indian Empire continue to remain subject to despotism—the people who were among the first civilizers of the world ? Modern world owes no little gratitude to these early civilizers of the human race. Are the descendants of the earliest civilizers to remain, in the present times of spreading emancipation, under the barbarous system of despotism, unworthy of British instincts, principles and civilization.

RIGHT NO. 3.—JUST FINANCIAL RELATIONS

This right requires no delay or training. If the British Government wills to do what is just and right, this justice towards self-government can be done at once.

First of all take the European Army expenditure. The Government of India in its despatch of 25th March 1890, says:—

> Millions of money have been spent on increasing the army in India, on armaments, and on fortifications to provide for the security of India, not against domestic enemies or to prevent the invasions of the warlike peoples of adjoining countries, but to maintain the supremacy of British Power in the East.

Again the Government of India says :

> It would be much nearer the truth to affirm that the Imperial Government keeps in India and quarters upon

the revenues of that country as large a portion of its army as it thinks can possibly be required to maintain its dominion there; that it habitually treats that portion of its army as a reserve force available for imperial purposes; that it has uniformly detached European regiments from the garrison of India to take part in Imperial wars whenever it has been found necessary or convenient to do so; and more than this, that it has drawn not less freely upon the native army of India towards the maintenance of which it contributes nothing to aid it in contests outside of India and with which the Indian Government has had little or no concern.

Such is the testimony of the Government of India that the European Army is for Imperial purposes.

Now I give the view taken in the India Office itself.

Sir James Peile was a member of the Council of the Secretary of State for India, and represented the Indian Secretary on the Royal Commission (Welby's) on Indian Expenditure. Sir James Peile in a motion, after pointing out that the military policy which regulated Indian Military expenditure was not exclusively Indian, urged that:

It is worthy of consideration how far it is equitable to charge on a dependency the whole military cost of that policy, when that dependency happens to be the only part of the Empire which has a land frontier adjacent to the territory of a great European power.

Here then these extracts of the Government of India and the India office show that the European Army expenditure is entirely for British Imperial purposes, and yet with flagrant injustice the burden is thrown by the Treasury upon the helpless Indian people.

In the same way all the Government expenditure in England, which entirely goes to the benefit of the people in England, and which is for British purposes, is imposed on the Indian people, while the Colonies do not pay any portion for similar expenditure in England. This expenditure should, in common justice, not be imposed on India. It is unjust. Here then, if we are relieved of burdens which ought not in common justice to be imposed upon us, our revenues, poor as they are at present, will supply ample means for education and many other reforms and improvements which are needed by us. This question is simply a matter of financial justice. I have put it on a clear, just principle, and on that principle India can be quiet ready to find the money and its own men for all her own needs—military, naval, civil or any other. For imperial expenditure we must have our share in the services in proportion to our contribution.

These just financial relations can be established at once. They require no delay or preparation. It only needs the determination and will of the British Government to do justice. Lastly as to self-government. If the British people and statesmen make up their mind to do their duty towards the Indian people they have every ability and statesmanship to devise means to accord self-government within no distant time. If there is the will and the conscience there is the way.

Now I come to the most crucial question—particularly crucial to myself personally.

I have been for some time past repeatedly asked whether I really have, after more than half a century of my own personal experience, such confidence in the honour and good faith of British statesmen and Government as to expect that our just claim to self-government as British citizens will be willingly and gracefully accorded to us with every honest effort in their power, leaving alone and forgetting the past.

Ladies and Gentlemen, I shall give you a full and free answer.

In 1853, when I made my first little speech at the inauguration of the Bombay Association, in perfect innocence of heart, influenced by my English education into great admiration for the character, instincts and struggles for liberty of the British people, I expressed my faith and confidence in the British Rulers in a short speech from which I give a short extract :—

> When we see that our Government is often ready to assist us in everything calculated to benefit us, we had better than merely complain and grumble, point out in a becoming manuer what our real wants are.

And I also said :

> If an Association like this be always in readiness to ascertain by strict enquiries the probable good or bad effects of any proposed measure, and whenever necessary to memorialise Government on behalf of the people with respect to them, our kind Government will not refuse to listen to such memorials.

Such was my faith. It was this faith of the educated of the time that made Sir Bartle Frere make the remark which Mr. Fawcett quoted, *viz.*, that he had been much struck with the fact that the ablest exponents of English policy and our best co-adjutors in adapting that policy to the wants of the various nations occupying Indian soil were to be found among the natives who had received a high class English education. And now, owing to the non-fulfilment of solemn pledges, what a change has taken place in the mind of the educated!

Since my early efforts I must say that I have felt so many disappointments as would be sufficient to break any heart and lead one to despair and even, I am afraid, to rebel.

My disappointments have not been of the ordinary kind but far worse and keener; ordinarily a person fights, and if he fails he is disappointed. But I fought and *won* on several occasions, but the executive did not let us have the fruit of those victories—disappointments quite enough, as I have said, to break one's heart. For instance, the "statutory" Civil Service, Simultaneous Examinations, Lord Lawrence Scholarships, Royal Commission, etc. I am thankful that the repayment from the Treasury of some unjust charges has been carried out, though the Indian Secretary's salary is not yet transferred to the Treasury as it was hoped.

But I have not despaired. Not only that I have not despaired, but at this moment, you may think it strange

I stand before you with hopefulness. I have not despaired for one reason and I am hopeful for another reason.

I have not despaired under the influence of the good English word which has been the rule of my life. That word is "Persevere." In any movement, great or small, you must persevere to the end. You cannot stop at any stage, disappointments notwithstanding, or you lose all you have gained and find it far more difficult afterwards even to begin again. As we proceed we may adopt such means as may be suitable at every stage, but persevere we must to *the end*. If our cause is good and just, as it is, we are sure to triumph in the end. So I have not despaired.

Now the reason of my hopefulness which I feel at this moment after all my disappointments, and this also under the influence of cne word "Revival," the present "revival" of the true old spirit and instinct of liberty and free British institutions in the hearts of the leading statesmen of the day. I shall now place before you the declarations of some of the leading statesmen of the day, and then you will judge that my faith and hope are well founded, whether they will be justified or not by future events.

Here I give you a few of these declarations, but I give an Appendix A of some of these declaration out of many.

SIR H. CAMPBELL-BANNERMAN

We believe in self-Government. We treat it not as an odious necessity, not as a foolish theory to which unfortunately the British Empire is committed. We treat it as a blessing and as a healing, a sobering and strengthening influence.

[Bradford, 15-5-1901].

I remain as firm a believer as ever I was in the virtue of self-government.

[Ayr, 29-10-1902].

But here is another self-government and popular control, and we believe in that principle.

MR. JOHN MORLEY

Yes, gentlemen, the sacred word 'free' which represented, as Englishmen have always thought until to-day, the noblest aspirations that can animate the breast of man.

[Palmerston Club, 9-6-1900].

In his view the root of good government was not to be found in bureaucracy or pedantocracy. They must seek to rouse up the free and spontaneous elements lying deep in the hearts and minds of the people of the country.

[Arbroath, 23-10-1903].

The study of the present revival of the spirit, instincts and traditions of Liberty and Liberalism among the Liberal statesmen of the day has produced in my heart full expectation that the end of the evil system, and the dawn of a Righteous and Liberal policy of freedom and self-government are at hand for India. I trust that I am justified in my expectations and hopefulness.

Ladies and Gentlemen, we have not only all the powerful moral forces of justice, righteousness and honour of Britain, but our birthright and pledged rights, and the absolute necessity and humanity of ending quickly all the sufferings of the masses of the people, from poverty, famine, plagues, destitution and degradation, etc., on our side. If we use those moral forces, which are very effective on a people like the British people, we must, we are bound to win. What is wanted for us is to learn the lesson from Englishmen themselves, to agitate most largely and most perseveringly by petitions, demonstrations and meetings, all quite peacefully but enthusiastically conducted. Let us not throw away our rights and moral forces which are so overwhelming on our side. I shall say something again on this subject.

With such very hopeful and promising views and declarations of some of the leaders of the present Government, we have also, coming to our side, more and more, Parliament, Press and Platform. We have some 200 members in the Indian Parliamentary Committee. The Labour Members, the Irish Nationalist Members, and the Radicals are sympathetic with us. We have several Liberal papers such as *The Daily News, The Tribune, The Morning Leader, The Manchester Guardian, The Star, The Daily Chronicle, Justice, Investor's Review, Reynolds, New Age,* and several others taking a juster view of India's rights and needs. We must make *India* a powerful organ. We have all sections of the Labour or Democratic Party, the British Nationalist Party, the Radicals and Liberals generally, taking larger interest in Indian matters. The large section of the British peeple to whom conscience and righteousness are above every possible worldly thing, are also awakening to a sense of their duty to the vast population of India in their dire distress and poverty, with all its dreadful consequences. When I was in Parliament and the only Indian, I had the support of the Irish, Radical and Labour Members. I never felt helpless and alone, and I succeeded in several of my efforts. We must have many Indian Members in Parliament till we get self-government. Under such favourable circumstances let us not fail to make the most of our opportunity for our political emancipation. Let us, it is true, at the same time do what is in our power to advance our social and industrial progress. But for our political emancipation, it will be a great folly and misfortune for us to miss this good fortune when it has at last come to us, though I fully admit we had enough of disappointments to make us lose heart and confidence.

I base my hope upon the "revival" of the old British love of liberty and self-government, of honour for pledges, of our rights of fellow-British citizenship. In the short life that may yet be vouchsafed to me, I hope to see a loyal, honest, honourable and conscientious adoption of the policy for self-government for India—and a beginning made at once towards that end.

I have now expressed to you my hopes and reasons for such hopes for ourselves. But as the Moral Law, the greatest force of the Universe, has it,—in our good will be England's own greatest good. Bright has wisely said :—"The good of England must come through the channels of the good of India......In order that England may become rich India itself must become rich." Mr. Morley has rightly said :—"No, gentlemen, every single right thing that is done by the Legislature, however moderate be its area, every single right thing is sure to lead to the doing of a greater number of unforeseen right things." (Dundee, 9-12-1889) If India is allowed to be prosperous by self-government, as the Colonies have become prosperous by self-government, what a vista of glory and benefits open up for the citizens of the British Empire, and for mankind, as an example and proof of the supremacy of the moral law.

While we put the duty of leading us on to self-government in the hands of the present British statesmen, we have also the duty upon ourselves to do all we can to support those statesmen by, on the one hand, preparing our Indian people for the right understanding, exercise and enjoyment of self-government, and on the other hand of convincing British people that we justly claim and must have all British Rights. I put before the Congress my suggestions for their consideration. To put the matter in the right form we should send our "Petition for Rights" to His Majesty the King-Emperor, to the House of Commons and to the House of Lords. By the British Bill of Rights of 1689—by the 5th Clause "The subjects have the right to present petitions to the Sovereign."

The next thing I suggest for your consideration is that the well-to-do Indians should raise a large fund of Patriotism. With this fund we should organise a body of able men and good speakers, to go to all the nooks and corners of India, and inform the people in their own languages of our British rights and how to exercise and enjoy them. Also to send to England another body of able speakers, and to provide means to go throughout the country and by large meetings to convince the British people that we justly claim and must have all British rights of self-government. By doing that I am sure that the British conscience will triumph and the British people will support the present statesmen, in their work of giving India responsible self-government in the shortest possible period. We must have a great agitation in England as well as here. The struggle against the Corn Laws cost, I think, two millions, and there was a great agitation. Let us learn to help ourselves in the same way.

I have said at the beginning that the duties of this Congress are twofold. And of the two, the claim to a change of present policy leading to self-government is the chief and most important work.

The second part of the work is the vigilant watch over the inevitable and unnecessary defects of the present machinery of the administration as it exists and as long as it exists. And as the fundamental principles of the present administration are unsound there are inherent evils, and others are naturally ever arising from them. These the Congress has to watch, and adopt means to remedy them as far as possible till self-government is attained, though it is only when self-government is attained that India will be free from its present evils and consequent sufferings.

This part of the work the Congress has been doing very largely during all the past twenty-one years, and the Subjects Committee will place before you various resolutions necessary for the improvement of the existing administration as far as such unnatural and uneconomic administration can be improved. I would have not troubled you more but that I should like to say a few words upon some topics connected with the second part of the Congress—Bengal Partition and *Swadeshi* movement.

In the Bengal Partition, the Bengalees have a just and great grievance. It is a bad blunder for England. I do not despair but that this blunder, I hope, may yet be rectified. This subject is being so well threshed out by the Bengalees themselves that I need not say anything more about it. But in connection with it we hear a great deal about agitators and agitation. Agitation is the life and soul of the whole political, social and industrial history of England. It is by agitation the English have accomplished their most glorious achievements, their paosperity, their liberties, and in short their first place among the Nations of the World.

The whole life of England, every day, is all agitation. You do not open your paper in the morning but read from beginning to end it is all agitation—Congress and Conferences—Meetings and Resolutions—without end, for a thousand and one movements, local and national. From the Prime Minister to the humblest politician his occupation is agitation for everything he wants to accomplish. The whole Parliament, Press and Platform, is simply all agitation. Agitation is the civilized peaceful weapon of moral force, and infinitely preferable to brute physical force when possible. The subject is very tempting. But I shall not say more than that the Indian journalists are mere Matriculates while the Anglo-Indian journalists are Masters of Arts in the University of British Agitators. The former are only the pupils of the latter, and the Anglo-Indian journalists ought to feel proud that their pupils are doing credit to them. Perhaps a few words from an English statesman will be more sedative and satisfactory.

Macaulay has said in one of his speeches:—

> I hold that we have owed to agitation a long series of beneficent reforms which would have been effected in no other way . . . . the truth is that agitation is inseparable from popular government . . . . Would the slave trade ever have been abolished without agitation? Would slavery ever have been abolished without agitation?

For every movement in England—hundreds, local and national—the cheap weapons are agitation by meetings, demonstrations and petitions to Parliament. These petitions are not any begging for any favours any more than that the conventional "Your obedient servant" in letters makes a man an obedient servant. It is the conventional way of approaching higher authorities. The petitions are claims for rights or for justice or for reforms,—to influence and put pressure on Parliament by showing how the public regard any particular matter. The fact that we have more or less failed hitherto, is not because we have petitioned too much but that we have petitioned too little. One of the factors that carries weight in Parliament is the evidence that the people interested in any question are really in earnest. Only the other day Mr. Asquith urged as one of his reasons against women's franchise that he did not see sufficient evidence to show that the majority of the women themselves were earnest to acquire the franchise. We have not petitioned or agitated enough at all in our demands. In every important matter we must petition Parliament with hundreds and thousands of petitions—with hundreds of thousands of signatures from all parts of India. Taking one present instance in England, the Church party has held till the beginning of October 1,400 meetings known, and many more unknown, against the Education Bill, and petitioned with three-quarters of a million signatures and many demonstrations. Since then they have been possibly more and more active. Agitate, agitate over the whole length and breadth of India in every nook and corner—peacefully, of course—if we really mean to get justice from John Bull. Satisfy him that we are in earnest. The Bengalis, I am glad, have learnt the lesson and have led the march. All India must learn the lesson—of sacrifice of money and of earnest personal work.

Agitate, to agitate means inform. Inform the Indian

people what their rights are and why and how they should obtain them, and inform the British people of the rights of the Indian people and why they should grant them. If we do not speak, they say we are satisfied. If we speak, we become agitators! The Indian people are properly asked to act constitutionally while the government remains unconstitutional and despotic.

Next about the "settled fact." Every Bill defeated in Parliament is a "settled fact." Is it not? And the next year it makes its appearance again. The Education Act of 1902 was a settled fact. An Act of Parliament, was it not? And now within a short time what a turmoil is it in? And what an agitation and excitement has been going on about it and is still in prospect. It may lead to a clash between the two Houses of Parliament. There is nothing as an eternal "settled fact." Times change, circumstances are misunderstood or change, better light and understanding, or new forces come into play, and what is settled to-day may become obsolete to-morrow.

The organizations which I suggest, and which I may call a band of political missionaries in all the Provinces, will serve many purposes at once—to inform the people of their rights, as British citizens, to prepare them to claim those rights by petitions, and when the rights are obtained, as sooner or later they must be obtained, to exercise and enjoy them.

"Swadeshi" is not a thing of to-day. It has existed in Bombay as far as I know for many years past. I am a free-trader, I am a Member, and in the Executive Committee of the Cobden Club for 20 years, and yet I say that "Swadeshi" is a forced necessity for India in its unnatural economic muddle. As long as the economic condition remains unnatural and impoverishing, by the necessity of supplying every year some Rs. 20,00,00,000 for the salary, pensions, &c., of the children of a foreign country at the expense and impoverishment of the children of India, to talk of applying economic laws to the condition of India is adding insult to injury. I have said so much about this over and over again that I would not say more about it here—I refer to my book. I ask any Englishmen whether Englishmen would submit to this unnatural economic muddle of India for a single day in England, leave alone 150 years? No, never. No, Ladies and Gentlemen, England will never submit to it. It is, what I have already quoted in Mr. Morley's words, it is "the meddling wrongly with economic things that is going to the very life, to the very heart, to the very core of our national existence."

Among the duties which I have said are incumbent upon the Indians, there is one which, though I mention last, is not the least. I mean a thorough political union among the Indian people of all creeds and classes. I make an appeal to all—call it mendicant, if you like—I am not ashamed of being a mendicant in any good cause and under necessity for any good cause. I appeal to the Indian people for this, because it is in their own hands only, just as I appeal to the British people for things that are entirely in their hands. In this appeal for a thorough union for political purposes among all the people, I make a particular one to my friends the Mahomedans. They are a manly people. They have been rulers both in and out of India. They are rulers this day both in and out of India. They have the highest Indian Prince ruling over the largest Native States, *viz.*, H. H. the Nizam. Among other Mahomedan Princes they have Junagad, Badhanpur, Bhopal and others.

Notwithstanding their backward education they have the pride of having had in all India the first Indian Barrister in Mr. Budrudin Tyabji and first Solicitor in Mr. Kamrudin Tyabji, two Mahomedan brothers. What a large share of Bombay commerce is in the hands of Mahomedans is well-known. Their chief purpose and effort at present must be to spread education among themselves. In this matter, among their best friends have been Sir Syed Ahmed and Justice Tyabji, in doing their utmost to promote education among them. Once they bring themselves in education in a line with the Hindus they have nothing to fear. They have in them the capacity, energy and intellect to hold their own and to get their due share in all the walks of life—of which the State services are but a small part. State services are not everything.

Whatever voice I can have, I wish Government would give every possible help to promote education among the Mahomedans. Once self-government is attained, then will there be prosperity enough for all, but not till then. The thorough union, therefore, of all the people for their emancipation is an absolute necessity.

All the people in their political position are in one boat. They must sink or swim together. Without this union all efforts will be vain. There is the common saying—but also the best common-sense—" United we stand—divided we fall."

There is one other circumstance, I may mention here. If I am right, I am under the impression that the bulk of the Bengali Mahomedans were Hindus by race and blood only a few generations ago. They have the tie of blood and kinship. Even now a great mass of the Bengali Mahomedans are not to be easily distinguished from their Hindu brothers. In many places they join together in their social joys and sorrows. They cannot divest themselves from the natural affinity of common blood. On the Bombay side the Hindus and Mahomedans of Gujarat all speak the same language, Gujarati, and are of the same stock, and all the Hindus and Mahomedans of Maharastra Annan—all speak the same language, Marathi, and are of the same stock—and so I think it is all over India, excepting in North India, where there are the descendants of the original Mahomedan invaders, but they are now also the people of India.

Sir Syed Ahmed was a nationalist to the backbone. I will mention an incident that happened to myself with him. On his first visit to England, we happened to meet together in the house of Sir C. Wingfield. He and his friends were waiting, and I was shown into the same room. One of his friends recognising me introduced me to him. As soon as he heard my name he at once held me in a strong embrace and expressed himself very much pleased. In various ways I knew that his heart was in the welfare of all India as one nation, He was a large and liberal-minded patriot. When I read his life some time ago, I was inspired with respect and admiration for him As I cannot find my copy of his life I take the opportunity of repeating some of his utterances, which Sir Henry Cotton has given in *India* of 12th October last.

Mahomedans and Hindus were, he said, the two eyes of India. Injure the one and you injure the other. "We should try to become one in heart and soul and act in unison; if united, we can support each other; if not the effect of one against the other will tend to the destruction and downfall of both."

He appreciated when he found worth and freely expressed it. He said: "I assure you that the Bengalis are the only people in our country whom we can properly be proud of, and it is only due to them that knowledge, liberty and patriotism have progressed in our country. I can truly say that they are really the head and crown of all the communities of Hindustan. In the word 'nation' I include both Hindus and Mahomedans, because that is the only meaning which I can attach to it."

Such was the wise and patriotic counsel of that great

man, and our Mahomedan friends will, I hope, take it to heart. I repeat once more that our emancipation depends upon the thorough union of all the people of India without any obstruction.

I have often read about the question of a constitution for the Congress. I think the gentlemen who raise this question would be the proper persons to prepare one like a Bill in the House of Commons in all its details. The Congress then can consider it and deal with it as the majority may decide.

Let every one of us do the best he can, do all in harmony for the common object of self-government.

Lastly, the question of social reforms and industrial progress—each of them needs its own earnest body of workers. Each requires for it separate devoted attention. All the three great purposes—Political, Social and Industrial—must be set working side by side. The progress in each will have its influence on the others. But as Mr. Morley truly and with deep insight says:—"Political principles are, after all, the root of our national greatness, strength and hope," and his other important utterance which I repeat with this one sums up the whole position of the Indian problem. He says:—"The meddling wrongly with economic things, that is going to the very life, to the very heart, to the very core of our national existence."

This meddling wrongly with economic things is the whole evil from which India suffers—and the only remedy for it is—"Political principles are, after all, the root of our national greatness, strength and hope." And these political principles are summed up in self-government. Self-Government is the only and chief remedy. In self-government lies our hope, strength, and greatness.

Well, Ladies and Gentlemen, I have finished my task. I do not know what good fortune may be in store for me during the short period that may be left to me, and if I can leave a word of affection and devotion for my country and countrymen I say, be united, persevere, and achieve self-government so that the millions now perishing by poverty, famine and plagues, and the scores of millions that are starving on scanty subsistence may be saved, and India may once more occupy her proud position of yore among the greatest and civilized nations of the world.

BABU SURENDRANATH BANERJEA

INDIAN NATIONAL CONGRESS, 1915

Mr. President, brother and sister delegates, ladies and gentlemen,—I am confronted with an initial difficulty in moving this resolution. A spectre is conjured up to frighten us out of this resolution. We are told by our critics—and they are as multitudinous as the stars of heaven (*laughter*)—and by our candid friends that to move a resolution of this kind at a time like the present and to formulate proposals of reform now is to embarrass the Government. If I could be persuaded of the soundness of this view, I, for my part, would have no part or share in this resolution; furthermore, I would ask you to drop it. For, Brother delegates, our attitude,—the attitude of the educated community—throughout the crisis of this war has been one of fervent devotion to the Throne (*applause*) and of active co-operation with the Government. Agitation is far from our minds. We may deliberate, discuss, even formulate proposals of reform, but we are resolved,—we, the men of the Congress are resolved—to embark upon no agitation, no controversy, and not to let loose the forces of public opinion so as to bring pressure to bear upon the Government.

Brother delegates, this war cannot last for ever. Peace must come. God grant that it may soon come.

We have to prepare ourselves for peace, for the situation in which we will find ourselves upon the conclusion of peace. I can think of no more patriotic task than that. We have to play the part of men, and let us equip ourselves for that exalted function. Brother delegates, the idea of re-adjustment is in the air, not only here in India but all the world over. The heart of the Empire is set upon it: it is the problem of problems upon which humanity is engaged. What is this war for? Why are these numerous sufferings endured? Because, it is a war of re-adjustment, a war that will set right the claims of minor nationalities, uphold and vindicate the sanctity of treaties, proclamations—ours is one (*applause*)—charters and similar "scraps of paper." (*laughter*). They are talking about what will happen after the war in Canada, in Australia; they are talking about it from the floor of the House of Commons and in the gatherings of public men and ministers of the State. May we not also talk about it a little from our standpoint? Are we to be charged with embarrassing the Government when we follow the examples of illustrious public men, men weighted with a sense of responsibility at least as onerous as that felt by our critics and our candid friends?

Brother delegates, the resolution says that the time is come when a definite advance must be made for the attainment of our goal, which is Self-Government. (*applause.*) But, brother delegates, there are those who tell us that we are unfit for self-government (*cries of "shame,"*) that the goal is distant, very distant, so distant as to be illusory (*laughter*), and not even with the tiny eye of hope can we obtain a glimpse of the promised land. A high authority speaking from his place in Parliament said that, so far as his imagination could pierce, he could not conceive of a time when India would be fit for Parliamentary institutions. The same authority is the author of the reform scheme. (*Laughter*). But, brother delegates, I am no prophet, and do not desire to be one (*laughter*,) though my ancestors were in their own humble sphere. But I will say this; that it will be one of the bitterest ironies of fate that will hand down Lord Morley to remote generations as the Simon De Montfort of the future Parliament of India. (*applause.*) We are not fit for self-government! Let us examine that proposition. (*laughter.*) Brother delegates, self-government is the ordering of Nature, the dispensation of Divine Providence, (*hear, hear*); every community must be the master of its own destiny. That is a part of the divine law, a part of the immutable order of the universe written in every line of Universal History, written in characters of life by the inscrutable hand of Divine Providence. If there is to be a deviation or a departure, it must be transitional and transient, and like the needle of a compass always pointing northwards; ours deflects steadily towards the goal, which is Self-Government.

Brother delegates, Self-Government, being the normal condition of things, it is incumbent upon those who say that we are not fit for self-government, that it is a distant possibility, so distant that it fades away into the mist of the unseen future,—I say it is incumbent upon them to prove their case. The burden of proof is upon them and not upon me, (*laughter*). But in a chivalrous spirit, imitating the chivalry of this Congress, I will come to their rescue, I will take upon myself the burden of proof, I will descend from the vantage ground I occupy, and fight my adversary in the open (*applause*) with his own instrument and upon terms of perfect equality. Let us survey the past, examine the present, look around us and then pronounce our verdict. Brother delegates, in the morning of the world, before Rome had been built, before Nineveh and Babylon had emerged into the historic arena, our ancestors had founded those village organisations (*applause*) which represent the first beginnings of self-government. So well organised, so tenacious of life and vitality they were that they survived the crash of Empires, the subversions of thrones, changes of dynasties, and they lived within living memory (*hear, hear*). Coming down to more recent times, what do we find? Wherever we have been tried, Sir, we have not been found wanting. We have been tried in the matter of local self-government, under conditions admitted by Lord Morley to be adverse; and yet the experiment has proved successful. We have been tried in the higher regions of self-government under the Reform Scheme of 1909 and again we have been successful. And let us look around. Here is this vast, this stupendous gathering of representative men from all parts of India. Is there any part of the world which can present an equal of a gathering like this. It has been said that self-government is government by discussions. How do we discuss here? How do we deliberate? How do we consult? How do we compromise? We do all that with a sense of moderation, of self-restraint, regard for constituted authority, which is proof positive of our capacity for deliberation. (*Hear hear* and *applause.*) But that is not all. The best training ground of self-government is the institution of self-government, and Mr. Gladstone is my authority for it. This is what he says: "Liberty alone fits a people for free institutions." If you do not give us liberty, if you do not give us free institutions, how can you say we are unqualified or unfit for free institutions? Then again, in another place, he says: "Free institutions alone qualify a people for Self-Government." If you deny a people free institutions, you take away from them the most useful academies and seminaries and institutions for training in self-government. Let me look abroad. Take the case of Japan. Japan was given full Parliamentary institutions immediately after Japan had emerged from the times of medieval barbarism and at the present moment, after a training of fifty years, all Europe, openly proclaims that Japan is qualified for the highest forms of self-government. Again, take the instance of the island of Phillippines. Only the other day, it became a province of America. America has given her, with the gracious generosity of a great republic, free institutions, and those institutions are working admirably. Therefore, let not our calumniators start the objection that we are disqualified for self-government. We say, you are out of court; because you have not given us free institutions: and it cannot be said that we are qualified or disqualified unless we are given these institutions.

Brother delegates, the resolution lays down the principles upon which the scheme of reform is to proceed. First and foremost is Provincial autonomy. In that resolution to which my Hon'ble friend Sir Ibrahim Rahimtulla spoke just now, there was a reference to this particular matter. In the forefront you have placed the question of Provincial autonomy. What is Provincial autonomy? It is the government of the province, not by the bureaucracy of the province, but by the chosen representatives of the people; it is the government of the province by the people of the province for the benefit of the people of that province. That is what I understand Provincial autonomy to mean. The basis of Provincial autonomy is financial independence. Brother delegates, the revenues of the province belong to the province. Many, many years ago, Sir James Westland, speaking from his place in the Imperial Legislative Council, said that the revenues of India belonged to the Government of India, (*laughter*). I wholly dissent from that view. The revenues of India belong to us, to you and to me, (*applause*). The revenues of India belong to the people of India (*applause*), held in trust by the Government of India for our benefit. And I am sure that a trustee is at liberty to delegate that trust to a subordinate authority. Therefore, we, who, I hope, shall soon become a sovereign people (*applause*),—we who represent the people, the majesty, the dignity, the authority, the throbbing aspirations of the people, we appeal to the Government to delegate its powers over the revenues of a province and entrust those revenues to the Government of that province. That is the first part of the programme that we suggest. Then, you will ask: "If you take all provincial revenues, what will the Government of India do?" Well, there are imperial revenues such as customs, salt, railways, post and telegraphs,—and opium there was, but it is dwindling, and it is a good thing too (*laughter*)—all these belong to the Government of India and the revenues of the Government may be subvented by contributions from the provincial Governments.

Ladies and gentlemen, we stand upon very firm ground in asking for Provincial autonomy, because it is contained in the great Despatch of the 25th August, 1911. An attempt has been made to attenuate the message contained in that document. Confronted with a hostile House, Lord Crewe, as Secretary of State, declared--I think he was a bit afraid of Lord Curzon and Co. (*laughter*)—confronted by a hostile House, Lord Crewe declared that this Despatch contained nothing more than the delegation of power from superior to subordinate authority. That is not borne out by the contents: and what is more, the assumption was promptly refuted by his lieutenant, who, in his free atmosphere of a Liberal Club,—I am speaking of Mr. Montague—said that this Despatch represented a new departure in Indian policy and opened up a new vision to the people of India. Truly, it is a new vision; truly, it is the beacon light which will guide us in the grand march which is to lead us to the promised land. We take our stand upon this Despatch, we resolutely adhere to it, and we ask the Government in season and out of season to redeem it.

Gentlemen, there are other suggestions made in this resolution. Mr. President, you have reminded me of the time (*Cries of* "*Go on*" "*Go on.*") I cannot be unfair to other speakers, there are other points in the resolution and only to one or two of them I shall refer (*cries of* "*no*" "*no,*" "*more, more.*") I shall be here the whole night in that case. The resolution refers to the expansion and the reconstitution of the Legislative Councils. Well, gentlemen, I am a member of two Legislative Councils, and I know something about them. In my own province, it was declared with a flourish of trumpets that we had a non-official majority, a very captivating phrase, "a non-official majority;" but a pure undiluted myth, this non-official majority. This non-official majority is a very different thing from a popular majority. We have occasionally to fight the Government, we occasionally have to be in the opposition,—not always—but I do not remember that we have ever been able to defeat the Government except on one occasion. Therefore, the myth of a non-official majority must be dispelled. We must have a living, absolute, unqualified majority of the representatives of the people (*applause*) in the Legislative Councils. Further the powers of the Legislative Councils must be enlarged. We move resolutions—I am one of the greatest sinners in that respect—and these resolutions are sometimes graciously accepted, and more often ungraciously rejected (*laughter*). When they are accepted, what does it matter? A resolution, after all, is a pious hope and aspiration: the Government are under no statutory obligation to give effect to it, though I must say as a matter of great credit to the Government of Lord Carmichael (*applause*) so far as he is at least personally concerned as the head of the Government,—he is full of liberal instincts—resolutions accepted by that Government would not always be a pious hope. But, gentlemen, in a matter of this kind we cannot allow ourselves to be dependent upon individual discretion, which would often lead to individual caprice. We say, and I hope the All-India Congress Committee will say, that every resolution accepted by a majority in the Legislative Council shall be binding on the Government and be given effect to.

One or two other points. I have been encouraged by the attention which you are giving me, but it involves a reciprocal duty on your part, namely, that you will do your best to bring this controversy about self-government to a triumphant issue, (*applause*). Brother delegates, we have got Executive Councils. My friend was a member of that Council. He will not let us into the secrets of that prison-house. But I think if the depths of his heart were sounded, it might be possible that we may be able to extricate a residuum of sub-consciousness which would tell us that at times he felt isolated, that he would have felt better, happier, more comfortable if he was associated with an Indian colleague. And as a matter of fact, I need not leave this thing to your imagination. Sir Syed Ali Imam, in that admirable address which he gave,—my friend knows it, he nods assent—in that admirable address which he gave in reply to the dinner that was held in his honour, said that at times a cloud of depression hung over his mind, that at times he felt discouraged and was only encouraged and supported by the active sympathy of His Excellency the Viceroy (*applause*). Therefore, I say, we, the Congress, should come to the rescue of our Indian representatives in the Executive Councils, and demand that there shall be a substantial increase in the number of such representatives in the Executive Councils, and, what is more, they shall be the elect of the people (*applause*). A Raja or a Maharaja, a Nawab Bahadur will not do, (*laughter*). We want popular representatives, who, if under the statute are not answerable to us, would, under a moral obligation, be responsible to us. Therefore, my suggestion would be: at least one-half of the members of the Executive Council must be Indians and they must all be elected.

Gentlemen, my last point is that to which reference was made by my friend Sir Ibrahim Rahimtulla. Fiscal domination is even more disastrous than political domination. That was uttered from this platform by a friend of mine. Well, we say, in one part of the resolution, "the readjustment of the relations between the Secretary of State for India and the Government of India." We have asked for Provincial autonomy, we have asked for Provincial independence, the independence of the revenues of the province. We must also ask for the independence of the Government of India. We must ask that the fetters now imposed by the India Office on the Government of India should be withdrawn, and the Government of India should reflect the public opinion of our people, not the public opinion of Manchester or Lancashire, (*laughter*). For instance, if those fetters are removed, I am confident that excise duties on cotton goods would disappear in a trice. And, therefore, it is of very great importance. Brother delegates, I will not dwell any more upon this point of the resolution. The resolution says further that a Committee should be appointed to confer with the Moslem League, with the Committee of the Moslem League, (*applause*) and to draft a scheme of reform. I have noticed with satisfaction the cheers which have greeted that statement. The Moslem League meets to-morrow in this City. I rejoice that they are going to hold a session (*applause*). Our fraternal greetings go to the Moslem League (*applause*). We sympathise with them in their patriotic efforts (*applause*) and may the Divine Dispenser of all blessings preside over their deliberations (*applause*). That is what we feel, that is what I feel, and I am sure that is what the Congress feels (*applause*) about the Moslem League. We are brothers, standing shoulder to shoulder, practically upon the same platform (*applause*) for the advancement of the common interests of the same Mother, (*applause*) the mother of Hindus, of Mahomedans, of Parsis, of Sikhs. And this disconsolate mother lies prostrate at our feet and it is our most sacred duty to wipe off her tears, to uplift her, to elevate her, to bring her back to her own position. And can you do so alone ? I say no. Hindus, Musalmans, Parsis, Sikhs must stand upon the same platform before this great accomplishment is achieved. And Brother delegates. in this matter the goal of the Congress and of the Moslem League is the same. They want self-government within the Empire. We want Self-Government within the Empire. I am sure a scheme of reform, a combined demand put forward by the League and the Congress, backed by the voice of United India, and supported with unflinching tenacity, is bound to be irresistible. Brethren, let us stand together, Hindus and Mahomedans, under the same banner of Self-Government. Let it float aloft and let us carry it to a triumphant issue. (*Applause.*)

Brother delegates, there is one little matter referred to in this resolution which I desire to call attention to. Mr. President, I won't take more than five minutes. The Subjects Committee have authorised the All-India Congress Committee to prepare a programme of continuous work of an educative and propagandist character for the spread of our ideals of self-government. As an old Congressman, this appeals to me most powerfully. Self-Government has been our watch-word from the very beginning of the institution of the Congress. In 1890, we sent a deputation, and we got, as the result of that deputation, the first instalment of Council reform by the Parliamentary Statute of 1892. Then, Mr. Gokhale, of honoured memory, (*applause*) used to visit England every now and then as our delegate and helped materially in the elaboration of the reform scheme. In 1914, just before the outbreak of the war, my friends the Hon'ble Mr. Bhupendranath Basu, the Hon'ble Mr. Samarth, Mr. Jinnah and one or two others went as a deputation to England in connection with the reform of the India Council. Well, brother delegates, the psychological moment has now arrived. Let us make a supreme effort which will culminate in the crowning triumph that will give to us and to our country the inestimable boon of self-government.

One word more and I have done. Mr. Asquith observed in the passage which you, Sir, were pleased to read the other day—he said in the course of a great speech that the Empire rests not upon the predominance of artificial and superficial rights of men based upon colour, but upon the loyal affection of free communities built upon the basis of equal rights. Well, we want to be free communities, we want to enjoy equal rights with the rest of the Empire. The angle of vision in England has changed. But has it changed here ? I think the answer must be in the negative (*laughter*). The Press Act with its severity has caused great uneasiness; the rigours of the Arms Act have not been relaxed; we are barred out of the commissioned ranks of the Army; we are not permitted to be enlisted as volunteers. In England, the cry is for more men and more men for the front. Why do not they appeal to us? Our manhood and our youth are anxious to draw the sword in the defence of the Empire. (*applause*). But the call never comes to us. A little more trust in the people is needed. (*Hear, hear*); and if that trust was forthcoming, it would be reciprocated with enthusiastic gratitude. Let our rulers read the open page of Indian history and note the lesson it teaches. A stranger, the son of an adventurer, Akbar, has enthroned himself in the hearts of his people. What was the fascination that enabled him to do that? He loved and trusted the people, and they loved and trusted him in an abounding measure. Centuries have passed since he has been laid in his quiet grave; his princely dynasty has disappeared; the Moghul Empire has crumbled into dust; but the name of Akbar excited the profoundest veneration amongst Hindus and Mahomedans alike. That is the outstanding lesson that it has taught.

Brother delegates, we want self-government—And why? Because we want to be a nation. We want self-government for the highest ends of national and moral regeneration, for uplifting our people. Our sense of civic responsibility cannot develop to its fullest height so long as the brand of political inferiority is marked on our brow. We must be free men before we can be good, responsible and well-meaning citizens. And therefore, this campaign is a moral as well as a political campaign; and we have on our side the sympathies of civilised countries and the good wishes of the true-thinking in all parts of the world, the majestic forces of time, and above all, the blessing of Almighty Providence. Thus equipped we are irresistible, invincible. Armed with that faith, we have started this campaign and, God willing, in the fulness of time, we shall have established in this great and ancient land the inestimable blessings of Self-Government under British ægis. (*Loud and long continued applause.*)

THE BISHOP OF MADRAS

INDIA AFTER THE WAR

It may seem premature to discuss what is to happen after the War, till the War is over and the victory won. So far as Europe is concerned, this is probably the case. It will be time enough to consider how the map of Europe is to be re-arranged when we can see the end. Before that comes many things may happen which will greatly modify the final settlement of accounts. On the other hand, in India the War is clearly bringing us face to face with definite problems of great difficulty and complexity, that will need long and anxious study before they can be rightly solved, and it is not too soon to begin at once to consider the problem that we have got to solve and the difficulties which lie in the way of its solution.

In the first place, then, we must frankly recognise that the War is bound to have an enormous influence on Indian life and thought and upon the whole political situation. The Russo-Japanese War had an extraordinary effect on India and one could feel the thrill of a new hope passing over the whole continent when it was over; but this War will have a far more potent and widespread effect on the peoples of India than the war between Russia and Japan. To begin with, India is taking a direct part in it. Indian blood is being freely shed, Indian treasure is being lavishly spent. In the Russo Japanese War India was only an interested spectator: in this War she is one of the actors. And while the former was a mere local War for material interests, this is a great world struggle of conflicting moral and political ideals. The liberty and civilisation of the world are at stake, and the princess and peoples of India feel to-day that they are making history. The day that Indian troops, therefore, landed at Marseilles marked the beginning of a new epoch in Indian history, it put India into a new position not only as regards the British Empire, but also as regards the progress and civilisation of the world. Never before has India taken part in a great world-movement. Shut off from the rest of the world by the great barrier of the Himalayas, she has lived her life, dreamed her dreams and thought her great thoughts apart in solitude. Now her long period of isolation is at an end. She is taking her part in a great War that is to decide the future progress of the world's civilisation for the next hundred years.

It is well that we should try to realise what a change this sudden entry on to the stage of the world's history must make in the outlook, the feelings and the ideas of the Indian peoples. If we may compare great things with small, it will be like the change that comes over a boy when he goes to school. The sudden passing into a new world affects his whole way of looking at things and even his attitude towards his parents. We must expect that there will be a similar change in India and that when the War is over she will enter upon a new stage in her history.

Even before the War, the political situation in India was one of unstable equilibrium. On the one hand it is acknowledged by all reasonable men that the great needs of India—peace, justice, unity, social reform, education and the development of its material resources—can only be satisfied by the maintenance of British Government. The outburst of loyalty to the British Empire and to our Sovereign at the beginning of the War was a striking testimony to the strength of this feeling among Indians of all classes. There is undoubtedly a very small body of anarchists in Bengal who still carry on a criminal campaign of outrage and assassination against the police and the British officials and there is a section of the Nationalist party who are now starting a campaign in favour of Home Rule for India immediately; but with these exceptions it is true to say that the desire for the maintenance of British rule is universal among the great mass of the peoples of India. On the other hand, the last fifty years have seen the rapid growth of an educated class throughout India who have received a Western education, are imbued with English political ideals and by reason of a common language and civilisation have been inspired with a sense of National unity, and which the Indian National Congress is the outward and visible sign. Among this class of educated men there has been growing up for the last half-century an increasing desire for a larger share in the

Government of their own country, a longing that India should have its place in the sun, and the vision of an Indian Nation, independent and Self-Governing, taking its place with the Colonies of Canada, South Africa and Australia, as an integral part of the British Empire. We must not imagine that the War will alter the fundamental facts of the political situation and lead the educated classes of India to abandon their ideals. People in England are apt to imagine that the great outburst of loyalty in India at the beginning of the War has put an end to political unrest, and that, when the War is over, we shall find ourselves in smooth waters: but that is an utter mistake. If educated Indians desired a large share in the Government of their own country before the War began, that desire will be far stronger when the War is over; if the desire to realise the ideal of Self-Government and to play an honourable part in the history of the world was strong in the hearts of the Indian peoples before the Indian troops landed in France, it will become incomparably stronger after the War.

All Englishmen would acknowledge that these are honourable ambitions and that the vision of the India that is to be is a noble and inspiring ideal, and that there is, nothing in this ambition or this ideal in any way inconsistent with perfect loyalty to the British Empire or with the full and frank recognition of the fact that for many years to come the strength and efficiency of the British Government are absolutely necessary if the ideals are to be attained. There is, therefore, no reason in the nature of things why we should look forward with any apprehension to the fact that the War is bound to give an immense stimulus both to the honourable ambitions of the educated class and also to their longing to realise the ideal of a Self-Governing India. At the same time there has undoubtedly been a conflict between the ideal of the Englishman in India and the ideal of the educated India during the last few years, and we must expect that the conflict will be more acute after the War. It is not due to the fact that the two ideals are necessarily irreconcilable, but simply to the fact that each of the two races naturally tends to look at the political situation from a different angle and to take an onesided and partial view of the problem it presents. It is perhaps natural that this should be so, simply because Englishmen and Indians differ so widely in temparament and mental characteristics. We English people are by temperament suspicious of ideals: we naturally fix our attention on present facts and deal with them as best we can: our whole interest is in the *status quo*: we live and work for the present and do not look forward to the future, and that to a very large extent is the secret of our success in the building of the Empire. It has been said that England conquered India in a fit of absent mindedness, and this is partly true: we did not come to India with any idea of Empire or with any intention of conquering India: we came as traders; we established factories because they were necessary for the security of our trade;

we assumed the Government of Districts and States because it seemed necessary to do so for the security of our factories, and so we were led on by the practical necessities of the case step by step until at last there came out this Empire! We are doing much the same thing now; we are taking one step after another by the education of the people, the extension of railways and telegraphs, the spread of the English language, the training of the people in the arts of Government, the creation of a sense of unity among the peoples of India, and we are thus preparing the way for great political changes in the future; but we never trouble ourselves to look ahead or seriously to think what is the inevitable goal towards which we are tending. Sufficient unto the day is the good and evil thereof.

On the other hand, Indians are essentially idealists; their whole interest in the past has been centred in religion, philosophy, and the abstract sciences of logic and mathematics. They have never taken much interest in history; their tendency is to concentrate on ideals, to go back to first principles, to dream dreams and see visions, and largely to ignore the intermediate steps by which the visions and ideals must be realised. In this respect there is a strong resemblance between the genius of the Indians and that of the Germans. Bernhardi remarks in one of his books that the most important fact about a politician is his conception of the universe; and the debates of the German Reichstag are full of fervent appeals to these general conceptions of the universe. Appeals of this kind would be greeted with shouts of laughter or with cold contempt in the British Parliament. Mr. Balfour is a philosopher and as his conceptions of the universe, but he would never dream of appealing to them in the House of Commons. But, as I have said, this love of ideals and abstractions is thoroughly Indian. A few years ago, when I was visiting a college in India, I attended a debate, got up for my benefit by some college students. They had chosen as the subject of debate the superiority of celibacy over matrimony. The subject was a purely abstract one so far as they themselves were concerned, as they were all married men, and the discussion was equally remote from the ordinary facts of life; the leader of the opposition began his speech by standing with great fervour and conviction. 'Celibacy is contrary to the categorical imperative of Kant.' As another illustration of the same characteristic of the Indian mind, I may quote the effort of an orator in a humbler rank of life. When I was in Calcutta, I formed a guild of Indian Christian servants; at our first meeting the question was discussed whether the limit of age for admission to the guild should be seventeen or eighteen. The Bishop's butler spoke first and solemnly began. 'In the beginning God created the heaven and the earth'; the intermediate facts necessary for deciding the question before us were entirely ignored.

When people with such utterly different mental characteristics look at the political situation as it now exists in India, they naturally view it in an entirely different way. English officials in India as a rule fix their thoughts on the facts and needs of present and ignore the ideals of the future; educated Indians fix their minds on the ideals of the future and to a very large extent ignore the facts and needs of the present.

On the one hand, the English officials do not at all realise what a natural and honourable ambition it is on the part of the educated class to desire a greater share in the Government of their own country, nor how splendid the vision is of a self-governing India; nor can they understand how difficult their position must necessarily be in India from the mere fact that they are foreigners governing a people with an ancient civilisation and history of their own. They forget that no educated and civilised people like to be governed by foreigners, however well they govern, and that the desire for independence and Self-Government is a simple elementary fact of human nature. They have always imagined that because they have governed well, their Government must necessarily be popular. It was once said by Sir Henry Campbell-Bannerman that good Government is no substitute for Self-Government; opinions may differ on this point, but we ought to realise more fully than we do the enormous disadvantage we labour under owing to the mere fact that we are governing India as a foreign bureaucracy.

Then, again, it is hard for us to realise the fact that India has a civilisation of its own, which it ought to develop upon its own lines. There are certain principles of thought, morality, social life and political progress which are common to all mankind. It is our duty and privilege to establish these principles in India; but, on the other hand, the exact form which these principles will assume in India is necessarily different from that which they have assumed in England. Our function is to sow seeds and let them grow in accordance with the genius of the Indian peoples. India has got its own contribution to make to the thought, the religion, the social and political life of humanity; but it can never make this contribution unless it is allowed ultimately to grow and develop upon its own natural lines in accordance with its own genius, and this is not possible without political Self-Government. At the present moment the progress of civilisation in India necessarily proceeds upon Western lines; it is at every point governed and directed by Englishmen; but our ultimate aim ought to be the development of a truly Indian civilisation on Indian lines.

And then, again, it is difficult for Englishmen in India to realise that in spite of the facts of past history, it is still true that the ultimate basis on which the British Government in India must rest in the future, is the will of the Indian peoples. Englishmen have been accustomed in the past to talk of India as a conquered country. We constantly hear it said that after all we have won India by the sword and intend to keep it by the sword; in the same way English people in India have often spoken of themselves as the ruling race. Such language has always been foolish and mischievous;

it has tended to wound the self-respect of educated Indians and it has made more galling than it need have been the yoke of foreign Government. But what we need to realise now is that as a statement of our future position in India such language will be a complete anachronism. Whatever may have been the origin of the British Government in India, its only justification now is the fact that it is necessary for the welfare, the happiness and the future progress of the Indian peoples themselves and that the great mass of the Indian peoples wish it to continue. Were the peoples of India ever to become fit for independence and to wish for independence, the British Government would have done its work and would retire. The idea that we can ever maintain our Government by force against the general will of the Indian people is unthinkable. Even if it were physically possible, our conscience would never allow us to use force and shed blood to maintain a foreign Government in India, if the mass of the people wished for a Government of their own. And the present War is making it doubly impossible for us ever to try to impose our Government upon the peoples of India by force. We are fighting now to the death against the claim of a single nation or race to impose its civilisation on the world and to dominate the other nations of Europe; but if it is wrong for Germany to attempt to impose her *Kultur* upon unwilling nations, it is equally wrong for England to attempt to impose her Government and civilisation upon India against the will of the Indian peoples. We cannot fight for one set of principles in Europe and then apply another set of principles in India.

At the same time the present War is surely striking proof that the British Government can take its stand upon the will of the Indian peoples with perfect safety. It has been a wonderful demonstration of fundamental loyalty of the great mass of the princes and peoples of India to the British Empire; and, if it has revealed the loyalty of India to the people of England, it has also revealed to the people of India the value to them of the British Empire. This ought to make a great difference to the practical policy of the British Government in India. Hitherto undoubtedly the policy of England in India has been to a very large extent dominated by a latent fear for the security of British rule. One result of the War surely ought to be to exercise this fear and to lead Englishmen as a body boldly to face the realities of the situation and to base their Government on the will of the people.

The outbreak of sedition in the Panjab at the beginning of 1915 and the revelations made at the trial of the conspirators of a plot to massacre Europeans, raise a revolt among the Indian troops and drive the British out of India may seem at first sight to show that this fear is by no means without justification even now, and that the will of the people is a very shaky foundation on which to base our rule. But in reality this very plot only supplies a strong additional reason for trusting the masses of the Indian peoples. The plot itself was hatched in America and British Columbia. It was probably engineered mainly by the German influence and German money. The conspirators were the men who went over to British Columbia in the *Komagata Maru*, and the people who brought the plot to the knowledge of the British Government were the Sikh peasantry. The fact that the conspiracy utterly failed and was nipped in the bud was due entirely to the staunch loyalty of the mass of the Sikh peasants and soldiers in the Punjab. If the plot proves anything, it is that the British Government need not fear fór one moment to take their stand on the will of the great mass of the poeple of India.

I hope it will not seem presumptuous to suggest that politicians in India may well learn a lesson from the experience of the Christian Church. As a rule, no doubt, the children of this world are in their generation wiser than the children of light. But I venture to think that for once the children of light have shown the greater wisdom. The Missionary Societies in India have to deal on a much smaller scale with precisely the same problem as that which confronts the State. They are administering the affairs of a large body of Indian Christians through a small body of foreign missionaries, who correspond very closely to the foreign bureaucracy of the State. There is the same tendency to apply Western methods to an Eastern people, the same discontent with foreign rule, the same claim on the part of the educated Indians for a larger share in the administration of Indian affairs, the same spirit of unrest; but the Anglican and Protestant missionary societies throughout India have always recognised the fact that, however good and efficient foreign rule may be, and however necessary it may be for the foundation of the Church, it is essentially a temporary expedient which cannot possibly be regarded as a permanent substitute for Self-Government. They have always maintained that the only possible ideal for the Church in India is an independent Indian Church managing its own affairs, living its own life, and developing on its own lines. They realise that the Self-Government of the Indian Church is necessary to enable it to play its proper part in the life and thought of Christendom. There may be, and there are legitimate differences of opinion as to the steps that ought to be taken in the immediate future for the realisation of this ideal and as to whether it is expedient at a particular time to take a particular step forward or not. But there is no difference of opinion whatever with regard to the ideal itself.

The result of this attitude on the part of the Missionary Societies is that, while there undoubtedly is occasional friction between individual missionaries in the field and their Indian fellow-workers, and difference of opinion with regard to the exact measure of Self Government for which any particular section of the Christian community is fitted, at the same time Europeans and Indians alike are working consciously for a common end, and are inspired by a common ideal. And this fact dominates the whole policy of the Missionary Societies, each step that they take being intended definitely to be a step onwards towards the one goal. They are intent not on securing their own position or ensuring the permanence of their work and influence in India, but on preparing for the time when their presence in India is no longer necessary. When, therefore, Indian Christians speak or write about the future Self-Government of the Indian Church, the missionary societies do not accuse them of disloyalty or regard them in any way with suspicion. The more talk there is about the Self-Government of the Indian Church the better we are all pleased. We do our utmost to encourage ideas of this kind and to stimulate the Indian Christians to realise their responsibilities and prepare themselves to meet them, and we can look forward to the natural development of their ideas and aspirations with equanimity. Our greatest triumph will be the final establishment of an Indian Church entirely independent of foreign missionaries and foreign control.

I cannot help thinking that in the same way the British Government would enormously strengthen its position in India if it were to make the Self-Government of India as an integral part of the British Empire its avowed object and ideal, encouraging educated Indians definitely to look forward to this ideal and shaping its own policy consistently with a view to this one great end. The Government would then practically adopt the platform of the Nationalist party. There would be no differences between them as to the end at which they are aiming, and though there would naturally be much difference of opinion, not only between Englishmen and Indians, but also between Indians and Indians, and Englishmen and Englishmen with regard to the particular steps that might wisely be taken at any particular time, still both alike would be working for a common ideal. The difference that this would make in the relations between the Government and the educated Indians as a body, as represented by the National Congress, would be immense. It would alter the whole of the political situation and would do more than anything else to allay the unrest which has been such a disquieting feature of Indian politics during the last fifty years, and it would give a consistency to our work and policy which at the present moment they do not possess. The danger of the present situation consists largely in the fact that, with notable exceptions, Englishmen in India are not only opposed to the feelings and sentiments of educated Indians, but also to the inevitable tendency of their own work and policy. Western education, the influence of British civilisation, British literature and British political ideals have all been tending for the last seventy years to stimulate strongly among the educated classes the desire for national liberty and Self-Government. And yet Englishmen have managed to give the impression that they regard this desire as dangerous and disloyal.

But if, on the one hand, Englishmen in India used to cultivate the spirit of idealism, on the other hand there is an equal necessity for a change of attitude on the part of educated Indians. They need to realise far more than they do at present, the enormous difficulties that lie in the way of the realisation of their ideal of a self governing India.

To begin with, India is a continent, not a country. It is inhabited not by one race but by forty. Its vast population is split up by divisions of race, religion, and caste. The Dravidian races in the South are widely different in temperament and character from the races of the North. The Bengalis are utterly different from the Punjabis, while the Maharattas of the Bombay Presidency are different from them both. The antagonism between Hindus and Muhammadans is notorious; they differ not only in religion but in their ideals of social life and Government So, too, within the Hindu community there is no real homogeneity. The Brahman and the outcaste are as wide asunder as the poles, much wider asunder than the slaves and their master in the Roman Empire. How to enable these heterogeneous elements to work together as members of one body for the development of a common civilisation is a problem that will tax to the uttermost all the resources of British statesmanship. The political development of India, indeed, must in the future be the work of Indians and not of Englishmen. All that the English Government can now do is to prepare the way and to create those conditions which will enable the Indian peoples to work out their own political and social salvation. But still the preliminary work of creating these conditions rests in the immediate future mainly with the British Government, and no statesmen in the world have ever had set them a more difficult task.

Then, again, to add to the difficulty, there is a singular lack of ordinary business capacity, governing power and political instinct among the vast majority of the Indian people. To govern an Empire of 320 million people is a big business proposition. It requires great financial ability and power of organisation. But these are just the weak points in the Indian character. The Parsis in Bombay have a genius for business. A few Hindus are successfully managing large business concerns in Bombay and elsewhere. A few Muhammadans are successful merchants; the Indians in South Africa owe their unpopularity largely to their talent for petty trade; but owing to the circumstances of their history for the last five thousand years, the Indian peoples have had no training in business that would at all fit them to administer the affairs of a large Empire. At the present moment, I doubt whether it would be possible to get together a body of Indians who could successfully manage the railways of India; and there is a wide gap between the management of the railways and the administration of the Empire. And this particular difficulty is increased by the fact that State socialism is far more developed in India than in England. People look to the State for everything.

The land is owned by the State; most of the railways are owned by the State; if a new industry needs starting, everyone clamours for the State to start it. The Government is expected to play the part of fairy godmother on a much more extensive scale in India than in England. And that means that it is constantly called upon to embark on enterprises that demand a great deal of business capacity. It is unfortunate, therefore, that so very few of the graduates of the Indian Universities ever embark on a business career. All of them, with very few exceptions, either go into Government service or become lawyers, doctors or teachers. It would be a great step towards Self-Government in India if half of our graduates would devote themselves to business, instead of to Government service or the law.

Then, again, there is the further difficulty that there is at present very little foundation on which to build any form of popular Government, really expressing the will of the Indian people as a whole. There is hardly any trace of democracy in India; the only forms of Government known are despotism and bureaucracy. The Native States are for the most part governed on the principle of despotism, in some cases tempered by bureaucracy, and British India is governed by a bureaucracy tempered by a narrow oligarchy. There is a Legislative Assembly for each Province and a Legislative Council for British India as a whole; but the various constituencies which elect the members of these Legislative Assemblies differ very little in size from the small boroughs in England a century ago. The number of electors is astonishingly few, and in South India, where more than 80 per cent of the educated classes belong to the Brahman caste, the Legislative Councils practically represent a minute fraction of the population. It is broadly true, therefore to say that at the present moment popular Government in India does not exist. It is possible that the germ of democracy may be found in the old Village Panchayats; but the highly centralised administration of the British Government has so far destroyed their power and importance that they are at the present moment almost non-existent.

There is yet one more difficulty which must be faced. It is the old familiar difficulty of putting a new patch on an old garment. We have got a system of Government in British India at the present moment which on the whole works fairly well, which has given to India the signal blessings of peace, order, justice, unity, material progress, and civilisation, and no reasonable man would be mad enough to propose that it should be swept away and an independent Indian Government of some kind or other suddenly put in its place. But it is extremely difficult to develop any system of real Self-Government under the shadow of the existing bureaucracy. It is one thing to associate Indians with Englishmen in carrying on a European system of government and developing a European system of civilisation; but it is another thing altogether to train the peoples of India to govern themselves and to develop their own civilisation or their own civilisation on their own lines. Here again the experience of the Christian Church is much to the point. The English Church has been introduced into India and has established among a large body of Indian Christians the Anglican system of doctrine, discipline, and worship; we have translated the English Prayer Book into the vernaculars of India; we train our clergy in Anglican theology and administer discipline in accordance with the law of the English Church. Thus the whole system is Anglican through and through, and it is not the less Anglican because we administer it among our Indian congregations mainly through Indian clergymen; we do not imagine that, because an Anglican system is administered by Indian clergymen, it becomes thereby any the more fitted to be the true expression of the faith, devotion, and spiritual life of Indian Christians. What we look forward to in the future is not an Anglican system administered by Indians, but an Indian system of faith, worship, and discipline, developed and managed by Indians themselves. We fully recognise that the fact of the system being administered by Indians does not make it truly Indian or suited to the genius and the needs of the Indian people, and that it will be impossible for a truly Indian Church ever to develop on its own lines until it can grow up independent of English control.

Assuming, however, a spirit of sweet reasonableness on the part of both Indians and Europeans, each trying to see the other's point of view and both working together with their different gifts and temperaments towards the common end, what possible lines of advance are there towards the great ideal of a Self-Governing India?

The first is obviously to increase the number of Indians in Government service and promote them continually to positions of greater responsibility, with the idea that ultimately the British element in the Government will to a very large extent disappear and India be governed almost entirely by Indians. This is practically the policy which has been steadily pursued for the last sixty or seventy years. Lord Morley's reforms were a great step in this direction, and the further reforms which have for some years past been advocated by the Nationalist party all tend to the same end. This policy undoubtedly is valuable, inasmuch as it serves to train a large body of Indians in the art of administration and to bring the Government more in touch with Indian thought and feeling; but on the other hand, as has been pointed out above, it cannot be regarded as a true solution of the problem that has ultimately to be solved. When it has reached its end it will only be the substitution of an Indian for a foreign bureaucracy. But what is needed in India in the future is a Government based upon and expressing the will of the Indian peoples. The problem before us is not the creation of an Indian bureaucracy, but the development in India of some form of popular Government. One of the foremost Indian politicians remarked very truly a few months ago, 'Even if all the posts in the Civil Service were filled with Indians, that would not constitute Self-Government for India. Self-Government must begin from below. There can be no such thing as Self-Government until the people in every village have learnt to govern themselves.'

The second line of advance is the development of Local Self-Government in municipalities and villages. This policy has been steadily carried out in India so far as municipalities and districts are concerned since the days of Lord Ripon, and it has achieved a certain measure of success. It has opened out to Indian gentlemen throughout the country an opportunity of useful public service in towns, cities, and districts; it is giving in a certain number of them a training in public affairs; it has accustomed people to the working of representative institutions, and it has undoubtedly sown the seeds of popular Government. It would be unreasonable indeed to expect that a system of this kind would be an unqualified success from the very beginning. It started with a body of men untrained in public business, very often, it must be admitted, deficient in public spirit and more prone to talk than to act; but I think that it is true to say that during the last thirty years Municipal Government throughout India has made steady progress. It remains to extend this system to local Self-Government from the towns and districts to the villages. This is one of the reforms which the late Mr. Gokhale advocated in the statement submitted by him to the Royal Commission on Decentralisation.

He propcsed that, in all villages with a population of 500 and over a Panchayat (lit. a Committee of five) should be constituted by statute, to consist of five or seven members, and that the villages below 500 should either be joined to larger adjoining villages or grouped into unions. These Panchayats, he said, should be invested with such powers and functions as the disposal of simple money claims, the trial of trivial offences, the execution and supervision of village works, the management of village forests, the carrying out of measures of famine and plague relief, the control of village water-supply and sanitation, and the supervision of school attendance.

The Village Panchayat is a very ancient institution, dating from the days when the village was a Self-Governing community with a very large measure of independence. The institution of village Panchayats, therefore, would not be a new thing in India. We have utilised them for the purposes of Church discipline in many mission districts with great success. They are institutions which the people understand and which they are capable of working by themselves. There seems to be no reason why they should not be as successfully revised by the State as they have already been by the Church.

A third possible line of advance is much more open to criticism. The ideal towards which we ought to aim in British India is, as has already been said, not a bureaucratic system administered by Indians, but a truly popular Government; but we are confronted with the difficulty that, on the one hand, we cannot make any advance towards that ideal so long as we maintain the existing system of Government; while on the other hand in British India as a whole the maintenance of the existing bureaucratic form of Government is for the present and in the immediate future absolutely necessary. The suggestion, then, has been made more than once that it might be possible for the State to make some such experiment in particular areas as is now being made by the Church. We are confronted by precisely the same difficulty in the development of our Church life as the difficulty that now confronts the State; the affairs of our Indian Christian congregations are administered by European missionaries appointed by the Committees of Missionary Societies at home, and while this system continues it is very difficult to make any real advance towards the independent life of the Indian Christian Church. What we have done, however, is to take a particular district and put that entirely in charge of Indian clergy and lay-workers under an Indian Bishop; the whole work is supported by Indians and managed by Indians and carried on in accordance with Indian ideas. The experiment met at the beginning with very severe criticism, and obviously there was the possibility of failure; but, even had it failed, failure in a particular district would not have been a great disaster; as a matter of fact, it has proved an unqualified success. Would it not be possible for the State to make a similar experiment? There are already a very large number of independent States in India under despotic forms of Government tempered by bureaucracy. Why should not one or more of these States establish a popular form of Government? This could of course, only be done by the Indian rulers or princes of these States themselves acting on their own initiative. It is not a reform that could be or ought to be forced upon them by the British Government, and it is also not a reform that could be introduced into any State that had not been previously prepared for it by the spread of education among the mass of the population. But I believe that a few, at any rate, of the more progressive Native States would very soon be ready for an advance in this direction, and that the more enlightened Indian Princes would be glad to introduce this reform, and for the good of their people limit their own autocratic powers and accept the honourable position of constitutional ruler. Even if the experiment was not altogether a success, it would not be a great disaster; it is not likely that such States would be worse governed than some of the existing Native States under autocratic rule. On the other hand, if it was a success it might form a model for the extension of popular Self-Government not only among the Native States generally, but also in British India.

It is a minor point, but I venture to think that it is a mistake to discourage the serious study of Indian politics in our Indian Universities. There is at the present moment a good deal of wild talk and writing on political subjects, but there is extraordinarily little serious and sober study of them. We greatly need in

India a large body of thoughtful Indian politicians of the type of the late Mr. Gokhale, and a great deal might be done to create such a body of men for the service of the State by fostering and encouraging the study of political and social questions in the Universities. I fully believe myself that a school of Political Science in each University, with a body of really able professors to teach the subject, would have a very wholesome and steadying effect upon Indian politics. It would create in each Province a sound body of public opinion; it would discourage wild and thoughtless talk, and it would raise up a body of men who in time would be able to apply the universal principles of political science to the special conditions of Indian life and society.

A more important point is the cultivation of friendly social relations between Europeans and Indians. It may be true that social relation between Europeans and Indians cannot be quite satisfactory so long as there is political inequality; and it may also be true, as is constantly urged by Europeans, that Indian customs, especially the seclusion of women and the caste rules of the Hindus with reference to food, place great obstacles in the way of social relations between the two races. At the same time it is a great exaggeration to say that there can be no social relations at all between the two races until these obstacles are removed. I can bear witness from my own experience of thirty years in India, both in Calcutta and Madras, that a very large amount of social intercourse between Europeans and

Indians is perfectly possible in spite of all obstacles, and that such intercourse is of the utmost value to both parties. There can be no doubt, I think, that more friendly social relations would do a great deal to enable Europeans and Indians to understand one another and to soften down on the part of educated Indians the inevitable dislike of foreign rule. The existing aloofness of Europeans from educated Indians in social matters necessarily gives the impression of haughtiness and a sense of superiority, and this is exactly what we ought to try by all means to avoid. It may be quite true that as rulers and men of business Europeans are superior to Indians, but it is not desirable that we Europeans should be constantly asserting the fact.

What we both need to recognise far more fully than we do at present is that Indians and Europeans have different virtues, different faults and different gifts, and that the collossal task of creating a Self-Governing India needs the gifts and virtues of both races. It is utterly impossible for the Europeans alone or for the educated Indians alone to accomplish so great a task. It is imperatively needed that we both work together in harmony and sympathy. We have long ago learnt that lesson in the Christian Church; it is high time that it was fully learnt in the State as well; but it never will be learnt so long as Europeans as a body maintain their present attitude of aloofness and will not make the effort needed to make friends with educated Indians. I do not overlook the difficulties in the way of this. Social intercourse is not easy between two sets of people who have different interests, different social customs and a different outlook upon life. The mere fact, that, when they meet together socially, they do not know what to talk about, undoubtedly makes social intercourse somewhat constrained. A little while ago the first Indian Bishop, the Bishop of Dornakal, was staying with me at Ootacamund. He was asked to dinner at Government House, and there he sat next to a young English officer who was very anxious indeed to make himself pleasant to the Indian guest, so he started conversation at once. 'Do you play polo, Bishop?' 'No.' Then, after a pause. 'Do you hunt?' 'No.' A longer pause. 'Do you play cricket?' 'No.' A still longer pause. 'Do you fish?' 'No.' And at last, in desperation, 'Do you dance?' A more emphatic 'No' still. But happily the Bishop saw an opening here; he at once plunged into the subject of the differences between dancing in India and dancing in England and proceeded to discuss the ethics of the Nautch. This incident may serve to illustrate the difficulty that naturally exists in the way of pleasant social intercourse between the two races, even where there is every desire to be pleasant and amiable on both sides. It is undoubtedly the case, too, that social intercourse between the two races is greatly limited by the fact that Indian ladies with few exceptions do not come out into society. But, true as all this is and real as these difficulties are, still a certain amount of social intercourse is possible, and it is our interest and duty in India to cultivate it to the utter most.

A great deal can be done by inviting Indian gentlemen to small tennis parties. It is one of the few forms of social amusement in which both races can join with mutual pleasure, and it is one in which Indians can hold their own against Europeans. Subalterns and vakils may have very little to talk about, but when they play a good set of tennis together, a bond of sympathy at once springs up between them. To suggest lawn tennis as one of the means for consolidating the British Empire in India may seem like trifling with a serious subject; but it is not a small matter to discover some method of social intercourse which is pleasant to Europeans and Indians alike, which serves to create mutual respect and mutual sympathy and which will help them to know one another better and so gradually to come and understand one another's point of view more fully. The main point, however, that is of supreme importance is that Englishmen and Indians alike should henceforth make a real and serious effort to understand one another to see clearly the goal for which they ought to strive and to work together in a spirit of brotherhood towards a common end. The War is a great call to brotherhood not only to the British Empire but to the Nations of the world, and the only solution of the great problems which it will create in the world and the Empire alike will be found in the cultivation of the Christian spirit of brotherhood instead of the old pagan spirit of race pride, class prejudice and what has well been called 'private mindedness,' which has hitherto been the root of all evil in international relations and in the social and spiritual life of States and Empires.

A more serious and difficult question that the War is bound to bring to the fore is that of National defence. Two grievances have for some years past been acutely felt with reference to this matter. The first is the exclusion of Indians from the ranks of commissioned officers and the second their exclusion from the volunteers. At present no Indian can be appointed to a Commission in the Indian Army and no Indian can join the volunteers. The poorest Eurasian can become a volunteer, but not the son of an Indian Member of Council. This is naturally resented as a stigma on the loyalty of the Indian people. The only reason that can be given for it is that a large body of Indian volunteers would constitute a danger to the stability of the British Government.

But whatever the reason for these two disabilities may be, it is clear that the question will have to be reconsidered after the War. At the meeting of the Indian National Congress held in Madras in December 1914, a resolution was passed urging on Government 'the necessity, wisdom, and justice of throwing open the higher offices in the Army to Indians and of establishing military schools and colleges where they might be trained for a military career as officers of the Indian Army'; and also the reorganisation and extension of the present system of volunteering so as to enable Indians, without distinction of race or class, to enlist as citizen soldiers of the Empire.' This demand was renewed in the National Congress held at Bombay in December, 1915, and has found expression in numerous local Conferences during the last few months. These questions, therefore, are bound to come up immediately after the War, and it is well that Englishmen in India should begin to consider what is going to be their attitude towards them. Ultimately, it must depend on whether they hold to the old idea that the British Government in India rests on British bayonets or realise that the time has now come to base our policy frankly on the principle that the only possible foundation of the Government of India is the will of the Indian peoples. If that is once realised and admitted, there can be no possible danger in allowing the peoples of India to undertake the responsibility for the defence of their own country. And we need to remember that the lessons of the War have shown us clearly that in the future the only people who can possibly defend India from an attack by land will be the Indians themselves. Happily, there is no prospect of an attack on India by any Great Power, at any rate, for the next fifty years. But if ever the time comes when it is necessary to defend India against serious aggression, her present army will be in numbers hopelessly inadequate. It does not number nearly a million men, and even three millions would be insufficient for a great war upon the modern scale. England might possibly be able to send 5,00,000 men to India at a crisis, but the vast majority of the troops would have to be raised and equipped in India. Surely this ought to be taken into account when we are considering the question of National defence in India at the present day.

But after all the main point that ought to be strongly emphasised at the present time is that what we need after the War is a change of attitude on the part of both Indians and Europeans. On the one hand, we need a more statesmanlike attitude on the part of the general body of Indian Nationalists and a fuller recognition of the work that has to be done in co-operation with the British Government before Home Rule can become a question of practical politics. The worst enemies of Home Rule are the people who clamour for it to be established at once. The Home Rule for India League has recently circulated a leaflet in England which askes that 'when peace returns to the world, such a change may be made in India's position in the Empire as will bind her by love to her fellow Dominions through the full enjoyment of Self-Government,' and demands that when the War is over 'Self-Government must be established in India.' This agitation is wholly mischievous, and can do nothing but harm to the cause it advocates. It will divert the minds of the less wise and less stable members of the educated class in India from the great works of education, social reform, industrial development and Local Self-Government that must prepare the way for Self-Government for India as a whole, and it will also alienate many Englishmen both in England and in India who are naturally inclined to sympathise with the Nationalist cause. It will be a serious disaster if the National Congress identifies itself with this agitation.

Then, on the other hand, we also need a new attitude on the part of Europeans in India, both official and non-official, towards the peoples of India and their aspirations, a new ideal for our work, a new conception of the ultimate basis of our power. The all important thing is that after the War we should cease to talk of the population of India as a subject people, cease to talk of ourselves as a ruling race, cease to base our Indian Empire upon force, cease the effort to impose upon the peoples of India a purely Western civilisation, and cease to allow our policy to be dominated by the fear of weakening the position of the foreign bureaucracy. We need to realise that we cannot now base the Government of India upon any other foundation than that of the will of the Indian peoples, that we are here as the servants of the Indian peoples and not as their masters, that a foreign bureaucracy can only be regarded as a temporary form of Government and that our ultimate aim and object must be to enable India to become a Self-Governing part of the British Empire and to develop her own civilisation upon her own lines. How exactly this change of attitude will affect the details of Government and administration in India is a different question. There is room for much difference of opinion as to what ought to be the next steps, how fast and how slowly we ought to proceed, and what will be the wisest methods of attaining our end. But the all-important thing is to have a definite conception of the end itself, a clear vision of the goal for which we are striving.

HENRY MADRAS.

Contributed to the Nineteenth Century, 1916

Mrs. ANNIE BESANT

In seconding the resolution on Self-government in the Congress of 1915, *Mrs. Besant spoke*:—

Mr. President and fellow-delegates,—The resolution which I have the honour to second before you to-day is perhaps the most momentous that has ever been laid before the National Congress during the thirty years of its splendid existence. For, not only does it proclaim the steps to be taken towards the attainment of self-government, but also it lays down principles of reform, which, if they are embodied in the Committee's report, will make self-government a reality not in the distant vista of time but within the lifetime of the present generation. (*applause*) for, I find the bold demand is made that we should have an expansion and reform of the Legislative Councils so as to make them truly and adequately representative of all sections of the people; and most vital of all, to give them an effective control over the act of the Executive Government. Now, if adequate representation is given, if effective control over the executive is granted, then it will be difficult to say that you have not got self-government in India. It is the largest step the Congress has ever taken, and it will make the Congress memorable in the grateful memory of the India of the future. Not only so, but there is the vital proviso that the All-India Congress Committee is to frame not only a scheme of reform but a programme of continuous work, (*hear, hear*), educative and propagandist (*hear, hear*); not agitation, you must understand, but education and propaganda. I am not clever enough to distinguish between that and popular agitation, but I beg you to cling to the words of the resolution which are doubtless statesmanlike and desirable. (*Laughter*).

In the brief time that is mine, I want to put you three reasons for which this granting of self-government is necessary. One is the practical reason of the need for legislation on certain vital points; the second, the economic condition of the country, the most pressing reason of all; and thirdly, and very briefly, the historical justification for the granting of self-government to India.

Now, as regards the first, the need for legislation. There are certain things that press upon the nation which would be rapidly altered if we had a majority, an effective majority, in the Legislative Councils, and if, as I hope, they be wholly elected. What we require has been laid down for us on very useful lines in the resolution. It was said, and I believe truly said, that it was impossible for England to train India on her literature, and, in the admiration for her hoary institutions, to teach her that taxation without representation was robbery and to expect her to remain taxed and unrepresented and without any effective control over the budgets which are passed year after year. Sometimes people say that an inscrutable Providence has brought Great Britain to this land.

I see nothing inscrutable in it. Great Britain, when England came here, was the only free country, sir, in Europe and Providence chose her to come that she might bring India into touch with Western liberty and especially Western institutions. (*applause*). The designs of Providence only become inscrutable when you have un-British rule in India instead of the British rule that she ought to follow. Then you may well have a conundrum that you will for ever find it impossible to solve.

There is another reason,—a very practical one—why we should believe that, if we have really representative institutions, we shall be able to carry the measures we desire. This Congress has been asking for 30 years for the separation of executive and judicial functions and has not gained it. But in Indian States that separation is already made. Baroda has done it, Gwalior has done it, some of the smaller States already possess it. And when you have self-Government you will not ask for it for thirty years, but you will make it in your first year. (*applause*). You have asked for panchayats Well, Gwalior, Baroda, Dewas and Patiala and other States have already established those village Councils successfully, and yet in British India it is impossible to get them thoroughly on foot. You will sweep away that Arms Act, of which our President so pointedly complained; you will get rid of the Press Act, which we have already protested against; you will get rid of the Seditious Meetings Act; you will get rid of the power to intern without trial and to imprison without justification (*applause*) ; you will get rid of that shameful revival of the old Bourbon barbarism, the old Regulation (Regulation 3 of 1818) which exists only in India to-day among all civilised nations of the world. Those are some of the reasons why we demand legislative assemblies with a majority at least of the representatives of the people.

But take the economic reason. Take first, the incidence of your taxation. It is admitted by the Government that in India there is no effective margin of taxation. It has been pointed out by Mr. Gokhale, among others, that the taxation of this country trenches on the subsistence of the labourer. Mr. Naoroji has pointed out that India's production is only Rs. 30 per head, £2 a head, and yet we find that in 1910 Imperial taxation was 3s. 7½d. a head. You need to read blue books, you need to understand what is going on around you. You have a taxation which threatens the bankruptcy of India by the ruin of her agricultural population. The Hon. Mr. Wacha has told us—and there is no better authority—that the indebtedness of the peasantry rises to 500 crores of rupees. (*Cries of "shame."*) Is that no reason for changing the system of Government which produces it? I ask you to consider in relation to this not only the question of taxation but the admitted fact that India is the most heavily taxed country in the world,—not in amount, remember, not in shillings or rupees, but in proportion to the production of the masses of her people (*applause*). You cannot measure taxation by counting the number of coins; you must find the produce of the labourers, and see how much of that you take when you tax him for the benefit of the State. And when you are dealing with taxation, the next point to remember is that you have admittedly the most costly Government in the civilised world, (*applause,*) and therefore the necessity for this crushing taxation. Nor is it only that the Government is costly, but you have to remember that the taxes that are raised largely go out of the country, in what is well-known as the drain—that which Lord Salisbury called "the bleeding of India," and he asked that the lancet should be used in the most congested place. You have to remember that the drain out of the country runs to 20 millions sterling. That Mr. Naoroji has calculated. Another 20 millions goes in various charges, interest on capital, etc., managed in the most extravagant fashion, you must remember. For, the railways and other companies have been dealt with by the State as no business people would deal with them, and had even sold their shares at par when they did not bring in the market even as much as half the money paid for them. I want you, younger men, "passionate youths" as you are, to turn your thoughts to these details of taxation and understand why it is that you demand self-government for India. Then I ask you to remember the result. Now, eleven resolutions in previous Congresses have spoken of the horrible poverty of the people. They say the Congress is a middle class and upper class organisation.

If the Congress were the Parliament of India, the poverty of the people would long ago have been redressed (*hear, hear*). I find the nineth Congress, Resolution No. 8, after concurring in the views set forth in the previous Congresses, states, 50 millions of the population,—the number is yearly increasing—are dragging out a miserable existence on the verge of starvation, and that in every decade several millions actually perish by starvation. I find Sir William Hunter saying that more than 40 millions of the people are always on the verge of starvation. I find Sir Charles Elliot saying that half the population never know what it is to have a full meal. And these, sir, are not "impatient idealists." They are historians (*applause*) and practical politicians. You have to consider that poverty; you have to realise what it means; you have to know the agony of hunger; and then think as Sir Charles Elliot declared, of 100 millions of the agricultural population who never have a full meal. Some amount of impatience is justifiable when the people are suffering to that horrible extent. For this I tell you: that my fear for India is not the passionate enthusiasm of misguided youths, but the spectre of hunger, the frightful spectre of coming bankruptcy, which means the most awful of revolutions, the revolution of starving people whom none can check or rein in, when once they despair of help. (*applause*).

The third reason is historical. Five thousand years ago, this country was trading with ancient Babylon, and 3,000 years before the Christ down to 1613 after

Christ, there is no break in the commercial and in the industrial prosperity of India. 5,000 years of self-government behind you. "But there were wars, there were revolts." Read history before you speak too glibly about the disturbances in medieval and in ancient India; for if there were wars here, there were wars there. Akbar was reigning when Queen Elizabeth was on the throne, and Queen Elizabeth gave the first charter to trade with India. In the reign of James I the first trading company was allowed to establish itself in Surat along the Western coast. Since that time, in England, one King was beheaded, a second king was driven out of the country, and two civil wars on behalf of the exiled Stuarts have taken place. I do not know whether Indian wars were so very much more mischievous than the wars that prevailed over the whole of Europe during those historical times (*applause*).

For, after all, is it not true that village organisation went on through them all? Is it not true that villages were left untouched, save when the Huns swept down with fire and sword? Is it not on record that while the soldiers were fighting, ploughmen were ploughing the land within sight of the battling army? I put this to you as a particular proposition: that the test of the goodness of a Government is the wealth and prosperity of the people. While India governed herself, so long her people were so well fed that every country in Europe fought for the right to have a charter to trade with this country. That was the result of self-government in this country. Whatever faults might have defaced that system, to-day our President has told us, that India* is the most poverty-stricken country in the world. I put the two things before you as the answer to the statement that we are not fit for Self-Government. I submit that 5,000 years of success are greater than the theories of a few Englishmen who consider that Indians are not their equals. (*applause*). We are told in the words of Mr. Edwin Bevan that India is a poor cripple with limbs broken, tissues lacerated, tied up in splints and bandages by the benevolent English physicians and she must not move lest the wounds should not heal. India is no sick man. She is a giant who was asleep and who is now awake. (*applause*).

Are you fit for self-government? Are you not sure? Mr. Gokhale said—and he knew his people well,—he said that you are compelled to live in an atmosphere of inferiority that made the tallest of you bow your heads and that the greatest moral wrong done to India was that she had changed in character under the present method of Government. These men who are here, representatives of India from every part of the land, these men are not the children of savages emerging from barbarism needing to be trained in the elements of self-government by a Western nation. They are the children of heroes, the children of warriors, worthy to govern their own land,—(*applause*), save for one reason: and that is that the very noblest amongst you seems to think himself inferior to the Englishmen around you. Oh, if only you would trust yourselves, if only you would believe in your own power (*hear, hear*), in your own strength and in your own knowledge (*applause*). If Sir Satyendra can tell us that he stood face to face with the Viceroy, has been an equal man in the Viceroy's Council, can we say that an Indian is not worthy to rule in his own land? Are we to think that he is the one swallow that does not make a summer? Are we not to believe, as I believe, Sir, that there are hundreds like you (*applause*) who would show your own ability if they had a chance to do so?

And so I urge that this resolution be thoroughly carried out and that full representation be given in the Legislative Councils, as a means of self-government, to India. And I pray of you by the memory of your past by the possibility of the greatness of your present, and by the splendid future that lies before you, if, as Sir Pherozeshah Mehta once said on this platform, you are not emasculated as a nation, stand up on your feet like men. For England understands when people meet her face to face (*applause*). England is a country of free men and she does not understand people being contented to be uuder the rule of foreign domination. Show England by your courage that you are grateful,—as I know you are—for what she has done, but be most grateful that she has taught you the value of free institutions and has shown you by the example of her history how freedom is to be won, and how a nation bcomes self-governing. (*Loud and continued applause*).

THE HON'BLE SIR IBRAHIM RAHIMTULLA

In supporting the resolution on Self-Government in the Congress of 1915, *The Hon'ble Sir Ibrahim Rahimtulla spoke as follows* :—

Brother delegates, ladies and gentlemen,—May I, in starting to support the resolution, make a personal grievance and a personal complaint against your President for having invited me to address this assembly after two of the greatest orators in India (*applause*) have dealt exhaustively and in all its bearings with the most important resolution that has now been placed before you. If the President has been cruel to me, I appeal to you for a little personal indulgence in listening to me with a little patience to enable me to put before you the reasons why I desire that you should all unanimously accept the resolution which is now before you.

Mr. President, ladies and gentlemen, it was two short years ago that, in speaking of the political atmosphere in India on a similar occasion, I compared the relations of the British Government with the people of India to those of a guardian and his words. I feel, and I believe every one of you will agree with me when I say, that it is with fostering care that the people of India are, in the words of Mrs. Besant, being gradually trained to appreciate the advantages, value and benefits of free institutions. It is owing to that connection that the guardian wishes the wards in their minority to come forward gradually and reach that goal of Self-Government which is laid down under our Constitution. Ladies and gentlemen, there is nothing more easy than to tell you that we have reached already the stage when we shall get self-government at once. No one would be more pleased or more grateful, no one will be more proud to realise that my countrymen have already reached a stage when they are capable of governing themselves without any outside help whatsoever (*Hear, hear*). If that is so, then there is nothing further to be said. The resolution which is placed before you carries out in spirit the declared creed of the Congress. The Congress lays down that we shall achieve self-government under the ægis of the British Crown, and the measures that are necessary to reach that stage are enumerated, some of them at least, in the resolution that is placed before you.

Ladies and gentlemen, there is one thing more I will say and that has reference to what I said before. I said India was the heritage of two minor sons, known as Hindu and Mussalman (*applause*). I appeal that the best, the most patriotic manner in which you can ever reach that goal, which is dear to the hearts of every one of us, is through the sincere and genuine co-operation (*applause*) of the two minor brothers, so that they might, hand in hand, go and appeal to their guardian for larger and larger, greater and greater political privileges, which I call the allowances for their maintenance. Ladies and gentlemen, you are all aware —I have stated once before—the cost of living is increasing, our needs are multiplying and we want from our guardian at every step more and more substantial reforms to take us to the goal which we have laid down for our guidance.

Mr. President, I say that it is a good augury that both the League and the Congress are proposing to appoint committees (*applause*) for the purpose of putting their heads together and to arrange and formulate proposals and demands which may carry the Indian nation to the goal so dear to the hearts of every one. (*Applause*).

DEWAN BAHADUR L. A. GOVINDARAGHAVA AIYAR

In supporting the resolution on Self-Government in the Congress of 1915, *Mr. L. A. Govindaraghava Aiyar said:—*

Mr. President, fellow-delegates, ladies and gentlemen,—I beg to support the resolution that has been moved by the Hon'ble Mr. Surendranath Banerjea and has been seconded by Mrs. Besant. This resolution, you will notice, ladies and gentlemen, lays stress on the fact that the ideal of this Congress is the attainment of self-government within the Empire. You will notice that this resolution accentuates our determination that we shall attain self-government by constitutional means. It shows that the form of self-government that we are anxious to have is one that is similar to what obtained in the self-governing colonies. It shows that we are determined to have a form of Government wherein the right that we shall exercise shall not be any the less than what any other component part of the Empire as such is entitled to exercise. This resolution also indicates that we are perfectly prepared to have our obligations and to discharge our duties, though they may be no less onerous than the obligations and duties of any other part of the Empire. Gentlemen, there is one other aspect of the resolution which to me is specially appealing, and I hope it is so to you as well. It is this, that the attainment of the objects indicated in the resolution will enable us to rise above that atmosphere of inferiority of which Mrs. Besant has spoken. That atmosphere has corroded our souls and stunted our growth. We are anxious that we should show to the world that we are capable of discharging more onerous duties than are entrusted to us, that we are prepared within the opportunities that might be allowed to us to rise equal to the obligations which the citizenship of the Empire means. We are also anxious that England and the Empire should know that we feel that in the exercise of the rights we have not been given as full and free a play as our past history, present conduct and possibility of the future justify.

Gentlemen, within the limited time at my disposal, I propose to deal with the very few objections that have been and might be raised to the passing of a resolution such as this. The objection drawn from the argument of embarrassment has been disposed of in his own inimitable way by the Hon'ble Mr. Surendranath Banerjea. Gentlemen, it is by not passing this resolution, by not taking the steps indicated in this resolution that embarrassment would be really caused to Government. For you will recognise that sooner or later the war will be over, and when the war is over, there is bound to be a readjustment of the relations among the various component parts of the Empire, and it will then be too late for India to take steps to know her mind, to formulate her own demand and to tell the Government what with one united voice she is demanding for herself. If there is to be embarrassment, it is not by taking steps such as are indicated in this resolution.

There is another argument that is also advanced; and that is, that if you insist upon a resolution such as this, you are trying to make a bargain with the Government and that far from showing spontaneous loyalty to the Government you are taking advantage of their difficulties in order to make a profit out of them. That argument I repel with all the force I am capable of. Who can say when the war had begun, when every one of us was anxious within the limitations under which we were placed to do what we could for the purpose of advancing the interests of the Empire, when from every lip rose the hope and prayer that success should attend the British arms and every thing that success to the British arms meant—which of us can honestly and conscientiously say that, when that prayer went forth, we thought of the ultimate benefit that we, as members of the Empire, could expect to realise by the cessation or close of the war? How can it be said that, when Province after Province has hastened to do what it could for the purpose of advancing the interests of the Empire, we ever thought of what it would be possible for us to get after the close of the war? It is perfectly reasonable that the Government recognise that we, who are members of this Empire, must have some legitimate and reasonable programme that we can place before them so that they might be in a position to realise what it is at the back of India, and what it is that goes to make up the loyalty of the people, what it is that goes to make up the consciousness with which the people have been content to have the British Government as one under which they think it their privilege to live, why this British Government above all is preferred. They are made to recognise that it is because Britain on the whole stands for freedom, for justice, for equality of treatment among its various subjects. It is because we recognise that Britain is that, that we are willing and have always been willing to live under the British ægis. I think we should prove false to ourselves and even more false to the Government under which we live unless we plainly speak out our mind and let them know what it is we want; and for that purpose this resolution is very important.

As has been already pointed out, there are to be two committees whose co-operation is to be secured. We feel that, if behind the recommendation that might be made, the Government understand that there is the united voice of the people, and that all sections of the people are agreed that particular demands are necessary—we feel that the Government will be then in a position to recognise that there is the living voice of the people asserting itself so that they might be in a position to do justice to that voice. It was on that account considered necessary that every effort should be made so as to be able to understand what the demands are that are to be formulated by the people. I have great pleasure in supporting the resolution (*Applause*).

Mrs. SAROJINI NAIDU

In supporting the resolution on Self-Government in the Congress of 1915, *Mrs. Sarojini Naidu said*:—

Mr. President, ladies and gentlemen, till one moment ago it was not my proud privilege to be able to say "fellow-delegates," because it is only at this very moment I have been—as a preliminary step, as a possible step to Self-Government that might come within a few years and about which, sir, you have asked for a declaration—I have been asked to speak for a Province that is not my own, the United Provinces, and I was asked to represent their desires for this great movement which your enthusiasm makes me believe is the real desire of the people of this country.

After the eloquent and brilliant exposition and interpretation of the ideals of self-government that have been formulated by the many speakers before me, whose knowledge of the subject is better than mine, and whose services in the cause for attaining that self-government are infinitely greater than mine can ever be you hardly need a word from me either to emphasise or to adorn the speeches that they have made and the ideals they have formulated. But since it is the desire of so many people here present that some woman from amidst you, some daughter of this Bharat Mother, should raise her voice, on behalf of her sisters, to second and support this resolution on self-government, I venture—though it seems presumption so to venture—to stand before you and to give my individual support as well as to speak in the name of many millions of my sisters of India, not only Hindu, but my Mussalman, Parsi and other sisters, for the sake of self-government which is the desire and the destiny of every human soul. This vast assemblage represents to-day in miniature the Federation of India to which we look forward not in the distant future. I see with the eye that is given to the world's poets who dream, and dream with a palpitating heart, that vision, that expectation, that ecstasy of desire, that prayer that we shall send forth every moment of our lives that the dream may be realised. What is your dream? What is it to be in the words of your resolution? What are the responsibilities that go with the privileges you demand as a free and self-governing people? I speak not of the privileges that you demand to-day but of the responsibilities that they entail upon you. What are those responsibilities, what is the high burden that will go with that honour that you have demanded, with the right that you insist as your destiny, that destiny of the children of India?

Friends, believe me, as one of the speakers before me has said, this is the psychological moment of our nation's history. For the first time, after centuries upon centuries of political antagonism, of bitterness that comes from division between creed and creed, between race and race, after centuries of feuds and bloodshed, this is the psychological moment when the Hindu and the Mussalman are met together in this cosmopolitan city to co-operate together, to weld together into a nationality with unity of feeling and purpose, of endeavour and achievement, without which there can be no India of to-morrow.

That is really the final burden, the final responsibility of this resolution that has been so brilliantly proposed and seconded. What is the purpose of the self-government that you demand? Is it that you wish to keep the privileges for this community or another, for this majority or another, excluding a minority of whatever caste or creed? No. You are demanding self-government that you may find in it your national regeneration, your national deliverance, so that you may be free not only from the despotism of political domination, but from that infinitely subtler and more dreadful and damming domination of your own prejudices and of your own self-seeking community or race. Having got arrested through the evolution of time and spirit, and seeking to obtain the right savouring of self-government, I ask you not to pause and say "We have found the ultimate goal," because it seems to me that we are likely to be left in the cold unless we are in by the open door of the great Federation of India and establish that national feeling of Unity that knows no difference of caste or creed. If the communities may keep their own individual entities, it is only for the enriching of the federated national life. And so working together, feeling together, co-operating together, subordinating all merely sectarian and racial interests to the larger hope and the higher vision of

United India, you will be able to say with one voice as children of one Mother :—

Waken! O Mother, thy children implore thee!
We kneel in thy presence to serve and adore thee!
The night is aflush with the dream of the morrow,
Why still dost thou sleep in thy bondage of sorrow?
O waken, and sever the woes that enthral us,
And hallow our hand for the triumphs that call us.
Are we not thine, O Beloved, to inherit
The purpose and pride and the power of thy spirit?
Ne'er shall we fail thee, forsake thee or falter,
Whose hearts are thy home and thy shield and thine altar.
Lo! we would thrill the high stars with thy story
And set thee again in the forefront of glory.
Mother, the flowers of our worship have crowned thee!
Mother, the flame of our hope shall surround thee!
Mother, the sword of our love shall defend thee!
Mother, the song of our faith shall attend thee!
Our deathless devotion and strength shall avail thee!
Hearken, O Queen and O Goddess, we hail thee!

(*Loud Applause*).

In supporting the resolution on Self-Government in the Congress of 1916, *Mrs. Sarojini Naidu said* :—

From the very beginning of time it has always been the woman's privilege to have the last word on any subject, and though that last word is sprung on her by the tyranny of the leaders that demand Home Rule, it is to vindicate the readiness of my sex to stand by the men of India in all that concerns their National welfare and honour that I rise to obey the mandate of this tyranny. Many speakers before me, gifted and famous, full of knowledge and full of experience, have laid before you a scheme of Self-Government, and it is not for me to add words to their practical wisdom. I am merely a spectator from the watch tower of dreams, and I watched the swift and troubled, sometimes chequered but nevertheless indomitable, time-spirit marching on in a pageant of triumphs to the desired goal. If to-day, Home Rule is no distant dream, if it is no mere fancy of Utopia, it is due to one thing more than to any other thing and perhaps you will let me enlighten you so that you may offer your gratitude to the right sources. Less than four years ago, in this very city of Lucknow, this city of memories, this city of dead kings, a new hope came to birth, because the younger generation of Mussalmans had seen a vision that made it possible for the leaders of the National Congress to realise within the scope of practicable vision, of practical work, of practical achievement, the national soul. It was my privilege to represent my great community on this occasion. It was the greatest honour of my life that I was invited to speak to this young generation of Islam that had seen this vision of Indian Nationality which succeeded in passing a constitution whose essential creed was co-operation with the sister community. Four years after in this very city of Lucknow we are now able to say that we shall have Home Rule. We will not ask for it. We will create it out of our own capacity, out of our inviolable unity, the unity of the Hindu and the Mussalman friends. Members of this Congress, citizens of India who have come from the farthest corners in this great country, I ask you in the name of that greater Nation that is born to-day in the city of Lucknow to offer your thanks to three men, though it might indeed seem invidious to make distinctions, where so many have been earnest, so many have been loyal and co-operating, but it would be indeed lacking in gratitude on the part of this great assembly were it not to offer a public recognition of gratitude to three most loyal, most brilliant, most faithful, most courageous Mussalmans—the Raja Sahab of Mahmudabad, that fearless and independent spirited Mazarul-Haque, and thirdly, Mr. M. A. Jinnah, of whom it was that the late Mr. Gokhale said to me immediately after the last Muslim League in Lucknow that he is the best ambassador of the Hindu-Muslim community. We are united to-day by the efforts of the Muslim League. We stand united, but united with such strength that nothing from outside, not even the tyrrany of Colonial domination, shall withhold from us our rights and privileges, withhold from us the liberties that are due which we claim by our united voice. Nothing can prevent us from achieving the desires of our heart, for the final issues are in your hands. The ultimate decision is yours, and who will deny you the birthright of freedom if the millions of India speak with one voice: "Ours is the right of freedom; we claim it; we take it; you dare not deny to us the birthright of humanity." Centuries have gone by; the old divisions are healed: old wounds have got cured. Instead of building our regeneration on hatred and division, we stand to-day building our national future on the secure, imperishable foundations of love and united service. To each of us has come that living consciousness that it is united service for the Motherland that constitutes the supremest hope of to-morrow. There is no one so mean, so weak, so selfish as not to think that in the service of the Motherland lies the joy greater than all personal joys, in suffering for her comes the supremest consolation in our personal sorrow and her worship is the absolution of sin, to live for her is the most victorious triumph of life, to die for her is to achieve priceless crown of immortality. Let us then offer our lives unanimously as a tribute at the feet of the Motherland, for as the great prophet of Islam says. "Under the feet of Mother lies Paradise."

THE HON'BLE RAO BAHADUR R. N. MUDHOLKAR

In supporting the resolution on Self-Government in the Congress of 1915, *The Hon'ble Rao Bahadur R. N. Mudholkar said:—*

Mr. President, brother and sister delegates,—It is rather hazardous for a man who is only a matter of fact man to come and address you on a subject which has been dealt with in his most characteristic eloquence by our greatest orator and in regard to which you had just now a most enthralling speech by a most enthralling speaker in this country, a lady whose achievements and whose powers of speech ought to make boastful man, boastful of his superiority, hang down his head in shame. Gentlemen, the only reason for my accepting the invitation of the President at this time is that there are one or two points which should be emphasised and which we ought to bear in mind. It is not a new departure that we make to-day. No doubt this resolution is the most important and the most momentous of the resolutions brought before the Congress to-day; but remember that it is not a new thing which we are asking to-day. What we are doing by this resolution is to carry on the work for which the Congress was called into existence and to put forward in the circumstances of the times the principles which have been the principles of this Congress ever since its foundation. The *raison d'etre* of our existence is the establishment of self-government within the Empire for India. As British subjects, all along we have been saying, we want to have the rights of full-blown British citizenship. That has been the demand from 1885, not only from 1885 but from long before that. It is this thing which we are formulating and which we are stating at some considerable length in order to meet the demands of the present situation.

It is said that by putting forward these demands at this time, when the fortunes of the Empire are still hanging in the balance we might be embarrassing the Government. That matter has been very effectively dealt with by the Hon'ble Mr. Surendranath Banerjea, but there is one fact which I would ask you to remember; that is, that in doing so we are only following the lead given by the highest officer in the land, the representative of His Majesty the King-Emperor. In the speech which he gave at Simla, His Excellency the Viceroy referred to the desires and aspirations of India and to the need of meeting those aspirations. In these circumstances, when the Viceroy pointed out to the Members of the Civil Service the great importance of their sympathising with the aspirations of the people, there is certainly nothing embarrassing on the part of the people assembled here putting forward a statement of the demands which have to be made at the present time. That is the thing which our critics have to remember, namely, that we are carrying out only our previous work and we are not embarrassing the Government.

Gentlemen, again in regard to Provincial autonomy and financial independence, we are taking our stand upon the Despatch of the 25th August, 1911 written by a very great statesman in which the Government of India contemplate an India consisting of provinces autonomous in their character. How are you embarrassing the Government when you say that you want Provincial autonomy in these provinces? When the question of fiscal reform and fiscal independence was discussed in the Viceregal Council, how can you again say that you are embarrassing the Government by asking for Provincial autonomy? For provincial autonomy and fiscal independence ought to go hand in hand.

Then the expansion and reform of the Legislative Councils has been put in a form very similar to this from the beginning. But now an occasion has arisen when we have to place it before the world and the Empire in a clear light. We quite see that after the war the reconstruction of the polity on which the Government of the Empire is to be carried on will have to be undertaken. In these circumstances, shall we be doing our duty, shall we, through a false sense of modesty, observe silence, shall we be guilty of treason to our country and of failure of duty towards our children, if, on this occasion, when the matter has to be dealt with when we know that the matter ought to be dealt with, we maintain silence and do not formulate our demands in a clear and proper manner? The best course is to authorise the All-India Congress Committee to frame a scheme, and to ask the All-India Congress Committee and the Moslem Committee to meet and deliberate together and prepare a scheme acceptable to the whole country.

With these words I commend this proposition to your acceptance (*Applause*).

THE HON. PANDIT JAGAT NARAIN

As Chairman of the Reception Committee to the Indian National Congress of 1916, the Hon. Pandit Jagat Narain in the course of his address spoke as follows:—

Gentlemen, in my opinion statesmanship demands that Great Britain should announce to the people of this country that Self-Governing India is the goal of her policy and grant us a substantial instalment of reform after the War, as a step towards that goal. Representative Government should be made a reality by the fullest control over civil affairs being given to the elected representatives of the people whose decisions should be binding on the Executive. Indians should no longer be debarred from an honourable participation in the defence of their hearths and homes, but should be given every opportunity of developing their martial spirit. The slow deterioration which is taking place in the manhood of the race is one of the saddest results of British rule in India, and steps should be taken to repair the injury as early as possible. It is also essential that in any scheme of Imperial Federation India should occupy the same position as the self-Governing Dominions. The memorandum submitted to His Excellency the Viceroy by our elected representatives, although not a complete statement of our demands, proceeds on these lines, and the same principles underlie the scheme of reform which has been prepared jointly by the All-India Congress Committee and the Muslim League Reform Committee, and which will soon come before you. But these reforms, which fall far short of Colonial Self-Government, cannot satisfy India for all time to come, and in any legislation undertaken to give effect to them, it should be provided that full responsible Government shall be conferred on her within a generation.

SOME OBJECTIONS ANSWERED.

I now crave your permission, gentlemen, to discuss a few objections urged against our modest demand. Is it in India's own interest, we are asked, that the reins of Government should be transferred into her hands? Is she fit to bear the responsibility of governing herself? Are Indians fitted by previous experience to discharge the duties associated with responsible Government or even to manage representative institutions? Has education made sufficient progress among them so that they may be expected to choose their best men as their leaders? And will they place national above communal interests or will sectarian rivalries draw them farther away from each other as soon as the bond of common obedience to their present rulers is dissolved? Gentlemen, I hope to answer these questions by appealing to the history of the British Empire, but I cannot help remarking that the recital of our shortcomings reflects little credit on British rule itself. "Never let a prince" says Machiavelli, "complain of the faults of the people under his rule, for they are due either to his negligence or else to his own example." England will do well to bear the saying in mind when it is tempted to justify its autocratic rule in India on the score of our unfitness.

In considering the objections advanced against India's demand for greater freedom, I am led to ask myself if Great Britain itself possessed all the qualifications which are now supposed to be the essential pre-requisites of Self-Government, when it was ruling not merely over itself but had extended its sway over a large part of the human race. I find that even so late as the beginning of the 19th century, its masses were steeped in ignorance and political power was concentrated in the hands of a few. Ireland was unquiet, religious bigotry had by no means died out and modern ideas of social duty had not made much headway among the upper classes. But the ignorance of the masses did not deter statesmen from putting more power into their hands and in view of the glorious success which has crowned their policy, who will say that they should have waited until the people had attained to ideal perfection ?

THE CASE OF CANADA

It may be said, however, that England has had a long experience in the art of Government and that she has arrived at the present stage after a slow process of evolution extending over several centuries. But this could not have been said of the colonies when responsible Government was conceded to them. I shall begin with Canada as being the first in the order of time and importance. The right of Canada to control its internal affairs received statutory recognition in 1840 and responsible Government was conceded a few years later. But the history of the colony during the few years preceding the grant of representative Government concerns us more nearly than the events which followed it. Upper Canada was inhabited almost entirely by Englishmen. Lower Canada too contained men of British origin, but the vast majority of the inhabitants were of French extraction. The relations of the two races were far from friendly. The difference of race led to quarrels between the French and the British and between Lower Canada and Upper Canada and seriously interfered with the Government of the provinces. At last things became so serious that the Imperial Government was forced to intervene and to pass laws in order to safeguard the interests of Upper Canada. The interference of the British Government was fiercely denounced by the French politicians and a rebellion broke out in Lower Canada in 1837, which however was soon put down. The ostensible cause of the rebellion was political, but the real cause lay deeper. Political strife was the outcome only of racial bitterness and was accentuated in proportion as the latter increased. The report of Lord Durham, who was sent to Canada by the Imperial authorities in order to bring peace to the troubled provinces, gives startling illustrations of the extent to which the alienation between the two races had proceeded. The

French hated the British and aspired to establish a Government in which the British would occupy a very inferior place. They looked upon the British as their commercial rivals and regarded their increasing trade and prosperity with dislike and jealousy. In consequence of this state of things, says Sir John Bourinot, "trade languished, internal development ceased, landed property decreased in value, the revenue showed a diminution, roads and all classes of local improvements were neglected, agricultural industry was stagnant, wheat had to be imported for the consumption of the people and immigration fell of." Juries were permeated with political prejudices. In purely political trials it was almost impossible to obtain justice. As to social intercourse between the two races, none of course existed. "French and British" writes Lord Durham, "combined for no public objects or improvements, and could not harmonise even in associations of charity."

The year 1838 witnessed another rebellion. This time the infection spread to Upper Canada as well. The policy pursued by the Government in Upper Canada had given rise to a great deal of dissatisfaction and there were loud complaints against the dominant influence of the official class. The colonists demanded that the legislature should be wholly elected and that the executive be made responsible to the legislature. The Imperial Government, however, showed no sign of complying with their demands while the Local Government practically made no secret of its hostility to the movement. The discontent consequently went on increasing and culminated in a rebellion.

Faced with such a serious situation, what did the British Government do? Did it decline to make any concessions? Did it forge repressive measures to put down disloyalty with a stern hand? No; on the contrary, be it said to its credit that it set itself resolutely to the task of removing discontent by removing the matter of it. Lord Durham's report was published about this time. This memorable document, which may be said to have laid the foundation of modern British colonial policy, awakened British statesmen to the gravity of the issues they were called upon to settle. Conceived in a spirit of far-sighted statesmanship, it proposed that England should withdraw from the direct Government of the colonies and by conferring freedom on them in regard to their internal affairs, bind them to itself by the strongest of all ties, the tie of self-interest. "The colonists" wrote Lord Durham, "may not always know what laws are best for them or which of their countrymen are the fittest or conducting their affairs, but, at least they have a greater interest in coming to a right judgment on these points, and will take greater pains to do so than those whose welfare is very remotely and slightly affected by the good or bad legislation of these portions of Empire. If the colonists make bad laws and select improper persons to conduct their affairs, they will generally be the only, always the greatest, sufferers; and like the people of other countries, they must bear the ills which they bring on themselves, until they choose to apply the remedy." Lord Durham's advice found ready acceptance with the Imperial authorities. An Act was accordingly passed in 1840 which affected the legislative union of Upper and Lower Canada and made the colonists masters in their own house. All discontent immediately subsided as if by magic. New interests were created, which provided healthy channels into which the energy of the people began to flow. Race was no longer the dividing line between different parties. Men grouped themselves, not according to their origin but according to the view that they took of political, social and economic questions relating to their country.

I have mentioned above that at the time Self-Government was conferred on Canada it was distracted by civil dissensions which had their origin in racial antagonism. Thus it was sadly wanting in one of the three qualifications without which, it is alleged, Self-Government can never be a success. It remains to be seen how far the people of Upper and Lower Canada were possessed of previous experience in the management of their institutions and what progress education had made amongst them. We find that Government disregarded the wishes of the popular assemblies and thought themselves bound to obtain the instructions of the Imperial authorities in difficult or doubtful cases. The executive officials were all appointed by the Crown and were not responsible to the legislature. "Their influence," says Sir John Bourinot, "permeated all branches of Government—the Executive, the Legislative council, and even the assembly where for years there sat several members holding offices of emoluments under the Crown." The judiciary was more or less under their influence. The Judges held office during the pleasure of the Crown and were nominated as members of the Executive and Legislative Councils. Even local Self-Government, which is said to be the cradle of political freedom, had not made much progress in Lower Canada at least. As for public instruction "popular education was at the lowest possible ebb. In 1837 there were in all the private and public schools of the Provinces only one-fifteenth of the total population," which did not exceed one million. In Lower Cananda not one-tenth could write. Children repeated the catechism by rote, but as a rule were unable to read. The record of Upper Canada was no better. It may be added that the means of communication were lamentably deficient. The roads were in a wretched condition and at times were impassable. Partly for this reason and partly because of the paucity of the police, the administration of criminal justice was very unsatisfactory. Thus, it is apparent that, judged by the high standard insisted on in the case of India, Canada did not possess the qualifications needed for Self-Government. Disunion flourished among the people. More than half the population belonged to a race which was a stranger to responsible Government in its own country, and there was no antecedent guarantee that they would be able to fulfil the responsibilities which their newly gained freedom imposed on them. In education, undoubtedly, India lags behind Canada as it was in 1840, though percentages are hardly fair standards of comparison where the difference of population is so vast. But we are now in advance of England as it was three-quarters of a century ago. And in any case the main point to be determined is the attitude of the people towards education. The enthusiasm which greeted Mr. Gokhale's Education Bill, which was rejected by those who taunt us with our educational backwardness, and the progressive increase in the number of pupils, in spite of the restrictive policy followed by Government, furnish unmistakable proofs of the recognition of the importance of education by the people. If they are still backward, it is not because of apathy, but because of the absence of proper facilities. Thus, practically speaking every argument used to advocate Self-Government for Canada can be applied with equal force to India. The statesmen of Lord Durham's day recognised that responsibility could be acquired only when adequate scope was given for its exercise. They believed that liberty would make the colonists wise and exercise a far greater educative influence on them than the irksome restraints of a distant Parliament. Events have fully justified their confidence. The progress and prosperity of Canada are a tribute to the wisdom of their policy. There is no reason why English liberties and privileges should not produce a like result in India. Indians have proved their fitness whenever and wherever they have been tried in responsible positions, and if the past is a guide to the future they may be safely entrusted with the direction and management of the affairs of their country to a much larger extent than hitherto. They make mistakes in the beginning but they will be all the better for them in the end.

THE CASE OF AUSTRALIA

I shall now deal briefly with the case of Australia. It does not seem to me that its earlier history makes a very inspiring or profitable reading. The attention of the Imperial authorities was not turned towards it until it became a matter of urgent necessity to find some place to which criminals could be transported. Some means had to be devised for disposing of the convicts who could no longer be sent to the American colonies and Australia offered a satisfactory solution of the difficulty. During the earlier years of its history it was thus a land of convicts, and it continued as a penal settlement, roughly speaking till the forties of the last century. Systematic efforts were made to introduce free immigrants in the twenties into New South Wales to which the earliest colonising efforts were directed, and although this had an appreciable effect in promoting the welfare of the colony and raising the moral tone of the settlement, it cannot be claimed that all the new settlers were a desirable kind, or that any serious efforts were made to grapple with the moral evils which were rampant in the colony.

Through carelessness or inefficiency women sent out to the settlement were for the most part such as to make the task of reforming the people more difficult. "New South Wales" writes a historian, "was, in fact, made the dumping ground for all the convicted as well as the unconvicted criminals of the United Kingdom." Drunkenness and immorality prevailed there to an alarming extent, and even so late as 1835 the moral condition of the colony gave cause for serious anxiety. As for education I cannot say how far it had progressed, but till 1848 it was entirely denominational. The State maintained no schools of its own. The economic condition of the colony, however, was much better than its social condition. Land was being steadily brought under the plough, great progress was being made in cattle-rearing, and trade and commerce were-undergoing rapid expansion. But even when these hopeful features are taken into consideration, I must say that the impression left on one's mind by a perusal of the early history of New South Wales is not particularly pleasant.

It is not necessary for me to go into the history of the other Australian colonies. Their development was not in every respect similar to that of New South Wales, but if I am not mistaken, it does not present any markedly dissimilar features.

As for the political condition of New South Wales, which is the chief object of our concern, a representative element was introduced into its Government with the advent of free-settlers in 1823. A further step was taken in 1842 when the popular element was increased. Finally, full responsible Government was conceded in 1853. It was also conceded to Victoria, South Australia and Tasmania at about the same time. If the facts I have stated above are correct, it does not appear to me that New South Wales or the other Colonies satisfied the tests that are now-a-days applied to India. A large proportion of the Colonists could not be said to have attained to a high social or ethical standard, and no systematic efforts had been made to educate them. And yet the Imperial Government showed itself ready, says Dr. Keith, to grant responsible Government because of "the discoveries of gold and the influx of population." Besides, the principle had been established by the example of Canada, and its acceptance there made its recognition inevitable in the case of other Colonies. If there is any substance in the objections advanced against the widening of Indian liberties, the conditions under which Australia was started on a career of full-fledged Self-Government were not very hopeful; but its progress during the regime of freedom exposes the utter hollowness of the contentions of our critics.

THE CASE OF SOUTH AFRICA

South Africa is the latest example within the British Empire of the benefit of Self-Government. Undeterred by opposition in Parliament and the wailings of "the men on the spot," the Government of Sir Henry Campbell-Bannerman conferred full responsible

Government in 1906 and 1907 respectively, on the Transval and the Orange River State, which less than six years before were engaged in a bloody struggle with England. While the events of the war were still fresh in the public mind, the Dutch were not merely placed on a footing of equality with the English but granted liberties which they had not enjoyed under their own rule. The rivalries of race and language, instead of finding free play, have as a consequence become less prominent than they were a decade ago, and the Dutch, so far from rising against England at the first favourable opportunity that offered itself, have been so completely won over by the magnanimous policy followed by her that they are to-day fighting side by side with her sons for the maintenance of her Empire.

Gentlemen, the three examples of Canada, Australia and South Africa which I have just quoted, bear convincing testimony to the potency of Self-Government as an instrument for the advancement of both National and Imperial interests. In all of them it has been found to be a healing and cementing principle, although according to the exacting standard set up by our critics not one of them could have made good its claim of Self-Government when it was granted to them. And where they have succeeded, why should India fail?

IMMEDIATE AGITATION NECESSARY

But the task of the advocates of Self-Government for India is not over when they have proved her fitness for it. Even if it be conceded, it is said, that free institutions should be introduced into India, this is not the time for stirring up controversy. Great Britain is engaged in fighting a powerful and determined enemy, to crush whom will be needed all the strength and resources of the Empire. It is the duty of every loyal citizen to do nothing at this juncture which will divert her attention from the successful prosecution of the War. We acknowledge our obligation to refrain from doing anything which will embarrass the authorities, and are cheerfully rendering every assistance we are capable of in the titanic struggle which will decide the fate of Europe. But at the same time we owe it to ourselves that we should make our people understand the inner meaning of the struggle and be in a position to make our wishes and sentiments known to the British Government when the reconstruction of the Empire is taken in hand. If Indian claims are to have any chance of being seriously considered, we must be able to place our views before the authorities when plans for the reorganisation of the empire are being discussed. This requires that our demands should be formulated in the form of a definite scheme and that sufficient time should be given to the country to discuss it thoroughly. Unless this is done, there is a great danger that we may be told that we do not know our own mind or that our views give expression only to the aspirations of a microscopic minority. Clearly, therefore, we cannot impose silence on ourselves till the conclusion of the war, for it may be too late then to do anything. On the contrary it is our duty to lose no time in educating public opinion and in discussing the vital question of India's position in the Empire after the War, in the press and on the platform. The time has certainly not come when we should press our claims on the attention of Government, but it is not a moment too soon for making up our own minds on the subject. As a matter of fact, more than a year has passed since the public discussion of the problem began, and it is only now that unanimity has been reached with regard to the changes which must be made in the Indian constitution in order that we may have adequate room for expansion and a fair field for the employment of our talents and energies. If Hindus and Mahomadans had neglected to take counsel among themselves beforehand and to make efforts to arrive at a common understanding they would have found themselves totally unprepared to represent the Indian case properly after the war at the tribunal of the Empire. The task of re-modelling the fabric of Empire could not have been postponed till the political lotus-eaters of India had made up their minds, and with the best will in the world imperial statesmen would have been forced to leave her out of account in determining their future policy.

There are other reasons also why we cannot sit still till the War is over. England herself was not postponed till the end of the war the considerations of questions affecting her vitally. In spite of it she is busy devising means for increasing her national efficiency. She has already taken steps to overhaul her system of education and is actively concerting measures with the Allies to promote her economic development after the War. The Colonies too are not silent. They are insisting loudly on their right to be associated with the mother-country in the control of foreign affairs and to be consulted in matters relating to peace and war. Their responsible spokesmen have declared that the matter cannot be kept in abeyance during the War, but that advantage must be taken of the present state of public opinion to bring about a satisfactory settlement. Mr. Bonar Law, as Secretary of State for the Colonies publicly stated that the present was the most favourable opportunity for promoting unity between England and the Dominions, and that the enthusiasm created by the war should be utilised to draw closer the bonds that unite them to her. Why should England be embarrassed if, following her own example and that of the Colonies, India too bestows a little attention on some of the most vital questions affecting her future?

Again the change in the attitude of British statesmen towards India during the last year and a half gives cause for serious anxiety. During the earlier months of the War there appeared to be a change in their angle of vision. India's services found a grateful mention in their public declarations and she was promised a reconsideration of her position after the war. But an ominous silence now prevails, in regard to her. While the Colonies have continued to receive generous attention and the Prime Ministers of Canada and Australia have been invited to meetings of the British

Cabinet as a proof of England's sincere desire to give the Colonies a greater share in the control of Imperial affairs, the enthusiasm created by India's magnificent response to the call of the Empire has to all appearances cooled down, and her services are in danger of being forgotten.

More disquieting than the careful omission of all references to India in their public pronouncements, is the almost studied disregard of Indian opinion recently shown by the Imperial authorities. When at the invitation of Lord Hardinge India agreed that she should raise no new questions calculated to stir up controversy during the War, she had a right to expect the Government too, on its part would refrain from doing anything calculated to create a feeling of uneasiness in the public mind, but she has been sadly disappointed.

Our faith in British statesmen was sorely tried when the Civil Service Act was passed which altered the system which regulated appointment to the Indian Civil Service. The Government of India Amendment Act gave another rude shock to our feelings. It cannot be contended that it was an emergency legislation. It might never have been undertaken without any detriment to our interests. It involved constitutional questions which it was, to say the least of it, impolitic to raise during the currency of the war. Yet the measure was introduced into Parliament without the public being given an opportunity of discussing its provisions, and was passed in the teeth of the vehement opposition of educated India.

THE REVOLTING SUGGESTION

The foregoing considerations make it plain that if Indians do not make their voice heard they cannot expect that their interests will be borne in mind when the Empire is reorganised after the War. But there is even a greater danger ahead, *viz.*, that the interests of India may be subordinated to those of the colonies. British statesmen have pledged themselves to give the dominions a greater share in the direction of Imperial policy. They are to be associated with the mother-country in the control of foreign affairs, and to share much more largely with her the burden of the defence of the Empire. Now it is argued that they cannot be made responsible for the foreign policy of the Empire, unless they are allowed to have a voice in the Government of the dependencies. In one of the recent books which deals with the reconstruction of the Empire after the War and which has attracted some public attention in this country—"*The Problem of the Commonwealth*" by Mr. L. Curtis—it is contended that "a British citizen in the dominions cannot be made responsible for the foreign affairs of the Common-wealth, without also becoming responsible for the Government of its subject peoples and sharing in the long and difficult task of training those peoples to govern themselves. The two things are by nature inseparable." The concern of the colonies for the welfare of India would be touching if only one could be sure of its existence. The bitter experience of India, however, does not allow her to share the hopes of those who have never suffered at the hands of the dominions. Her children are treated as undesirables in every dominion. Every colony has so framed its laws as to bar ingress to Indians and to drive out those already settled there, and as Dr. A.B. Keith points out in his recently published book, *Imperial Unity and the Dominions*, the policy of South Africa, in particular, has been a "record of extraordinary meanness." The race prejudice of the self-governing colonies has spread beyond their borders. We have it on the authority of Mr. Gokhale that the presence of colonial students at British Universities has increased the difficulties of Indian students, and Mr. H. S. L. Polak—to whom we accord a cordial welcome—tells us that South African influence in British East Africa is responsible for a steady deterioration in the position of the Indians, to whose industry the protectorate owes all its prosperity. India is not so blind to her own interests, or so lost to all sense of self-respect, as to willingly accept the domination of the colonies which evince an overweening contempt for all Indians and deny their own Indian subjects the right to live like human beings. She will bear a great deal before submitting to such an indignity. If the Government of India by the dominions is an inevitable consequence of Imperial Federation, then all attempts at federation are foredoomed to failure. As Dr. Keith says, Imperial unity is impossible so long as India does not enjoy the liberty to develope the best that is in her and is not placed on a footing of equality with the self-governing dominions.

Gentlemen, in order to achieve the object we have in view, sustained work is an essential preliminary. We must enlighten the people in our country. But it is equally necessary that we should knock at the door of the British democracy. It is true that our first task is to educate our own people whose united strength nothing will be able to withstand but British public opinion is the final arbiter in our case and its education should be an object of special concern to us.

OUR DUTY

Ladies and gentlemen, we are living in momentous times. On every side we see the stirrings of a new spirit, a yearning towards light and freedom, and the time is at hand for the realization of the glorious dreams of those who sowed the seed of western knowledge in India. The call of the Motherland is sounding, in our ears. The Press Act cannot quell our ardour, nor can the Defence of India Act cool our enthusiasm. They only reinforce the lesson that "where freedom lives not there live no good things." Unjust opposition, instead of daunting us will only stimulate us to greater effort, for to us Self-Government is not a privilege but a duty. Inspired by a clear-eyed faith in the ultimate victory of our cause, which nothing can shake, and a passionate patriotism which rejoices in service and self-sacrifice, we shall march forward resolutely to the goal that we have set before us of winning for our country its rightful place in British Commonwealth. I earnestly trust that England will read the signs of the times aright, and add a glorious page to her history by helping three hundred millions to cast off the shackles that bind them. " The menace, the real peril, as Mr. Bernard Houghton says, " lies not in the grant of more popular Government to India; it lies in the continuance of the present system, a system which has served its purpose but which India has now over grown." These are wise words which Great Britain will do well to ponder over. India has been too long at school. She can no longer be persuaded that her liberties are safer when held in trust for her by others than in her own hands. And the unrest in India is the greatest tribute to British rule. In the words of Mr. Kerr, the Editor of the *Round Table*, " If British rule, however benevolent and well intentioned, did not produce this uneasy striving after better things, it would carry within itself its own condemnation. Englishmen ought to welcome with pride the desire of India to govern herself." To quote again the words of Mr. Houghton, who was himself a member of the Indian Civil Service, with a slight change, their representatives in India should " now stand aside, and in the interest of that country they have served so long and so truly, make over the dominion to other hands. Not in dishonour, but in honour proudly, as shipbuilders who deliver to seamen the completed ship, may they now yield up the direction of India. For it is the inherent defects of the system, which no body of men, however devoted, can remove, which renders inevitable the change to a new policy. By a frank recognition of those defects they can furnish a supreme instance alike of loyalty to the land of their adoption and of a true and self-denying statesmanship."

THE HON. BABU AMBIKACHARAN MUZUMDAR

In the course of his Presidential address of the 31*st Indian National Congress of* 1916, *Babu Ambikacharan Muzumdar spoke as follows*:—

Gentlemen,—Call it Home Rule, call it Self-Rule, call it "Swaraj," call it Self-Government, it is all one and the same thing—it is Representative Government. The idea is not a new one, nor is it the revelation of any evangelist. As far as I am aware, the idea dawned upon the people in 1882 when the agitation on the Ilbert Bill first revealed to the people the helplessness of their situation. A "National League" was then formed and a burning pamphlet called the "Star in the East" was issued which was written in a style and language which if employed at the present day would have surely stranded the writer in serious difficulties. Lord Ripon fully anticipated the demand when in his famous Resolution of January 1882 he told the people that "local self-government must precede national self-government." Although the first Indian National Congress passed no resolution directly bearing on the question, the notification under which it was called into existence clearly stated that one of the objects of the future assembly was "indirectly to form the germ of an Indian Parliament which, if properly conducted, will constitute in a few years an unanswerable reply to the assertion that India is still wholly unfit for any form of representative institution." And Mrs. Annie Besant in her admirable book, "How India Wrought for Freedom," has pointedly referred to the utterance of the Grand Old Man of India which clearly foreshadowed the coming demand of the Indian people of self-government. Ever since then the idea worked and matured itself when in the brilliant session of the Congress in 1906, it found an emphatic and equivocal pronouncement from the very same patriarch of the Indian political world in his trumpet call for "Swaraj" which has since then stirred the Indian mind to its utmost depth to find the true remedy which it had so far sought in vain. A generation has passed away, but a generation has risen whose sole and whole-hearted demand is nothing short of self-government as the sovereign remedy for the present unsatisfactory situation. A cry has, however, been raised that we are not yet fit for self-government. Procrastination is the proverbial thief of time. It is also the orthodox plea of a frame of mind which, unable to cope with an untenable position, only asks for an adjournment to seek for a compromise on the most favourable terms.

But before we proceed to discuss this question, we must first divest ourselves of the dogmatism which prevails with equal force, though not with equal authority, on both sides, and try to understand the question in the light of the unanswerable logic of facts. Let us see what are the requisites of self-government and how far the Indian people possess these requisites to reasonably demand-self-government.

THREE CONDITIONS OF MILL

John Stuart Mill in his book on Representative Government lays down three conditions for self-government which are now universally accepted by all writers on political philosophy. These conditions are:—1st, that the people for whom the form of Government is intended should be willing to accept it; 2nd, that they must be willing and able to do what is necessary to keep it standing; and 3rd, that they must be willing and able to do what it requires of them to enable it to fulfil its purposes. To these three tests I will add a fourth, by way of a rider, directly to meet the argument of our critics—have the people given satisfactory evidence of their capacity for Self-Government?

EDUCATION NO TEST

It will be noticed that Mill nowhere lays down Education as a separate and independent test for Self-Government and this is for a very good reason. Education no doubt sharpens and stimulates the other tests; but it cannot be the sole or even the main test for a National Government. The Hindus in the 13th century and the Mussulmans of India in the 18th century were the masters of no inconsiderable share of unprofitable learning; but it neither developed their national solidarity nor strengthened their national character, and both in their turn fell an easy prey to a superior force. The Mahomedan historian admits that India was conquered not by superior education but by superior Islamic national solidarity and strength. On the other hand the Slave Republic of Liberia was established by an uneducated mass of emigrants from America upon their liberation towards the beginning of the 19th Century. Then take the case of Europe. There also education has not played a very important part in determining the form of government suited to each country. According to the latest satistics available Norway and Sweden carry the largest percentage of educated population, it being 97, England has a percentage of 87, France 78, Germany 91 and Portugal 56. If education had been the determining factor, Norway and Sweden would not have been practically an absolute Monarchy and France or Portugal a Republic, while Germany would have long ceased to be a military despotism where a subaltern can with impunity punish judges and magistrates for the grave offence of not being deferential to his uniform and the theory of the " Superman " sways the minds of 80 millions of human beings of the highest culture and erudition in the world. What was the education of England during the reign of Charles I, and was not the Magna Charta wrested from a despotic king by a band of uneducated barons who could sign their names only by scrolls and marks?

In 1821 there were nearly 18,500 schools with 65,000 scholars in Great Britain. In the year 1858 the number of schools rose to 122,000 and the scholars to over 3,000,000. We have it on the authority of the Education Commission of 1882 that prior to 1854 when the first Educational Despatch of Sir Charles Wood was issued there were merely a million of students in British India receiving elementary education in the various indigenous institutions. The statement of the member of Education in 1914 shows that there are at present 127,000 schools with over 5,000,000 scholars receiving such education. It would thus appear that the number and the percentage of literates in Great Britain in the reign of George IV were not higher than those of India in the reign of his Gracious Majesty George V, and that the number, though not the percentage, of literates in India in 1914 does not compare very unfavourably with that of Great Britain in 1858. And yet what 'was' the constitution of Great Britain in 1821 and what 'is' the constitution of British India in 1916! Education therefore, though it may help and promote Self-Government, is not an indispensable condition or a condition precedent to Self-Government.

FIRST CONDITION

The first condition needs not much elaboration, as the willingness of the people for Self-Government is not only admitted, but is said to be premature and somewhat extravagant. The press and the platform even in their present muzzled condition are ringing with the cry for Self-Government and on every occasion whether in the heated Council Chambers or in the serene atmosphere of literary discussions there is an insistent demand for Self-Government as the only remedy for the present situation.

SECOND AND THIRD CONDITIONS

The second and the third conditions may be considered together. India, self-contained and contented, with its natural defences and internal resources presents a bulwark against all foreign aggression. Its danger is not from without but from within. During the last sixty years since the Crown has assumed the reins of government it must be admitted that there has not been even the ripple of disturbance and the people educated or uneducated, despite all their vexations and disappointment, their hardships, their grievances and the irritating measures which have so often provoked their patience, have throughout stood fast by the Crown. They have protested but have nowhere resisted the measures of the Government. Since the outbreak of the war, India has been practically denuded of soldiers and it has been possible for Government to maintain peace and order throughout the vast country with only the help of the police as it exists in India. Those who recklessly cry "the wolf," ought to know that if the wolf had really been anywhere in the field, it would not have been possible long to indulge in this foolish trick. It ought to be fairly conceded that the credit of this remarkable achievement is evenly divided between the Government and the people,—the confidence of the people in the Government and the trust of the Government in the people; and that any attempt on the part of either to appropriate it to itself the whole credit is an absurd pretension. The spirit of co-operation and self-help infused into the minds of our people mainly by the inspiring breath of the Congress, and the numberless societies, missions and associations which have sprung up throughout the country with philanthropic and other aims and objects are sufficiently indicative of the quickening of a national life, and the courage and endurance displayed by our young men in every public cause, are all unmistakable evidence of the readiness of the people to support the administration. In flood and famine, in fires and fairs and in other positions of dangers, difficulties and distress there are thousands of young men who eagerly rush forward to help the administration without waiting for recognition or expecting any reward and despite police surveillance to which they are subjected. The Hospital ships furnished by Bombay and Madras, the Ambulance Corps and the Double Company provided by Bengal and the various war funds raised throughout the country are no mean evidence of the willingness and readiness of the people to co-operate with the administration. All these, in my opinion, afford striking evidence of the devotion and the capacity for self-sacrifice which our countrymen are prepared to incur in the public interests and which constitute the most valuable qualification for self-rule. This shews that our people are willing and able to make the Government stand and are ready to make the necessary sacrifices for the establishment of National Government. Lapses no doubt there are, but do they not occur even among people invested with full measure of self-government? A National Government would shift the burden as well as its odium and unpopularity from the state to the people and would necessarily make them still more alive to their responsibilities. It is power which creates responsibility. Responsibility without power is a debt without security which cannot be enforced if left undischarged.

It was George Yule who, twenty years ago, speaking at the first Congress held in the United Provinces, said that all political agitations have to pass through three stages—that of Ridicule, Opposition and Concession. We have long passed the stage of Ridicule and almost passed the second stage and we are now practically on the debatable ground between Opposition and Concession, standing more on the firm soil of the latter than on the slippery ground of the former.

"NOT YET"

There are however those who say "not yet." Not yet! Then "when"?—asks the Indian Nationalist. But here the Oracle is dumb and Echo only answers—"when"! Edwin Bewan's parable of "the Patient and the Steel frame" is cited and the people are strictly enjoined to lie in peace and possess their souls in patience, until their political *Nirvana* is accomplished. Similies and metaphors are not safe guides in practical life, for all fables are but fallacies clothed in equivocal language which captivates the imagination and deludes the reason. For even the patient in the "steel frame" requires a gradual relaxation and occasional readjustment of his splints and bandages and, above all, a steady, substantial improvement in his dietary arrangements, as after all it is the food and nourishment and not the splints and bandages, that are calculated to give him strength and cure him of his injuries. You cannot indefinitely keep him on milk and sago to help either the "knitting of the bones" or the "granulation of the flesh." Our critics however would enjoin "perfect quiet and repose" without prescribing any kind of diet until the people shall have in their spirit of quiescence fully recovered themselves in their steel frame. If any illustration were actually needed, one might fairly suggest that the case of either the swimmer or the rider would probably furnish a more opposite object lesson. You cannot expect the one to be an expert jockey without training him on the back of a horse, as you cannot expect the other to be an expert swimmer without allowing him to go into water. There must be repeated falls and duckings before any efficiency can be attained by either. Admitting for argument's sake—and there can be no prejudice in such an admission—that the Indians are not yet as fit for Self-Government as the Europeans are, does it follow that they must only patiently contemplate in their steel frame without a stir till the day of their release? If that be so the day of their redemption will, in all probability, maintain its ever receding distance and the vision of the patient never be realised. There is a school for the lawyer, the physician, the educationist and the Engineer where he can obtain his passport and begin his profession; but is there any school or college where an aspirant can be admitted to his degree for Self-Government? It is through Self-Government that the art of Self-Government can be either taught are acquired. One must be drilled in the art of administration before he can acquire steady use of his faculties in the work of practical administration. In the words of Mr. Gladstone, it is the institution of Self-Government which constitutes the best training ground for Self-Government. It is through failure that success can be achieved in practical politics. Such failure was fully anticipated by Lord Ripon in his famous Resolution of 1882 and it is through such failures that the British people have obtained the constitution of which they are so justly proud. In the reigns of James I., Charles I., and his successors, what was the British constitution and the status of the British people when Parliament could be summoned or dismissed at the pleasure of despotic sovereign, and titles and offices were freely bought and sold without any regard to public interest? The mass of the people were steeped in ignorance, while the highest officers in state were not sometimes free from intrigue and corruption. Yet the British people fought for their rights and liberties and obtained them in the midst of these unfavourable conditions. If they had ever allowed themselves to be kept in a steel frame until "nature resumed her active process," where would have been the splendid fabric of British constitutional freedom to-day? Nature never helps those who do not help themselves.

ARE INDIANS FIT FOR SELF-GOVERNMENT

Now let us turn to a discussion of the rider which was started at the beginning of this question. Gentlemen, our critics have already begun sorting our politicians, I do not pretend to be a politician; but even if I were one, I would far rather go with the "politicians of the baser sort" than agree to rise one degree higher, or one degree lower as you may choose to call it in the estimation of our critics, while as to the superlative degree. I would ungrudgingly have it reserved for those who have so far forgotten the traditions of their own race as to completely divest themselves of the instincts of a free and liberty loving people to which they ethnologically belong. The question to be answered is.—Have the Indian people given fair proof of their capacity for Self-Government? I do not like to indulge in theories: Let facts answer.

IN THE NATIVE STATES

India possess an area of 1,800,000 square miles with a population of 316 millions, of which over 700,000 square miles, or more than one third of this area, with a population of over 70 millions, or close upon one fourth, belong to the independent Native States. Now these States are entirely managed by Indian administrators, and it has to be admitted that some of them are marching ahead of British India in certain directions, particularly in respect of education, judicial reforms and industrial development which are the most sacred functions of a constitutional Government. It must be borne in mind that not a few of these distinguished administrators who have achieved such brilliant results in the administrations of these States are sometimes drawn from His Majesty's subjects in British India. Men like Sir Salar Jung, Sir Dinkar Rao, Sir T. Mahadava Rao, Mr. Dadabhai Naoroji, Rao Bahadur Surdar Sansar Chandra Sen, Dewan Bahadur Raghunath Rao, Mr. Romesh Chandra Dutt, Sir Seshiah Sastri, Mr. Ranga Charlu, Mr. Gouri Shankar Ojha, Mr. Seshadri Aiyar, Mr. B. L. Gupta, Mr. Nilamber Mukherjee and Mr. A. R. Banerjee who have governed various Native States with such consummate ability and conspicuous success, have indisputably vindicated the capacity of their countrymen for the highest administrative offices. They have shown that if commanded by their Sovereign they were fit to hold any portfolio in the Government of India. If these distinguished administrators had had their lot cast solely in British India many of them would have in all probability ended their careers as Deputy Magistrates, a few as District Officers, and fewer still as officiating Commissioners of divisions.

IN THE VARIOUS SERVICES

Then, have not Indians in British India given practical proof of their administrative capacity to qualify themselves for Self-Government ? Have they not in the charge of districts both as judicial and executive officers, and have they not in charge of divisions or of a board of revenue, or in the intricate department of audit and account given sufficient evidence of their ability and capacity for efficient administration? Have they not been tried in the humbler stages of local Self-Government as well as in the higher legislative assemblies? They have been tried in the inner circles of the Provincial as well as the Imperial administration, and they have been also tried at the real seat of authority in Whitehall? True, Sir S. P. Sinha, might never have aspired to the chair occupied by Maine and Macaulay; but has England sent any more Maines and Macaulays to fill that chair? Or was Sir S.P. Sinha, or Syed Ali Imam an altogether unworthy successor of Sir James Stephen or Sir C.P. Ilbert? In the great department of administration of justice they have been tried in the highest tribunals of the land where they have acted and are acting as Chief Justices with as much credit and distinction as any brought out from England, while in the domain of education they have as Vice-Chancellors managed important Universities in a way which has extorted the admiration, if not the envy, of the most captious critics. They have also managed with remarkable success the affairs of one of the foremost, if not the foremost, corporations in the country. All these they have done, and if they have not done more, it is their misfortune and not their fault.

OTHER QUALIFICATIONS

Self-control, strength of mind and fidelity are among the highest virtues of an administrator, and judged by these tests, have not Indians acquitted themselves in a manner worthy of the best traditions of any service in the world? Sir Satyendra Prasanna Sinha's resignation of his seat in the Executive Council is still a mystery to the public. But whatever may be its solution, it is an open secret that at a critical time he withdrew the resignation that he had tendered and stood loyally by the Government. Has any body ever heard the faintest whisper of this incident from the lips of Sir Satyendra Prasanna Sinha? Then take another case. The partition of Bengal had stirred the people of Bengal to a state of feverish excitement unprecedented in their history. Petitions and protests to Viceroys and Ministers were of no avail and after seven years of persistent agitation the people were awaiting in breathless suspense the decision of His Majesty. A despatch from the Governor-General in Council recommended a modification of the partition in August 1911 and Sir Syed Ali Imam was one of the signatories to this eventful document. Yet on the 12th December the Royal Proclamation came as a complete surprise both upon the local Governments as well as upon the people. The Partition was said to have been effected in the interest of the Muhammadans. But did Sir Syed Ali Imam either in his quivering lips or tell-tale eyes betray in the slightest degree the dead secret of the prison house within this anxious period of five months.

THE OBJECTIONS

The most orthodox argument, in fact the only argument, now advanced against this natural and legitimate demand is that the mass are silent and have not joined in the cry. This is an ingenuous argument for an inarticulate mass will never speak and the reforms will not come. But have the mass at any time and in any country spoken out before any reform has been granted? The hydra headed mass speak only in times of rebellion or revolution, and even then under the inspiration of their leaders who rise out of the educated minority, but their voice is not heard amid a process of silent evolution in the benefits of which they are bound to participate. Did the mass in England cry for the *Magna Charta* or the Petition of Rights, or the Reform Bill? The educated few have everywhere represented the ignorant many and history tells us that they have always been their unaccredited spokesmen. And then whose fault is it that the masses in India are dumb and illiterate? The Congress has cried and Congressmen have tried their utmost for the spread of elementary education and they have been told that the time has not yet arrived for universal compulsory education for the masses. We do not know if the Astrological Almanac is being consulted for an auspicious day for such an undertaking. It all looks like the trite, old, yet never hackneyed, game of "head I win, tail you lose."

SOLICITUDE FOR THE POOR CASTE SYSTEM

Then as a corollary to the above a further argument is advanced that there are so many communities and sub-divisions in this caste-ridden country that if Self-Government were conceded King Stork would one by one swallow up all the frogs, and a Babel of disorder would follow in which men would run at one another's throats and render settled Government impossible. Such keen solicitude for the poor and the weak is no doubt highly creditable to an enlightened administration; but in a country where more than two fifths of the population live on insufficient food where in 42 years there were 22 famines carrying away millions of human beings; a country which is admittedly the poorest and yet the most heavily taxed as well as burdened with the costliest of administrations; where the average earnings of the free citizen are almost half of what the prisoner in the jail gets for his food and raiment; where floods devastate and Malaria decimates without any remedy or redress, while piles of reports and recommendations of Commissions and Committees cover the archives of the Secretariat; where the poor have often to drink muddy liquids to appease their thirst; and where five out of every six children even in moderately decent families of the poor are allowed to grow up in ignorance—I say in a country like that men may not be wanting who might consider such paternal solicitude as too much of a protestation. I do not at all suggest that the Government of the country is solely or even primarily responsible for everyone of these untoward circumstances; but what I do maintain is that the apprehensions of the Government and its organs are ill-founded and unjustified. No doubt there is the baneful caste system, but there is also the counter-balancing distribution of labour and profession. The caste imposes only social restrictions and no political disabilities. Caste system in one shape or other and to some extent obtains in almost every society, but has nowhere stood as an insurmountable bar in the way of its political or economic development. Then is there no redeeming feature of the Indian social system with all its defects? Is there any country where every home is an asylum for the poor, and where the poor and the destitute are fed and clothed by their richer countrymen so generously? Is there any other people among whom the prevailing religions enjoin public charity without distinction of caste, colour or creed to such an extent that it has led the advocates of modern civilisation to characterise it as encouraging "professional mendicancy?" Government no doubt honestly tries to mitigate the sufferings of the poor in the hour of their distress; but is any notice taken of the millions who are silently succoured by the well-to-do Hindus and Muhammadans out of their own pocket in accordance with the injunctions of their religions? Then, has not the Congress cried for 30 years for the amelioration of the condition of the masses as persistently as for political rights and privileges? If such be the case, where is the ground and where the evidence for the apprehension so keenly felt and so persistently echoed and re-echoed? The Labour Party in the British Parliament is only of yesterday's growth and were

Parliamentary institutions deferred till the grant of a nominal representation of its vast working population? And was it Cobden or Kier Hardie that organised the Anti-Corn Law League or improved the wages of the labouring classes of Great Britain? And Cobden did not belong to any labouring class. And then are not caste prejudices fast dying out under the inexorable pressure of our environment, and are not men of talents rising out of the ranks of the so-called depressed classes who are receiving the ungrudging homage of the Brahmans and other superior castes? Lastly, would not there always be the paramount authority of the Government to correct abuses and remedy injustice wherever committed? Blood is always thicker than water and people are not therefore wanting amongst us who honestly regard the question of the strong and the weak only as a plausible pretext and not as a serious argument.

HINDU MOSLEM QUESTION

Another difficulty put forward is the eternal question of the differences between the Hindus and the Muhammadans of India. But the game has been nearly played out, and the Hindus and the Muhammadans have practically solved the question. It is more than five years ago that some of us dreamt a dream which appears now not to have been all a dream. The Congress and the League have come to meet at the same place and the day may not be far distant when in spite of the Siren song which has so far diverted their course they will come to meet in the same pavilion and at the same time. The Hindus and Muhammadans are rapidly converging towards each other and indeed it would be a miracle if they did not so converge and if they continued to fly off at a tangent despite the irresistible attraction of the great centripetal force which is drawing them towards their common centre. The stock argument based upon occasional differences and disturbances between Hindus and Mussalmans cannot have much force. These are confined mostly to lower classes of people on either side. It is neither fair nor judicious to exaggerate their importance. There are Hindus and Muhammadans side by side in every Native State. In the Muhammadan State of Hyderabad with a Hindu population of nearly 70 per cent. and the Hindu State of Kashmere with 60 per cent. Muhammudan subjects, we do not hear of any cow killing riots or Mohurrum disturbances or of any ill-feeling between the two communities. And one wonders why a different state of things should prevail in British territories. A nationality is now no longer either a religious or a social federation, but a political unit. Diverse races professing different forms of religion and following distinct varieties of manners, customs and traditions easily submit to a common political faith to work out their common destiny. The Piets and the Scots, the Saxons, and the Normans, the Protestants and the Catholics are now all welded into the great British nation. The Teutons and the Slavs, the Prussians and the Poles have formed one of the mightest empires which has lit up a world wide conflagration ; while in that curious Dual Monarchy of Austro-Hungary the Magyars, the Hungarians, Czecks, the Poles, the Slavs, the Serbs, the Croates and the Rumanians have formed themselves into a national federation of no ordinary solidarity and strength. The Hindus and Mussalmans are both of common Aryan stock, while Hindu anthropology traces them to a common descent within the legendary period of their ancient history. Neither the Parsis nor the Muhammadans of India owe any temporal allegiance either to the Shah of Persia or the Sultan of Turkey. They are now Indians as much as the Hindus. But why indulge in speculations against a settled fact? I think I break no secret when I announce to you that the Hindu Moslem question has been settled and the Hindus and Mussalmans have agreed to make a united demand for Self-Government. The All-India Congress Committee and the representatives of the Moslem League, who recently met in conference at Calcutta, have after two days' deliberations in one voice resolved to make a joint demand for a Representative Government in India. There are little differences on one or two minor points of detail, but they count for nothing. The vital issue has been solved and the main point has been gained. The report of the Conference will shortly be placed before you and I need not enter into details. We have many historic days but I believe the 17th November will rank among the brightest and the most notable of them all. I would now appeal to both the communities to sink all their minor domestic differences and present a solid united front for the realisation of their common destiny within the Empire. Only the seeds having been sown, the seedlings have just sprouted and for God's sake let us not quarrel over the division of the crop which still demands our combined labour and attention before the harvest comes. What are special electorates and communal representations when there is really no electorate and no representation among people? What matters it if Dinshaw Edulji Wacha or Surendra Nath Banerjee or Muzural Haque were to represent us in our National Assembly? They are three in one and one in three. Remember what the great Yudhishthra said addressing the Kauravas and the Pandavas.

Making a different application of this noble saying of the wise and saintly Yudhishthra we may say that we may be five brothers on one side and a hundred brothers on the other, but in a common cause we are a hundred and five brethren undivided and indivisible.

Gentlemen, an ounce of fact is said to be worth a ton of theories, and while we here are quarrelling over the first principles of the problem, the Americans have quietly and speedily solved it in the Philippines.

THE PHILIPPINES

The Philippine islands from their discovery by Lopezide Villalobos in the reign of Philip of Spain were under a form of despotic Government compared to which the despotism of John Company was an unmixed blessing. The archipelago is inhabited by a congeries of people speaking different languages and observing different forms of religion of the most primitive type. The Negritoes, the Negroes, the Panayas, the Mindanos, a dark wholly people, Indonassians, the Malayans, the Chinese, the Spaniards and a number of non-descripts inhabit the island. Of ancient civilisation and tradition these people have none, while as to their enlightenment and culture the world has heard nothing. The Americans conquered the islands in 1898, and the only claim of the people to the consideration of their liberators was that they had at first formed themselves into a band of insurgents under the leadership of an ambitious man named Aguinaldo who afterwards aspired to expel their benefactors. A provisional Government was however soon established by the Americans and peace restored in the country. Quite recently a proposal was brought forward in the House of Representatives of the United States for the granting of Home Rule to the Philippines, and in the discussion which followed some maintained that it should be accomplished in two years, some in four years, while others held that there should be no time limit; but all agreed that the islanders must be given their freedom and the archipelago should not form a permanent appendage to the United States which since the Civil War had positively refused to go in for territorial aggrandisement even in the face of the splendid opportunities which the New World presented to them. The last resolution was carried; and the American Governor in addressing the Philippinos on the occasion of granting them a substantial majority in the Legislative Assemblies of 1913, said:—" We regard ourselves as trustees, acting not for the advantage of the United States, but for the benefit of the people of the Philippines. Every step we take will be taken with a view to the independence of the Islands and as a preparation for that independence. The administration will take one step at once. It will give to the native citizens of the islands a majority in the Commission and thus in the Upper as well as in the Lower House of the Legislature. . . . We place within your reach the instruments of redemption. The door of opportunity stands open, and the event, under Providence is in your hands. The triumph is as great for us as it is for you." Noble words these, and nobly have the Americans come forward to fulfil them. As a result of this announcement the following measures have been introduced.

The Central Government in the Philippines is composed of the Governor-General, who is the chief executive and president of the Philippine Commission, and eight Commissioners, three Americans and five Philippinos. The Philippine Commission constitutes the Upper House and the elective Philippine Assembly the Lower House of the Legislative body. The members of the Assembly hold office for four years, and the Legislature elects two Resident Commissioners to the United States, who had office for the same term. These are members of the United States House of Representatives with a voice but not a vote. The islands are divided into 36 provinces of which 31 are regular and the rest special. The Government of each of the regular provinces is vested in a provincial board composed of a Governor and two *vocals*. The Governor is the chief executive of the province and presiding officer of the board. He and the *vocals* of the board are all elected by popular *vote*. The Government of towns is practically autonomous, the officials being elected by the qualified voters of the municipalities and serving for four years. The Jones' Bill of Independence introduced in the United States Legislature proposed to confer complete independence on the Philippinos not later than four years from the passing of the bill. In place of the present Philippine Commission, which is abolished, the Philippinos are to elect a Senate. The house is already elected by the people, and with election of the Senate, the electorate is to be increased by about 600,000. As about 200,000 Philippinos vote now the new law will grant voting rights to about 800,000. The office of Governor General is retained and there is to be a Vice-Governor, an American, whose duties are to be fixed by the Governor-General. The functions of the Legislature are limited so as to provide that the coinage currency and immigration laws shall not be made without the approval of the President of the United States. Finally, all Americans residing in the Islands who desire to vote must become citizens of the Islands. *The Republican* points out also that the preamble of the bill fixes no specific date for the granting of independence, but simply states that it has always been the purpose of the people of the United States to withdraw their sovereignty over the Philippine Islands and to recognise their independence as soon as a suitable Government can be established therein. Therefore, as justly pointed out by the *Indian Patriot* "enlarged powers of Self-Government are granted in order that by the use and exercise of popular franchise and Governmental powers, they may the better be prepared fully to assume the responsibilities and enjoy all the privileges of complete independence."

Thus a complete autonomous federal Government has already been established in the islands in which the Philippinos largely preponderate over the Americans and in which the actual administration has been substantially transferred to them. There is no bureaucracy in the Philippines nor Jingo Press there. No, there is no ruler and ruled, no sedition and no internments. Self-Government has established a reign of peace and contentment. Every Philippino is now a free citizen unemasculated by the operation of any Arms Act and unfettered by any Press Law. Are the arm chair critics who so lavishly indulge in abusing the Indian Nationalists for their "extravagant hopes" and "unrealisable demands" prepared to give any explanation of this phenomenal progress of the Philippines under the suzerainty of America? What is the difference between the Union Jack and the Star and Stripes? Let Sir William Wedderburn, who was as distinguished a member of the Indian Civil Service as his views have always commanded respect for their sobriety, soundness and moderation, answer Sir William commenting on the question of Self-Government as viewed on a reference to the Philippines pertinently asks,—" Can anybody show valid cause why this good example (of America) should not be followed by the British Government with regard to India? Are the Philippinos in any respect superior to the people of India? Or is it that the British people are inferior to the Americans in love of principle and moral courage?" We pause for a reply as to which of the alternatives is correct. Sir William then adds,—" the problem in India is much simpler, for India does not ask for a termination of the British connection, but I can say with certainty that among our best friends in India there exists grave disquiet, produced by the silence of the Government regarding their future policy, accompanied by irritating retrogressive legislation in Parliament and fresh activity of police repression in India." If the Philippinos have developed an instinct for Self-Government within 18 years no amount of reasoning or argument can satisfy the Indian mind that the Hindus, the Muhammadans, the Parsis and the Christians of India have not made even a near approach to it within 160 years; and if they are not yet fit for Self-Government, I despair of a time when they may be so.

AMENDMENT OF CONSTITUTION

There is yet another question which ought to be clearly understood in connection with our demand for

Self-Government. Is it any appreciable increase in our share in the administration that we demand on the permanent basis of the present system of Government? Or is it a thorough change in the constitution irrespective of all considerations of larger employment of the children of the soil in the public services? To be more explicit, let us put the question in its naked form. Supposing the Public Service Commission, whose report is still a sealed book to the people of this country, have recommended that no less than one half or even two thirds of the appointments in the different civil services should be filled up by Indians, but that the present bureaucracy must always continue to be in power, would such a recommendation, even if accepted by the Government, satisfy Indian aspirations? I know the answer will be in the negative. Such an arrangement will only serve to add a number of Indian bureaucrats without adding a bit to the powers and privileges of the people, and there would not be much to choose between the present bureaucracy and its proposed substitute. It is the system and not the *personnel* of the administration from which the people suffer. It is the rotten soil that breeds rank weeds. It is only a radical change in the form and constitution of the Government, however slow or tentative in its character, but steady and continuous in its development, that can satisfy the growing spirit of the Indian people and remove their grievances. If the British Parliament were after the War to hold in one hand a very high percentage of the public employments and a small modicum of real Self-Government in the other and to ask India to choose between these two, I am sure, she would unhesitatingly grasp the one and let go the other.

ANARCHY AND REPRESSION

Gentlemen, the new spirit to which I have already referred frankly refuses to believe in the liberalisation of a bureaucratic administration. The spirit is common both to the young and the old with this difference only that, while the old would proceed cautiously and steadily, the young are moved by the enthusiastic ardour natural to their age. If the Congress has so far persistently advanced the claims of the people to a larger share in the various public service, it has done so more from an economic point of view than for the satisfaction of its demands for a National Government. Irresponsible critics who denounce the new spirit ought to remember that it is not a sudden and abnormal growth in the Indian mind. It has appeared in Egypt, in Turkey, in Persia and in China and in fact in every country where autocratic rule has prevailed. All these countries have undergone the hammering process and everywhere hammering has served only to beat soft metals into hard ones. Anarchism and lawlessness have in all these countries followed in the wake of misrule.

The appearance of anarchism in the land has been a source of the deepest concern to the Government and the people alike. Both are interested in its irradication, alike for the ends of peaceful Government and the progressive development of the country on constitutional lines. But we must know what the disease is before we can apply the remedy. Anarchism has roots deep in economic and political conditions. One asks how is it that free countries like England and France or America are free from this taint ? There the blessings of freedom, of industrial progress and peace and contentment which follow in their train reign over the land. Let those great blessings be ours and anarchism will disappear. It is of western origin. It is an excrescence which ought to disappear with healing measures calculated to diffuse broadcast the blessings of political contentment and of material prosperity. By all means punish evil doers and iniquitous breakers of the law who commit wanton assaults on the lives and properties of their fellow-country men. But repression is not the true remedy. Repression when unwisely enforced and against the sober sense and judgment of the community must aggravate the situation and strengthen those forces of discontent which are the breeding ground of anarchism. "The sovereign remedy for public distemper," says Burke, "is conciliation and not coercion, for though coercion may succeed for a time it always leaves room for coercing again." A sufficient trial has been given to the orthodox method of the bureaucracy and the Congress urges that the other method should now be tried.

THE ASSURANCES

Gentlemen, we are roundly charged with ravelling in "extravagant hopes" and indulging in "unrealisable demands." But we have long refused to profit by the very friendly and eminently practical suggestions of those whose only claim to be regarded as *Statesman* or *Englishman* consists in the proud names which they have like the "bogus medical degrees" assumed for themselves. We do not judge the great British nation by specimens of this kind who do no honour to the English name. If we had done, that the Congress would have long ago wound up its business and gone into voluntary liquidation. The descendants of Howard and Wilberforce, of Burke and Bright, of Macaulay and Main, and of Canning and Ripon are not yet extinct. It is a nation of giants who refuse to tolerate injustice and perpetuate serfdom wherever they may exist, if only they are satisfied of their existence, and who possess a responsive heart to the call of freedom. It has been truly said that it is not Britain's heart but Britain's ear, that has been so long deaf to the wail that has been raised in this country. But the din of War has risen above all and the thrilling demonstrations of India's fidelity to the British connection have disabused many a robust mind in England of the hobgoblin stories to which they have been so lavishly treated in the past; and liberals and conservatives have therefore, with equal emphasis come to recognise as rational what has been denounced as "extravagant hopes" and "unrealisable demands" of the Indian people. Let us recall to-day only a few of the many assurances that have been given to India by some of the responsible ministers and men who are now guiding the destinies of the Empire.

The *Times*, the leading organ of conservative opinion in England, has been struck with the unexpected demonstration in India and frankly admitted that the Indian problem must be henceforth looked at from a different point of view. "On our part," says the great journal, "when we have settled account with the enemy, India must be allowed a more ample place in the councils of the Empire." Both Mr. Montagu and Mr. Roberts, as Under-Secretary for India, have from time to time expressed themselves in no uncertain voice as to the correct lines upon which the Indian administration requires to be revised and modified. Mr. Montagu's honest interpretation of Lord Hardinge's despatch of August 1911 is well-known, while Mr. Roberts speaking from his place in the House of Commons has frankly acknowledged that with the intellectual classes in India this outburst of loyalty is a "reasoned sentiment based upon considerations of enlightened self interest," and has at the same time asked the British public to alter "the angle of vision" in their perspective of the Indian problem. Following the *Times*, the *Review of Reviews* has, in one of its latest numbers, fairly admitted that "India to-day occupies a higher place in the Empire than ever before and has materially advanced her claims towards Self-Government and it is inevitable that, after the War her outstanding demands should receive the most sympathetic consideration." "We have," the *Review* adds, "made promises of Self-Government to Egypt, and it is inconceivable that we should deny the same privileges to India. At present India is not pressing her claim, but patiently awaits her just due, not as a reward, but as a right which her conduct has shown her worthy of possessing." Lord Haldane who till recently occupied a commanding position in the cabinet said:—"The Indian soldiers were fighting for the liberties of humanity, as much as we ourselves. India had given her lives and treasures in Humanity's great cause, hence things could not be left as they were. We had been thrown together in the mighty struggle and had been made to realise our oneness, so producing relations between India and England which did not exist before. Our victory would be victory for the Empire as a whole and could not fail to raise it to a higher level." Then at a recent meeting held at Guildhall at the instance of the Lord Mayor, Mr. Asquith, the premier and Mr. Bonar Law, the erstwhile leader of the Opposition, and both now united in coalition ministry, have given a joint pledge for the readjustment of India's position in the councils of the Empire after the War is over. But, to quote the words of Mr. Bonar Law, why the thing should not be done "while the metal was still glowing red-hot from the furnace of the War" and the promised rewards of India's comradeship and co-operation should be all relegated to the indefinite future and not one of them even shadowed forth in the present programmes of the Imperial Government, seems to be inexplicable. Quite recently Lord Chelmsford is reported to have said that "the War by giving India an opportunity to show its practical importance to the Empire had stirred Indian aspiration for development politically and economically. It would be his endeavour to secure a practical response to this new desire for progress." His lordship is said to have added: "My task is to guard India from cramping influences of undue conservatism equally with unpractical revolutionary tendencies."

Now, are these men of less authority, foresight and responsibility than the members of the Indian bureaucracy or its exponents in the Anglo-Indian Press, who are ever so loud and positive in denouncing our claims? Or are these assurances all a hoax intended to delude the Indian mind? We positively refuse to accept any such view which would be a gross columny on the great British nation. We have much greater confidence in British statesmanship which may have blundered in many places but has failed nowhere. Gentlemen, we indulge in no gloomy anticipations; but we shudder to contemplate the serious effect which the non-fulfilment of these pledges is likely to produce in the minds of the Indian public. The Partition of Bengal which was after all a provincial question brought in its trail an outburst of discontent which like wild fire spread throughout the whole country and necessitated a full brigade of repressive measures to put it down, although its smouldering sparks are not yet fully extinct. And how widespread and far-reaching must be the unrest which is sure to follow a light hearted treatment of these solemn pledges and assurances upon which the people have so firmly and so confidently built their future hopes of advancement ? God forbid that such a calamity should befall India. As loyal subjects of His Majesty, we of the Congress deem it our duty to tell all whom it may concern not to treat the Indian problem after the War as lightly as some irrespons.ble and mischievous critics are evidently disposed to do. Already a subdued note of the " Scrap of paper " has been raised in certain quarters. The Charter Act of 1833, the Queen's Proclamation of 1858 and the two gracious message of King Edward VII and George V. still remain unredeemed, and it would be no wise statesmanship to add to the burden of unredeemed pledges. England has been drawn into the vortex of a titanic struggle for the deliverance of Belgium and Servia. God grant, she may come out with her brave allies completely triumphant in her heroic efforts. She has however a much greater State in India and India has a much greater claim to her consideration. Let us hope she will not fail to be at least as just as she is generous. After the War is over a complete re-adjustment of the Empire will have to be made; all its component parts will have to be co-ordinated and harmonise with one another and with the parent state India alone cannot be left out of this programme. She must be admitted into common and equal partnership with the colonies on terms of equal rights and obligations of the Empire, enjoying equal laws and equal rights of British citizenship throughout that Empire. The collar of a dependency should be removed from her neck and the coronet of an autonomous, Self-Governing state placed upon her head. What a glorious federation it would then be, more glorious than that of the Roman Empire or of any that the world has yet seen. England would be well to remember in her own interest that she cannot maintain a condition of perpetual pupilege any where within her world-wide possessions without slowly and imperceptibly innoculating herself with its poison in her own home. Demoralisation in one part of a body however remote must inevitably result, if not remedied, in the ultimate deterioration of the whole system. Present experience has shown that for greater cohesion and solidarity of the Empire its component parts must be brought into closer touch and more intimate relations between one another and the mother country. India alone cannot be excluded from equal consideration in the coming re-adjustment, for if she were to be so excluded, India's position is sure to be worse than even at present. If the colonies are allowed a representation in the federal council of the Empire they will undoubtedly have a voice in the administration of India and, for ought we know, their representatives may sometimes find a place in the Cabinet and also become the Secretary of State for India. If India is denied such representation she will be further regarded as being subject also to the colonies. There is a serious danger in admitting the colonies to a participation in determining the policy that is to be followed in relation to India, for the colonial mind is saturated with the colour prejudice which would thus be reflected in the Government of India. Such a change in the 'angle vision' it would be dreadful to contemplate. If the equilibrium of the Empire is to be maintained, India must also be thrown into the scale: She must be freely admitted into the partnership and given a free constitution like that of the self-governing dominions and a fair representation in the federal council along with the colonies.

OUR DEMANDS

Ladies and Gentlemen, I now propose as a summary to the foregoing discussions to submit a few "daring and impertinent" proposals for the consideration of the Government both in England as well as in India. A memorandum presented by nineteen members of the supreme Legislative Council has met with the criticism of both sides. Some have regarded it as premature and falling short of our demands, while others have denounced it as extravagant. The circumstances which brought about the submission of this memorandum have already been explained to the public; while, as I read it, this memorandum represents neither the irreducible minimum nor the unenhancible maximum of our demands; nor do I understand the signatories to it to mean that their proposals are to be carried out on the morning following the day on which the Treaty of Berlin may be signed. The signatories to the memorandum have, however, done me one great service. They have borne the brunt of the fusilade and made my passage less difficult, so as to enable me to press forward unnoticed under cover of their fire. As to the other side of the shield our misfortune is that we are unable to see where the extravagance comes in. We have no superfluities in any direction and for such a people as ourselves to indulge in extravagance seems to be out of the question. Extravagance may seize the minds of those who have got enough and to spare. However that may be, here are our demands which God willing are bound to be fulfilled at no distant date.

1. India must cease to be a dependency and to be raised to the status of a self-governing state as an equal partner with equal rights and responsibilities as an independent unit of the Empire.

2. In any scheme of re-adjustment after the War, India should have fair representation in the Federal Council like the colonies of the Empire.

3. India must be governed from Delhi and Simla, and not from Whitehall or Downing Street. The Council of the Secretary of State should be either abolished or its constitution so modified as to admit of substantial Indian representation on it. Of the two Under Secretaries of State for India one should be an Indian and the salaries of the Secretary of State should be placed to the Britain estimates as in the case of the Secretary for the Colonies. The Secretary of State for India should, however, have no more powers over

the Government of India than those exercised by the Secretary for the Colonies in the case of the dominions. India must have complete autonomy financial, legislative as well as administrative.

4. The Government of India is the most vital point in the proposed reforms. It is the fountain head of all the local administrations and unless we can ensure its progressive character any effective reform of the local Governments would be impossible. For this the Services must be completely separated from the State and no member of any service should be a member of the Government. The knowledge and experience of competent members of a Service may be utilised in the departments, but they should not be allowed to be members of the Executive Council or the Cabinet of the Government itself.

5. The Executive Government of India should vest in the Governor-General with a number of ministers not less than one-half of whom should be Indians elected by the elected non-official Indian members of the Supreme Legislative Council. These members should hold office for five years. Thus this ministry of the Viceroy will possess the composite character of a parliamentary and non-parliamentary cabinet.

6. The Upper House of Representatives in Canada is composed 90 members. The Supreme Legislative Council in India should consist of at least 150 members. These members should be all elected. But for the transitory period one-fifth may be appointed by the

Cabinet, not more than one-fourth of whom may be officials.

7. The annual budget should be introduced into the Legislative Council like Money Bills, and except the military estimates the entire Budget should be subject to the vote of the Council.

8. The Provincial Governments should be perfectly autonomous, each Province developing and enjoying its own resources, subject only to a contribution towards the maintenance of the Supreme Government.

9. A Provincial administration should be vested, as in the case of the Supreme Government, in a Governor with a cabinet not less than one half of whom should be Indians elected by the non-official elected Indian members of its Legislative Council.

10. The Provincial Legislative Council should in the case of major province consist of 100 members and in the case of a minor province 75 members all of whom should be elected by the people and each district must have at least one representative of its own. For the transitory period there should of course be the same conditions and restrictions as in the cases of the Supreme Legislative Council.

11. As the executive and the legislative functions are to be separated, so there must be complete separation of the judicial from the executive functions of the State. The judicial administration, whether civil or criminal, should be wholly vested in the High Courts both as regards control as well as the pay, prospect

and promotion of its officers. The High Courts should be subordinate only to the Supreme Government.

12. The Arms Act should be repealed or so modified as to place the Indians exactly on the same footing with the Europeans and Eurasians. The Press Act should be removed from the Statute Book and all the repressive measures withdrawn.

13. India should have a national militia to which all the races should be eligible under proper safeguards and they should be allowed to volunteer themselves under such conditions as may be found necessary for the maintenance of efficiency and discipline. The Commissioned ranks in the army should be thrown open to His Majesty's Indian Subjects.

14. A full measure of local Self-Government should be immediately granted throughout the country, and the Corporations of the Presidency towns the District and the Taluq Boards and the district municipal corporations should be made perfectly self-governing bodies with elected members and elected chairmen of their own. They should be freed from all official control except such as may be legally exercised by the Government direct.

15. Mass education should be made free and compulsory. Suitable provisions should also be made for the development and encouragement of indigenous industries.

The above is a summary of our demands. We do not fix any time-limit, for the duration of the war is uncertain and there must be a transitory period through which the process must pass. But if we fix no time limit, we agree to no indefinite postponement either. Some of these proposals can and ought to be immediately carried out and there is no reason why they should wait for the termination of the War: while there are others which cannot of course be settled until the time for the readjustment of the Empire arrives; but we must be distinctly understood to maintain that this period should not be treated as a further extension granted to the present system of administration and its methods. There must be henceforth a distinct tendency visible in every branch of the administration to conciliate the people and inspire trust and confidence in the future policy of the Government. As words without thoughts never to heaven go, so promises without performance and sympathy without action can never touch the hearts of the people. Patience has often been prescribed as the sovereign remedy for all distempers; but it cannot be denied that when the most skilful physician is unable for a long time to show any sign of improvement and on the contrary there are continued symptoms of aggravation, a suspicion naturally may arise in the mind of the patient as to the skill of the physician or the efficacy of his methods. On our part, gentlemen we must be content to ascend.

STEP BY STEP

It is no argument to say that you have long acquired the capacity to make the ascent. You might have ten years before safely tried the experiment; but it does not follow, that you can therefore cover ten steps or even two steps at a time. Whenever you have to ascend you must begin from the base and rise steadily and cautiously upwards. Of course it would be no progress if you gain one step and lose two. Doubtless we ought carefully to see that we lose no ground and then even if our progress be slow we may be sure of reaching our destined goal.

THE BRITISH COMMITTEE

Gentlemen, one word about our British agency in London. It is perfectly superfluous for me to point out that no business concern can be successfully carried on without a well-equipped and efficient agency as its principal place of business. In England is the real seat of power and the battle of India must be fought on the British soil. Though it is we who must fight it out we must have the British public as our ally. That public must be informed and influenced so as to enable it to come to a correct judgment of our case. There is an erroneous impression in certain quarters that as our grievances are so numerous and so palpable they must be known to the British people also. But who is there to carry your message to England? You certainly cannot expect *Reuter* to do it. You certainly do not believe that retired Anglo-Indians will proclaim their own defects and short comings. On the contrary there are the standing official reports always to present a roseate view of the administration taking credit for whatever is good, throwing the entire blame for all that is bad on your shoulders and justifying all sorts of repressive measures. The British public in their ignorance easily swallow all these *ex parte* cock and bull stories and consider the Indian administration to be a perfect Utopia. So you must have a counsel of your own to represent your case before the great tribunal of public opinion in Great Britain if you do not wish judgment to go against you by default. Sir William Wedderburn is performing this function at no small sacrifice to himself. India cannot repay the deep debt which she owes to him and his colleagues on the British Committee, and the poet's words are her only satisfaction that a grateful mind by owing owes not, but always remains indebted and discharged. Mr. H.E.A. Cotton, the worthy son of a worthy father, following in the footsteps of his illustrious parent has been doing yeoman's service to India. The British Committee and its sole organ *India* must be maintained at all costs if we are to carry on our operations at the vital front. It has always seemed to me of the utmost importance to associate with the British Committee at least one competent Indian permanently located in England. The great services rendered there some years back by the late Mr. W. C. Bannerjee and recently by our distinguished countrymen Sir Krishna Govinda Gupta ought to be an object lesson to us. But for all these a permanent Congress Fund is an imperative necessity. The granting of small doles by the Congress every year which are always larger in their arrears than in their payment and the undignified spectacle of one of the leaders every year extending his beggarly Brahmanical hand for such pittance, is not the way of practical men engaged in practical business. There is no dearth of men who are rolling in the superfluities of their unearned heritages. Large sums of money are still spent throughout the country in mere shows and ceremonies of the most temporary interest; and if we cannot even raise so much as twice a couple of *lakhs* of rupees for the uplifting of the nation, then are we rightly treated by our rulers as an inferior race and twitted by our critics as mere men of words indulging in "extravagant hopes" and "unrealisable demands."

CONCLUSION

Ladies and gentlemen, I am afraid I have exhausted your patience although I have failed to exhaust my theme. My last words are to those bright young faces whom I see before me. My dear young friends and countrymen, you are our hostages to posterity. Every generation has a perpetual devolution and succession of rights and responsibilities. The acquisition of one generation becomes the heritage of the next, and it is the duty of each generation not only to enjoy what it receives from its predecessor, but also to transmit its heritage consolidated, augmented and improved to the one coming after it. Many of those who preceded you in this national struggle have been gathered to their fathers, while those who are still in the field belong to a fast vanishing generation. You ought now to press forward to take their place and hold aloft the banner which is dropping from their sinking hands. Like the mother of the Grachi India, poor India, shorn of her prestine grandeur and glory, has only to boast of *you* as her "precious jewels." Remember of what great nation you are born. It was for you that in the early morning of the world the *Vedas* were revealed and in a later period demoratic Islam came with *Koran* and the practical Parsi with the *Zend Avesta*. Yours is the heritage of three of the most ancient civilisations of the world which have formed as it were a glorious confluence of three streams in this sacred land of yours while to these in the dispensation of an inscrutible Providence a fourth has recently been added to constitute a *Sagara-Sangama* for the deliverance of your race. It was for you that Vyasa wrote and Valmiki sung, and it was for you that Patanjali evolves the loftiest of philosophies and the *Geeta* expounded the sublime mysteries of life. It was here that more than two thousand years ago *Buddha Gautama*, the truest and greatest benefactor of mankind, first taught the doctrine of universal brotherhood of men, which now sways the minds of one fifth of the population of the habitable globe; and it was here that five hundred years ago Sree Chaitanya preached the gospel of love, fraternity and equality from the banks of the Ganges to the banks of the Narbudda; and now modern civilisation is prostituting science, filling the air, land and water with deadly engines for the destruction of God's creation. But let us not be great only in the worship of a great past. A mighty wave of changes is surging throughout this world and India is passing through a momentous transition. Her future is in your hands. You can either make or mar that future. If I were asked, what was the first demand of the Motherland upon her children at this juncture, I would unhesitatingly answer that it is Patriotism. And the second?—Patriotism. And the third?—Patriotism. I do not mean that morbid sentiment which rises like a rocket and falls like a stone; not that sentiment which takes a man off his feet and lands him in disasters: not that sentiment which panders to passion and does not appeal to reason; but I mean that supreme virtue which enlightens the head and ennobles the heart, and under the heavenly inspiration of which a man forgets his self and merges his individuality, like a drop in an ocean, in the vast all-absorbing interest of his country, feeding only on self-sacrifice and ever growing on what it feeds. To the Indian Nationalists their country must be their religion "taught by no priests but by the beating hearts" and *her* welfare their common faith "which makes the many one." Hushed be the whispers of jealousy and spite, and silenced be the discordant notes of rancerous dissensions amongst you. Sink all your differences in a supreme common cause. Unite and stand solidly shoulder to shoulder, resolved either to conquer or to die. Or, what is life worth if we cannot live like men ? Firm and resolute in your purpose, be always manly and dignified in your attitude and sober and cautious in your steps. Be loyal to your king and devoted to your country. Difficult as your task is constitutional must be your method: There is, no royal road to freedom. Reverses there must be, but reverses should only stiffen your backs. Do not despair, for despair is the keynote of failure. The pendulum may be swinging forward and backward; but look up and see the hand of invisible. Time is perpetually marking its progress on the dial of the destiny of your country. Above all, remember that nations are not born but made. They must grow from within but cannot be made to grow from without. You must stand on your own legs and be prepared to fight it out with heart within and God over head. *Dieu-et-Mon-Droit* is the motto emblazoned on the British Coat of Arms and as citizens of the British Empire "God and My Right" ought to be your watch-word and battle-cry in the bloodless revolution which is taking place in this country. Be ambitious but not proud; be humble but aspire to a nobler manlier and healthier life. What have you to boast of but your vanished glories ! You are Utilanders in your own country. In the burning words of the Father of the Congress—

"What avail your wealth, your learning,
Empty titles, sordid trade ?
True Self-rule were worth them all !
Nations by themselves are made."

VANDE MATARAM.

BAL GANGADHAR TILAK

In supporting the resolution on Self-Government in the Congress of 1916, *Bal Gangadhar Tilak said*:—

I thank you sincerely for the reception that you have given me on this platform, but let me tell you I am not fool enough to think that this reception is given to me personally. It is given, if I rightly understand, for those principles for which I have been fighting. The resolution which I wish to support embodies all these principles. It is the resolution of Self-Government. It is that for which we have been fighting, for which the Congress has been fighting for the last thirty years. The first note of it was heard ten years ago on the banks of the Hugli, and it was sounded by the Grand Old Man of India, that Parsi Patriot of Bombay, Dadabhai Naorojee. Since the note was sounded, difference of opinions arose. Some said that the note ought to be carried on, and ought to be followed by a detailed scheme at once, that it should be taken up and made to resound all over India as soon as possible. There was another party amongst us that said that it could not be done so soon, and the tune of that note required to be a little lowered. That was the cause of the dissension ten years ago, and I am glad to say that I have lived these 10 years to see that we are going to put our voices and shoulders together to push on this scheme of Self-Government. Not only have we lived to see these differences closed, but to see the differences of Hindus and Muhammadans closed as well. So, we have now united in every way in the United Provinces, and we have found that luck in Lucknow. So I consider it the most auspicious day in the most auspicious Session of this 31st Indian National Congress. There are only one or two points on which I wish to address you. It has been said by some that we, Hindus, have yielded too much to our Muhammadan brethren. I am sure I represent the sense of the Hindu community all over India when I say that we could not have yielded too much. I would not care, if the rights of Self-Government are granted to the Muhammadan community only. I would not care, if they are granted to Rajputs. I would not care, if they are granted to the lowest classes of the Hindu population, provided the British Government considers them more fit than the educated classes of India for exercising those rights. I would not care if those rights are granted to any section of the Indian community. Then the fight will be between them and another section of the community, and not, as at present, a triangular fight. We have to gain this from a powerful bureaucracy, an unwilling bureaucracy naturally unwilling, because the bureaucracy now feels that these rights, these privileges, this authority will pass out of their hands. I would feel the same if I were in that position, and I am not going to blame the bureaucracy for entertaining that natural feeling, but whatever that feeling may be, it is a feeling which we have to combat against, it is a feeling that it is not conducive to the growth of Self-Government in this country. When we have to fight against a third party, it is a very important thing that we stand on this platform united as regards all shades of different political opinion. That is the most important event of the day. When Dhadhabai Naoroji declared that "Swaraj" should be our goal, its name was "Swaraj;" later on, it came to be known as Self-Government and Constitutional Reform, and we Nationalists style it Home Rule. It is all the same in three different names. There is the objection raised that "Swaraj" has a bad odour in India and "Home Rule" had a bad odour in England, and hence we ought to call it Constitutional Reform.

I do not care to call it by any name. I do not mind for the name, but I believe you have hardly realised the importance and character of that scheme of reform. Let me tell you that it is far more liberal than the Irish Home Rule Bill, and then you can understand what possibilities it carries with it. It may not be complete Home Rule, but it is more than a beginning of it. It may not be complete Self-Government, but it is far better than Local Self-Government. It may not be "Swaraj" in the wider sense of the word, but it is far better than "Swadeshi" and "Boycott." It is, in fact, a synthesis of all the Congress resolutions passed during the last 30 years, a synthesis that will help us all to proceed to work in a definite and responsible manner. We cannot now afford to spend our energy on all the resolutions on the Public Services, the Arms

Act and sundry others. All is comprehended and included within this one resolution.

I would ask everyone of you to try to carry out this one resolution with all your effort, might, and enthusiasm and everything that you can command; your intelligence, money, enthusiasm, all must now be devoted for carrying out this scheme of reform. Do not think it is an easy task. Nothing can be gained by passing resolutions on this platform, by the simple union of the two races, the Hindus and the Muhammadans, and the two parties, the moderates and the Nationalists. The union is intended to create a certain power and energy amongst us, and unless that power and energy are exercised, you cannot hope to succeed, so great are the obstacles in your way. You must now prepare to fight out the scheme. In short, I do not care if the Sessions of the Congress are held no longer. I believe it has done its work as a deliberative body. The next part is the executive and that will be placed before you afterwards.

When "Swaraj" was declared to be our goal, it was a question whether it was a legal goal. The Calcutta High Court held it was a legal goal a year afterwards. Then it was a question whether it was legal. Finally it was decided that it must be carried out, and expressed in such words as would not cast any slur on the Bureaucracy which was the master of the time. That too, has been decided judicially, that you can make any criticism in order to further your objects and justify your demand, and that it comes within the bounds of law. So, the goal of "Swaraj" is declared legal, and here you have a specific scheme of "Swaraj" passed by the united communities of the Hindus and Muhammadans. All the thorns in your way have been removed. It will be your own fault if you do not succeed in attaining what is now described in this scheme. This is a very serious responsibility. Do not shirk it, but work for it.

The days of wonders are gone. You cannot feed now 100,000 people on a few crumbs of bread as you did in Jesus' day. The attaining of this object cannot be achieved by the wonders of Heaven. You have to do it. These are days of work and incessant labour, and I hope that, with the help of Providence, you will find that energy and those resources which are required for carrying out that scheme. I hope that by the end of 1917, when I expect that the War will be closed, or at least, in 1918 we shall meet at some place in India where we shall be able to raise up the banner of Self-Rule.

THE HON. MAZUR-UL-HAQUE

In supporting the resolution on Self-government in the Congress of 1916, *the Hon. Mazur-ul-Haque said*:—

In all my political life. I have been of this opinion that our Motherland cannot advance without the unity of the Hindus and the Muhammadans. Having been of this opinion, I have worked for the attainment of union, and that has been achieved to-day in this town of Lucknow. I consider it my duty here to mention the name of one who has been the chief instrument of attaining that unity, I mean the name of my revered friend the Raja of Mahmudabad. I assure you that he is an asset for India. I hope there will be many like him in my country. May he live long! The time for speechifying and talk has long gone by and the time for action has come. You are talking about Self-Government and Home Rule. and do you for a moment believe that you will get it by talking? Unless and until you make your Rulers believe that you are earnest, serious in your demand, you will never get anything. I am sure of it. So my advice to my countrymen is this: try to work now. You must have propaganda throughout the country, and let our Rulers see for themselves that every man, every woman, and every child of India is bent upon, and determined to have, Self-Government.

SIR DINSHAW PETIT

In supporting the resolution on Self-Government in the Congress of 1916, *Sir Dinshaw Petit said* :—

I have taken upon myself, to answer the command of our leaders, to address you, lest my refusal should be construed into some sort of apathy on the part of the community to which I belong. Towards the just and the righteous aspirations of the people of this country, there cannot be the slightest doubt as to what could be the views of the community which has produced a Dhadhaboy Naoroji and a Pherozeshah Mehta. It is said by those who do not like the advancement of the people of this country towards the attainment of Home Rule, that the Parsis under the British Government have been enjoying too many high offices and high posts, that they do not know what they would gain by casting their lot with the Hindus and the Muhammadans in making the demand. Do not for a moment think that the Parsis, when they are under the Government of Home Rule will, in any way, suffer in that direction, but admitting for arguments' sake for a moment that they did, would it be right and sensible to expect that for the benefit of a few thousand Parsis, 313 millions of people should be denied their birthright and their privilege?

It is always said that the Parsis are the most loyal community in India. They are second to none in their loyalty to the Crown, and therefore it is they support this movement because everybody must feel that there is nothing which would contribute more towards the permanence of British connection in India than Home Rule under British guidance. I shall throw out one suggestion towards the speedier attainment of the objects of this Congress, and it is this: I speak with some personal experience of public life in the Presidency from which I come. That the people who do the greatest harm to our legitimate aspirations are not the people who rule us, but unfortunately, some of our own people. I know there are people who go to the Government House to carry tales. I know there are people in the Legislative Council and in the Municipal Corporation who barter away the rights and the privileges of their country and city to get a Khan Bahadur or a C.I.E. It is my advice that we must ostracise such people. If we do not admit them into our clubs, let us see if they will be admitted by their English friends in their clubs. Now, on behalf of my community, I congratulate you on the union which you Hindus and Muhammadans have made this time by sinking into oblivion all your little differences. United you must fall, whether it be for good or for evil.

BABU BEPIN CHANDRA PAL

In supporting the resolution on Self-Government in the Congress of 1916, *Babu Bepin Chandra Pal said*:--

I can hardly tell you how happy I feel to meet you all, my dearly beloved members of the United National Congress, after an absence of 10 long years. These 10 years have not gone in vain, and the fruition of our efforts is seen in every word of the resolution that has been placed before you to-day. We divided: the result of that division has been a closer union than had been before between us, and the proof of it is seen in every word of the resolution to-day. We fought; we wrangled; but every fight is justified not in itself, but by a closer and more organic reconciliation to which it leads, and our fight has, in the providence of God, led to more organic reconciliation between all parties, all ideals and all principles that we represented and fought for during the past. Here you have in the resolution the word "Self-Government," divested of every adjectival or adverbial, or any other phrase to take away its quality or quantity from it. Self-Government pure and simple is the resolution to which our leaders have spoken to which you have already given your acceptance. It is the first article of the Congress; it is the first article of the Indian Nationality; it is the first article of every self-respecting nation, every civilised nation in humanity. It is the first article of every man and woman who feels within himself or herself the call of the Divine. It is the first article of every Yogi, of every Gnani, and of every Bhaktha, because Self-Government is the pith and foundation, not only of the life temporal but also of the life spiritual. Yesterday you passed a resolution from the Chair avowing sincerely and honestly your allegiance to the British connection. It seems to me that the resolution to-day follows as a necessary corollary to that resolution of yesterday, because the only condition upon which British connection with India can be perpetuated is the realisation of the resolution that has been placed before you to-day.

This resolution divides itself into three parts. The first part demands that there must be a Royal Proclamation. Why do you demand a Proclamation? You do not know that. I will tell you why I demand it. I know there is deep despair upon the face of India at the present time. I have talked to the young. I have met old men of my age and men older than myself, and the one thing that one and all of them have said to me is, what is the good of it? Deep despair and despondency sit upon the face of India at the present time. I believe we have a future. I am fully assured that you and I shall live in our own country just as every other civilised people in the world are living in their own country. I have no doubt about the future. I see clearly, as I see the grey beard of the President from here, that Self-Government for India is absolutely assured, but my people do not believe it. The old men do not believe it. They say " What is the good, let us die in peace." The young men do not believe in it. " (They say ?) What is the good ? Let us earn money and leave a generation behind us." And the middle-aged gentlemen say the same. We want a message of practical hope, a message of objective hope, and therefore we want this message from the British Crown and the British Parliament to tell us that we shall live in our own country as other people live in their own countries. But that will not do. We have had declarations, and we have been disabused of being taken in by politicians' words. We want something substantial and a substantial assurance that this declaration will not go the way of similar declaration in the past.

We want the Reform Scheme placed before the Congress, prepared by the Congress and the Muslim League, to be immediately put into action. That is the second, but that is not all. You are talking of the reconstruction of the Empire, but I want to know what this Empire is without India. Is there a British Empire without India ? They talk of man-power. The total man-power of the British Empire all told of the age from 15 to 35, is something like 11 crores and 1½ crores of that man-power consists of white humanity and 9½ crores of brown and black humanity. What is the British Empire then in man-power if you leave out the 7½ crores of the youth of India ? You talk of brain-power. Where is the brain power of the Empire ? As it is, we have no opportunity for the exercise of our brains for the application of our intellect to the solution of the larger world problems of the day. We have no place in the councils of the statesmen. If we had, we might have proved our power as we have already proved in the bar, on the bench, in every walk of life. Wherever we had an opportunity we have proved that the Indian brain is not a negligible quantity in the Empire. Why have we only one J. C. Bose, only one P. C. Rai, only one Professor Paranjpe, not for want of brain-power, but for want of opportunities to realise to the full extent the brain-power of our nation. Give us that opportunity, or rather remove the obstacles from it, and we shall take the opportunity and utilise it for ourselves to the fullest extent and therefore we say that we want this.

The third thing is about the reconstruction of the Empire. We say it is impossible if India is left out worse than impossible. It will be the death of the Indian National aspirations on the one side and the death of the Imperial ambitions on the other, if India is left out in the reconstruction of the Empire. Thirty years ago it might have been conceivable to leave India out of the Imperial family, to keep India as a helot, a drawer of water and hewer of wood. To-day, with this new awakened National consciousness, this sensitive patriotism throbbing through the heart of the young and the old, the thing is unthinkable, inconceivable, dangerous and fatal to the permanence of the British connection with India. Therefore we say that these 3 parts of the resolution should have not only your acceptance, but should command the serious attention of the "Round Table" and the square table and every table on earth.

MR. JOSEPH BAPTISTA

In supporting the resolution on Self-Government in the Congress of 1916, *Mr. Joseph Baptista said:—*

I can assure you that it is not without fear and trembling that I venture to support this resolution. I understand that in this Province a new commandment has been issued: "Thou shalt not be emphatic" (laughter), you could be phlegmatic if you like, but not emphatic. In other words, you must not call "a spade a spade." That would be too emphatic. You must call it diamonds and hearts (pearls?). You cannot call Home Rule Home Rule. But if you call Home Rule Self-Government, it is all right. Whether it is all right or all wrong, I prefer to call Home Rule Home Rule. To my great surprise I find that within the past few months Home Rule has become the popular cry throughout the whole country. There are no heretics among us. All believe in the creed of Home Rule. No dissenters, no quakers or shakers, we are all militant Home Rulers. To what is this great change to be attributed and to whom must we be grateful in this great hour of trial. You must give the credit to the person who deserves that credit, and I say most emphatically that credit is due to the magnetic personality and dynamic energy of our friend and sister, Mrs. Besant. She is the Simon-de-Montfort that guided us all to victory. You know she has suffered for it while devoting herself to our cause. May I in your name say that we love her, that we trust her, and that we stand by her. This question is not merely a question of our growing aspirations. It is a question of all questions, the question of the destiny of India.

Allow me to tell you that so far as the destiny of India is concerned, it is the most momentous and the most transcendent question that can occupy the minds of the educated Indians. Believe me that the destiny of India depends upon political principles that are applied to the Government of this country. You may be quite sure that the destiny will not be achieved unless we combine the principles of liberty, the principles of Nationalism and the principles of federation in the Government of this country. The task before us is to rescue India from her present plight, and place her on a pedestal upon which we can look with pride and pleasure. What is the present plight of India? Is there anyone who is satisfied with the present position of India? Go outside British India; India is a mere political cypher in the political world; nobody cares a fig for her; and nobody thinks of her. Is that a proper position for 300 millions of people to occupy in this Empire. What do you find if you go to the Colonies? The curse of colour. In the South African War, Indians stood by Englishmen and fought beside and shed their blood for them. What is the reward? Exclusion from the country or confinement in isolated places subjected to regulations so odious that it makes our blood boil. Such is the reward and such is the gratitude of a civilised and Christian country. Coming home, what do you find?—the curse of distrust, distrust everywhere, excluded from the army as you know, excluded from the use of arms by the Arms Act on account of distrust, and there by emasculated, subjected to Press Laws and God knows to what other laws as Mr. Surendranath Banerjea said. Apart from that, what do you find with the fauna and flora which can produce everything to minister to the comforts of all people and with men who are skilful in production? You have 50 to 60 millions of people pledged to starvation from day to day. (Cries of Shame.) Is this the structure of the Empire with which you are satisfied? The Anglo-Indian architects have had their free hand for the last 150 years, and this is the Empire they have produced. I ask you is there any man, with sense or sensibility, that can look upon this and say that this is a proper thing for us? Can any one say that this a mansion befitting the ancient civilisation and latent potentialities of the country? Is this not a glorified chawl? This is entirely due not to men that administer, but entirely due to the system under which it is administered. There cannot be the slightest doubt that no improvement is possible unless the centralised system is done away with. At the present moment what are we? We are under a centralised system of Government. The Government of India is, after all, a mere administrative department of Government in England and no more.

THE HON. Dr. TEJ BAHADUR SAPRU

In supporting the resolution on Self-Government in the Congress of 1916, *the Hon. Dr. Tej Bahadur Sapru said*:—

If I was asked to sum up our demand in one word, I would say unhesitatingly that what we want is not so much of reforms as the power to reform ourselves. Reforms in driblets, in instalments, we have had in the past, and we may expect to have them in the future but they will not satisfy the rising and growing aspirations of our countrymen now. Self-respect alone demands that, like other self-respecting nations of the world, we should be allowed a free hand to work out our own destiny and that we should not be treated as perpetual school boys in politics. (Hear, hear). Gentlemen, there are just one or two points which I should like to touch upon if you will permit me. My time is limited, but I consider that they are worth hearing.

It has been said by a distinguished writer, whose name has come up before you during the last two days, that the real cement of the Empire is devotion to the Empire. Granted. In this land of spirituality we do not want a Westerner to teach us a lesson in devotion. (Hear, hear.) But may I be permitted to ask whether it is possible for any human being to be devoted when there is no response to that devotion. (Hear, hear). Devoted to England we have been in the past, devoted to England we shall be in the future. But if by devotion to the Empire is meant that we should be devoted to the colonies then I, for one, will have no hesitation in saying that India will refuse to allow the Colonies to rule over her. Let us not mince matters over this. Let us be plain and out spoken. To England we have been devoted, we are and we shall be, but India will not be so short-sighted and so foolish as to allow the colonies to have a finger in her pie.

Gentlemen, the next point that has been urged against us is, that we have not got the capacity to rule ourselves. When was the discovery made, may I ask? Until at least 60 or 70 years ago before England took over directly the control of affairs in India into her hands who were ruling us? We ourselves. Is it really intended to be said that during the last 60 or 70 years since the control of affairs in India has passed into England's hands, that we have lost all capacity? If the answer is 'Yes,' I say the discredit is to those who have deprived us of the capacity. I venture to submit with all respect and with all sincerity that we have not lost the capacity for Self-Government. Witness the Native States of Hyderabad, Baroda, and Mysore. Who is ruling them? Our own countrymen. It really comes to this, that so far as the power of initiative is concerned, so far as the scope for talent is concerned, that is denied to us here, and it is not denied to the people in the States like Hyderabad, Baroda and Mysore. Gentlemen, assuming that we have lost something of the capacity, how are we going to recover that capacity. By being denied admission to the inner circles of the Government or by being allowed to commit mistakes and to learn thereby? The answer is obvious.

Now, gentlemen, there is one more objection which I wish to notice and then I will retire. It has been said by that very writer Mr. Curtis, that the 'one great and supreme objection to self-government being conferred just now on this country is that we have not got sufficiently large electorates. And I may tell you in confidence that I was told personally that if we could show to England that one-fifth of the population possessed sufficient political capacity, then they would not object to our getting self-government. Now, gentlemen, you have got 315 million people in this country—I am very poor in arithmetic—I believe one fifth of that comes to 63 million. And at the rate of progress we have been making in the matter of primary education, I should think it would take us 400 or 500 years before we get political capacity (Laughter). I know, gentlemen, that India is always famous for patience. But the time has come now for us to say definitely and without equivocation that Self-Government is no longer to us a far-off adorable dream, that we want to achieve it as soon as possible by all constitutional means open to us without mincing matters and without equivocating on that point. Let it not be held to us as an ideal to be reached within 100 years or 200 years. Of course patience is a great virtue, but, gentlemen, outspokenness too if, I may be permitted to say so, is sometimes a greater virtue. Let us not deceive ourselves, let us not be deceived by others by saying that we are going to be content with these small driblets of reforms. The time for that has gone by. The time has come when England should call upon its statesmen to exercise their higher gifts of statesmanship, to exercise their gifts of imagination, to exercise their gifts of political judgment and feel the political temperature of this country and act accordingly. (Loud applause).

THE HON'BLE
RAO BAHADUR B. N. SARMA

In supporting the resolution on Self Government the Hon'ble Rao Bahadur B. N. Sarma said:—

We ask for provincial autonomy in domestic matters with a central legislature armed with extensive powers and completely dominating all domestic concerns, with an executive armed with extensive powers subject to the will of the Imperial Parliament as it exists at present, and if there should be a revision, with India as a partner, as an equal partner, in every sense of the term with the self-governing Dominions of the Empire. A question then naturally would be, are we fit for it? Are we asking for reforms along lines, lines along which we have not experimented in the past. Turn to past history, all history alike tells us that Indian peoples with rulers of their own race have been able to rule countries far more extensive than the Indian Empire of the present day; for those rulers have been holding sway over Khandar and Ceylon and other vast colonies which the genius of our ancestors created first in times past. Was this domination only for short periods? No; for long centuries, for periods longer than that of any empire, modern or past. Then comes the question, have we still capacity? I assure you, gentlemen, that the skill and capacity, enough dormant in us, are not yet completely dead. If you read history aright what does it tell us. We see a large number of autonomous states linked together by loose federal tie, paying tribute and acknowledging the supremacy of the central authority of the government to the Maharajadiraj, Sultan, or Emperor. Our Maharajadiraj, Sultan or Emperor is the British Imperial Majesty. Our autonomous states are the Native States of India and the Provincial Governments which we create under our scheme with self-governing powers. The central authority is the Government of India, and the Viceroy is the deputy of the Maharajadiraj. The central authority is armed exactly as the old Emperors were armed with a council of elders. They are given by our scheme advisedly vast powers over the military and over the national army, which has to be created under our scheme. Gentlemen, have we weakened the British Power? If the Resident of a Native State with the British power at his back can keep Government going, cannot our, a Governor with two executive councillors, nominees of his, with the British power at his back, rule a Province? We have provided for democratic institutions. The Allies say that they are now engaged in crushing Prussian military despotism, that the future safety of mankind lie in the increase of democratic institutions and we have provided for them. Gentlemen, we have not weakened the British power in any the slightest degree? We have not lost the capacity. Then comes the question, are there not various insuperable difficulties in our way, are there not barriers? They existed in the last year in Switzerland and yet there is no difficulty. The religious difficulty is the same. Then I come to the educational test. Now remember, gentlemen, that the number of literate people in India is 18 millions, nearly the same as the total male population of England, and are we to be told that with this literate population we cannot find enough men to rule this country when only an infinitesimal fraction thereof are able to govern India in the best interests of India? Our universities are turning out graduates nearly as numerous as the British universities. Then comes the question; if we are not educationally backward, what is it that stands in the way? The colour bar. I hope that the Government will not repeat the supposed mistake and land the Empire in disaster. The true difficulty seems to be that a fear is felt that in a federal common wealth, India might in a short space of time become the paramount power. That is the real difficulty. But sufficient safeguards may be provided and the day is far off because it is only in proportion to the contribution to national defences that any state can have representation. We are economically poor, and we cannot therefore, contribute much, and consequently we shall take a place superior to that of the colonies but inferior to that of England, and there is no very great danger that we will be able to swamp the rest of the Empire in the councils of the country. Revise the history of the past, review its pages and what do you find? A foreign bureaucracy is always ready to tax people for the sake of the defence of the country, for the sake of protecting its power. But the moment they come to domestic reforms, they do not know where they will be, they do not know whether the vast masses will support them and hence they say they cannot tax. What have you done? We have revised the electorate, broadened it so that no harebrained reformer may go forth with proposals of taxations which would not be supported by the country. It is said that we shall oppress the depressed classes. May I ask whether the Government, the British Government, were dissuaded in self-governing South Africa, because the Kaffir and the weak Indian population were likely to be oppressed? Their conscience were not touched then. Why should it be touched now when it comes to dividing the people of this country? To me the problem is distinctly clear. We cannot afford to efface ourselves economically and from a military point of view with growing China, growing Japan and growing Russia. Friends of to-day may be enemies of to-morrow, and we cannot have Belgium repeated here. Primary education must be spread and the number of reforms must be achieved, and all this can be done only under self-government. Therefore it is we ask for Self-Government, and if the Britishers are true to their destiny, they will confer it at no distant date.

MR. JEHANGIR PETIT

In supporting the resolution on Self-Government in the Congress of 1916, *Mr. Jehangir Petit said*:—

The proposition before you obtains the quintessence of the desires and demands of the Indian Nation, passed year after year at different sessions of the Indian National Congress. 'I have no faith in the so-called change of the "angle of vision." If the Indian Nation is determined to have what is embodied in this resolution and what is its great and determined resolution, the only way to get it is to show to the Government and the powers, that the population of this great country is determined at all cost to have what is embodied in this resolution. What is it that secured for South Africa immediately after its annexation its independence and Self-Government? What is it that secured for other Colonies their independence and Self-Government? By making the administration impossible they obtained Self-Government. Once you declared your determination in unmistakable terms, Home Rule or Self-Government will not be delayed or withheld from you one day longer. Remember in this country we have to deal with what is more pernicious than any thing that we had to deal with before. If we have to deal with great democracy in England, our work is simple enough, but democracy in England is impotent before obstinate Bureaucracy.

THE HON'BLE PANDIT MADAN MOHAN MALAVIYA

Speech delivered at the Special Provincial Congress held at Lucknow, on the 10th August 1917.

Sisters and brethren,—In order to understand the present political situation in India it is necessary to take a survey of the past which has led up to it. In doing so we must remember that the two great communities which inhabit India, the Hindu and the Mahomedan, are inheritors of two ancient civilizations. The Hindus ruled over this empire for thousands of years and attained a high degree of civilization which compared favourably with the other civilizations of the past or the present. When the Mahomedans came to India they brought with them their own special civilization, which had left its mark in Europe, and settled down in this country as its permanent inhabitants. Their best representatives achieved a high degree of success in the administration which they established here. Thus until a little over 150 years ago, when the British established a footing in India, with a short interval, India had been governed mainly by its own people. And even to-day nearly one-third of India is being governed by Indians. In the face of these facts it is absurd for anybody to suggest that Indians are not fit for governing themselves. But like every other great country India passed through a period of national decadence. It was at such a time that the representatives of certain European nations endeavoured to obtain political power in India. Of these the English were successful in doing so. They were distinguished among all the nations of Europe for having a liberal and popular system of administration. They were the first in modern history to establish the principle of the government of the people by the people on a sound and unshakable basis. Other nations of Europe and America and Japan have taken their lessons in parliamentary government from England and prospered under it. Indians reconciled themselves to the English system of administration because it was based on liberal principles. So long as the administration of what had come to be British India was in the hands of the East India Company, the Charter which that Company held from the English Parliament was limited to the short period of 20 years. Every time the Charter had to be renewed, that Parliament made an enquiry into the administration of the country to satisfy itself that their administration of India was carried on in a manner calculated to promote the moral and material well-being of its inhabitants. On one of such occasions, in 1833 an Act was passed by the English Parliament which laid down that natives of India shall without distinction of race or creed be admitted to the highest offices in the public services of their country for which their education and character qualified them. When after the mutiny in 1858 the Government of India passed directly under the Crown, the great Queen of England, speaking as the representative of the people of the United Kingdom, gave solemn pledges to the people of India that they would be regarded as the equal fellow-subjects of the British people. When the Government of India Bill of 1858 was under discussion in Parliament objection was taken to it on the ground that the principle of popular representation had not been recognised in the measure. It was urged that there was 'no better security for good government than national representation and the free expression of public opinion.' But it was said in reply that 'national representation you cannot at present have in India.' But education was to be promoted and Indians were to be employed in high offices with the view, among other reasons, to fit them for the anticipated enlargement of their political powers. It was thus made clear that the intention was gradually to let the people of India have their proper share in governing themselves through their representatives.

CONGRESS DEMAND FOR SELF-GOVERNMENT

Under the Indian Councils Act which was passed in 1861 some Indians were appointed as members of the Legislative Council, but their presence counted practically for nothing, and as education advanced Indians began to feel that the affairs of their country were not being properly administered and would not be so administered unless and until they were allowed a proper share in the administration. The very first Indian National Congress which met at Bombay in 1885 gave expression to this general conviction in its third resolution. Speaking in support of that resolution our revered countryman Mr. Dadabhai Naoroji said that 'they had learnt from the English people how necessary representation is for good government;' without it 'what good is it to India to be under the British sway. It will be simply another Asiatic despotism. . . . . We are only British drudges or slaves.' At its second session, which was presided over by Mr. Dadabhai Naoroji, the Congress recorded its fixed conviction that the introduction of representative institutions would prove one of the most important practical steps towards the amelioration of the condition of the people, and that the reform and expansion of the imperial and provincial legislative councils had become essential alike in the interests of India and England. The Congress put forward a definite, well considered scheme of such reform. It is important to recall the essential features of that scheme. Not less than one-half of the members of such enlarged councils were to be elected. Remember, this was thirty years ago. Not more than one-fourth were to be officials having seats ex-officio in the councils, and not more than one-fourth were to be nominated by Government. All legislative measures and all financial questions, including all budgets, whether they involved new or enhanced taxation or not, were to be necessarily submitted to and dealt with by these councils. The decisions of the legislative councils were to be ordinarily binding upon the executive Government, but the executive Government was to possess the power of overruling the decision arrived at by the majority of the council in every case in which in its opinion the public interests would suffer by the acceptance of such decision. It was provided, however, that whenever this power was exercised a full exposition of the grounds on which this had been considered necessary should be published within one month, and in the case of local Governments they should report the circumstances and explain their action to the Government of India, and in the case of the latter, it was similarly to report and explain to the Secretary of State; and in any such case, on a representation made through the Government of India and the Secretary of State by the overruled majority, a Standing Committee of the House of Commons was to consider the matter, and, if needful, report thereon to the full House. You will note that in its essential features that scheme was similar to the one that was adopted last year by the Congress and the Muslim League as a definite step towards self-government. In moving the resolution by which it was recommended, our esteemed countryman Mr. Surendranath Banerjea said in 1886: 'Self-government is the ordering of nature, the will of Divine Providence. Every nation must be the arbiter of its own destinies—such is the omnipotent fiat inscribed by nature with her own hands and in her own eternal book. But do we govern ourselves? The answer is No. Are we then living in an unnatural state? Yes, in the same state in which the patient lives under the ministrations of the physician.' Other speakers spoke in a similar strain.

You know what happened afterwards. At the request of the Congress, Mr. Bradlaugh introduced a Bill in Parliament to bring about a reform of the legislative councils. Thereupon the Government introduced a Bill which became law in 1892 by which the Councils were somewhat reformed. The reform, however, did not satisfy the needs of the country, and in 1905 our lamented brother Mr. Gokhale, speaking as President of the Congress at Benares, urged the further enlargement of the imperial and provincial councils and an expansion of their powers. He said that the goal of the Congress was that India should be governed in the interests of the Indians themselves and that in course of time a form of government should be attained in this country similar to what exists in the self-governing colonies of the British Empire. In the following year, Mr. Dadabhai Naoroji, presiding in his 82nd year at the Congress at Calcutta, spoke in clearer and more emphatic language of the pressing need of the introduction of self-government in India. The whole of his address deserves to be read and re-read many a time. He claimed for Indians in India all the control over the administration that Englishmen had in England. He urged that this was a necessity if the great economic evil which was at the root of Indian poverty was to be remedied and the progress and welfare of the Indian people was to be secured. "The whole matter," said our Grand Old Man, "can be comprised in one word self-government, or Swaraj, like that of the United Kingdom or the colonies.' In concluding his memorable address, our late revered countryman said: 'Self-government is the only and chief remedy. In Self-government lie our hope, strength and greatness...I do not know what good fortune may be in store for me during the short period that may be left to me, and if I can leave a word of affection and devotion for my country and countrymen, I say: Be united, persevere and achieve self-government so that the millions now perishing by poverty, famine and plague, and the scores of millions that are starving on scanty subsistence may be saved and India may once more occupy her proud position of yore among the greatest and civilized nations of the world.'

Mr. Dadabhai Naoroji did not say that complete self-government should be introduced at once. 'Has the time arrived' asked he, 'to do anything loyally, faithfully and systematically as a beginning at once, so that it may automatically develop into the full realization of the right of self-government?' And he answered: 'Yes. Not only has the time fully arrived, but, had arrived long past, to make this beginning...... If the British people and statesmen make up their mind to do their duty towards the Indian people they have every ability and statesmanship to devise means to accord self-government within no distant time. 'If there is the will and the conscience there is the way.'

It was in response to our agitation that the Minto-Morley Reforms were introduced in 1909. They fell far short of the requirements of the situation, but we accepted them as a liberal instalment of the reforms needed to give the people a substantial share in the management of their affairs. But the experience of four years of the working of the reformed councils, showed the utter helplessness of the representatives of the people in those councils and a desire for a further substantial measure of reform began again to be urged at the Congress and in the press.

The desire for a substantial step towards self-government continued to express itself more and more in an emphatic manner in the years that followed. In the Congress that was held at Bombay in 1915, the President—Sir S. P. Sinha—urged that the only satisfactory form of government to which India aspires 'is government of the people, for the people and by the people.'

You will thus see that the cry for self-government was not raised merely during the present war and because of it, but is at least as old as the Indian National Congress itself. I have dwelt at such length upon this aspect of the question because efforts have been made in some quarters to create a prejudice against our proposals by the unfounded assertion that the cry for self-government or home-rule was for the first time raised by Mrs. Besant two years ago and has since been taken up by the Congress. Mrs. Besant has done perhaps more than any other person during the last twelve months to carry on an active propaganda in support of the scheme of self-Government passed by the Indian National Congress and the All-India Moslem League. But she has not put forward any new or separate scheme of her own. There are not different schemes of the Indian National Congress and of the Moslem League and of the Home Rule League before the country and the Government. There is but one scheme, and that is the scheme jointly adopted by the Congress and the Moslem League. The Home Rule League has declared that it is carrying on a propaganda in support of the Congress and Moslem League scheme. If anybody is to blame for that scheme, it is the Congress and the Moslem League and not the Home Rule League. But this is by the way.

OTHER DEMANDS

From what has been stated above it is clear that Indians had been endeavouring for nearly a generation to obtain a real measure of self-government in their country's affairs when the present war broke out in Europe. She had also been complaining for thirty years that the invidious distinction which the Government made between Indians and Europeans in the military administration of the country should be obliterated. She had long and repeatedly asked that the unmerited slur which the Arms Act, as at present administered, cast upon Indians and the disadvantages to which it exposed them should be removed and that the rules under the Act should be suitably modified to achieve these objects. She had asked that the commissioned ranks in the Indian army should be thrown open to all classes of Indians subject to reasonable physical and educational tests, and that a military college or colleges should be established in India where proper military training should be given to Indians. She had asked that Indians should be allowed, to join or raise volunteer corps as their European fellow-subjects were allowed to do. These were some of the other long standing grievances of India when the war broke out.

THE IMPETUS OF THE WAR

At the outbreak of the war his Majesty the King-Emperor was pleased to send a gracious message to the princes and people of India that he had entered upon the war in defence of treaty rights and obligations and the cause of justice and liberty and the unmolested independent existence of nations small and great. The princes and people of India loyally responded to his Majesty's appeal to stand up to fight for the right and the Empire. India will ever be grateful to Lord Hardinge for the courage, sympathy and statesmanship which he showed in deciding to send the Indian Expeditionary Force to Europe to fight for the King and the Empire at a critical period of the war. India's loyal response and the splendid heroism of her sons in the battlefield won the hearty admiration and just appreciation of the leading members of the two Houses of Parliament, and of the press of England.

Such was the situation. What did it demand of the Government of India? In view of the splendid rally of India to the cause of the Empire, the first thing it demanded was that all invidious distinctions between the Indian and European fellow-subjects of his Majesty should once for all be obliterated. But it was a matter for deep regret that except the limited unencouraging opening made under the Indian Defence Force Act, these distinctions remain as they were before the war broke out. Along with many others I have been urging for the last three years that commissions in the Indian army should be thrown open to Indians. I have been repeatedly told that the matter has been under consideration. I cannot but regret that the consideration has been so prolonged. The matter is one of simple justice. Expediency also demands that the exclusion of which Indians have so long complained should no longer continue to hurt and discourage them, particularly in view of the fact that the end of the war is not yet in sight and that there may yet be an unending call upon Indians to fight for the King and the country. For the same reasons the rules under the Arms Act which have produced a deplorably emasculating effect upon a large section of the people should be suitably modified. It is also essential that the recommendations which were made in the shape of amendments to the Indian Defence Force Bill and which were unfortunately rejected should be accepted by Government and provision made for the military training of Indian youths between the ages of 16 and

18 as has been made in the case of Europeans, and for the enrolment of Indians of higher age for local military service as also had been made in the case of Europeans.

CONSTITUTIONAL REFORMS

As regards constitutional reforms, the Congress and the Moslem League have recommended that his Majesty the King-Emperor should be pleased to issue a proclamation announcing that it is the aim and intention of British policy to confer self-government on India at an early date. In view of the pronouncements of responsible statesmen of England and some of the highly placed officials in this country I cannot understand why the Government cannot make such a pronouncement at once as there is evidently no serious difference of opinion about self-government being the goal of British policy in India.

As regards the definite steps towards self-government which the Congress and the Moslem League have recommended should be taken after the war, there is no doubt a difference of opinion between some of the officials of the Government and the representatives of the public. The difference reduces itself in reality to a question of the pace at which progress should be made towards self-government. One should have thought that such a difference of opinion would not lead to a quarrel. But unfortunately this has not been so. There are some highly placed officials in the Government of India and in several of the local Governments who evidently think that the proposals of the Congress and the Moslem League in this direction are extravagant. His Excellency the Viceroy has told us that he and his councillors were engaged for six months during the last year in framing proposals of reform which in their opinion should be adopted at the end of the war and which they have submitted to the Secretary of State for the consideration of his Majesty's Government. Judging from the utterances of several provincial Governors these proposals seem to be of a minor character and to fall far short of the demands of the Congress. The public do not yet know what those proposals are. Our repeated request that they should be published has not been granted. They know that those proposals have been pressed upon the Secretary of State for his acceptance. It therefore clearly became our duty to carry on an educative and demonstrative propaganda in support of the proposals which the Congress and the Moslem League have jointly placed before the Government.

If the scheme of reforms which we have urged is adopted in full at the end of the war, as we desire it should be, it will not alter the form of our Government. It will not break up the existing machinery and replace it with something new. The institutions and departments which exist will continue. But what will happen will be that except in certain non-domestic matters, the voice of the Legislative Council, which will contain an elected majority of members, shall ordinarily prevail over the voice of the executive Government, that all financial proposals shall be laid before the

Legislative Council and passed by it; and that in the Executive Council half the number of members shall be Indians. It is true that if these changes are adopted the character of the Government will be radically altered. To the extent it will be, it will become a representative government but no untoward results need be apprehended from it. The Viceroy will have the power to veto any decision of the Legislative Council whenever he will deem it fit in public interest to do so. If this safeguard should not be considered sufficient to allay apprehension and to inspire confidence among our English fellow-subjects, further reasonable safeguards can be provided. But there is nothing in our proposals which can justify an attitude of anger and alarm on the part of any of our European fellow-subjects. I was amused to hear the other day that one of these—and a quite sober and respectable gentleman, he—said that he did not object to our desiring home-rule for ourselves but that he objected to his being placed under our rule. Well, nobody will force him into that position. If he is not prepared to live and work with us as an equal fellow-subject, he will be quite free to quit our country. But the steps towards self-government which we desire to be taken after the war will not yet convert the Government of India into an Indian government. They will convert it into a mixed government of Indians and Englishmen. We are not working for a separation from England. We desire that even when full self-government has been established in India, the connection between India and England should continue for our mutual advantage. There is nothing in that idea to hurt our national sentiment. The most powerful of nations have found it necessary or advantageous to maintain friendly alliances with other nations. But whether our connection with England will continue will depend very much on the attitude of our British fellow-subjects towards us. Nor is there any occasion for those of our European fellow-subjects who are engaged in trade and commerce, to be alarmed at our proposals. If they are carried out, and if we get a fair chance of promoting the trade and prosperity of our country, we shall be able to do much greater trade with each other than we do at present. The history of several countries proves this beyond question.

REPRESSION

But unfortunately some of the advocates of the official proposals seem to have been so convinced of the reasonableness of their own proposals, and of the extreme undesirability of the proposals of the Congress that they seem to have thought it their duty to use their official authority to discourage agitation in support of the popular proposals. I have not seen the circular which the Government of India are said to have issued to provincial Governments. But I have no doubt in my mind that such a circular was issued and that several provincial governments based upon it the policy of repression which they have followed. It is also my conviction that the order of internment passed against Mrs. Besant and Mr. Arundale and Mr. Wadia was passed in pursuance of that policy. I do not say that Mrs. Besant never wrote anything which was open to legal objection nor do I say that she did. What I do say is that if she infringed the law in speaking or writing, and if the infringement was serious enough to deserve action being taken upon it, she should have been proceeded against according to the ordinary law of the land. I consider that in proceeding as the Madras Government did against her and her two colleagues, they had abused the power which they possessed under the Defence of India Act.

The Defence of India Act was clearly meant to be used against the enemies of the Government. I do not believe and Indians generally do not believe that Mrs. Besant is an enemy of the British Government. It is in this view that a feeling of great injustice is rankling in the public mind and it will continue to do so until she and her colleagues are realised. It would be evidence of strength and not of weakness on the part of Government, if out of deference to Indian public feeling, it would cancel the orders of internment in question. It should similarly cancel the orders of internment under which Messrs. Mahomed Ali and Shaukat Ali have so long been deprived of their freedom of movement, without any definite charge being formulated and proved against them.

We are often told that we ought not to agitate while the war is going on. Everyone will agree that those who are really busy with work connected with the war should not be disturbed. But how many people are really absorbed in work connected with the war? A war cabinet has replaced the ordinary British cabinet and has set a number of British statesmen free to consider and work out many proposals of reform, even constitutional reform of a far-reaching character. The Electoral Reform Bill has been passed. The Irish problem is nearing solution. Various committees have been busy formulating schemes for the development of British trade after the war and schemes of improved national education. In India also it is but a few who are really so absorbed in work connected with the war as not to be able to devote time to other questions. His Excellency the Viceroy and his councillors did find time to formulate proposals of reform. Owing to the war activity in several departments has been curtailed, and I hope I am not wrong in thinking that at no previous time did the officers of Government here find themselves so little pressed for time as many of them do at present. So far as we Indians are concerned, while we must do our duty in making such contributions to the war in men and money as we can, I shall be glad to know that outside the army there are many Indians in the country who have the honour of any responsibility connected with the actual conduct of the war being placed upon them. Anyhow, many of us feel that as matters stand, we should be failing in our duty to our country and countrymen and to our King-Emperor if we did not do what lies in our power to press the reforms which we consider to be essential for the progress and welfare of our people upon the consideration of the Government. And this brings me to the question of

WHAT THE SITUATION DEMANDS OF US

The first thing is a clear realization of what we desire to achieve. And the second, a firm determination to do all that is necessary to achieve it. As regards the first, I am sure that we educated men understand what self-government or home-rule means. I am equally sure that there is a vast body of our countrymen and countrywomen who have to be taught to understand what self-government means and to feel an earnest desire to obtain it. Let us remember that our English fellow-subjects are not easy to persuade. You must convince them that not only a few but the great bulk of our people desire self-government. And in this connection I cannot better than remind you of the earnest advice given to us by Mr. Dadabhai Naoroji in his presidential address in Calcutta in 1906. Said our revered leader: 'While we put the duty of leading us on to self-government on the heads of the present British statesmen, we have also the duty upon ourselves to do all we can to support those statesmen by, on the one hand, preparing our Indian people for the right understanding, exercise and enjoyment of the government, and on the other hand, of convincing the British people that we justly claim and must have all British rights. I put before the Congress my suggestions for their consideration. To put the matter in right form, we should send our "Petition of Rights" to his Majesty the King-Emperor, to the House of

Commons and to the House of Lords.' 'The next thing I suggest' said Mr. Dadabhai, 'for your consideration is that the well-to-do Indians should raise a large fund of patriotism. With this fund we should organise a body of able men and good speakers, to go to all the nooks and corners of India and inform the people in their own languages of our British rights and how to exercise and enjoy them; also to send to England another body of able speakers, and to provide means to go throughout the country and by large meetings to convince the British people that we justly claim and must have all British rights of Self-Government. . . .

'Agitate, agitate over the whole length and breadth of India in every nook and corner—peacefully of course —if we really mean to get justice from John Bull. Satisfy him that we are in earnest. All India must learn the lesson—of sacrifice of money and of earnest personal work. By doing that I am sure that the British conscience will triumph and the British people will support the present statesmen in their work of giving India responsible self-government in the shortest possible period. We must have a great agitation in England as well as here.'

Further on, our grand old leader said: 'Agitate; agitate means inform. Inform, inform the Indian people what their rights are and why and how they should obtain them and inform the British people of the rights of the Indian people and why they should grant them.'

'The organization which I suggest, and which I may call a band of political missionaries in all the provinces will serve many purposes at once—to inform the people of their rights as British citizens, to prepare them to claim those rights by petitions and when the rights are obtained, to exercise and enjoy them.'

It was a matter of regret and reproach to us that we had not carried out this earnest advice of our revered leader so long. The Minto-Morley reforms of 1909, lulled us into the belief that we had got a liberal instalment of reform. But the experience of the last few years had shown that those reforms have not given any effective voice to the representatives of the people in the administration of the country's affairs; and now that the need for a substantial measure of reform towards self-government is more keenly realised and the time forces are in a special degree favourable to the cause of freedom and self-government, I hope that we shall loyally respond to the exhortation of our departed Grand Old Man and earnestly carry on agitation for self-government on the lines indicated by him. I may here inform you that a petition to Parliament is under preparation, and will soon be ready and begin to be circulated for signatures. I trust you will obtain as large a number of signatures to it as you can. It is essential that between now and the meeting of the next Congress, we should thoroughly organize ourselves in the way suggested by Mr. Dadabhai Naoroji and should preach the doctrine of self-government or Swaraj in every nook and corner of cur provinces. We should establish self-government or Swaraj Leagues or Home-Rule Leagues, to propagate the idea and to enlist the intelligent and earnest support of our people for our proposals. I hope you will all endeavour to carry out this idea. I expect that the next Congress which will meet at Calcutta will be attended by a very large number of people. I presume you are aware that the joint session of the All India Congress Committee and of the Council of the Muslim League has recommended that on the day the Congress will be held in Calcutta, a Congress Durbar should be held in every district at which a translation of the presidential address should be read, and the resolutions on self-government which were passed by the last Congress and the Moslem League in December last at Lucknow should be adopted. I feel certain that if we shall carry out the advice of Mr. Dadabhai Naoroji we shall demonstrate that we deserve self-government, and we shall win the first substantial step towards it, urged in the scheme of the Congress and the Muslim League, within twelve months of the end of the present war. Right and justice are on our side. The time-spirit is with us. English statesmen have acknowledged that India has freely given her lives and treasure in the cause of the Empire and that things cannot therefore be left as they are. If we do not win self-government now the fault will be entirely ours. To ensure success it is necessary that our agitation should be universal and intense. It is equally necessary that it should be strictly constitutional. Our position is clear and strong. We are not asking for separation from England. We are asking for self-government within the Empire under the British Crown. The cause of self-government does not require to be supported by arguments showing wherein a foreign system of administration has failed. Self-government is the natural system of government. An alien government even at its best entails many inevitable disadvantages. Macaulay truly observed that 'no nation can be perfectly well governed till it is competent to govern itself'; and we are familiar with the dictum of Sir Henry Campbell-Bannermann that 'good government could never be substitute for government by the people themselves. As Mr. Dadabhai Naoroji put it we claim self-government as our right as British subjects, and even if the British system of administration in India were much less open to just criticism than it is, even then we should have been justified in asking for self-government. But while we frankly acknowledge the good that the British Government has done us in many directions, we cannot shut our eyes to its many shortcomings. Take for instance the question of education. Think of the state of general education in India when the English came to this country and compare it with what it is at present, and you cannot but feel grateful for what has been accomplished. But consider at the same time what remains to be done in the field of education. Compare the progress in education which self-governing Japan achieved in thirty years with what has been achieved in double that period in India. In 1872, when Japan introduced its system of national education only 28 per cent. of the children of school-going age were at school; by 1903 the percentage had risen to 90! It stands most higher now. In India, after nearly 60 years of the great education despatch of 1854 and the organizations that followed the percentage of the children of school-going age is still below 20!' For decades past we have been urging that more and more should be done for the education of the people, but the progress achieved has been woefully slow. You will remember our lamented brother Mr. Gokhale introduced his Elementary Education Bill which would have permitted elementary education being made compulsory in certain areas in certain conditions, and you will remember that the Bill was defeated by the opposition of the bureaucracy that governs us. Is it surprising that we have come to the conviction that we shall ever be able to properly promote the education of our people until we have a voice in the administration of our affairs? Similarly there is much to complain of in many other departments. Let us take the question of the employment of Indians in the higher public services of the country. You know that the examination for admission into the Indian Civil Service is held in far-off England only. It is a manifest injustice to Indians. Mr. Dadabhai Naoroji began an agitation in 1867 that examinations for admission into the Indian Civil Service should be held simultaneously in India and in England to enable the youths of this country to have a fair chance of competing for the higher services of their own country. But half a century of agitation has not sufficed to secure that small justice to us. The result is, as has been pointed out by my friend Pandit Hriday Nath Kuszru in his recently published and excellent pamphlet on the public services in India, that on the 1st April 1917, out of 1,478 posts ordinarily reserved for the members of Indian Civil Service, only 146 or about 10 per cent. were held by statutory natives of India! It hardly needs saying that if India had been governed in the interests of Indians, we should have found the very reverse of this, *viz.* that 90 p. c. of the posts in question were held by Indians and only 10 p. c. by Europeans. The state of affairs out of the Indian Civil Service was hardly better. The total number of appointments, carrying a salary of Rs. 500, and upwards was 5,390 in 1910, and of these only 924 or 17 per cent. were held by Indians and 83 per cent. by Europeans and Eurasians! This is on the civil side. So far as the army is concerned, it is entirely officered by our British fellow-subjects. Notwithstanding our repeated prayers, the commissioned ranks of the Indian army have never yet been opened to Indians. Notwithstanding all the fidelity, devotion and heorism with which Indians have served his Majesty and his predecessors for over a century they cannot yet rise beyond the position of subadar-major risaldar-major!

I will draw attention to only one other matter. We appreciate at its proper value the growth of Indian trade and commerce. But it is largely in the hands of Europeans. We have not been helped to obtain our fair share in it.' And our industries have not been developed as they could have been developed and as they ought to have been developed. What is it that is responsible for these and many others of our grievances? It is the existing system of administration. Generally speaking, our English fellow-subjects who come to this country at the age of 25 or 21 and who retire from it for good at 55, cannot take that keen and abiding interest in promoting the interests of India and Indians as we Indians can do; and, in matters where there is a conflict between the interests of India and Indians on the one side and of England and Englishmen on the other, many of them not unnaturally place the interests of their own country and people before our interests. These and many other economic and administrative considerations which vitally affect the moral and material well-being of our people and determine our political status in the scale of nations, have ingrained the conviction in us, so well expressed by Mr. Dadabhai Naoroji, that self-government is the only and chief remedy, and that in self-government lies our hope.

Sisters and brethren, let us now put forth a sustained effort commensurate with the depth and earnestness of this conviction for achieving that which we consider to be best for our country and our people. Let us act without fear and without reproach, doing no wrong ourselves but not desisting from our duty even if a wrong should be done to us. It is a matter for thankfulness that unlike some of the other provincial

Governments the Government of these provinces have taken up the correct attitude of not interfering with constitutional agitation for self-government. I have every hope that they will continue in that attitude and that so far as these provinces are concerned there will be no unnecessary obstacles placed in our path. But notwithstanding this, and whether our work lies here or in other provinces, it is essential that in taking up serious constitutional agitation, we all should have a clear mind and a firm determination as to how we shall discharge our duty. We should take every care to do nothing that is wrong, nothing that will expose us to just reproach. But if in spite of it, trouble should overtake us in the exercise of our constitutional rights, we must suffer it with calm determination and not run away from it. If we shall so bear ourselves. I feel sure that either obstacles will not arise in our path, or if they do, they will not take long to melt. We have really no enemies to be afraid of, if we do not harbour in enemy within ourselves, which makes us slaves or fear and of personal selfish considerations. The path of our duty is clear. Let us tread it as men.

Sisters and brethren, I have detained you very long, but before I resume my seat I should like to say just a few words which I wish would reach the ears of our fellow-subjects of the Indian Civil Service and the non-official European community in India. They both possess great influence and power in this country and they can influence opinion in England also. Many of them have lived long in or been connected with this country. We are entitled to claim sympathy from them in our aspirations and help and co-operation in realizing them. It is possible that some of our proposals appear to some of them as impracticable and even extravagant. We are prepared to justify them, and where we cannot, to modify them. We do not claim infallibility for our judgment. I appeal to them to approach a consideration of our proposals in a spirit of friendliness and sympathy, and to help in bringing about a change in the constitution of the Government of our country which will be in consonance with the principles of liberty, justice and the free and unmolested existence and development of every people, for which the British Empire has been making an enormous sacrifice of life and treasure and which alone can ensure the right measure of happiness and prosperity to India and glory to England. I have the privilege of knowing several men among them who, though they do not see eye to eye with us, take a large-minded view of the relations which should exist between India and England in the future, who desire that justice should be done to India's claims. I appeal to them actively to throw the weight of their influence in favour of justice and freedom. And I hope I do not appeal in vain.

But however that may be, my countrymen, let us remember that the duty of working out our salvation lies principally upon ourselves. Let us do it faithfully and unflinchingly. Let us organize ourselves without any further loss of time, and arrange to preach the

16

great *Mantra*, the humane religion of self-government or *Swaraj* or home-rule in every home, in all parts of our country. Let us teach every brother and sister, Hindu, Mussalman, Parsi, Christian, &c., young and old, humble as well as high, to understand the meaning of self-government, to desire it and to work for it, each to the extent of his or her ability with all the earnestness he or she can. In one word, let us put our soul into the business, and God willing success will crown our efforts sooner than many of us at present imagine.

THE HON. Mr. NABIULLAH

In the course of his address as Chairman of the Reception Committee the Hon. Mr. Nabiulluh spoke a follows:—

Gentlemen, through the supreme and searching test of this war the loyalty of India has emerged untarnished and proved to be one of the greater and most precious assets of the Empire. I need not dwell on the character and quality of its widespread manifestations. It has shown itself in a variety of ways and through acts and deeds in which all classes of His Majesty's Indian subjects have shared with equal enthusiasm. In such an atmosphere it may be a piece of irrelevance to talk of Muslim loyalty. However, in this great Muslim assembly it may not be wholly out of place to note with deep satisfaction the unswerving fidelity with which the Mussalmans have borne their part of the Imperial burden. The sense of this satisfaction is immeasurably enhanced when it is borne in mind that Muslim soldiers have cheerfully gone into the fight against the forces of their Caliph in defence of the cause of the Empire to which their secular destinies are linked.

"MASTERLY INACTIVITY" SUICIDAL

Gentlemen, at a time when all efforts and energies are concentrated on the conduct of the war, it is natural that all schemes of normal and peaceful developments and advance should be held in abeyance.

At the beginning of the war a sort of political truce was declared in India and the voice of controversy has since been hushed. All public activities have been suspended that could even remotely have the effect of distracting the mind of the Government in its task of organising victory. Even some of the most urgent needs of the country have been allowed to wait till peace comes to restore to the affairs of mankind their true proportion and balance. This does not, however, mean that we are to remain in a state of suspended animation while the hammer blows of facts are fashioning the frame work of a new and we trust a better and a freer world. The organisation of peace after the war is, in the opinion of most thinking men, a more complex and anxious problem than the winning of the war itself. In Great Britain and the countries of her Allies no less than among the peoples of the Central Alliance, strenuous thought and energies are being applied to the discovery of stable foundation for a new political economic and social order. Is India alone to stand still and take no thought for the morrow, when that morrow is to usher in a new era in the history of the world and the nations saved from perils of militarism are to undertake their planning of their lives with the freedom and joy of a new resurrection? The war is not to last for ever. I would not be surprised if 1917 brings the end definitely in sight. Are we to wake up one fine morning when the peace has been signed, to collect our scattered thoughts hastily together and start a wild, academic discussion about the future of our country? The Indian public man who has grasped the psychology of the existing conditions, and yet helps to waste through a policy of masterly inactivity the all too brief interlude for planning and preparation, is a traitor to the cause of India.

DIFFICULTIES AHEAD

Gentlemen, substantial changes in the administration and Government of India have become inevitable and it is the duty of the intellectual and political leaders of the Indian people to participate actively in the evolution of the new order of things and determine what those changes should be. If solemn public declaration count for anything, we may take it that the British nation and responsible British statesmen have discovered the true heart of India in this great crisis of their history. The scales of ignorance and prejudice have fallen from their eyes, and in the stress of common sacrifice and common emotion there has come to birth in England genuine movement of sympathy for the aspirations of our people. Early in the war we were definitely assured by an Under Secretary of State for India that a new angle of vision would henceforth be applied to Indian affairs. As a recognition of the need by a responsible British Minister to broaden the basis of Indian governance nothing could be more explicit. It must be remembered that a new "angle of vision" cannot be picked out at will from a text book on political philosophy. It is an intellectual process, an adjustment of policy and principles to new aspects of a case. In the case of India it would be a mere empty phrase if it does not mean the introduction of a policy of trust, of allowing Indian opinion steadily and increasingly to assume the ultimate control and direction of the affairs of this country.

Now, with this broadening of the intellectual horizon of India's responsible rulers and with the goal clearly set before our eyes, it now rests with the Indian people themselves to take heart of grace close their ranks and shrink from no effort and sacrifice that may be needed to bring the coveted prize within their grasp. Gentlemen, with all the sympathy and good will that may come to us from quarters where a short time ago we used to meet with indifference and cold reserve, the path that lies before us is neither easy nor smooth. The temper of the "man on the spot" in India is yet an incalculable factor in the situation. And you are well aware how formidable "the man on the spot" is and what tremendous weapons he can employ, if it is his whim and pleasure to thwart the will of the people. Then there are other forces, representing interests of alien origin and frequently hostile to the needs of Indian nationalism, which we have to take into full account. These forces are controlled by a section of the Anglo-Indian Press, and all of us know how easily they can be set in motion against the forces of Indian progress. These and a host of other difficulties we have to overcome, and you can well imagine what patience, cool headedness, clear thinking, organisation of will and effort and above all that sustained inspiration for public service which patriotism and unity alone can give, are needed if these difficulties are to be effectually removed from our path. India has much to do and much to learn in all conscience, before it attains to its full stature as a self-governing nation. But unity and patriotism are the sovereign remedies for the ills that afflict our body politic at this critical period of our history.

PATRIOTISM OF MOSLEMS

Fellow members of the All-India Moslem League, this brings me to the central point that lends exceptional value and significance to the sessions we are holding to-day. The affairs of the country, which we Moslems are proud to call our motherland, have reached a stage, where they call for the sinking of all petty differences of race and creed and demand united action. An overwhelming responsibility lies on the shoulders of every community in India at this juncture. Their patriotism and sense of duty to the generations yet unborn are on trial. The future of India hangs in the balance. If their lives are touched with the Divine spark that moves men to vaster planes of common duty and service, the petty anxieties and pre-occupations of self will be burned to ashes and the dream of the Indian patriot will become a glorious reality. But, if these groups of human beings have never known the light of a common purpose, nor has the reality of a common ideal ever entered their lives, if they are so many diverse atoms held together by the accidents of

Geography, political subjection and the narrowness of little creeds, then there is absolutely no "future" for India and all this sterile din and clamour of politics should cease. Need India wait for an answer from the followers of Islam in this great crisis of her fate? We know what our answer ought to be and will be. Let me assure our fellow countrymen of other creeds, that a Mussalman cannot betray the cause of India without betraying his whole past. He shall, God willing, be in the vanguard of the forces that are to fight the battles of our constitutional freedom. His active political life is of a short duration, but during this brief period he has traversed the ground that the great Hindu community took about a quarter of a century to cover. The history of the All-India Moslem League is a faithful reflex of the political growth of Indian Mussalmans. Within six years of its birth this great Moslem political organisation emerged from its original shell and set before itself a goal to which the rest of India was gradually moving. This widening ot purpose and outlook was not due to the fact of any masterful personality but was the result of the strong pressure of popular opinion. If the League had not adopted its policy and programme to the urgent demand of the Moslem democracy it would have probably ceased to exist. Its present position is solely due to the fact that it works in close touch with Moslem opinion and is, in the widest sense, the representative of the will of the community.

OBJECTS OF THE LEAGUE

The All-India-Moslem League stands to-day for two principal objects, namely, for the safe-guarding of the political position of Mussalmans and for co-operation with the other communities for the attainment of self-Government. The realisation of the first object is, as all fair-minded persons would be ready to admit, an essential condition of the success of the second. It would be idle to talk of co-operation if the Mussalmans did not feel a complete sense of security as regards their communal future. They are the "minority" and in all political developments a minority must have certain definite safeguards. The Moslem demand for such safeguards is therefore, natural and legitimate and the "majority" which in any case holds the balance of power, cannot oppose this demand without laying itself open to the charge of selfishness and political insincerity. Let our Hindu brethren remember that an adequate and effective separate-representation of Mussalmans in self-governing institutions can in no case deprive them of the decisive power of the majority. When such power is guaranteed to them by their number I fail to see why should some of their communal enthusiasts deny to Mussalmans the right to secure their political existence. Opposition of this character breeds distrust and the good faith of those who base such opposition on grounds of unity and nationalism comes to be questioned by Moslem rank and file.

Let me take a recent unfortunate episode by way of

illustration. Some months ago the Legislature of this province passed an act relating to the Municipalities in which the Mussalmans were given the right of separate representation slightly in excess of their numbers; the Hindu majority on Municipal Boards was in the aggregate complete and decisive. And yet some of the Hindu leaders allowed themselves to forget the infinitely larger interests of the country, took up the cry of "Hindus in danger" and rushed the whole province into the throes of a bitter and violent agitation. This exhibition of uncompromising temper had scared a considerable section of the Mussalmans and there was a serious danger of the new born movement for Hindu-Moslem co-operation being nipped in the bud, if the Moslem leaders had also lost their heads and had allowed a counter agitation to grow up with sectarian cries to match. It would indeed have been a bitter irony of fate if the whole of India were to be punished for the sins of a few unbalanced individuals.

GOAL OF UNITED INDIA

Gentlemen, it has given a considerable relief to us to refind that the responsible Hindu leaders in all parts of India realise the Moslem standpoint and are ready to offer all reasonable guarantees for the safety of the Moslem political position. With the settlement of this fundamental question relating to the progress of India nothing else should remain in the way of a complete Hindu-Moslem co-operation for the end we both have in view. That end I need hardly say is United India, alive to her destiny and recoiling from no toil and sacrifice to rise to the submit of her aspiration, *i.e.*, to position of a self-governing member of the British Empire. Is there a single Mussalman present here to-day, nay is there a single Indian in and outside of this hall, born of Indian woman, whose heart fails to warm up and whose pulse does not beat faster as he gives even a moment's thought to that glorious conception? If there is such a miserable wretch in existence, he is a freak and a monstrosity. For such ideal no effort, can be spared, no sacrifice can be too great.

Gentlemen, our task to-day is essentially a task of reconstruction. In concert with the rest of our fellow-countrymen we have to prepare a scheme of reforms for the administration and government of India to be introduced as soon as possible after the end of the war which would go a long way towards securing an effective voice to the Indian people in the conduct of public affairs. Your best energies will no doubt be directed to the consideration of such a scheme and I need not therefore waste your time by making suggestions of my own. I need not also embark on a long recital of the customary grievances that are the stock in trade of the Indian political reformer. Nor need I undertake a detailed review of the administrative sins of omission and commission from the point of view of an Indian and a Mussalman. The grievances like the poor are always with us. For the present we have a far bigger and more essential task in hand and on its satisfactory accomplishment all our energies should be bent.

THE PRESS ACT

I cannot, however, close without referring to the administration of the Press Act and the Defence of India Act and the grave feelings of anxiety and alarm to which they have given rise. I need not argue at length to point out the lawless character of the Press Act. It is a harsh and drastic measure. The highest tribunals in the land have shown its provisions to be of a nature that have reduced the freedom of the press to a farce. It confers arbitrary and absolute powers on the executive and public opinion can be expressed only on sufferances. Many of the most influential and independent Moslem newspapers like the "Comrade" and the "Hamdard" have succumbed to the operation of this Act. Free and independent journalism in the country has become a most hazardous and risky undertaking. The whole of educated India has been demanding with one voice its removal from the statue book, and the sooner this is done the better it would be for the peace and contentment of the country.

THE DEFENCE OF INDIA ACT

The Defence of India Act is an emergency measure which confers extraordinary and exceptional powers on local Governments with the object of preserving public safety during the period of war. No Indian public man has ever questioned the right and the duty of the state to arm itself with exceptional weapons in a crisis like the one through which the Empire is passing. However, the administration of this measure which was previously intended to deal with the enemies of the State, has become a matter of growing concern of the public. The Defence of India rules have been used with alarming frequency throughout India and some of the most distinguished and popular Moslem leaders like Messrs. Mahammed Ali and Shaukat Ali have been deprived of their liberty and interned. No definite charges have been brought against them, there has been no public trial for any known offence under the law, and they have been given no opportunity to explain the grounds on which the order for their internment may have been based.

It is, therefore, no fault of the people if they regard these two brothers as innocent victims of some cruel misunderstanding or suspicion. I need not speak of the great hold that Mr. Mahommed Ali has on the esteem and affections of his people. Within his comparatively short but crowded career as a devoted servant of his community he has won his way to the heart of the Moslem India. The feeling for him and his brother is one of deep sorrow and sympathy and if this feeling has not found an organised public expression it is because the Moslem community has exercised wonderful self-restraint and has refrained from embarrassing the Government at such a time as this. May we hope that the Government will be pleased to take the Moslem sentiment into consideration and restore Messrs. Mahammed Ali and Shaukat Ali to liberty, thereby earning the deep and abiding gratitude of the entire Moslem community.

CONCLUSION

Gentlemen, I have done. It only remains for me to step aside and make way for my distinguished and able friend whom we have summoned to preside over our deliberations at this important session of the League. The Hon'ble Mr. Mohammed Ali Jinnah stands in no need of introduction to an assembly of Indian Mussalmans. Though comparatively young in years, he has already made his mark in the public life of this country. His clear gaze and ripe judgment, his cool, imperturbable temper, his sweet reasonableness, his fearless courage and devotion to duty have stood the test through serious crisis in public affairs and have helped to save many an awkward situation. I have no doubt that under his guidance the work of the ninth Session of the All-India Moslem League will be crowned with success.

THE HON'BLE
Mr. MOHAMMED ALI JINNAH

In the course of his Presidential Address to the All-India Muslim League, Lucknow, 1916, *The Hon'ble Mr. M. A. Jinnah spoke as follows :—*

This is primarily the time for an annual stock-taking for the testing of our position in the light of the experience of the past year, for an intelligent preparation of the ways and means for meeting the demands of the future, and above all, for refreshing, so to speak the ideals that feed the springs of our faith, hope and endeavour. This, I take to be the fundamental object for which the annual sessions of political bodies, like the All-India Moslem League are held.

A NEW EPOCH

The circumstances however in which we meet to-day are exceptional and mark a new epoch in the history of our country. All that is great and inspiring in the common affairs of men for which the noblest and most valiant of mankind have lived and wrought and suffered in all ages and all climes is now moving India to its depths. The whole country is awakening to the call of destiny and is scanning the new horizons with eager hope. A new spirit of earnestness, confidence and resolution is abroad in the land. In all directions are visible the stirrings of a new life. The Mussalmans of India would be false to themselves and the traditions of their past, had they not shared to the full the new hope that is moving India's patriotic sons to-day, or had they failed to respond to the call of their country. Their gaze like that of their Hindu fellow-countrymen is fixed on the future.

MUSLIM RESPONSIBILITY

But, gentlemen of the All-India Muslim League, remember that the gaze of your community and of the whole country is at this moment fixed on you. The decisions that you may take in this historic hall at this historic session of the League will go forth with all the force and weight that can legitimately be claimed by the chosen leaders and representatives of 70 millions of Indian Mussalmans. On the nature of those decisions will depend in a large measure the fate of India's future, of India's unity and of our common ideals and aspirations for constitutional freedom. The moment for decision has arrived. The alternatives are clear and unmistakable.

INDIA'S LOYALTY

What India has given in this fellowship of service and sacrifice, has been a free and spontaneous tribute to the ideals of the great British Nation as well as a necessary contribution to the strength of the fighting forces of civilisation which are so valiantly rolling back the tides of scientifically organised barbarism. In this willing service of the people of India there has been no distinction of class or creed. It has come from every part of the land and from every country with equal readiness, and devotion. In this service has been no cold calculating instinct at work, there it has sprung from a clear compelling sense of duty and moral sympathy and not from any commercial desire to make a safe political investment. India's loyalty to the Empire has set no price on itself.

THE TASK OF RECONSTRUCTION

These tasks have a peculiar urgency and significance in the case of the vast and various communitics comprising the British Empire and among the complex series of problems relating to the Imperial reconstruction awaiting British statesmanship. None is of more anxious moment than the problem of reconstruction in India. I need not set about to discuss in detail the Indian problem in all its bearings; it has been discussed threadbare by all manner of men from every conceivable angle of vision. However, there are two cardinal facts about the Indian situation which practical statesmanship will have to take into account while addressing itself to the study of the problem and its adequate solution.

TWO CARDINAL FACTS

There is first the great fact of the British rule in India with its western character and standards of administration which, while retaining absolute power of initiative, direction, and decision, has maintained for many decades an unbroken peace and order in the land and administered even-handed justice, brought the Indian mind through a widespread system of western education into contact with the thought and ideals of the West, and thus led to the birth of a great and living movement for the intellectual and moral regeneration of the people. His Excellency Lord Chelmsford said: "The growing self-respect and self-consciousness of her [India's] people are plants that we ourselves have watered."

Secondly, there is the fact of the existence of a powerful unifying process, the most vital and interesting result of western education in the country, which is creating out of the diverse mass of race and creed a New India fast growing to unity of thought, purpose and outlook, responsive to new appeals of territorial patriotism, and with nationality stirring with new energy and aspiration and becoming daily more purposeful and eager to recover its birthright, to direct its own affairs and govern itself. And, to put it briefly, we have a powerful and efficient bureaucracy of British officers responsible only to the British Parliament, governing, with methods known benevolent despotism, a people that have grown fully conscious of their destiny and are peacefully struggling for political freedom. This is the Indian problem in a nutshell and the task of British statesmanship is to find a prompt, peaceful and enduring solution of the problem.

ASPECTS OF THE INDIAN PROBLEM

If it were possible to isolate the tangled group of social and political phenomena and subject it to a thorough investigation by reason, unalloyed by sentiment, it would be infinitely easier to find a safe and sure path for Indian political development and advance; but, as you know, pure unalloyed reason is not the chief motive power in human things. In the affairs of our common secular existence we have to deal not with angels but with men with passions, prejudices, personal idiosyncrasies, innumerable cross currents of motive of desire, hope, fear and hate. The Indian problem has all such formidable complications in its texture. We have for instance the large and trained body of English officials who carry on the administration of the country and exercise power over the well being and happiness of the teeming millions of this land. They are most of them hardworking, efficient, and conscientious public servants and yet they are beset by the prejudices and limitations that mark them as a class apart. They are naturally conservative, have a rooted horror of bold administrative changes or constitutional experiments, are reluctant to part with power or associate Indians freely in the Government of the country. Their main concern appears to be to work the machine smoothly, content to go through their common round from day to day, and they feel bored and worried and upset by the loud, confident and unsettling accents of New India. All this is eminently human, but it also means an enormous aggravation of the difficulties in the path of final settlement.

CONFLICTING INTERESTS

It means in actual experience the growth of a tremendous class interest, the interest of the governing class is distinct from, if not wholly opposed to, the interest of the governed. It is in fact the existence of this vast, powerful and by no means silent interest that explains the origin and wide currency of certain shallow, bastard and desperate political maxims which are flung into the face of Indian patriots on the least provocation, and they are familiar enough to all students of Indian affairs. As a sample, I may add, the following :

A BASTARD MAXIM

(1) "Democratic institutions cannot thrive in the environment of the East." Why? Were democratic institutions unknown to the Hindus and Muhammadans in the past? Was there no Village Panchayat? What are the history, the tradition, the literature, and the precepts of Islam? There are no people in the world who are more democratic, even in their religion, than the Mussalmans.

(2) "The only form of Government suitable to India is an autocracy tempered by English [European] efficiency and character." All nations have had to go through the experience of despotic or autocratic Government at one time or another in the history of the world. Russia was liberated to a certain extent only a few years ago. France and England had to struggle

before they conquered the Autocracy. Is India to remain under the heel of a novel form of autocracy in the shape of a bureaucracy for all time to come, when Japan and even China have set up constitutional Governments on the democratic lines of Great Britain and America?

(3) (*a*) "The interests of the educated classes are opposed to those of the Indian masses" and (*b*) the former would oppress the latter if the strong protecting hands of the British official were withdrawn." This astonishing proposition beats all reason and sense. It is suggested that we who are the very kith and kin of the masses, most of us springing from the middle classes, are likely to oppress the people if more power is conferred; that the masses require protection at the hands of the English officials between whom and the people there is nothing in common; that our interests are opposed to those of the masses, in what respect is never pointed out, and that, therefore, the monopoly of the administrative control should continue in the hands of non-Indian officials.

The suggestion which is so flippantly made is intended to secure the longest possible lease for the bureaucracy and to enjoy their monopoly, but it can neither stand the light of facts, nor the analysis of truth. One has only to look at the past records of the Congress for more than a quarter of a century and of the All-India Muslim League to dismiss this specious plea. The educated people of this country have shown greater anxiety and solicitude for the welfare and advancement of the masses than for any other question during the last quarter of a century.

(4) "Indians are unfit to govern themselves." With this last question I propose to deal later in my speech.

These are a few of the baseless and silly generalities in which the advocates of the existing methods of Indian governance indulge freely and provocatively when the least menace arises to the monopoly of the bureaucratic authority.

THE INTERNAL SITUATION

Again if we turn to the internal situation in India we meet with a set of social ethnological and cultural conditions unparalleled in recorded history. We have a vast contingent inhabited by 315 millions of people sprung from various racial stocks, inheriting various cultures and professing a variety of religious creeds. This stupendous human group thrown together under one physical and political environment is still in various stages of intellectual and moral growth. All this means a great diversity of outlook, purpose and endeavour. Every Indian Nationalist who has given close and anxious thought to the problem of Nation-building in India fully realises the magnitude of his task. He is not afraid of admitting frankly that difficulties exist in his path. Such difficulties have no terrors for him. They are already vanishing before the forces which are developing in the New Spirit. Well, these are the broad aspects of the Indian problem, and they will give you a fairly general idea of the obstacles that stand in the way of a full and speedy realisation of the ideals of Indian patriots. We have a powerfully organised body of conservative interest on the one hand, and a lack of complete organisation of the National will and intelligence on the other.

INDIA FOR THE INDIANS

There is, however, one fundamental fact that stands out clear and unmistakable which no sophistry of argument and no pseudo scientific theories about colour and race can disguise. Amid the class of warring interests and the noise of foolish catchwords no cool-headed student of Indian affairs can lose sight of the great obvious truism that India is the first and the last resort for the Indians. Be the time near or distant the Indian people are bound to attain to their full stature as a Self-Governing nation. No force in the world can rob them of their destiny and thwart the purpose of Providence. British statesmanship has not become bankrupt or utterly bereft of its faculty of clear political perception, and it is therefore bound to recognise that the working of the law of national development in India, which came to birth with the British rule itself and is daily gathering momentum under the pressure of the world forces of freedom and progress, must sooner or later produce a change in the principles and methods of Indian governance. It is inevitable. Then why fight against it, why ignore it? Why should not, rather, there be honest straight forward efforts to clear the way of doubts, suspicions and senseless antagonisms to that glorious consummation? Leaving aside the hair brained twaddle of the tribe of scientific meddlers who love to sit in judgment on the East and ape political philosophy, no man, with the least pretensions to common sense, can affect to maintain that the Indian humanity is stamped with a ruthless psychology, and cramped for ever within the prison of its skull.

SELF-GOVERNMENT, THE ONLY FUTURE

If the Indians are not the pariahs of nature, if they are not out of the pale or operation of the laws that govern mankind elsewhere, if their minds can grow in knowledge and power and can think and plan and organise together for the common needs of the present and for the common hopes of the future, the only future for them is Self-Government, is the attainment of the power to apply through properly organised channels the common National will and intelligence to the needs and tasks of their National existence. The cant of unfitness must die, the laws of nature and the doctrines of common humanity are not different in the East.

THE OFFICIAL ATTITUDE

It is a great relief to think that some of the responsible British statesmen have definitely pronounced in recent years that India's ambition to attain Self-Government is neither a catastrophe nor a sin. Indeed that great and sympathetic Viceroy, Lord Hardinge, whose memory will always be cherished with affection by the people of this country, for the first time recognised the legitimacy of that vital Indian aspiration. Neither indications have not been wanting of late which go to show that our National dream and purpose is gaining the stamp of even official approval. There is, however, a world of difference between a theoretical approval of an ideal and its practical application.

DEEDS NOT WORDS

The supreme duty of the men that lead the forces of Indian progress is to insist that India's Rulers should definitely set the ideal before them as the ultimate goal to be attained within a reasonable time and should accelerate the pace accordingly. All our difficulties now arise from the steady reluctance on the part of Indian officialdom to keep this end definitely in view and move faster. Sympathy, divorced from a resolute and active progressive policy can hardly ameliorate the situation. Honeyed words alone cannot suffice. We may congratulate each other about a changed angle of vision and yet remaining where we are till doomsday. The time for a definite decision and a bold move forward has arrived. The vital question to-day, is: Is India fit to be free and to what extent? There can be no shelving of the issue at this juncture. It must be settled one way or the other. If she is not fit to-day she has got to be made fit for Self-Government. This I maintain is no less a duty and responsibility of the Government than of the people themselves.

THE TEST OF FITNESS

Is India fit for freedom? We who are present here to-day know full well that from the Indian standpoint there can be but one answer. Our critics would probably challenge our conviction. Our only reply to them would be to go forward and put the matter to the proof. After all, what is the test of fitness? If we turn to history we find that in the past only such people have been declared to have been fit for freedom who fought for it and attained it. We are living in different times. Peace has its victories and we are fighting and only fight constitutional battles. This peaceful struggle is not, and will not be, wanting in the quality of vigour and sacrifice, and we are determined to convince the British Empire that we are fit for the place of a partner within the Empire, and nothing less will satisfy India. But apart from the numerous other considerations that have repeatedly been urged in support of the claims of India to a responsible and representative form of Government, the one that has grown to be of infinitely larger weight and urgency is the living and vigorous spirit of Patriotism and National Self-Consciousness which is chafing under irksome restraints, and is seeking wider and legitimate outlets for Service and Self-Expression. The strength and volume of this Spirit, this pent-up altruistic feeling and energy of youths can be easily realised by those who have their finger on the pulse of the country. The most significant and hopeful aspect of this spirit is that it has taken its rise from a new-born movement in the direction of National unity which has brought Hindus and Mussalmans together in loving and brotherly service for the common cause. Bombay had the good fortune to see the Indian National Congress and the All-India Muslim League met for the first time in the same city last December. These simultaneous Sessions were brought about with no little labour, anxiety and trouble. I do not wish to go into past controversy but I venture to say that the Session of the All-India Muslim League at Bombay will go down to posterity as peculiarly interesting in its results. The so-called opponents of ours, although for the time being they caused the utmost anxiety and individual risks, which after all do not count in a National Movement, have, I cannot help saying, rendered the greatest service to our cause. Their unjust attitude served only to stiffen the back of the community. The League rose phœnex-like stronger, more solidified and determined in its ideals and aspirations, with an added strength of resolution in carrying out its programme. And, to-day, in your historic city of Lucknow the centre of Mussalman culture and intellect, where three years ago the All-India Muslim League laid down our cherished ideal of Self-Government under the aegis of the British is witnessing the simultaneous sessions of the Indian National Congress and the All-India Muslim League once more.

THE HINDU-MUSLIM RAPPROCHEMENT

Indeed the person who fails to read in the Hindu-Muslim rapprochement within the last two years the first great sign of the birth of a United India has little knowledge of the political conditions of a few years ago, and has no business to talk of India.

FUTURE IDEALS OF THE LEAGUE

I need hardly say that the Hindu-Muslim question had hitherto lain as a colossal riddle athwart the numerous unifying forces that make for the evolution of a common Indian Nationality. The new temper that we witness to-day is the measure of the change that has happily come over Hindu-Muslim relations. What this change really signifies can only be judged by a reference to the state of things that obtained only a few years ago when mutual distrust and suspicion were rampant and communal bigots on either side ruled the roost. Everyone of us can easily recall the frame of the Muslim mind and the feeling in which the All-India Muslim League was founded at Dacca. To put it frankly the All-India Muslim League came into existence as an organisation with the main object of safe-guarding Muslim interests. The Mussalmans as a community had till then abstained from all manner of political agitation, and they were naturally moved by the loud and insistent demand for constitutional and administrative reforms which Hindu politicians were pressing on the Indian Government. They felt, and rightly, the need of organising themselves for political action lest the impending changes initiated by a liberal Secretary of the State should swamp them altogether as a community. This was perhaps the only course open to a community proud of the traditions of its past, yet weak in numbers and lacking the strength that organised political activity alone can give. The main principle on which the First All-India Muslim political organisation was based, was the retention of Muslim communal, individuality, strong and unimpaired in any constitutional readjustment that might be made in India in the course of its political evolution. The creed has grown and broadened with the growth of political life and thought in the community in its general outlook, and the ideal as regards the future. The All-India Muslim League stands abreast of the Indian National Congress and is ready to participate in any patriotic efforts for the advancement of the country as a whole. In fact this readiness of the educated Muslims only about a decade after they first entered the field of politics to work shoulder to shoulder with the other Indian communities for the common good of all is to my mind the strongest proof of the value and need of this great Muslim political organisation at present. I have been a staunch Congressman throughout my public life and have been no lover of sectarian cries, but it appears to me that the reproach of "separation" sometimes levelled at Mussalmans is singularly inept and wide of the mark when I see this great communal organisation rapidly growing into a powerful factor for the birth of a United India. A minority must above everything else have a complete sense of security before its broader political sense can be evoked for co-operation and united endeavour in the national tasks. To the Mussalmans of India that security can only come through adequate and effective safeguards as regards their political existence as a community. Whatever my individual opinion may be, I am here to interpret and express the sense of the overwhelming body of Muslim opinion of which the All-Indian Muslim League is the political organ.

HINDU MUSLIM RELATIONS

It is a matter of infinite gratification to me as well as to all patriotic Mussalmans that the Muslim communal position in this matter has been recognised and met in an ungrudging spirit by the leaders of the great Hindu community. This was so amply demonstrated by the happy and unanimous decision that was arrived at by the Committees of the Indian National Congress and the All-India Muslim League that met at Calcutta only last November. Our joint Conferences in Lucknow were marked by honest efforts on either side to find a lasting solution of our differences, and I rejoice to think that a final settlement has at last been reached which sets the seal on Hindu-Muslim co-operation and opens a new era in the history of our country. A few irreconcilable spirits in either company still exist here and there, but the atmosphere has on the whole been rid of the menace of sectarian thunder, and the prospects of the future are bright with a promise that gladdens the hearts of India's devoted sons. Just as I have no sympathy with a member of my community who even with an assured communal existence would not extend the hand of fellowship to his Hindu Brother, so I cannot appreciate the attitude of the Hindu Patriot who would insist on his pound of flesh, though in this struggle the entire future of the country for the sake of a small gain to one side or the other may be marred for ever. As an instance I would like to point the recent unfortunate controversy that was raised in these Provinces over the passing of the Municipal Act, but surely we are not wanting in political wisdom and sagacity. Let us remember, whether Hindus or Mussalmans that New India wants a wholly different type of public worker of more generous spirit and ampler mould, free from the egoism of sect and the narrowness of bigotry, one who can resist the temptation to crush the weak and yet would not quail before the aggression of the strong; who can rise above the petty preoccupations of the day to the higher plane of devotion and service which alone can give to a people faith, hope, freedom, and power.

THE SCHEME OF REFORM

With the satisfactory solution of the most formidable problem that stood in the path of Indian progress towards political co-operation and unity our constitutional battle may be said to have been half won already. The united Indian demand based on the actual needs of the country and framed with due regard to time and circumstances must eventually prove irresistible. It must also be recognised that those responsible for the Government of India have already shown a disposition to treat the existing grievances of the people a broader spirit of understanding and sympathy. With the restoration of peace the Indian problem will have to be dealt with on bold and generous lines and India will have to be granted her birthright as a free, responsible, and equal member of the British Empire. How this change is to be effected and what are to be the lines of development and methods of solution are matters that have been fully occupying the thought of Indian publicists for the past two years, and authoritative schemes of readjustment have already been formulated and placed before the Government by the nineteen Elected Representatives of the Imperial Council. You are aware that a Committee of the All-India Muslim League was formed last year and was authorised to draw up a scheme of reform in consultation with the Committee of the Indian National Congress. That scheme is ready and will at this Sessions be submitted to you for your consideration and judgment. After you have adopted the scheme of reforms you should see that the Congress and the League take concerted measures to have a Bill drafted by constitutional lawyers as an Amending Bill to the Government of India Act which embodies the present constitution of our country. This Bill when ready should be adopted by the Indian National Congress and the All-India Muslim League, and a deputation of leading and representative men from both the bodies should be appointed to see that the Bill is introduced into the British Parliament and adopted. For that purpose we should raise as large a fund as possible to supply the sinews of war until our aims and objects are fulfilled.

THE POSITION OF INDIA IN THE EMPIRE

The first and the foremost question that requires to be put at rest is the position of India in the Empire. This should be defined in the most unequivocal terms, it should be made clear by the Government in an authoritative manner that Self-Government is not a mere distant goal that may be attained at some future indefinite time, but that Self-Government for India is the definite aim and object of the Government, to be given to the people within a reasonable time. That should be the aim and object of the reconstruction and reformation of the present constitution of the Government of India; and immediate steps should be taken after the War to introduce the reforms with that end in view, both by the Government and the Imperial partnership. Reading the signs of the times it appears that the claims of the Overseas Dominions such as Canada, Australia and even South Africa, *viz.*, to allow them a voice in the declaration of war and the making of peace and the Imperial foreign policy, if they are to bear the responsibilities of the Empire, cannot well be resisted, and it might follow that an Imperial Parliament may be constructed and established, England, Scotland and Ireland having their internal and domestic affairs such as the dominions already have. Sir Joseph Ward, addressing the meeting of the Insurance Institute at Gresham College, only last month, said that in the future reconstruction of the Empire there could not be any interference with local authority, and though an Imperial Parliament was a long way off they might now work for some effective Imperial Council and that before an organic parliament was possible there must be devolution in Britain to make the way for a federal legislature. The Overseas Dominions had no right even to a minority voice as to whether the Nation should go to war or what the peace terms should be. He quoted Mr. Asquith's speech at the 9th Imperial Conference in which the Prime Minister stated: An Imperial Parliament scheme would impair the authority of the British Parliament. "Since then," Sir Joseph said, "there had been a great evolution of opinion on the subject. Mr. Bonar Law had declared as a result of the War that the time was coming when the Overseas Dominions would share in the Government of the Empire with Britain. He hoped that before the War ended some *modus vivendi* would be established." In the political reconstruction, India as the largest part of the Empire cannot possibly be allowed to continue a Dependency as an adjunct to England, Scotland or Ireland, or to be ruled and governed by the Dominions. Hitherto the responsibility for the control and the supervision of India has been vested in

Great Britain. The question naturally arises: What will be the position of India if an Imperial Parliament, with full representation of the Dominions, is constituted? Is India to serve new and additional masters? Is India, ruled jointly by England and Scotland and Ireland, to be handed over to this Imperial Parliament, and to be thus ruled and to be governed by the Colonies? Are we not to have a status or *locus standi* in the Imperial Parliament? I feel sure that I am expressing the opinion of the entire educated people of this country that India will never allow herself to be relegated to such an intolerable position. Indeed she does not want a change of masters nor additional masters. If an Imperial Parliament as indicated above is established, India's right should be recognised, and her voice in that Imperial Parliament must be fully and properly secured and represented by her own sons in the Councils of the Empire.

MINIMUM DEMANDS

Next, it is well known that the reforms that are sought by the people of India to be introduced into the constitutional Government of India were fully adumbrated recently by the nineteen elected members of the Imperial Legislative Council, and I do not wish to repeat them here, as I believe you are all familiar with them already. As one of the signatories I would urge upon you to follow them substantially so far as the fundamental principles are involved in those proposals. Those demands were formulated by responsible men who owe a duty to the Government and people alike as their chosen representatives, not in a spirit of bargaining. Those demands are the minimum in the strictest sense of the word. It is said that these are extravagant demands; it is said it is a big thing; it is said that we are not yet ready for them; it is said that if these reforms are introduced there will be chaos, and particularly the Anglo-Indian Press is not only most unreasonable and disappointing but alarmed. These are mere destructive methods. Similar fears were raised and arguments advanced when the Minto Morley reforms were on the Legislative anvil, but what is the verdict now, official and non-official after nearly seven years of actual trial? I give an answer: We have not been favoured either by our critics or by the Government with a reply as to what is the alternative scheme, we are not taken into the confidence of the secret chambers of the Government where the Government of India, it is said, have been deliberating upon and preparing a despatch containing their proposals of reform to be submitted to the Secretary of State for India. In England the representatives of the Colonies and the press and the people and the ministers are freely discussing the reconstruction of the constitution of the Empire after the War. Nay, even before the War is over it is suggested to set up an Imperial Council; whereas in India we are denied the opportunity of knowing even what the Government are contemplating. It will be a great misfortune if any decisions are arrived at with regard to the future ot India by the Government and the Secretary of State for India without the proposals being published and placed before the country at large for public criticism and opinion. I most earnestly urge upon the Government that before any final decision is arrived at the proposed reforms should be published and the people should be taken into their confidence. I feel that if the people are bitterly disappointed at this juncture it will mean the greatest disaster to the future progress of this country.

THE QUESTION OF THE CALIPHATE

I should be failing in my duty towards my own people and the Government if I did not at this crisis make it clear that of the many delicate questions there is none that requires a closer attention and study by the Government and the Minister of Great Britain than the question of the Caliphate. The sentiments and feelings and the religious convictions, not only of the Mussalmans of India but of the Mussalmans of the world, are not to be lightly treated. The loyalty of the Muhammadans of India to the Government is no small asset. From the very commencement of the great crisis through which the British Empire has been passing the allegiance of the Mussalmans to the Crown and their loyalty to the Government has remained whole-hearted and unshaken. May I, therefore, urge that the Government should have regard for their dearest and most sacred religious feeling, and under no circumstances interfere with the question of the future of the Caliphate. It should be left entirely to the Mussalmans to acknowledge and accept their own

Caliph. I do not desire to dilate on this grave and delicate subject, but much deeper currents underlie this exceptional exhortation of mine, which I have ventured to make in the interests of the Mussalmans and the Government of Great Britain, than it would be expedient at present to discuss on public platform. But the Mussalmans may well claim that their feelings and sentiments relating to their most cherished traditions should receive consideration in the general policy of the Empire, particularly when they coincide with the demands of justice, human pity and international obligations.

THE HOLY PLACES OF ISLAM

As a spokesman of the Mussalmans of India, I must here acknowledge that the noble assurance of the British Government given to them through H. E. Lord Hardinge, the late Viceroy of India, as regards the Holy Places of Islam, was received by them not only with the utmost satisfaction but with profound gratitude.

THE MUSLIM ATTITUDE

I may say a word as to the attitude of the Mussalmans of India towards the Government. Our clear duty is to be loyal and respectful, without stooping to a cringing policy. We want no favours and crave for no partial treatment. That is demoralising to the community and injurious to the State. The Mussalmans must learn to have self respect. What we want is a healthy and fair impetus to be given to our aspirations and ideals as a community, and it is the most sacred duty of the Government to respond to that claim. Towards the Hindus our attitude should be of good will and brotherly feelings. Co-operation in the cause of our Motherland should be our guiding principle. India's real progress can only be achieved by a true understanding and harmonious relation between the two great sister communities. With regard to our own affairs we can depend upon nobody but ourselves. We should infuse a greater spirit of solidarity into our society ; we should remove the root causes and the evil effects of the process of disintegration, we should maintain a sustained loyalty to, and co-operation with, each other. We should sink personal differences and subordinate personal ambitions to the well-being of the community. We must recognise that no useful purpose is served in petty disputes and in forming party combination. We could not lose the sympathy of our well-wishers in India and in England by creating a wrong impression that we, as a community, are out only for self-interest and self-gain. We must show by our words and deeds that we sincerely and earnestly desire a healthy National unity. For the rest, the 70 millions of Mussalmans need not fear religious differences. A few days ago I came across a paragraph in the *Bombay Chronicle* the well-known daily paper of Bombay, with its editor, Mr. B. G. Horniman, a friend of the Mussalmans, who has rendered great services to us. It is as follows: The following incident reported by the *Amrita Bazar Patrika*, may well be read with profit by those whose perverse imaginations, in spite of proofs to the contrary, always see in the difference of religions in India an irremovable bar against placing Indians in high offices of trust and responsibility. This is how H. H. the Nizam just disposed of Hindu-Mussalman dispute in his territory. Well, for about a year or so there sprang up a quarrel between the Hindus and the Mussalmans of Warrangal about the building of a mosque in a prominent Hindu locality. In spite of many protests from the Hindu population the other party persisted in constructing one. The Hindus then appealed to His Highness with the result that he was pleased to appoint a Committee of enquiry, consisting of two Mussalmans and one Hindu to report on the matter. The report was in favour of the Hindus, and His Highness has been pleased to pass his orders accordingly. The action taken by H. H. the Nizam, it need hardly be added, was in accordance with the traditional policy adopted by the Rulers of Hyderabad.

CONCLUSION

The Renaissance of India really lies in our own hands. Let us work and trust to God so that we may leave a richer heritage to our children than all the gold of the world—FREEDOM—for which no sacrifice is too great.

THE HON. Mr. ABDUL RASUL

Speaking on the resolution on Self-Government in the All-India Muslim League, Lucknow, in 1916. *The Hon. Mr. Abdul Rasul said :—*

It is known that England is the most freedom loving country in the world. It was pointed out in another place how all political refugees of Europe, found shelter in England. When England along with other powers advocated the cause of freedom, did England think that India was not as educated as some of the other countries following? Most of you know that England along with other powers advocated Self-Government for the Balkan States. The people of India are better educated than the people of the Balkan States. Are we less educated and advanced than what Japan was fifty years ago when Self-Government was granted to the people of Japan? We find that even the Negros in Siberia have Self-Government. The wording of our resolution is most moderate, and reforms, that we now ask for are only steps to a further measure of Self-Government. That is our goal. I hope the Government will not consider our demands extravagant. It has been stated in some papers that after the War the Colonies would have a large share in the administration of India. I do not know, if that is correct or not. We have been ruled by the English people, but certainly we shall object to be ruled by the

Civilians who come from the Colonies which do not treat our people in a way that they ought to, having regard to the fact that that the Indians, South Africans, Australians, etc., are all subjects of the same Sovereign. We know what our people want better than the Civilians who come from South Africa, Australia, New Zealand and England. I do not mean any disparagement to the members of the Indian Civil Service when I say that in 95 cases out of 100 they do not understand our languages. There is a great deal of misunderstanding about this question of Home Rule or Self-Government. Our rulers and Anglo-Indian editors of papers say that our object is to drive the English out of India. It is not the intention either of the Hindus or the Mussalmans to drive the English out of India. If it is to be a settled fact that the Colonies are to have control over our affairs, we must insist on having our share in the control of the affairs of the Empire. Do not think that anybody can say that ours is an unreasonable demand. Understand that Mr. L. Curtis, who is here on the dais has written a book called *The Problem of the Commonwealth* and that it is also his object that we, Indians, should have a place in the Empire not as a Dependency, but as a dominant partner. If so, we welcome the suggestion in his book, but if it is not so, we must strongly object to the Colonies having any share in controlling the affairs of India. The Governor-General said the other day in Calcutta that he would be dishonest if he held out any hopes that our progress would be rapid. I say equally determinedly and equally respectfully that, if our rulers do not grant us reforms, which are so reasonable, yet if we go on appealing and appealing to the British people in spite of what he, Lord Chelmsford said, our progress will be rapid. The English people have been very cautious, but at the same time if we can show to them the justice of our cause, I have no doubt the British public would come forward to grant what we want within a few years. After the Boer War the British statesman granted Self-Government to South Africa. When we are shedding blood in the cause of the British Empire, are we to be debarred from having that measure of Self-Government which, Boers, who were enemies of Britain, obtained within a few years of the annexation of South Africa? (Loud and continued applause).

SIR RABINDRANATH TAGORE

The following is a running summary of a lecture recently delivered by Dr. Tagore at Calcutta on "Things being shaped as the Master desires."

"I have grown grey as I have watched, year after year how, at the least shower of rain, Chitpore Road, in front of our lane, becomes flooded, and how the discomfort of its being under water is emphasised for us and the wheels of our luckless carriages by the underlying tram tracks, which on this road, are in a chronic state of being under repairs.

I have latterly begun to think that it is possible not to allow this kind of thing to go on· that, in fact, one gets on ever so much better for not allowing it to go on—and that the contrast between Chitpore Road and Chowringhee is driven home to every one who goes about with his eyes open. They both belong to and are part and parcel of the same city, the same municipality, but what we are willing to suffer in the northern part, they are not willing to stand in the south. We await our Master's voice; they insist on being their own masters.

The right of being one's own master is the greatest of man's rights. So this country, in which all teachings and injunctions, all rules and observances, have been directed towards keeping this greatest of rights suppressed, where paths are destroyed lest footsteps should stray, where in the name of religion man is humiliated and abused,—has naturally become the greatest of slave factories.

Our modern bureaucratic rulers have taken to gravely offering us the same counsel: "You are unfit, you will make mistakes, self-government is not for you." These teachings of Manu and Parashar sound strangely out of tune when repeated in English and rouse us to give the reply which the spirit of European civilisation itself has taught us:—"To make mistakes is not so serious a matter as not to be one's own master. Truth can only be arrived at, if one is free to err."

We may go further and remind our bureaucratic masters that the automobile of self-government, which they now so proudly drive in their own country, was not always there; and that the creating of the old parliamentary cart, which first began its journey in the night jolting its way from the rut of one precedent to another, did not sound exactly like the music of a triumphal progress. How it used to sway from interest to interest,—of the king, of the church, of the land lord, of the brewer! Was there not a time when its members could only be made to attend under threat of penalty? And talking of blunders what a tale could be unfolded of its old relations with Ireland and America and its blazing indiscretions in the Dardanells and Mesopotamia, to say nothing of the not inconsiderable list which might be made out for India alone.

And we have finally a still more important point to

urge. Self-Government not only leads to efficiency and a greater sense of responsibility, but it makes for the uplifting of the national spirit, when those whose minds are now confined within the parochial limits of community of village are given the opportunity of thinking and acting imperially, then alone can they realise the vision of mankind in its larger sense.

Therefore in spite of all risks of muddies or blunders we must have Self-Government—this and this alone is the sovereign cure of all our national distempers.

The same helm serves to steer to the left as to the right. And we must not forget that there is a fundamental principle which must be grasped before man can become true either socially or politically. Each individual has no particular law to guide him. He must have a command of the universal law if he would be successful. The mental cowardice which compels us to await the master's voice before we can act has shaped the very fount of all our national aspirations and endeavours. What master? Any master, be he the elder at home, the police "daroga" the priest or pundit or anyone of the numerous evil spirits in whose altar we have sacrificed all our individuality and independent thinking.

And yet there was a day in India when the Upanishads taught of the Eternal and Universal law, the knowledge of which is science. It is this same science which has given Europe the courage to say :—"Malaria shall be driven off the Earth. Lack of food and lack of knowledge shall not be allowed in the homes of men.

Harmony shall reign in the political world between the commonweal and the rights of the individual."

To-day, all the world is praying to be relieved from sub-servience to the dictates of masters and super-men. Awakened by the modern spirit, we are yearning to join in the universal chorus of democracy. It would have been our eternal shame had we failed to do so, had we proved our undying yearning for some master's voice. It is of happy augury that we have caught a glimpse of the truth and are still able to respond to it.

I know that we are open to the same retort, which the Brahmin gave to the Sudra of old that this fundamental principle of British policy does not apply to us. But, for all that, let us not refuse to believe in humanity and human justice. Let us continue to behave as though power is not the only thing great in the British regime, but that the principles on which it is based are even greater. When the Sudra joined his palms in submission to the Brahminical decree of inferiority, on that very day was dug the pit for the Brahmins' downfall. The weak can be no less enemies of the strong than the strong of the weak. We shall not do the British the dis-service of weakly assisting them to belie their own greatness.

That the people are most concerned in their own Government is a truth greater than the Government itself. This is the truth which gives strength to the British people. This is the truth which is also our strength. If we fail to hold on to this truth, the Government will lose sight of it likewise. If we do not believe and trust in the British ideal of Self-Government, then the police must needs tyrannise over us and the efforts of the Magistrate to protect us will be unavailing; then will the god of Prestige continue to demand its human victims and British rule in India give the lie to historic British ideals.

After a hundred and fifty years of British rule we hear to-day that Bengal is not even to be allowed to sigh over the troubles of her sister province of Madras. Up till now we had been led to believe that the fact that under the same British sovereignty the provinces of Bengal, Punjab, Madras and Bombay were all being welded into a uniformity of ideal and aspiration was one of the brightest jewels of the British crown. We are told in the West that Britain entered this war and faced death accounting the sorrows of Belgium and France as her own; and are we to be told in the same breath in the East that Bengal must not bother her head about the troubles of Madras? Is this a command to which we are prepared to bow the head? Do we not know for certain, in spite of the vehemence of its utterance of the load of shame which lurks behind?

England came to India as representing European civilisation. The ideal of that civilisation is the word she has pledged to us. We must hold her to that word. It is our duty not to allow her to forget it. Unless both parties do their duty forgetfulness and fall will be the inevitable consequence. Science, comradeship and self-respect of the people, this is the wealth

Europe has acquired. This is the consideration on which must be based England's title to the Empire.

The Englishman may point to his own history and say "This great ideal of the government of the people by the people was evolved by us through many a struggle and at the cost of much striving and sacrifice." I admit it. All pioneer peoples of the world, in the pursuit of their several quests, have had to pass through much error and sorrow and strife. But when they have gained the truth they sought, it has become available to others without their having to tread the same long road of error and sacrifice.

In America I have seen Bengal youths becoming experts in the manufacture of machines without their having had to retrace the whole history of the steam engine beginning from the boiling kettle. What it took centuries for Europe to evolve it took but little time for Japan to transplant, roots and all, to her own soil. So, far from being convinced of any reason for delay, we may on the contrary urge that it is just because we are deficient in the qualities which are necessary for self-government that practice in governing ourselves is all the sooner necessary. What of the democracies which are the boast of the West? Can we not rake up enough of sin and crime and every kind of enormity from amidst the European peoples? Had there been any Over Lord to say that till all these continue to exist Europe shall not have self-government, then not only would all these have remained as they are, but all possibility of their cure would have departed.

I do not deny that we have our weaknesses in our individual characters and in our social system. Still we want self-government. In the great democratic festival of the world no one people have all their lights burning—yet the festival goes on. If for sometime our light has gone out, may we not ask for it to be lit at the wick of England's lamp without thereby raising a howl of indignation? It will not detract from England's light but surely add to the brightness of the world's illumination.

H. H. THE MAHARAJAH OF ALWAR

At a banquet given in honour of H. H. the Maharajah of Bikaner at the Taj Mahal Hotel, Bombay, the Maharajah of Alwar in the course of a long speech said;—

Your Highness, if at this War Conference there should be any question regarding the future of our country, it will not be necessary for you to speak of our great past. Our ancient civilisation is still a source of admiration to the people of other lands, and cannot but be the cause of legitimate pride to the sons and daughters who have been born of the soil. But no nation can live on its past alone. We are determined that the superstructure shall be built to completion on the same religious foundation, and that the future of our mother country shall be as equally great, if not greater than what it was in the ancient days. We are all naturally anxious to raise India's position in accordance with her ancient glory. India has nothing to beg. But at the present time, it has not even the opportunity to claim or ask that our Aryavarta may at least be put in such a position that she may be able to hold her head alongside of other sister nations of the Empire. We are not going to embarrass the Government who guide the destinies of this country with such questions at the present moment, as it is necessary for us to concert all our energies towards our common aim of ultimate success. We feel confident that, when the moment arrives, we shall not be forgotten or left behind. Is it possible that a nation which has drawn the sword for protecting the liberties of weaker nations, such as Belgium, will overlook our rights and claims to raise our heads on a footing of equality with the other Dominions? When the War is successfully over and the British people extend to India their hand of comradeship, entrust us to wield the destinies of our own country, Your Highness can assure them we shall be as ready to grasp their hand with feelings of warm gratitude and emotion, as we have been to discharge our duties in the present crisis. When such constitutional changes take place, it is not possible to think that the destinies of our one-third India are likely to be ignored. We rest in confidence at the present moment.

H. H. THE MAHARAJAH OF BIKANER

At a banquet given in honour of H. H. the Maharajah of Bikaner at the Taj Mahal Hotel, Bombay, His Highness, in the course of his reply, said:—

We have every reason to feel confident as to the future of India, and I think that, if we reflect on the ready response and gratitude which stir the hearts of millions of loyal Indians at each new sympathetic step or generous measure taken by the British Government for the amelioration of the condition and status of the people or the political advancement or the moral or material development of our mother country, we can feel proud of our countrymen. And most of all we may be proud when we regard the sacrifices in blood or treasure that have been cheerfully made by prince and peasant alike in this colossal struggle, when our countrymen have fought shoulder to shoulder with our English and Colonial brethren for God, King and Country, and in the cause of freedom and humanity without any idea of reward or recompense, but glad firmly to grasp the hand of comradeship and friendship extended to them by their brethren of Great and Greater Britain, for whether we come from the territories of British India or those of the Indian States we are all Indians who are entirely united in loyalty and attachment to our King-Emperor, in our affection for our mother country and in our deep and genuine solicitude for our brethren of all creeds and communities throughout India. And I know I am voicing the feelings and sentiments of Your Highnesses when I further state that we of the Indian States, who yielded to no one in the whole of the British Empire in steadfast loyalty and deep devotion to the Person and Throne of our King-Emperor, happily find it quite consistent to be at one and the same time in the best and truest sense of the term staunch loyalists and Imperialists as well as true patriots of our mother country, deeply sympathising with all the legitimate aspirations of our brother Indians in British India, just as much as we feel sure our brethren in British India sympathise with the legitimate aspirations of the Princes and people of the Indian States, and our desire to see maintained unimpeded our dignity, privileges and high position. The beginning now made in according India her proper place in the Empire is wise and sagacious measure that will knit England and India still closer together, and that it will further strengthen the ties connecting India with Great Britain which all well-wishers of the Great British Empire earnestly desire. I would like to be permitted to say that I am not speaking any idle words in an irresponsible or light hearted manner, but that I am expressing, my honest and firm conviction when I say that this and many other signs are good omens, full of bright promise for the future of India. The daughter State has proved that it would, as of old, always faithfully stand by England through thick and thin for the honour and glory of the mighty British Empire; of which she considers herself an integral part. After the end of this terrible world-wide War, who can doubt that the angle of vision as regards India will be still further altered in favour of every reasonable and right political reform? Close personal comradeship on the battle-fields and the common bond of loyalty for the Sovereign and love for the Empire have further more led to a similar favourable change in the angle of vision of the Self-Governing Colonies and the other parts of the British Dominions which for the first time are beginning to realise and understand India at her true worth. Big changes are in the air, including the reconstruction and reconstitution of our Empire, and though at present the immediate energies of all of us must be devoted to winning the War, yet when by God's infinite grace the arms of His Imperial Majesty the King Emperor and those of our brave Allies are crowned with victory, an event which happily is already in sight, I sincerely believe that British statesmanship and British sense of justice and fairness will rise equal to the occasion, and accord to our country that place to which her position in the Empire and her loyal services to the Crown entitle her. We may, therefore, confidently assume that Great Britain and the British nation who have so bravely made, and are still making, such tremendous sacrifices to uphold the cause of justice and humanity, will not forget the just claims and aspirations of India to enable her to work out her destiny under Britain's guiding hand and protection.

LORD BISHOP OF CALCUTTA.

The Lord Bishop of Calcutta in the course of his sermon at the St. Paul's Cathedral on the War Anniversary day, 1917, *said:—*

Our cause remains to-day what it has always been, the cause of justice, mercy and good faith, the cause of truth and of liberty. We are still fighting to prevent one Power from destroying the liberties of some states and dismembering others, and from imposing upon the whole world the theory that 'might is right.'

But there are signs that under the strain and exasperation of protected warfare we are tempted to be unfaithful at heart to the object for which we are fighting. We have all realized that if Germany won this war, the world would have to accept all the atrocities which the Germans have committed in it as parts of the recognized custom of war. Yet in this last year both in Parliament and in the newspapers men have urged that we ought to commit atrocities upon the Germans under the name of reprisals. If we did this we should be giving the sanction of our example to the commission of atrocities in war. If we do not uphold the customs of civilized warfare, who will be left to do it? We must be very straight and plain with ourselves. If we commit, or approve of our soldiers committing unjust or merciless or dishonourable acts, we have but little right to say that we are fighting for justice, mercy and good faith. It is then hypocrisy for us to bring our cause before God to-day.

But it is not only against the German method of conducting war that we are fighting. We are fighting against the German principle that the strongest nation ought to subdue and enslave weaker ones. If this principle were accepted, there would be no end to wars, and the strongest nation might always plead the excuse of Germany that it was making these conquests with the object of spreading its own superior civilization. We stand for the right of nations to live and grow according to their own God-given nature, whether they be great or small. Here again we must keep our own conscience clear. We have become the paramount power in India by a series of conquests in which we have used Indian soldiers and had Indian allies. We have remained the paramount power in India because the Indian people needed our protection against foreign foes and against internal disorder. We must now look at our paramount position in the light of our own war-ideals. The British rule in India must aim at giving India opportunities of self-development according to the natural bent of its peoples. With this in view, the first object of its rulers must be to train Indians in self-government. If we turn away from any such application of our principles to this country, it is but hypocrisy to come before God with the plea that our cause is the cause of liberty.

But while our cause has remained the same as we have professed it since the war began, recent events have given it a new meaning. The adhesion, of the United States to our side and the revolution in Russia have added a new element to the idea that we are fighting for liberty. We have hitherto been fighting for the liberty of nations from enslavement by other nations. Now we realise that we are also fighting for the masses of the people within each nation. We are fighting for the democratic idea. With eyes enlighted and with hearts uplifted, understanding our great cause more clearly than in the beginning of the War, let us pray that we may be more worth of our cause.

Mr. SYED WAZIR HASAN

At a meeting of the London Indian Association held at the Caxton Hall, Westminister, (1913 October 11), Mr. Syed Wazir Hasan, Secretary of the All-India Moslem League, delivered an address on " The Hindu-Mahomedan Problem in India." Dr. J. N. MEHTA presided, and there was a considerable attendance of members and friends, including Sir Mancherjee Bhownaggree, Mrs. Sarojini Naidu, Mr. Mohammed Ali (Editor of the Delhi " Cômrade ") Mr. M. A. Jinnah, Mr. J. M. Parikh, and Mr. H. P. Lal (Secretary).

Mr. SYED WAZIR HASAN, who was cordially greeted, then addressed the meeting. The subject (he said), with which he was to occupy their time was of very great significance and importance to the inhabitants of a country which contained, as it did, about one-fifth of the whole human race, and it was of no less importance to Great Britain, of which India, in the words of Lord Morley, was practically the only Empire. Upon the right solution of it depended the future of their mother land, and also to a great extent the future of the great Empire to which they belonged. Of course, India was neither wholly Moslem nor wholly Hindu, nor, indeed, was India synonymous with a combination of Hindus and Mussulmans. But he meant no disrespect to other communities in India when he said that the Hindus and the Mussulmans formed the two main communities of India, and her future depended far more on the establishment of proper relations between them and the adjustment of those relations to the position of India in the British Empire than on the relations and position of other communities inhabiting India. It would be obvious to any but the wholly insane that it was possible neither for the seventy millions of Mussulmans to exterminate in any manner or way the two hundred and twenty millions of Hindus, nor for the two hundred and twenty millions of Hindus to get rid of the seventy millions of Mussulmans. They should not go back too far into the remote past, and rake up old rivalries, nor were they likely to get at the truth in histories most often read by the educated Indians of to-day, for it was only too often that the honest and laborious chronicler's hand was invisible therein while the shadow of the politician loomed only too large. But about six years ago, when a new educational policy came to be pursued in India the position of the two communities were not exactly the same. The Mahomedans had practically lost their Indian Empire, but like all proud but fallen people, they disdained at the time to learn anything from their new teachers. However natural this spirit of defiance and this habit of sulking might have been, no Mussulman could look back upon it except to lament the criminal neglect of opportunities which were provided for Mussulmans as well as the Hindus in India by a generation of English men whose name was blessed in all educated and cultured Indian households, and would continue to be so blessed by coming generations educated on the lines marked out by those illustrious and benevolent Englishmen. He was inclined to find the causes of present-day antagonism to the extent that it existed in the difference of temper of the two communities when education on modern lines was first introduced into India. Wisely enough, and quite naturally, the Hindu community began from the very first to take full advantage of the new education, and its present evolution was due to the foresight and adaptability of its leaders sixty years ago. Unfortunately for the Mussulmans, they remained for a long time in the stupor that followed upon their decline, and the disappearance of their dominion, and it seemed very unlikely that they could be roused from that condition by any individuals or forces working at the time. But happily for them, just at the time that the Hindus began to attend in increasing numbers, every day the schools and colleges established, by Government and missionary societies in India, there lived amongst the Mahomedans one who, although the product of ancient Eastern education, and surrounded by the environments of a period of decline had a sufficiently clear vision, and a far-sightedness that made him realise the importance of a change in the form and the content of education. He meant, of course, Sir Syed Ahmed Khan, the greatest Mussulman of the last century, and one of the greatest Indians of that period. No one in India had worked harder or on sounder lines for the unity of India than did Sir Syed Ahmed, because it was due to him that Indian Mussulmans took to English education, and when once the two communities shared the same temper as regards Western education, and the educational disparity between them was removed, national unity would be assured. The Calcutta University was founded in 1857, and thirty years after that memorable event India witnessed the establishment of the Indian National Congress.

THE EXAMPLE OF THE CONGRESS

In this interval a new generation of men had come into prominence, and was beginning to guide the destinies of their fellow-countrymen. The teachings of Western poets and political philosophers had now begun to bear fruit, and the first manifestations of the effect of the training which India received at the hands of its rulers now became visible in an organised form in the Indian National Congress. The Congress was, therefore, the result of the ordinary process of evolution working during the preceding thirty years, and was, as such, an embodiment of Indian political consciousness. These thirty years were unfortunately not utilised by Indian Mussulmans in the same manner. But the cogitation of Sir Syed Ahmed, for whom the downfall of Mussulman and the cataclysm of the Mutiny of 1857 were a rude awakening, resulted in the foundation of the Mahomedan Anglo-Oriental College at Aligarh in

1877, and it was no mere coincidence that it took the Mussulmans also exactly the same period of thirty years after this epoch-making event to establish their first political organisation. In the space of these thirty years intervening between the foundation of the Aligarh College and the establishment of the Moslem League in 1906 a new generation of Mussulmans had come into prominence, and had begun to shape the destinies of their co-religionists. The foundation of the League was, therefore, the first manifestation of the dawn of political consciousness on the Moslem horizon in India. The study of the poets and philosophers of the West which had brought about a new political consciousness to the Hindus twenty years ago, brought about the same consciousness to the Mussulmans twenty years later. In 1886 the Mussulmans could have taken no useful part in Indian politics, and, in fact, he felt certain that with their ignorance at that time, and in the temper in which they then happened to be, their participation in Indian politics would have reacted unfavourably on their Hindu fellow-countrymen also. " He who plucks an unripe fruit must expect to find it sour."

THE MAHOMEDANS AND THE MOVEMENT

It might be asked that if the Mahomedans became conscious of their political entity twenty years later than the Hindus, why did they not join an already existing political organisation instead of forming, as they had done, a separate organisation of their own. His reply to this question would be two-fold. In the first place, the growth and evolution of the two communities, although similar in character, was not the same in point of time. Those who started on their journey late in the day could not hope to catch up those who began theirs with the dawn. But it was possible for Mussulmans to learn a great deal from the lessons which experience has taught to the Hindus, and either by discovering short-cuts or making forced marches to catch up their fellow wayfarers on the road of progress. And here he would make an appeal to his Hindu fellow-countrymen to lend every assistance they could to the Moslem laggards, for if they were to work together with the Hindus the two must march shoulder to shoulder. Even in politics magnanimity was often the best policy, and in thus appealing to Hindu fellow-countrymen to be magnanimous, he was not appealing only to their magnanimity but also to their political sagacity. The continuance of educational disparity between Hindus and Mussulmans would retard the growth of a common nationality, as the existence of such a disparity retarded common action in the past. Political unity could only be established between those who were equally well educated, and if Moslem co-operation appeared at all necessary, it was the duty of his fellow-countrymen to assist in removing the existing disparity, and any help offered to the Mussulmans in education was one more stone put on top of the others in the construction of the national edifice. Considering that so many things and institutions which were common to-day in India were the results of study of English people and their institutions, and of a conscious or unconscious imitation of them, it was not to be wondered as if in gazing into the future of our country they were liable to think a little too often that it would be similar to that of the country which brought to them their newly-found political consciousness. But it was only too true that India was in a hundred and one things unlike England, and they would once more be quarrelling with the laws of Nature if they anticipated a political future for India exactly the same as the present condition of England. The history of India for many, many centuries, and the temperament of our people in the East had to be taken into account, and it appeared to him that they would be failing in their duty as nation-builders if in deciding upon the method of attaining salvation, they attached the same value and significance to differences of religion in India as was done in England. In the East religion was something more than a matter of ritual, something more than a set of spiritual conceptions. It often provided a social polity, and gave a distinct colour and shape to culture. When he scanned the skies he saw the vision of the future to be one of a united India, but the union appeared to be one not of individuals but of communities—a political entity on federal lines as unique in constitution as their circumstances—a federation of faiths no less strong than a federation of States in America or of kingdoms in Germany—a union of people "not like to like but like in difference, self-reverent each and reverencing each." The main thing to consider was not whether two people enter the same house from two different doors or from one door, but whether they entered the same house or not, and whether they came to it animated with the same desires and cherishing the same ideals. If he might be permitted to say so, too much time had been spent in discussing the question of different doors, and it had been forgotten that they had to live in the same house, and that if they wished to live together, it was better to live in concord and harmony than in conflict and hostility.

THE GROWTH OF GOOD FEELING

Often and often enough the political organisations of the two communities had worked on the same lines in recent years, and the representatives of the two communities in the various legislative bodies of India had fought shoulder to shoulder against despotic measures and policies. The most recent manifestation of the desire to work together had been the series of meetings which had been held in Allahabad, Calcutta, Madras, and Bombay. The last of which had taken place at Cawnpore, and an account of this had come to hand by the mail. They would find that Mr. Mazar-ul-Haque, the distinguished champion of Indian unity, had made a remarkable speech. In this meeting, he might add, more than two thousand Mussulmans participated. It would not do to mistake these signs for an ebullition of Moslem temper which would subside as quickly as it had arisen. These were symptoms of the effect that education on similiar lines had produced on two communities living side by side and recognising a common destiny above the existence of separate entities and the din of communal claims. The new ideals which were being cherished by the present generation of the Mussulmans could not but open new vistas before their vision. They saw—and saw with a steady gaze—that the progress of their common mother-land must depend on a hearty co-operation among all her sons. Side by side with the recognition of their peculiar conditions the Mussulmans, too, had begun to form conceptions of broader obligations and wider responsibilities to their country as a whole, and while not quarrelling with the existence of separate communities as separate political entities, it was possible to progress towards the formation of a nation in India evolved out of a gradual process of eliminating and minimising the points of difference and developing and increasing the points of concord between the two great communities. Even if he differed from some of his fellow-countrymen in his solution of the problem of nationhood, he was not any the less sincere and ardent in his desire to achieve the goal which they all had in view. The glaring monotony of Indian public life was the result of forcing the awakening mind of the people into a cast-iron mould that might break, but would not bend. It was a shallow philosophy that sought to find unity of effort through a uniformity of opinion. It was idle to expect public men to respond to fresh inspiration, and to initiate fresh forms of public endeavour so long as freedom of thought was suppressed by those who controlled the only efficient instrument that democracy had evolved for the organisation of public will and intelligence.

THE MOSLEM LEAGUE AND ITS OBJECTS

He would now place before them certain recent developments in the organisation of which he was the chief executive officer—the All-Indian Moslem League. It was felt that there must be a political ideal for a political organisation. In April, 1912, there issued a circular letter from the office of the All-India Moslem League to all its members and other leading Mussalmans inviting their opinion on the subject. It was a matter of extreme satisfaction that the views of a large majority pointed to one and only one end, and it was that Moslems must place on their programme as their ideal a system of self-government suitable to India under the ægis of the British Crown. This ideal was placed before a meeting of the council of the All-India Moslem League held on December 31, 1912, under the presidentship of his Highness the Aga Khan, and eventually the League gave its confirmation. That ideal runs in the following resolution :—

"The objects of the League shall be inter alia attainment under the ægis of the British Crown of a system of self-government suitable to India through constitutional means by bringing about amongst others a steady reform of the existing system of administration, by promoting national unity, by fostering a public spirit among the people of India, and by co-operation with other communities for the said purposes."

This clause indicated not only the ideal towards which a steady march was being made, but it also attempted, to a limited extent, of course, to point out the steps by which they might approach nearer to the goal in view. Let them now analyse the clause—"By a steady reform of the existing system of administration." This indicated that although no revolutionary reforms were contemplated, nevertheless, the Mussulman mind was not unconscious of the defects in the administration of the country at present. It was obvious that the machinery with the help of which India is governed was more or less a century old. It was preposterous to contend that the India of to-day could be well governed with the help of the same machinery.

THE IDEAL OF SELF-GOVERNMENT

The second portion of the clause stood thus—"By promoting national unity." Howsoever they might wish for a speedy formation of an Indian nationality, it must evolve out of the circumstances which arose under political activities in different directions. It could not be "let there be a nation, and there is a nation." The Indian nationality must be founded upon the bed-rock of a unity of ideals. The methods of working for the attainment of those ideals might differ. He maintained, therefore, that the ideal of self-government which the

All-India Moslem League had placed on its programme was an important step towards the formation of that great nationality for the building of which all Indians were aspiring. The last portion of the clause ran as follows:—"By co-operating with other communities for the said purposes." Their Hindu brethren had been invited to meet the Mussulmans in conference in which they could discuss the preliminaries to concerted action, and if he was spared the strength to take up this pleasant task, the conference should be convened. He would now quote a short passage from a message which his friend, Mr. Mahomed Ali, and himself, left behind for his fellow-countrymen when leaving the shores of India:—

> "But the object of our journey is by no means sectarian or exclusively communal. We firmly believe that the progress and well-being of the Mussulmans are bound up with the progress and well-being of the country in which they live. The present carries in its womb the hopes and fears common to every community in India, and we shall be failing in our duties not only as Indians, but as Mussulmans also, if we do not strive during our sojourn in England to convert our fears into hopes, and to materialise the hopes which we share with all our fellow-countrymen."

He hoped they would accept this as a true index of the Moslem heart, and he appealed to his fellow-countrymen for patience, toleration, and good-will.

THE CRITICS OF THE NEW MOSLEM

He could not conclude without passing reference to chimerical dangers pointed out and needless warnings indulged in by a certain section of the Anglo-Indian press, which had found an echo in the correspondence columns of an important English journal, but it was not only to these people that he addressed himself when he said that the unity of Hindus and Mussulmans was not to be a unity in opposition to the British Government. Often and often in the history of political organisations a unity in opposition had proved to be both ephemeral and weak. It was true that they wished to unite in attacking from two different sides the citadel of bureaucratic, and, in fact, despotic rule, and all the abuses which it inevitably brought in its train, but he was astonished to find that the unity between Hindus and Mahomedans which every British administrator in India had so long preached was giving rise in the official mind to considerable embarrassment and uneasiness, now that it was at last going to be practised. He would not insult these illustrious administrators by accusing them of hypocrisy, but they must realise that the education which Indians had received, made them somewhat critical, and unless they dissociated themselves from all ideas of being hostile to Hindu and Mussulman unity, Indians would not be equally disposed to give them credit for perfect sincerity. They were not so foolish as to believe that self-government could be achieved in a day. It would only follow the growth and development of a common nationality. If they were to believe the journals to which he had referred, the Mahomedans seemed to be very much like the child in the nursery rhyme—" When he is good, he is very, very good, but when he is bad he is horrid." Was it sane to imagine for a moment that Indian Mussulmans meant to exterminate the British and oust the British Government from India simply because, following slowly in the wake of the Government of India, they had now come to cherish the ideal of self-government, to which such a clear reference was made in the now memorable despatch of that Government, August 25, 1911? Was it natural to expect that in spite of years of Western education which had guided other communities of India on the path of progress, Indian Mussulmans would be content to live like the women of ancient Rome in a state of perpetual tutelage? Was it wise, was it even in the interests of the continuance of the British connexion with India to distort for the ultimate rulers of India the legitimate hopes and aspirations of educated Mussulmans into a moment of anarchical character? If it was believed that a wise Providence could not neglect the growth and progress of a fifth of the whole human race, they must believe that British rule in India to-day was providential. The sheet-anchor of the Oriental mind was a faith in Providence. Let them all hold fast to that faith, but let them not forget those beautiful lines which may be addressed to unity.

"Thou wilt come, join men, knit nation unto nation.
But not for us who watch to-day and burn.
Thou wilt come, but after what long years of trial,
Weary, watching, patient louging, dull denial."

LALA LAJPAT RAI

A remarkable article by Lala Lajpat Rai has been published in a Boston (U.S.A.) newspaper. The following is the extract:—

I have often been asked how India feels about the war, and what is her position. India's interest is neither purely altruistic nor absolutely disinterested. She is interested in the results of the war as she hopes for a radical readjustment of her political relations with England, or, for the matter of that, with the whole world. She aspires to a position worthy of her past. Her people desire to be in their own country what other people are in theirs, as it is only then that she can make her proper contribution to the world ethics and the world culture.

READJUSTMENT AND REVALUATION

Then, again, this war must result not only in the revaluation of political standards, but also in a revision of ethical and moral ideals. India has a valuable contribution to make towards this revaluation. This readjustment and revaluation must spring from a spirit of co-operation and goodwill, not only between the different nations of the world, but also between the different religions of the world. That is only possible if India is treated justly and generously and given her legitimate place in the comity of nations, and if her political disqualifications and disabilities are removed.

THE POLITICAL AWAKENING

At present the world sees India with other than Indian eyes, and generally with the eyes of prejudice—the eyes of Empire builders and Empire rulers. She suffers a great deal from misrepresentation and misapprehension.

However, we need not unearth the past; what we are just now concerned with is the present. There can be no denying the fact that ever since the Russo-Japanese war India has been astir. A keen desire for political liberties has been shown by all classes of her people. The general awakening of India has attracted world-wide notice. A national party has come into existence who do not accept the present political arrangement as satisfactory or honourable. Some of them desire complete independence; others would be contented to remain within the British Empire on the same footing as Canada or Australia or South Africa. They have proved their fitness by every test recognised under the sun.

INDIANS AS FIGHTERS

It is now an established fact that even as fighters Indians are inferior to none. Many a position lost by the purely white troops in this war has been regained by the Indians. Their valour, their resourcefulness, their stamina, their indifference to death, their skill, have all been put to test. The unanimous opinion of all competent observers is in their favour. The British press and the French press, and even the German press, are full of praises for them. Yet they are fighting in strange environments, in a climate of which they have had no experience before, among people (both friends and foes) whose language they do not know.

THE GRIEVANCE OF THE ARMS ACT

The fighting capacity of India is simply inexhaustible. India can throw into the war millions of fighting men, if they are properly armed. At present a General Arms Act prohibits the use of arms by Indians in general except under a license from the magistrate, which is granted very sparingly, and for very strong reasons. Even the constitutional party among the Indian Nationalists feels the humiliation of being a disarmed nation and strongly objects to a continuance of this policy. It demands the repeal of this act or such modification of its provisions as will enable the bulk of men of property and education to carry arms. When the war ends this demand is sure to gain in volume and intensity, and it will be impossible for the authorities to resist without creating a serious disaffection in the country.

THE INDIAN "INTELLECTUAL"

As for intellectual equipment, their intellectual capacity has never been denied. But education is neither compulsory nor free. The populations of 300,000,000 in an area of over a million square miles has only five universities to satisfy their craving for intellectual food. In the matter of scientific, technical, and vocational education, India is decades behind Europe and America. There is hardly a high-class technological institute in the whole country. To get up-to-date education Indians have to go to Europe or seek the hospitality of American universities.

It is obvious that this can be done by few only, and sometimes the best of the Indian students cannot get proper education to enable them to show the best in them. Yet the few that have gone to Europe or have come to America have held their own against local students. In the British universities, Indians have on many occasions beaten Britishers on their own ground; occupied the highest positions in all departments of knowledge, mathematics, classics, history, political economy, science, medicine, surgery, law, and philosophy. In India itself the opportunities for original and research work are almost nil. Post-graduate work is very little provided for. Yet in less than fifty years the country has produced a Tagore and a Bose—one on the literary side and the other on the scientific.

AS LAWYERS AND STATESMEN

As for capacity for legal and political work, it is admitted by the British administrators that the world knows no more keen and acute lawyers and clever debaters than the Indians. With the Indian Press Act laying down limitations on the liberty of the press and with "sedition" laws always hanging over their heads like the sword of Damocles, the Indian politicians have held their own. There is no lack of statesmanship and public spirit in India if there were only fields for its display.

There is another part of national life in which India lags decades behind the other big countries of the world, namely, on the industrial side. For sometime it was said that Indians were lacking in enterprise and in commercial genius. The difficulty is that India is not free to determine and follow its fiscal policy. That policy is laid down for it from London, and the interests of Great Britain loom very large. Even if the Government of India, as at present constituted, were to determine a policy in the interests of India' primarily, they would not be allowed to do so if it is in any way militated against the commercial interests of Great Britain.

WHAT SELF-GOVERNMENT WILL DO

With Self-Government the industrial regeneration of India will come as a matter of course. It will remove the present embargo on Indian immigration to other countries outside of Asia. Self-governed India will loom large in world politics, not as aggressor or exploiter, but as a contributor to the general happiness of mankind, and to the moral and ethical uplift of the race. Hindus are the most tolerant people on earth. With self-government gained India will be a great moral force. It will add to the glory of Great Britain if she gets it without bloodshed. She has deserved it by her conduct in the past. She is earning it now on the battlefields of Europe. She can be a never-ending source of strength to the British Empire, if dealt with justly and liberally.

WHAT INDIA WANTS

The "Christian Science Monitor" contains the following report of an interview which its representative at San Francisco has had with Lala Lajpat Rai.

The well-known Indian Nationalist leader, who has recently arrived in the United States from Japan, said that while a majority of the educated and half-educated Indians, as well as the lower classes, were in favour of Indian self-government, and while there had been outbreaks and acts of sedition, there was no possibility of an upraising of the people against the British Government.

In regard to the concessions that the British Government is likely to make at the close of the war in favour of Indian autonomy, he observed that the talk of a more liberal Indian policy among British publicists, and even by the Tory Press, led by the London "Times," at the beginning of the war, had recently ceased or changed its tone, indicating, in his opinion, that the prospects of substantial concessions in self-government were not now so bright as they seemed to be at the beginning of the war.

Indian politicians might be divided into three classes. First, there were the extreme Nationalists; second, the moderate Nationalists; and third, those who were frankly in favour of the rule of the British Government. The Extremists based their propaganda on fundamental grounds. They did not believe that the British would ever voluntarily grant them freedom. They were, therefore, opposed to making petitions and sending memorials. Some of them wanted absolute "swaraj," and some of them qualified "swaraj" on Colonial lines; but everyone of them believed that neither was possible except by active revolt or successful passive resistance. They felt that they were not now in a position to organise, but that, in the meantime, it was their duty to do as much as they could to embarrass the Government by following the tactics of guerrilla warfare and by conducting a terrorist campaign. They said that they must keep the flag flying, no matter how heavy their losses. In their opinion it was the only way to carry on their propaganda and make it effective for impressing the country and gaining fresh recruits to their cause.

The Moderates, on the other hand, those of the Indian National Congress, who wanted to conduct their agitation on constitutional lines within the limits of law, were not in favour of embarrassing the British Government. They were opposed to all agitation, leaving everything to the good sense of the Government. Many of them believed that after the war the Government would make large political concessions, and that the country would make a material advance on the road to self-government on Colonial lines. Many of the members of this body, however, could scarcely be distinguished from those of the third class, who were out-and-out loyalists.

The programme of the Moderate party, that is, the demands that they were likely to make on the British Government at the close of the war, had not been completely formulated, but the substance of the demands might be classified as follows: Repeal and modification of the Arms Act, making it possible, at least for men of education and property, to keep arms without license; some provision for the military training of Indian youths; army commissions to Indians; improvements in the position and prospects of the Indian soldier; a change in the constitution of the Imperial Executive Council so as to admit of more than one Indian being appointed to it; changes in the legislative councils; a non-official, elected majority in the Viceroy's Council; direct election; removal or restrictions in the choice of candidates; freedom of debate; freedom from the embargo of the Secretary of the State for India in fiscal legislation. Similar changes in the provincial councils with provincial fiscal autonomy and greater freedom in provincial legislation; executive councils for the provinces that were without them; a provision that each council should have at least two Indian members, and that the latter should be elected. Compulsory primary education, with ample provision for technical, commercial and scientific education; complete separation of judicial from executive functions with high courts in place of chief courts in each of the provinces, and an extension of jury trials; governors in place of lieutenant-governors and chief commissioners in all the provinces; exclusive or at least larger employment of Indian agency in the public services; inauguration of industries under Government patronage with a protective tariff and ample provision for technical and industrial education in the country. The holding of simultaneous competitive examinations in India for all branches of the Indian services for which examinations are held in England; the repeal of the Indian Press Act and other coercive and repressive laws put on the statute book within the last ten years; better treatment in the Colonies with freedom of travel and emigration or freedom to bar the Colonials from holding any position in India; freedom of education; local self-government, freed of official control from village unions upwards.

HOME RULE FOR INDIA

The "Christian Commonwealth" for July 29, 1914 contains a lengthy interview with Lala Lajpat Rai.

It is observed at the outset that since the rejection of the India Council Bill by the House of Lords the question of British rule in India has ceased almost as suddenly as it began to interest the British people. But at the best of times interest in India is confined to a small section of the people.

Sometimes, but very rarely, we have a dim apprehension of the fact that the blessings of British rule are not altogether appreciated by the Indian people. We hear of a Nationalist movement. Travellers tell rather disturbing stories of the unrest that prevails. A few

Anglo-Indians who have spent years among that people warn us in grave tones that this unrest will one day come to a head. But on the whole, the British public and the British Parliament never think about India in any sense as a country with a soul of its own, which sees visions and dreams. And we are shocked and startled by the suggestion that in her dreams India sees herself as a self-governing country.

Yet to this conclusion events in India are certainly tending. The rejection of the India Council Bill is another step on the road that leads to the formulation of a claim for Home Rule.

THE REJECTION OF THE INDIA COUNCIL BILL

We regret the rejection of the Bill, not because we regarded that measure as a considerable step in the direction of associating educated Indian opinion with the Government of India, but because the refusal of even that small concession of representation in the Bill will make the progress of our constitutional agitation very difficult.

It gives the extreme section a handle against us. The constitutional movement in India is viewed with suspicion on both sides: by the younger generation of the Indian Nationalists as well as by the Government. This result will make it harder for us to confine the Nationalist movement within constitutional limits. We are strongly opposed to violent methods of propaganda. But we shall find ourselves powerless to stem the tide flowing in that direction if we are to have our proposals rejected in this way. It can only foment unrest and lead to conspiracy and violence if the mass of the people of India become convinced that our constitutional propaganda is shown to be powerless to secure the reforms we have set out to win.

While leaving the next step to be decided by the Congress at its meeting in December next, Lala Lajpat Rai is personally in favour of abolishing the Secretary of State's Council altogether, as serving no useful purpose.

It is a citadel of bureaucsacy. It stands in the way of the government of India being reconstituted on proper lines and of Indian claims being considered. It can only be justified in its continued existence by making it an organ for the expression of Indian opinion. If it is not to be that, it is worthless. Either it should be abolished or Indian opinion should have adequate and effective representation upon it. And we hoped that might be achieved by allowing some form of election, at least as far as the Indian members are concerned.

THE DIFFICULTY OF THE INDIAN REFORMER

The difficulty of the situation is this. The present constitution of the Legislative Councils leaves much to be desired, in spite of the " reforms." The value of the municipal boards as popular assemblies is largely discounted by the preponderance of official members and Government nominees. Any sort of vigorous outside propaganda is hindered by the Press Act and the Public Meetings Act.

We are muzzled. We cannot bring any strong pressure

to bear upon the Government. It proves the ineffectiveness of ordinary political propaganda, and drives all agitation underground. Educated people can only take part in public life by speaking and writing, and our activities in this way are restricted to a degree that the English people cannot realise. The only other channel of service open to us is social service, and that is limited by the fact that there is little we can accomplish by means of reform from within.

THE DEMAND FOR SELF-GOVERNMENT

Self-government for India on the same lines as it has been granted to other parts of the British Empire is one of the ideals of the National Congress. Anglo-Indians say that it is impracticable. The extremists among the Indian Nationalists say that it is impossible: they do not believe that the British rulers of India will ever consent to it. The direction their propaganda takes is therefore obvious. They do not believe in the ideal of self-government within the Empire. They want absolute autonomy and independence. The moderate section among the Indian Nationalists are prepared to accept the continuation of British rule. They desire self-government within the Empire. We have already some sort of municipal franchise. It is limited, as I have shown. But it can be extended to the Councils and gradually developed. This is our answer to those who say that it is impracticable, We have no answer to those who say that it is impossible, and who point to the refusal of our very moderate claims for representation by the British rulers as evidence tha constitutional methods of agitation are futile.

It is admitted that the mass of uneducated Indian

opinion is not vocal, and that the only vocal section of the people is the educated class. But it is that class that leads the others. It is drawn from all classes, and represents all grades. From them the unrest spreads to the masses, as definite ideals and claims are more and more clearly and firmly formulated. And Lala Lajpat Rai's last word to the interviewer is that unless something substantial is done quickly to associate the Indian people more closely with the government of their own affairs, "the situation, already sufficiently serious, is likely to become more grave."

Mr. SYED HASAN IMAM

In the course of his Presidential address at The Bihar Special Provincial Congress held at Patna, on August 26, 1917, *Mr. Hasan Imam, spoke as follows*:—

Gentlemen:—I have always been of opinion that the education imparted to us in this country is calculated to impress upon us too much of our duties to the State but very little of our rights. Perpetual insistence on our duties to the State and its visible embodiment—the officials—is the one keynote of a foreign educational policy, and one sees it at the very first glance. For example in a book recently brought out by a member of the Indian Educational Service in this province—called *Select Passages on Duty to the State* for the purpose of 'reading, analysis and translation in schools and colleges' the learned compiler declares in the preface to it that the extracts collected 'have been chosen with a view to emphasising the duty we owe to the state and to one another.' Now I have nothing to say against and in fact much in favour of teaching our boys the duties they owe to one another, but I venture to think that infusing young minds with the notion that they but owe duties to the State, without teaching them in the same breath that the State also owes, in a corresponding measure, duties to its subjects is not to fit our young men to become self-respecting and useful citizens of the Empire. It is hardly fair to our young men to ransack classical writers on politics, from Plato and Aristotle to Mill and Spencer—as the compiler of the book in question has done—with a view to stuff their brains with passages on their duties to the State, without simultaneously enjoining on them the one great lesson our people stand badly in need of learning, that the State is for the benefit of the people and not the people for the benefit of the State, whether in India or in any other country. Viewed in this light it is not so much the people who owe duties to the State as the latter to the former. But unfortunately this very necessary teaching is not imparted to our young men either in schools or colleges or even when they have entered the world. The political atmosphere in this country, in which we live and move and have our being, is so redolent of 'Duty to the State' and laden with official vapour to such an extent that even meetings expressly called to record our loyalty to our Sovereign are not supposed to be able to do so unless presided over by a high executive official. It is therefore that in the absence of any insistence on the State's duties to the people, it devolves upon us to carry on as vigorous, active and earnest a constitutional agitation as we can with a view to teach the people the great lesson that the State exists for them and not they for the State. It was this lesson which our revered and patriarchal leader, Dadabai Naoroji, who has just gone to his rest, emphasised from the presidential chair of the Indian National Congress when he presided over it for the third and last time, at Calcutta, in 1906. His memorable words—so full of deep significance and earnest patriotism—may well be recalled by us at this time and laid to heart. Our great leader exhorted us in words of burning eloquence as follows :—

' Agitate, agitate over the whole length and breadth of India in every nook and corner. All India must learn the lesson of sacrifice of money and of earnest personal work. By doing that I am sure the British conscience will triumph and the British people will support the present statesmen in their work of giving India responsible self-government in the shortest possible period. We must have a great agitation in England as well as here. Agitate; agitate means inform. Inform, inform the Indian people what their rights are and why and how they should obtain them and inform the British people of the rights of the Indian people and why they should grant them. The organization, which I suggest, and which I may call a band of political missionaries in all the provinces will serve many purposes at once—to inform the people of their rights as British citizens, to prepare them to claim those rights by petitions and when the rights are obtained, to exercise and enjoy them."

In meeting to-day we are to some extent carrying out the mandate of our revered leader, who has been rightly designated the father of constitutional agitation in this country. The two points which the Provincial Congress Committee have thus kept in view in convening this session of the Congress are firstly, the declaration of Richard Cobden that 'repetition is the essence of agitation' and secondly, the lesson embodied in Herbert Spencer's famous dictum that alien truths can be forced on minds reluctant to receive them only by means of repeated iterations.

PERSISTENT AGITATION AND THE BUREAUCRACY

These two dicta, the first of the most persistent and the most successful of British constitutional agitators and the second of one of the greatest political thinkers of the 19th century, should constitute the watch-words of our public activities. I have not had the same advantage which some others in this province have had of coming in contact with the members of the great bureaucracy who have been the arbitors of our destinies for now over a century and a half, ever since that memorable date, 12th of August, 1765, on which the grant of the Dewany of Bengal and Behar was made by the Emperor Shah Alam to the East India Company. But in this official-ridden country where, as I have already pointed out, even demonstrations of loyalty are organized and presided over by officials no one can live without feeling sooner or later the impact of the Indian bureaucracy. Now as I fully believe that there is a soul of goodness in things evil. I shall be the last person to deny the virtues of the bureaucrats who have wielded and still wield the destinies of our country. These virtues are being so constantly dinned into our ears by themselves that it is not likely that we can forget them. The latest glorifier of bureaucratic self-complacency, a member of the Indian Civil Service, in his recently-published book called *The Economic Life of Bengal District*, sketches with a rare modesty the unparalleled achievements in this country of the great service of which he is a member, in the following passage:—'The Indian bureaucracy has supplied India with cheaper railway communications than any possessed by European countries, has provided for her the greatest irrigation works in the world, has created a judicial system which will bear comparison for fairness and expedition with any system elsewhere, has maintained order and security of life and property in the most unlikely conditions, has grapled successfully with widespread failure of crops and has attempted of late years the stupendous labour of providing an ignorant and densely populated country with a modern system of education and a modern system of sanitation. It has done all this at a cost which is an infinitely lighter burden upon the resources of a poor country than any of the Governments in Europe has placed upon the resources of a rich country.' Here are the alleged achievements of the Indian bureaucracy put by a member of that body presumably at the highest and certainly not at the lowest. I have no desire—since it is not germane to the subject before me—to find myself in controversy with the writer of the passage I have quoted for your special behoof, but what I desire to point out is that in this very flattering and almost idyllic picture of the achievements of the

Indian Civil Service—painted by the sympathetic hands of one interested in showing his own class in the most favourable light and in which the super-excellences of that body are brought into most prominent relief—there is no reference at all to any sense of responsiveness on the part of the civilian to the just aspirations of the Indians for what the Greeks called the 'higher things of life. That writer does not allege that, and it but goes to conclusively confirm us in our impression of the character of the Civilian administration as mechanical, unresponsive, and doctrinaire, in fact, as absolutely impervious to popular aspirations and to public opinion. Nor is it surprising since the very essence of the bureaucratic government is a belief in its own infallibility and its right to do for the people not what they want but what they ought to or are supposed to want. It is one of the well-established maxims in the science of character-study that the exercise of unchecked and irresponsible power inevitably corrupts some of the finer qualities of humanity and is calculated to tarnish, in the end, even the pure metal of which the Nietzcshean superman is made. When you have to deal with such a class of men, the only way, it seems to me, which is likely to be effective is to iterate and reiterate your demands with a force and intensity which cannot be overlooked or ignored. I do not subscribe to the view that such demands can be more properly made in our Legislative Councils. True I am at some disadvantage in speaking on the subjec since I have never aspired so far to a seat in either the Provincial or the Imperial Legislative Council. But I have had the benefit of the experience of several of my friends who have been members of the Councils and and their 'confessions' have comfirmed my view that our Legislative Councils—as at present constituted—can and do afford very little scope for the expression of the public opinion of the educated and advanced sections in the country. Regard being had to these two obvious facts, the limitations of our Legislative Councils and the absolute imperviousness of the bureaucracy to public criticism and popular demands, it behoves us to earnestly and seriously take to heart the exhortation of Dadabhai Naoroji to agitate, agitate and agitate on constitutional lines till our people from the Himalayas to Cape Comorin become permeated with one uniform idea that they have not only duties to discharge to the State but rights against it--the rights to think their thoughts aloud, the rights of free association and expression and above all the right to rule themselves on such lines as they believe will be conducive to good government, without let or hindrance from any foreign bureaucracy. It is in this view of the matter, that this Special Congress is calculated to serve a very useful purpose.

OUR ONE GOAL: HOME RULE FOR INDIA

It is because we are satisfied that there can be no political and economic progress in our land till the bureaucracy is replaced by popular legislatures with full control over the executive and the judiciary, that we have placed before us as the goal of our aspirations, the establishment of self-governing institutions in this country. It is idle to tell us that the bureaucracy have done for us this, that and the other, that they have given us good government with its concomitants of peace and contentment. Good government which the bureaucracy profess to have given us is no doubt better than no government but in the first place good government need to be necessarily synonymous with bureaucratic government. Even a fair-minded member of the Indian Civil Service.—Mr. Bernard Houghton—has had the candour to admit in his well-known work called *Bureaucratic Government* that 'the menace, the real peril, lies not in the grant of more popular government to. India; it lies in the continuance of the present bureaucratic system—a system which has served its purpose and which India has now outgrown.' We are grateful for this unequivocal admission in our favour by a retired Civilian but as a matter of fact we scarcely need any such outside support. Our knowledge of the deficiencies and limitations of the Indian bureaucray is too subjective to make us require any objective proof. The wearer whom his shoe pinches feels it but too keenly to need any confirmations on the point from the on-looker. We who have lived these many years under the administration of the Indian bureaucracy do but too well realize its inevitable shortcomings—the inelasticity of its system, the rigidity of its method, the soullessness of its administration, the super-sensitiveness to and impatience of even the most moderate criticism, the intense anxiety to retain, at all cost, the power and influence it has so long enjoyed and last but not least the passion for docile obedience subservience to its authority. These are realized in a more or less large measure in all parts of India, but in a somewhat backward province like ours they stand out in bold relief—especially the last. However it be, it is quite clear to us that now that we are demanding self-government, we shall not be placated by the good government offered to us by the Indian bureaucracy—be it howsoever best intentioned, conscientious or benevolent.

THE BUREAUCRACY AND OUR ASPIRATIONS

Such then is the situation facing us at present—on the one side a growing phalanx of educated and cultured Indians daily getting more and more qualified to manage their own affairs and desirous of coming into their own deeply dissatisfied with the present system of administration and the political constitution which affords hardly any scope for their talents, capabilities, and legitimate aspirations for administering their own affairs; on the other a close foreign bureaucracy actuated by strong *esprit de corps*, an unbending determination to preserve in their own hands all power in the State, and an inflexible resolve to cherish and maintain these great vested advantages which they have so long enjoyed. But there is nothing new in this. It is after all the repetition of what has transpired in every country in its onward march from bureaucracy to democracy. It is just what was occurred before our own eyes in China and Russia and we in India must, profiting by the examples before us, be fully prepared to pass through the necessary struggle—a settled political phenomenon—which precedes the birth of a new nation, for as no sentient being can be born without the pains of labour on the part of the mother so each people must undergo the process of travail incidental to its being born as a nation, with a political consciousness. Now there is no doubt in our mind that the Indian bureaucracy has outlived its day and outgrown our requirements and it must now be at once replaced by popular Government. But whenever we urge this plea we are met with the official reply:—'True, you are entitled to self-government in the fulness of time.' We concede it is—as Mr. Percy Lyon put it to a Calcutta audience shortly before he retired from the Executive Council of Bengal—'the inherent right of a nation to govern itself and Englishmen learn and understand that from their birth and it has been their policy from time immemorial.' But—and now comes the very important 'but'—'You are not yet fully qualified. You need still a long period of growth and culture. The growing child cannot be treated as we treat the adult. You require to be trained and disciplined before you can be entrusted with a full measure of liberty and the full responsibility belonging to man's estate.' I daresay you have all noticed these sentiments finding a place even in the otherwise statesmanlike declaration made in the House of Commons by the Right Hon. Mr. Montagu about the Indian reforms. The Secretary of State told us that 'the British Government and the Government of India'—mark 'the Government of India' also which itself is the great bureaucratic citadel—' must be the judges of the time and measure of each advance in conferring self-government on India.' Contrast this pronouncement of the Secretary of State with that of the Prime Minister, recently made with reference to the German colonies, at present in British occupation. Said the Right Hon. Mr. Lloyd George:—'The dominant factor in settling the fate of the German colonies must be the people's own desires and wishes and the leading principle is that the wishes of the inhabitants must be the superme consideration in the re-settlement—in other words the formula adopted by the Allies with regard to the disputed territories in Europe is to be applied equally in the tropical countries.' Any extended comment upon these two declarations—of the King-Emperor's Indian minister and his Prime Minister—would be but an act of supererogation. Obviously India, which in the recent memorable words of the Lord Bishop of Calcutta came under British Rule, 'by a series of conquests in which we (the British) have used Indian soldiers and had Indian allies is to be shown not even that consideration which is to be extended to the German colonies conquered during the present war. It is then at all surprising that holding the views he does as to 'training Indians in self-government,' the Metropolitan exclaimed 'that if we turn away from any such application of our principles to India, it is but hypocracy to come before God with the plea that our cause is the cause of liberty.' No gentlemen, we cannot and should not accept the view propounded by Mr. Montagu—while giving him full credit for the very best of motives and intentions—that the Government of India should be 'the judges of the time and measure' of our each advance towards self-government. True, he refers in this connection to the British Government also but we know from our past experience that that means on effect and substance nothing more than the acceptance of the views of the Government of India and the retired officials who occupy comfortable berths in that Cave of Adullam—the India office. We desire to remodel and reconstitute the Government of India and the provincial Governments by making them subject in all matters of administration and legislation to popular control, that is to subordinate the Executive to the views and wishes of popular legislatures—and yet it is the very instruments of our proposed reconstitution that are to be the judges of our capacity to do so! Verily Indian problems seem calculated to pervert the sense of logic even in great statesmen. Mr. Montagu's statement—if really acted up to—will but serve to confer on the Indian bureaucracy the additional power to hinder our progress, perhaps even more effectively than they can do at present. But the proposal has its humorous side which has not escaped the vigilant editor of the *Amrita Bazar Patrika*, who shrewdly remarks that 'if the custodian of a minor whose property he enjoys be given the privilege of determining his ward's age of majority, the latter will ever be in a state of minority.' There is great force and wisdom in these sagacious comments, and just as the declaration of the age of the ward's majority does not depend upon the wishes of the guardian but is fixed by law independent of the latter's self-interested opinion, so should the question of our capacity for each advance be determined by the British Parliament upon due enquiries made from time to time by means of Parliamentary committees, in consultation with the representatives of the National Congress and the Muslim League. Of one thing we are all sure, that if the Government of India and the British Government —which latter practically means the India Office —are to be the judges of our progress in self-government, the time will not have arrived till the crack of doom, when we may hope to attain even a fair—let alone a full—measure of self-government. This matter is in my opinion one of most vital importance and I can but hope that these observations of mine will assist you, to some extent, in formulating your views in your resolution on the subject.

'Apply any test that may be considered reasonable and you will find that the results of the Anglo-Indian administration are like the fabled apples on the shores if the dead-sea rich and tempting to the view but "ashes to the tastes."

THE REPLY TO REPRESSION

Now all this cannot conduce to peace and contentment and above all there can be no peace till Mrs. Besant and her two associates are released and restored to full liberty. Reforms may or may not be introduced in our constitution, commissions in the army may or may not be granted to Indians, Mr. Montagu may or may not come to confer with his Excellency Lord Chelmsford's Government—in fact whatever may not happen—but if I am certain of one thing it is this, that there shall be no peace in the land so long as Mrs. Besant and her associates remain interned. We want the Government to distinctly understand that we are not prepared to be content with any measure of self-government until Mrs. Besant, who is to us symbolical of all that is good, great, ennobling and vivifying in the Home Rule movement, is restored to our ranks to be able to preside over the next session of the Indian National Congress. If the Government are not aware of the true feeling of the country on the subject and the temper of the people the more is the pity, the more it is to their discredit. Already a wave for passive resistance is surging through the land and will—unless the Government realize even at this late hour their responsibilities in the matter—very probably carry everything before it. Now passive resistance is the last weapon of the constitutional agitator. It includes what is popularly known as boycott and comprises amongst other things the withholding of all co-operation till the wrong to be righted is duly redressed.

That it is a perfectly constitutional method of bringing moral pressure to bear upon the Government does not admit of any doubt. Sir Charles Russell—afterwards Lord Russell of Kallowen, Lord Chief Justice of England—in his address to the Parnell Commission dealt at length with the subject and in the course of it he observed that 'individual boycotting or boycotting in combination is neither actionable nor criminal.' At the same time, though a perfectly legal and constitutional weapon, resort to passive resistance requires careful consideration, and on this subject I cannot do better than read out to you what Mrs. Besant herself wrote in her paper *New India* in the issue of the 4th January, 1915—'The conditions of successful passive resistance are a clearly defined grievance deeply felt by the great majority of people, a public whose sympathy can be obtained, a small area in which practically all the people concerned exercise such resistance. Vague discontent, general dissatisfaction, these are not suitable for passive resistance. Moreover, there must be a reasonable hope of success within a comparatively brief time. In India none of the conditions are present. Indian conditions resemble those against which the suffragists contend in England—a mass of inert indifference which cannot be roused into sympathy. Therefore while respecting the handful of patriots who adopt this policy, we say quite definitely that passive resistance cannot be wisely and usefully employed in working for self-government. A handful of passive resisters in 300 millions of passive acquiescers is futile and their abstinence helps the bureaucracy.'. There is a deal of truth in these observations, though the Government would do well to take note that the acerbity of feeling in the country is now ever so much greater thanks to the policy of persistent repression, culminating in the internment of Mrs. Besant herself and her two associates—and that they should therefore so modify their policy as to give some assurance to the people that hereafter they will not be thwarted in their efforts at securing constitutional reforms. And I feel sure that the most signal proof the Government could give—one that will afford us the utmost satisfaction and gratification—is the immediate release of Mrs. Besant and Messrs. Arundale and Wadia.

THE PROMISED REFORMS AND OUR LINE OF ACTION

And now, gentlemen, I have done. I fear I have trespassed on your valuable time too long, but the vital importance to us of the problem of the reform of the Indian constitution and my desire to be of some little assistance to you in the discussion of the subjects which will be placed before you, is my apology for my having detained you. You are aware of the announcement made by Mr. Montagu in the House of Commons on the subject of Indian reforms including the grant of commissions to Indians in his Majesty's Indian Army. For this definite and distinct declaration of policy promising the establishment of self-government in this country, we are grateful to his Majesty's Government and not the less to Mr. Montagu himself—the reflex of whose true liberalism and genuine sympathy with our aspirations is visible in the terms of the announcement. I have already taken exception to that part of the statement which refers to the question of the fitness for which further advance to be judged practically by the Government of India. But though we have a right to complain of this part of the statement nevertheless you may be sure that no Government of India will be able to resist our demand if it will be backed up by the weight of our educational and moral progress in a larger and larger measure. The Government of India may be and is all powerful and very influential but the great principles of righteousness that govern this Universe are after all ever so much and immeasurably stronger than the strongest bureaucracy. It is but a few years back that Lord Morley declared his conviction that his object in introducing the Indian reforms was not to establish the germs of parliamentary government in India and it is that what we have now been practically promised by Mr. Montagu. However, all that is for time to come. It is sufficient for our present purposes that as the result of this conference with the Government of India, the heads of provincial Governments and administrations and the leaders of public opinion, Mr. Montagu had promised to introduce substantial reforms. For myself I have great hopes from Mr. Montagu, since he has always given evidence of a critical faculty keenly alive to the inherent limitations and inevitable deficiencies of the Indian bureaucracy. But a few days before he assumed his present office, he delivered a remarkable speech in the House of Commons, during the debate on the Report of the Mesopotamian Commission, and I will commend a careful perusal of it to your earnest attention. Never before in the history of Anglo-Indian administration the bureaucracy were subjected to such a searching, withering criticism by one who had held the high office of Parliamentary Under Secretary for India. Just think of his delicious description of the working of that *Sanctum Sanctorum*, that holy of holies of retired Anglo-Indians—the India Office—as 'an apotheosis of circumlocution and red tape beyond the dreams of any ordinary citizen.' Similarly he declared the Government of India as 'too wooden, too iron, too inelastic, too antediluvian' and added that he did not believe 'that any body could ever support the Government of India from the point of view of modern requirements,' since it 'was an indefensible system of Government.' It is this refreshing candour—the Indian bureaucrat will perhaps characterise it as brutal—that leads me to hope that the scheme which Mr. Montagu will evolve may satisfy our aspirations for the present. He knows that that feeler thrown out by his assistant—Lord Islington—in his address at Oxford has already been condemned, as the proposals outlined in it are singularly inept, inane and jejune. Nor can we in the light of the revelations made by the Hon. Mr. Srinivasa Shastry as to the circumstances under which our late lamented leader Mr. Gokhale prepared his scheme which has been recently published accept as suited to our present requirements the proposals outlined therein. But shortly Mr. Gokhale's suggestions constitute a pre-war document and the last three years have brought about such a tremendous moral and intellectual revolution that what might have suited us then cannot do so now. Thus we are driven to fall back upon our own scheme—that jointly evolved by the National Congress and the Muslim League. That scheme, therefore, represents for us, at present, our irreducible minimum of claims and while we shall be grateful to Mr. Montagu were he to give us more it is quite certain that we cannot be and shall not be content with anything less than what is set out in our scheme. That is our plain and emphatic demand.

OUR FUTURE DESTINY

Whether we shall get at present all what we want is not known to us, since the future is on the knees of the gods. But about one thing we should be under no delusion and that is that whether we get it now or later, to-day or to-morrow, we *shall* come into our birth right and nothing—nay, no power on earth—can keep us out of our inheritance, if only we ourselves are not stack in pressing our demands earnestly, forcefully and constitutionally on the attention of the great British democracy who are the real sovereign power in the State. For though the King-in-Parliament is the supreme power in the British State from the legal point of view, it is the democracy of Great Britain that is for all political purposes the master of even the Parliament. What is therefore, essential to our success is an agitation on a gigantic scale to convince the British democracy of the justice of our claims to self-government and the moment their leaders are satisfied of it they will unhesitatingly bring to bear upon the House of Commons the force at their disposal. Already our hands have been materially strengthened in pressing our claims by the recommendation made in the Minority Report of the Mesopotamian Commission by Commander J. C. Wedgwood M. P., who concludes it as follows:—"My last recommendation is that we should no longer deny to Indians the full privilege of citizenship but should allow them a large share in the government of their own country and in the control of that bureaucracy which in this war uncontrolled by public opinion, has failed to rise to British standards." It now remains for us to follow up this advantage by a sustained, persistent and vigorous constitutional agitation both in Britain and in this country and we should not be satisfied till we have eventually succeeded in storming the bureaucratic citadels at Whitehall, Simla and Delhi and installing in their places free, popular government in the memorable words of President Lincoln as 'Government of the people, for the people, by the people.' Then and then only shall the genius of our Motherland which did so much for human culture and civilization in the days of yore, shall again find full play for the true service of humanity. You might have read the testimony recently borne by the well-known writer, Mr. H. C. Wells, to the Indian mind, which he described as possessed ' of singular richness and singular delicacy with a wonderful gentleness—a mind that in spite of all, that it has done in the past is still destined to make its chief contribution to the human synthesis in the years that lie ahead.' We Indians fully share this view and hope but we are equally satisfied that if the approach of that day is to be hastened it will be by the early establishment of Home Rule in this land—since of the many evils of a foreign bureaucracy perhaps the greatest is its pernicious effect in stunting the development of the mind of the people it rules over, and in perverting their moral nature. But we fully believe that we are the heirs of a better and larger hope and shall yet rise in the scale of nations. It rests with us to hasten its realisation by our earnestness, patriotism, sincerity and above all by possessing an illimitable faith in the great destiny that awaits us in being constituted a self-governing member of the commonwealths composing the greatest federal Empire the world has yet known.—*Bande Mataram.*

SIR KRISHNA GUPTA

They were passing through very stirring times—very moving and distressing times. A small people, but proud and independent, had been wantonly attacked, trampled under foot, pillaged and ravaged by a remorseless enemy, and England, true to her traditions as the champion of liberty, and upholder of righteousness and justice, had rushed to her rescue, and with the help of noble Allies, was fighting for all that made for humanity. In that great world-wide conflict, England had been well supported by all parts of her Empire. Men from the distant marches—from the uttermost regions of the Seven Seas—had come forward to prove that Empire was a reality stronger than the ties of blood and kin, of race, of creed, and of colour. It had proved to be stronger than mere self-interest, stronger even than death itself. Truly, in the hour of trial the Empire had found itself. (Cheers). India, his own country, had not lagged behind. Side by side with their British comrades, Indian soldiers were fighting in every theatre of war. In Flanders they were by the side of the Canadians, in the Near East they were at the side of the Australians and the New Zealanders; in the Persian Gulf, in Mesopotamia, in East Africa, it was the Indian Army, both Indians and British, who were carrying on operations. Truly, it might be said that India was bearing her part—her fair share in the fray. This was as it should be. India was the corner-stone of the Empire.

THE REAL EMPIRE

It was the possession of India that gave the British Crown the title and justification of calling the British Dominions an Empire. It was a curious fact that there was a disposition to draw a distinction between Empire and Empire. In the Press and in public and private conversations the talk was of the British Empire—Imperial, united. But the British people and the self-governing colonies did not recognise their ruler and sovereign as their Emperor; he was only their King, and it was solely in reference to India that they found the title employed. King George was Emperor of India, but only King of the United Kingdom and the Dominions. He did not profess to understand what was behind that. It might be that, although Empire was good enough, there was something uncanny about the word Emperor, and, judging from what was happening in other Empires, there might be some truth in that. (Laughter.)

THE SETTLEMENT AFTER THE WAR

The Colonies, as they knew, were very vigorous and pushful, and rather more vocal than themselves. They had already started the idea that, when the war was over, and a final settlement took place, they were to be directly consulted. They were quite right. But India also ought to have direct representation. (Cheers.) The Colonial request had met with a favourable response in the highest quarters. But when the turn of India came, they were told that they were represented by the Secretary of State for India. If that were the case, were not the Dominions also represented by the Colonial Secretary, by their Agents-General, their High Commissioners? If India was not to be content with the Secretary of State, why should not the Colonies be equally content with their representation? But India very properly also claimed to be directly represented. The Secretary of State was a Cabinet Minister with the collective responsibilities attaching to that office. He was like a butterfly fluttering from flower to flower; he passed from office to office and he had no permanent connexion with India. Hence if the Colonies were to be directly represented on Imperial questions, India had a right to the same treatment. At the recent meeting at the Guildhall, Mr. Bonar Law had said:—

> The dominions of the British Empire have not been created by the war but the conditions have been changed by the war. It is my hope, and if it is taken up in earnest while the metal is glowing red hot in the furnace of the war I believe it may be done, that as result we may see a Parliament of the British Empire in which every part of the Empire in proportion to its resources and numbers will share in the duty and honour of ruling the British Empire.

India wished for nothing more; if that were done, they would be satisfied.

A FUTURE OF SELF-GOVERNMENT

He would not be doing his duty did he not say a few words upon the great benefits which the British connexion had brought to India. But for that connexion, their condition would have been very much worse, and they therefore wished for the continuance of British rule. If India was at any time to be democratically governed, it must be under the guidance of Great Britain. To educated Indians, to all classes of thinking men, the British connexion was an absolute necessity for India. They were proud of the connexion. It was English education which had given them ideas of liberty. It was the English language in which the various peoples of India communicated with each other. Much of late had been said in deprecation of education, much suspicion had been attached to the educated Indian classes; they had been accused of disloyalty. But this great war had shown that the educated classes were loyal to the backbone—(cheers)—and to their credit must be placed the present peaceful state of the country. (Loud cheers.) He hoped that under the British connexion, under the guidance of England, the land of liberty, his country and their country would be raised from its present state of degradation, and become one of the great units of the Empire. When England had trained the people of India in the art of self-government, when she received complete autonomy, when they had the various Provinces as separate States, controlled by a Central or Federal Government, presided over by a representative of the

British Crown, preferably one of the reigning family, then, and then only, would England have discharged the great task imposed on her by Providence. She would reap her reward in the consolidation of the Empire, the stability of which would never be shaken, and in the everlasting affection and contentment of a people amongst whose faults certainly ingratitude is not one. That day, let us hope, would soon come. (Cheers).

SIR SATYENDRA PRASAD SINHA

The following are the extracts of an interview with the representative of the Christian Monitor, Calcutta :—

Asked whether it was probable that the Home Government had come to any decision as to the future of India after the war, Sir Satyendra expressed himself as doubtful. "I could wish that they had made up their minds about it," he remarked, "for I cannot help thinking that the longer they hesitate to declare themselves, the less likelihood is there that they will come to a bold and statesmanlike decision.

"India, of course, has got a great deal that she wanted. She is making steady progress socially and industrially, and she has the prospect, in the dim and distant future, of obtaining self-government. But that is not enough. India is painfully conscious of rigid limitations which come into play the moment she aspires to develop beyond a certain point. Indians have their own ideas of self-expression. Repress those ideas, and you dwarf us, even granting that you offer us more perfect ideas of your own. In the matter of government, for example, it is, from our point of view, less important now that we should have a perfect government than that we should govern ourselves."

HOW TO PROCEED

When we speak of self-government, not one of us ever contemplates any separation between Great Britain and India. We gladly recognise that the ties between the two countries are too strong to break, and, if they were not, we would not have them broken. Let the British Government retain the amplest powers of veto over all our affairs. But, subject to that veto, let us have now an instalment of self-government on colonial lines, and let the basis of these concessions be broadened as rapidly as we fit ourselves for their extension. Of course, we shall make mistakes—there will be many and big mistakes. Atrocities even may occur—never mind, even they will not prove that you have been wrong to trust us. Only be bold, and the outcome will be not merely a contented and prosperous India, but an India which will be ten times as strong a British asset as she is to-day.

"I am no sentimentalist. I do not rest these proposals merely on grounds of abstract justice to India, but also upon considerations of the highest expediency to Great Britain. It is to Britain's interest that India should be happy, prosperous, and self-governed. Such an India will be a source of strength to the Empire in every way. India only asks to be trusted. Surely she has earned a right to that."

"We are sometimes told that, because it took you centuries of struggle and development to work out your political freedom, therefore we must be content to progress at the same deliberate pace. Are we, then, to derive no benefit from your experience? Surely you were working out the problem of free institutions for all mankind. Railways were started in England less than a century ago, but you have not insisted on making us wait for them as long as you had to wait. I know Englishmen are cautious by nature and temperament, but extreme caution is sometimes no less harmful than its opposite. And for this purpose—that is, cautioning, as it were, against extreme caution—I would like to read to you a passage from Ruskin." Here Sir Satyendra took up a little book which lay on the table and read as follows: "All measures of reformation are effective in exact proportion to their timeliness. Partial decay may be cut away and cleansed, incipient error corrected; but there is a point at which corruption can no more be stayed, nor wandering recalled."

"GIVE REAL SELF-GOVERNMENT"

"What I am contending for," "is not merely a matter of better treatment for individuals. It is not enough to offer So-and-so a high position in your Government. You should give us real self-governing powers."

"Is it your opinion," he was asked, "that the Indians have made the best possible use of the limited powers of self-government which have already been conceded?"

"It is my opinion," he replied, "that, considering the very limited opportunities afforded to them of schooling themselves in the art and practice of self-government, they have done extraordinarily well. If we are to wait for true self-government until we are perfect, we shall wait for ever. In the words of Dr. Johnson, 'Nothing will ever be attempted if all possible objections must be first overcome.' "

"What," next enquired the "Christian Science Monitor" representative, "would be the effect of a self-governing India upon the position of non-official European residents?"

"Please remember," answered Sir Satyendra, "that we always postulate the continuance of British rule. That is a guarantee that we shall always welcome the British merchant and rejoice in his prosperity. For a long time to come we must look up to the British as our guides and mentors. As I said in my presidential address to the National Congress at Bombay, no other race could or would have done the work of the English in India. Let England trust us, and she will never regret it."

THE HON. RAJAH OF MAHMUDABAD

The Hon'ble the Rajah of Mahmudabad, who was interviewed at Simla, by a press correspondent on the present political situation in India, said:—

We thank the Prime Minister for appointing Mr. Montagu as Secretary of State for India. We know that he is a friend of the people of India and he knows India from the inside. We welcome his pronouncement in the House of Commons, as this is the first time in the History of British India that it has been definitely laid down that the British policy is to raise India to the status of a self-governing partner of the Empire at an early date. I appreciate fully the importance of Mr. Montagu's decision to come to India and examine Indian problems on the spot. But we must prepare ourselves to do all we can to enable him to understand what exactly the real situation is, and I might as well say here as emphatically as I can that we intend to support, and support as firmly and unflinchingly as possible, the Congress League reform scheme. While on the visit of Mr. Montagu, I wish to take this opportunity to declare my rooted conviction that the projected visit might be more likely to produce the desired result if a general amnesty were declared, and political prisoners were released. One of the chief difficulties no doubt which any Indian reformer would have to face and successfully overcome is the adjustment in as happy a manner as possible of the relations between the Ruling Chiefs and the British Indian Government. While not desirous of entering into the question fully, I would lay it down as a guiding principle that unless we of British India are allowed to have a voice in the affairs of the Native States, the Princes should not be given any hand in shaping our destinies at this critical juncture. I have great hopes in the statesmanship and liberal instincts of our present Viceroy.

Mr. MOHAMED ALI

SPEECH DELIVERED WHILE IN ENGLAND

Mr. Mohamed Ali, who was greeted with cheers, said that he and his colleague were very grateful for the kindness which had been extended to them during their visit. On a previous occasion when in England he learnt how much untruth was embodied in Kipling's lines, "East is East, and West is West and never the twain shall meet," and the impressions he then gained had been fully confirmed by his experience of the last few weeks. Speaking of his mission, he said that, though they had met with many disappointments, they did not despair. They had found a great deal of ignorance prevalent regarding India, but they had also realised that much of it had in recent years been dispelled, and he would suggest to those of his hearers who might be authors that, if they found they could not always get sufficient inspiration out of the threadbare themes of the West, there were vast worlds in the East from which they could gather fresh inspiration. There was a good deal of virgin soil which novelists could till but which journalists who were always in a hurry could only scratch. It was to the author he looked for the dissemination of information with regard to Eastern problems. It had always been a matter of wonder to him how the forty-five millions of people who inhabited Great Britain could be so oblivious of the fact that they had a big moral trust in connexion with the hundreds of millions who inhabited their Eastern Empire. Western people had lately been telling them that practically a ban had been put on the larger part of creation a sinister ban of colour—a ban which was to make the Asiatic an inferior being—they seemed to forget that Jesus Christ was an Asiatic, and that they had got almost all their civilisation from the East. The people of India had had Western education and Western ideas forced upon them; as a result they had learned self-respect, they had come to realise the dignity of their race, and they had come to know, too, that they must live their own life and work out their own destiny. They did not believe that Providence would be so unjust as to place a ban upon the larger half of humanity. If they felt dissatisfied with the present condition of things, was it to be said that they were consequently disloyal? Had they wanted to light the fiery cross, they could have done it much better in their own country than by coming to England. Had they wanted to embarrass the Government, they would not have made their speeches on public platforms; they would have worked underground. He wished to utter one word of warning, and that was, if they did not take care of their large Empire in India, if they were not true to the great trust which Providence had placed in their hands, they would run serious risk of losing India. In his opinion, the British connexion was indispensable for India's growth and progress. He was loyal to his Majesty, not because he was a British-born subject, but because he believed the British connexion meant the uplifting of his country, of his race, and of his religion. For these objects it was necessary that the British should be in India. He and his colleague came to this country to lay their case before the British public. In the first instance, it was their desire to see Ministers and to whisper into their ears the matters which it was sought to impress upon the Government. But they had not been able to see the Ministers they desired to meet. They would return and try again. When he was in Edinburgh the other day he was shown seven gates at Edinburgh Castle in close proximity to one another, which an enemy seeking entrance had to pass in turn. He could only say that if there were seventy gates preventing their access to British Ministers they intended to knock and knock again at each until they were opened. And although on this occasion they had not been able to reach the ear of Lord Crewe, they had, at any rate, succeeded in reaching the ears of those who ruled Lord Crewe, of those who were his masters, of those who had a vote to give. When they got back to their own country they would not wish to excite their fellow-countrymen by telling them how they had been compelled to return without seeing Ministers, but they would, at any rate, feel confident that, if Ministers would not see them, they would at any rate, have to hear them, both in this country and in India.

KHAN BAHADUR SARFARAZ HUSSAIN KHAN

In the course of his speech as President of the Behar Provincial Conference, Khan Bahadur Sarfaraz Hussain Khan said:—

I have followed with advantage the excellent precedent of my predecessors in seeking the co-operation of men of light and leading in the province by requesting them to favour me with their views and sentiments, and I am extremely grateful to such of my friends as have thus assisted me with useful suggestions. I shall utilize them as well as I can and—without the least desire to minimise my own responsibility—I feel all the better fortified that I am supported by the views of united Behar in what I am going to say on some of the current questions agitating the public mind in the province.

"It is a grievance of a very long standing—this of the practical emasculation of the higher classes of our people. It is morally indefensible, politically inexpedient and is at the root of much legitimate discontent which a wise Government would do well to remove."

The Secretary of State for India has announced in the House of Commons the decision of His Majesty's Government to remove the bar which has hitherto precluded the admission of Indians to the commissioned rank in his Majesty's Army and steps are accordingly being taken respecting the grant of commissions to nine Indian Officers belonging to native Indian land forces who have served in the field in the present war and whom the Government of India recommended for this honour in recognition of their services. Their name will be notified in the London Gazette and in the same Gazette they will be posted to the Indian army. The Secretary of State and the Government of India are discussing the general conditions under which Indians should in future be eligible for commissions. In due course the Army Council will be consulted with a view to the introduction of a carefully considered scheme to provide for the selection of candidates and for training them in important duties which will devolve upon them.

For years I gave the best of what God has given me to loyal co-operation with those in whose hands Providence has placed our destinies, but I feel bound to confess that of late the conviction has been growing upon me more and more that while co-operation with the officials is good, self-dependence and self-reliance are even better and that while good Government, such as has been established in this country by our British fellow-subjects, is to be appreciated and supported, yet Self-Government for India within the Empire would be even immeasurably better and should, therefore, be sought after by every constitutional means at our disposal. It is in the fulness of this conviction that I stand before you to-day as an avowed Home Ruler so that the few years that may yet be vouchsafed to me by Providence may be devoted to the service of my Motherland. I fear I may shock the delicate sensibilities of a few friends,—for whose views I have great respect—by declaring myself at the very outset as a Home Ruler who believes that India is even to-day quite fit for enjoying a fair measure of Self-Government—popular control over her administrative and legislative machinery. But I cannot help it. Apart from the fact that the conviction I have come to entertain is now shared by the vast bulk of educated Indians throughout the length and breadth of our country, there is the additional and even more important reason for my putting it in the forefront of my address, namely, that is the result of my life-long experience of public affairs. Even if my views on this most momentous question were not shared by my countrymen but, I stood alone in holding it, I would nevertheless have felt bound to press it on you, for as William Morris happily puts it :—

Stand upright, speak thy thought, declare
The truth thou hast, that all may share.
Be bold, declare it everywhere.
They only live who dare.

But when I find that the demand for Self-Government is echoed from end to end in this country, and that all classes and communities are united in its insistence as the first plank in Indian progress, I feel doubly strengthened in asking you to press it, with all the earnestness and enthusiasm you may command, on the attention of His Majesty's Government, and to strain every nerve in securing it by constitutional methods, buoyed up with the conviction that good government can never be a proper substitute for Self-Government.

"All demonstrations of the virtues of a foreign bureaucracy, though often conclusive, are as useless as demonstrations of the superiority of artificial teeth, glass eyes, silver wind-pipes and patent wooden legs to the natural products."

And here I would like to explain that our fight is with the system and not with the holders of the office. It is a mere accident at present that by far much the larger number of the members of the Indian Civil Service are British and Irish. Yet, if the whole of the Indian Civil Service consisted of Indians and Indians alone, our demand for Self-Government would be quite as keen and insistent, for we are against being ruled by a bureaucracy whether native or foreign, whether Indian or alien.

As a matter of fact, the alleged unfitness of our people has no existence apart from the Anglo-Indian mind which sees what it desires to see. It is idle to attempt to argue into conviction men or classes whose judgments are warped by prejudices incidental to threatened encroachments on their vested interests. To such I can do no better than present the following passage from Macaulay's famous Essay on Milton :—
"Many Politicians of our time are in the habit of laying it down as a self-evident proposition that no people ought to be free till they are fit to use their freedom. The maxim is worthy of the fool in the old story who

resolved not to go into the water till he had learnt to swim." "If men are to wait for liberty," continues Macaulay, "till they have become good and wise in slavery, they may indeed wait for ever."

I have been too long connected with our public affairs not to know that in a country such as ours considerations of communal representation cannot be brushed aside whether in the public services or in the constitution of our Legislative Councils. At the same time, I feel certain that we have reached a stage in our political evolution when we should declare that so far, at any rate, as the few very high executive and judicial offices are concerned, they should be offered to the absolutely best men amongst us without regard to their religious persuasion. It was no doubt declared by Lord Morley that he would not make the Executive Councillorship a see-saw between the Indian communities. But such has been the case in actual practice, just what Lord Morley reprobated as a see-saw. If the Government believe that no one sees through this little game of theirs they are very greatly mistaken indeed. In this connection I may quote an extract from a leading article in a recent issue of the *Statesman* which will speak for itself:—

"When Raja Kishori Lall Goswami retired, it was thought necessary to appoint a Mahomedan as his successor, though Lord Morley had definitely laid down the rule that in this part of the public service the rotation of religions was not to be taken into account."

As the appointments are made at present, a member of the Executive Council must feel that he owes his appointment not so much to his personal qualification as to the accident of his belonging to a particular religious community. Apart from this consideration there is the other very grave objection to the present practice that the Indian Councillor appointed on communal considerations is likely to be influenced in his work by the feeling that he sits there as the representative of the particular community to which he belongs and not as that of the whole province or the country. It is, therefore, highly expedient that the selection should be made from the most qualified Indians available—in the province or the country as the case may be—so that the Indian Councillor may be a broad-minded and enlightened public man imbued not with communal but territorial patriotism and possessing the confidence of all classes, by reason of his knowledge and experience of public affairs in general.

SHEIKH MUSHIR HOSAIN KIDWAI OF GADIA

THE DEMAND FOR SELF-GOVERNMENT

Everyone who has studied the problem in India is aware that it is the Civil Service, with its vested interests, which constitutes the chief obstacle to reform. Under the present system, the bureaucracy frames the laws and regulates the finances exactly as it pleases. And, so long as the Viceroy remains under the domination of the Civil Service, it is useless to imagine that even a Ripon or a Hardinge can undertake any genuine step forward in the direction of progress. I hold that it is only from this country that real constitutional changes in the nature of self-government can be expected. It is, therefore, most desirable that a deputation of Indian publicists should come to England in order to prepare the public here for the time when the claims of India must be discussed in connexion with the re-settlement of the Empire. The memorandum which has been presented to the Viceroy should be circulated to every member of both Houses of Parliament.

It has been stated that the signatories to the memorandum do not include any representatives of the "military caste" or of backward provinces. But

India does not seek transition through violent methods, and the support of the "military caste" is unnecessary. It is not revolution that is demanded, but reform,—radical, indeed but within sound constitutional limits. Nevertheless, the choice of the character of agitation is still, to a large extent, in the power of the educated Indians and the British public. Even now, in one of the provinces of India, the life of the leader of the constitutional party is being threatened by the anarchists. Self-government is the only concession that can avert the danger and satisfy the awakened consciousness of India.

Mr. J. S. COTTON

PROPHECY OF HOME RULE FOR INDIA

'The Future of India' of 'India' by Mr. J. S. Cotton (brother of Sir Henry Cotton) in *Colonies and Dependencies*, of the English Citizen series, published in 1883:—

'In India we have hitherto failed to look the facts fairly in the face. Inconsistent theories of our position there require to be reconciled, so that some deliberate policy may be enunciated, and acted upon. Englishmen in India are for the most part too deeply immersed in details to find time to formulate the principles of a new polity. The more incumbent is it for Englishmen at home, upon whom the responsibility ultimately rests, to ask themselves the question—What are we doing in India? Ought we to contemplate the existing connection as permanent, and merely attempt to alleviate the grievances that the nature of the case or ourselves have caused? Or ought we to regard the emancipation of India as the final aim of our continued presence there, to proclaim it as our duty, and to fit our policy so as to hasten its accomplishment? And here it may be observed that 'the emancipation of India' need not necessarily involve a total severance from the British Crown, though it would involve the destruction of English supremacy and the grant of a large measure of local independence. Home-Rule for India, as Home

Rule has been already conceded to Canada and the Australian colonies, is by no means inconsistent with the unity of the empire—least of all when we anticipate what the empire will probably be like fifty years hence. And we can press the analogy somewhat closer. Canada is a sort of confederacy; neither Australia nor South Africa has yet entered into the political stage of confederation. India, on the other hand, is only united in external show. In her case Home Rule would mean the restitution of local independence to twenty different provinces of states, which might well find their common head in England.'

Mr. E. S. MONTAGU

In the course of his speech on the Mesopotamian Commission Mr. E. S. Montagu said:—

As a goal I see a different picture! I see the great Self-Governing Dominions and Provinces of India organised and co-ordinated with the great Principalities, the existing Principalities—and perhaps new ones—not one great Home Rule country, but a series of Self-Governing Provinces and Principalities, federated by one Central Government. But whatever be the object of your rule in India, the universal demand of those Indians whom I have met and corresponded with is that you should state it. Having stated it, you should give some instalment to show that you are in real earnest, some beginning of the new plan which you intend to pursue that gives the opportunity of giving greater representative institutions in some form or other to the people of India, of giving them greater control of their Executive, of remodelling the Executive—that affords you the opportunity of giving the Executive more liberty from home, because you cannot leave your harassed officials responsible to two sets of people. Responsibility here at home was intended to replace or to be a substitute for responsibility in India. As you increased responsibility in India you can lessen that responsibility at home.

But I am positive of this, that your great claim

to continue the illogical system of Government by which we have governed India in the past is that it was efficient. *It has been proved to be not efficient.* It has been proved to be not sufficiently elastic to express the will of the Indian people; to make them into a warring Nation as they wanted to be. The history of this War shows that you can rely upon the loyalty of the Indian people to the British Empire—if you ever before doubted it! If you want to use that loyalty, you must take advantage of that love of country which is a religion in India, and you must give them that bigger opportunity of controlling their own destinies, not merely by Councils which cannot act, but by control, by growing control, of the Executive itself. Then in your next War—if we ever have War—in your next crisis, through times of peace, you will have a contented India, an India equipped to help. Believe me, Mr. Speaker, it is not a question of expediency, it is not a question of desirability. Unless you are prepared to remodel in the light of modern experience, this century old and cumbrous machine, then, I believe, I verily believe, that you will lose your right to control the destinies of the Indian Empire.

COMMANDER J. C. WEDGEWOOD, M. P.

Writing in his letter to the Home Rule League, Madras, Commander J. C. Wedgewood, M. P., says:—

Two new facts have brought Indian Home Rule into practical politics. The first is the wonderful result of giving Home Rule to the Boers of South Africa; the second is the Russian Revolution, with the inspiration that it gives to all subject people, with its hint to England that if we would remain the leading exponents of democracy, we too must do our part and subordinate old selfish aims.

The objections that the Bureaucracy raise are these. They say that the Colonial Home Rule would lead to corruption, and to inefficiency. The Report of the Mesopotamia Commission destroys the "efficiency" excuse; no uncontrolled Bureaucracy can ever be efficient. Public criticism and control alone can keep a Bureaucracy in check. As for "corruption,"—why, it is better to be even corrupt than to be servile.

What I have suggested is that the British Government should lay it down that Colonial Home Rule is the end they have in view though it may take even 50 years to complete the process. They should lay down the stages and the dates when each successive stage will become operative, provided that the previous stage works satisfactorily. The stages might be of the following nature: the power of imposing certain taxes for purposes desired by India or the provinces then complete control of the purse; free direct election and some representation; then full representative Government; lastly full Responsible Government;—all combined with real popular education. Whether the Province or the Nation be taken as the unit seems to me to be immaterial, provided you in India create and preserve the national spirit as a driving power.

Any man who sets himself up to oppose absolute Government incurs great risks. The loss of employment and promotion, petty persecution, even the loss of fortune and freedom; all these you may have to face. In proportion as your sacrifices are great so will your reward be. But keep your hands clean of murder and you will have the respect and honour of all that is best in this country and of millions throughout the world who believe in liberty. I hope the struggle need not be very long. My nation, which supported the Italian against the Austrian, the Pole against the Russian, which has fought with a single mind in this War, will not long allow itself to remain the oppressor of a nation that can make sacrifices. But you must not trust others alone: it rests with you to make the sacrifices.

In any case I salute you, the newest soldiers in an old fight; and I hope that a common cause may make us no longer aliens but brothers. We may not in our time achieve success (for there is no real end), but we can hand on the torch, burning brightly, to the next generation—and believe me, it is some satisfaction to do it in so goodly a company.

Dr. JOHN POLLEN, C.I.E.

THE LOYALTY AND DEVOTION OF INDIA

A large audience attended the Congregational Church, West Hill, Dartford, (November 29), 1915 when Dr. John Pollen, C.I.E., gave an address on "The Loyalty and Devotion of India."

There were (said Dr. POLLEN) five facts regarding India which seemed not to be fully realised by the British public. The first was that there was no such country as India in the sense of its being one nation. India was made up of many different nations and included races and peoples in every stage of advance of civilisation. The second fact was that India was not a conquered country, or rather that the Indians were not a subject people. They had not been subdued by British artillery or bayonets, but by something far higher, for they had come under British domination by consent and freely and voluntarily acquiesced in British control. The right policy then was to trust the Indian people all in all, for in India "Faith and Unfaith could ne'er be equal powers." The third great fact was that the peoples of India on the whole were devotedly loyal; fidelity to the salt of their King-Emperor being their leading characteristic. Of course, there was unrest in India as in any growing community. There were some turbulent spirits in the land and German intrigue had stirred up the dying embers of anarchism; but the intellectual and advanced classes of India, all the warrior castes and clans, and the whole of the agricultural population were whole-heartedly devoted to the King-Emperor and would shed their blood freely in the cause for which Great Britain was fighting. Millions of men and money could be raised in India to resist the common foe. The fourth fact to be realised was that the Indian Army did not consist exclusively of Sikhs and Gurkhas, but of many thousands of Dogras, Pathans, Baluchis, Rajputs, Mahrattas, and Madrassees, to say nothing of Afghans and other martial tribes on the frontiers. The magnificent way in which the Indian Chiefs with their Armies had rallied round the Flag was already a matter of history and the splendid endurance and bravery of the Indian troops at the fronts had been testified to by the British Commanders directing operations against the Hun on three Continents. The fifth fact to be borne in mind was that Indians were not "black men," and that nothing could be more insulting than to allude to or speak of them as "niggers." Only mischievous and ignorant people ever thought of using such language with regard to our Indian fellow-subjects.

As subjects of our Empire, Indians were entitled to the same privileges as ourselves, and under the Proclamations of the Great Queen, of King Edward the Seventh, and of King George the Fifth, Indians had the same rights as ourselves; "Leave to live by no man's leave underneath the law." The present war, it was to be hoped, had put an end for ever to "Top-dogism" and "D——d niggerism." In his opinion at the present moment the best thing for India would be that Lord Hardinge, a Governor-General who understood the people and was loved by them, should be continued in his Viceroyalty until the end of the war. If this could not be arranged it would be no bad thing to send Sir Edward Carson out as Governor-General; he was a warm-hearted Irishman and would soon learn to understand and appreciate the devoted loyalty even of the Home Rulers of India! At any rate, he would learn that there were other places in the world besides Ulster.

Dr. V. H. RUTHERFORD, M. P.

INDIA AND SELF-GOVERNMENT

An address on " Home Rule for India " was given by Dr. V. H. Rutherford, (June 30), 1916 at a meeting of the London Indian Association.

Mr. Syed Hossain, who was in the chair, introduced Dr. Rutherford as an old and staunch friend, who, both in and out of Parliament, had consistently served the cause of India. Dr. Rutherford's was no new-found infatuation for the rights and liberties of India. He had long been associated with those with whom the principle of self-government for India was a living faith.

Insisting that the time was appropriate for the discussion of the question of India's future, when Indians were sacrificing both their lives and their money in a war for national freedom, Dr. Rutherford advocated the setting up of provincial parliaments, with a central imperial legislature in which the so called " Native States " would be represented. All the members of these bodies should be elected on a franchise to be settled by Indians. At the same time the old village councils should be restored and Municipal Councils and district boards re-organised upon an elective basis. He would apply the principle of Home Rule strictly to the Civil Service. Indians should administer their own country. The present form of Government in India was pure despotism: and it was the worst in the world, however qualified it might be by benevolence. Arguments might, of course, be advanced against his proposals. It would be said that Hindus and Mahomedans were mutually antagonistic; but the signs of the times were all in favour of co-operation between the two great communities. The All-India Moslem League and the National Congress were about to meet in conference, and were united in a common desire to achieve the national aspiration. Next, it was urged by critics of the type of Mr. Balfour, that parliamentary government was not adaptable to India, because of the many races which inhabited the country. The suggestion was worthy of those who had denounced the grant of a constitution to South Africa as "a dangerous experiment." Again, it was pleaded that India was not fit for self-government. What a melancholy reflection this was upon British rule! It had been said so often that the English were in India to teach Indians to rule themselves, and yet after a century and a-half it was to be acknowledged that they had failed. As a matter of fact, he (Dr. Rutherford) had visited Baroda, which was administered entirely by Indians, and had found it better governed than any portion of India governed by Britons. He need only remind them of the one matter of free and compulsory education, in which Baroda was far ahead. Liberty, as Mr. Gladstone had said, alone fitted men for liberty. Surely Indians were as fit to govern themselves as Serbs, Bulgars and Greeks. Another favourite argument was that with self government India would fall a prey to some foreign Power. But it was self-government within the British Empire for which India was striving. Great Britain would be India's protector, just as much as she was the protector of Australia and Canada and South Africa. The Indian Army must be officered and commanded by Indians, and would then be ready to defend its own frontiers. How was the end to be achieved ? Indian Nationalists must develop the spirit of patriotism in India itself and at the same time strive to enlighten the British democracy as to the justice of their demand. That demand must be pressed by constitutional means, and by these alone; and he hoped that British statesmanship, taught by the lesson of Ireland, would prove equal to the occasion. Self-government had kept Canada, Australia, New Zealand, and South Africa within the British Empire, and it would do the same for India.

Mr. SIDNEY WEBB

BRITISH POLICY IN INDIA

In the course of a valuable article on "The Guardianship of the Non-Adult Races" in the "New Statesman," writes Mr. Sidney Webb on the subject of official practice in India as contrasted in the historic pledges made since 1858.

"We declare that we seek in India no advantage for England or its inhabitants; that our aim is exclusively the advancement and welfare of India and of the British Empire as a whole; that we will allow no considerations of creed or colour or race to interfere with the selection of the persons best fitted to fill the administrative posts. Unfortunately, as it seems, these principles are not always acted on, or are so changed by being put in operation as to be indistinguishable from quite an opposite set of principles. It is not difficult to meet Englishmen (and especially Englishwomen) of the governing class—including, we suspect, half the Indian Civil Service itself—who avowedly believe that 'England' holds India by the sword, and quite justifiably benefits by its possession, in salaries for its sons and profits for its traders; that anything tending to diminish these perquisites of Empire for the benefit of India itself must, of course, be resisted; that it is unnecessary, and indeed impracticable, to allow Indian public opinion to influence the administration; that it is not the advancement, improvement, or development of the Hindoo that we ought to promote by education or otherwise, but his remaining in the present tutelage that we find profitable to ourselves; and that, in particular, the admission of any greater proportion of educated Indians into the Civil Service of their own country—not to say the promotion of any such Indian official, however highly qualified to be Lieutenant-Governor of a Province—must, as calculated to diminish the authority of the English, be absolutely prevented. Unfortunately, as it seems to us, there is not in the Government of India any definite and persistent choice between these alternative policies. There is, in all the million details of Indian administration, too little real regard for the declarations of the King-Emperor, and too much acceptance of the opposite policy. The Secretary of State for India does not, as a matter of fact, allow the Government of India to settle the Indian Customs Tariff, or even its internal taxation, with reference solely to the interests of India and the British Empire as a whole; the Government of India does not set itself to organise Indian education in such a way as to produce the greatest advancement of the Indian, either physically, mentally or morally. When Lord Hardinge last year absolutely forbade to the natives of India the Boy Scout Movement, in any shape or form, he was not acting sincerely in the interests of the better physical and moral training of the Hindoo race, the virility of which the Government is not really anxious to promote; when, as happened lately, the officially dominated Universities of India, together with the Provincial Education Departments, prescribed, for the young men's reading, Charlotte Yonge's novels and Cowper's letters to the displacement of Macaulay and Burke, they were not acting single-mindedly, as universities ought to do, in the interest of their students' intellectual development; when the British Government declares that the Indian Civil Service is open to the competitive examination of all British subjects irrespective of race or colour, it is behaving disingenuously in adding, to this apparently literal fulfilment of Queen Victoria's proclamation, the limiting proviso that only those persons will be eligible (and then not for the highest posts) who can travel thousands of miles from their own country to sit, in a narrow street off Piccadilly, at an examination deliberately so devised as enormously to favour those candidates who have been through a particular curriculum at the University of Oxford. To the Socialist it seems as if a large proportion of the Indian Civil Service, and a still larger proportion of the English governing class, were not really in agreement with the repeated declarations of the Crown as to our policy in India. The child is growing up. Whereas it used to be only seven years old, it is now fourteen. Are we to try to prevent it from attaining manhood?"

Mr. HERBERT BURROWS

THE PASSING OF EMPIRE IN INDIA

Mr. Herbert Burrows gave an interesting address at South Place Ethical Institute, Finsbury.

He observed that few phrases had suffered more from ignorance and distortion than the word Empire. In its proper dictionary signification, it appeared harmless enough, but tyrannies and despotisms had clustered around it without number. With regard to the British Empire the remarkable fact was that there was no such thing except in India and the Crown Colonies. With regard to India there were two main schools of thought. There was the "Imperial school," represented in India by the hard-and-fast Anglo-Indian and in England by the governing classes in Parliament and at the India Office. Their views had been very crudely, but most truthfully, put by Mr. Joynson-Hicks, who, when he was member for North-West Manchester, blurted out that it was utter nonsense to say that the British were in India for India's good; that they were there for their own good and intended to remain there for the same reason. Then there were the other school which held that India should have complete self-government, and that Britain should see about giving it to her at the earliest possible moment, publicly declaring this to be her object. Between these two extremes there were, of course, many gradations, even among Indians themselves. Some said that Britain should remain in India, simply as suzerain, others desired to see her retain her grip of national administration: others, again, would turn India into a Colony on the model of Australia and Canada: and there were also those who were content with the wide extension of local municipal government. He did not propose to discuss these various shades of opinions. It was his belief that British rule in India had fallen far short of the ideal professed in 1858, when the Company's government came to an end. But he would leave that to discuss Mr. Fielding Hall's thesis that much of the so-called "unrest" was largely the Englishman's own fault. He would pre-suppose that the English were going to remain in India, and for more years than some of his Indian friends might believe. He was prepared to find he was mistaken: for India of all countries in the world was perhaps the most difficult to understand. Although he had not been to India, it had been his good fortune to come into daily contact with Indians—men of different castes, races, habits, thoughts, ideas, aspirations, and religions—and the more he saw of them, the more he realised the infinite patience which it needed for an European even to scratch the surface of the problem. He did not believe in much that Kipling had written, but he did feel the truth of the hackneyed quotation as to the gulf between East and West. In the mass there could be little *rapprochement* between two races which for centuries had differed so essentially in general evolution and training and in every sort of characteristic. Indians had exactly the same feeling towards the negro. The first thing, then, was to try to understand. It was because the English had not understood, and mostly had not tried to understand, that their so-called Empire in India was slowly passing away. They had always been except in rare instances, and still were an alien race in a strange land, counting the hours until they were released to spend in their own country the money they had made. No assimilation was possible under such circumstances. He was putting on one side the anarchists and terrorists. His thought was of the general type. The Government might pass Press Laws as bad as those of Russia, but 315 millions of people could not be permanently ruled by such means, however stringent they might be.

The "Daily Mail" had on December 16 published a letter from an "Anglo-Indian," which revealed a condition of affairs that stay-at-home Englishmen could not possibly imagine, namely, that a whole people could be barred because of their colour by a so-called superior race. As this Anglo-Indian put it, the arrogance and snobbishness of the Anglo-Indian was a festering sore to the body politic of India. Much was heard of the Jim Crow car in the United States. But let an Indian enter a carriage in which an Englishman was seated, and he ran the risk of being bundled out. The effect upon a proud and highly sensitive people could be appreciated by Englishmen, if they would only set to work to imagine India mistress of England, and Indians treating Englishmen in that manner. The iron would enter into their souls. Was it worth while to arouse such passions in India. Frankly, however, he did not believe any general disturbance was coming. There was as yet no real coherence in India. Her town life was sparse, her villages widely separated by jungle. Her races, languages, religions were of different types. Hindus and Mahomedans were coming together in a manner which was most hopeful: but the movement was slow, and many of the old prejudices and jealousies remained. Differences in India were very deep and very far-reaching. He was very strongly inclined to think also that the chief opponents for a long time to come of any real changes in India would be the Indian women. As for the caste system, the social salvation of the country would never be accomplished until Indians ate together, lived together, and intermixed without restriction. The same observation applied to England, where, in some respects, the class system was as bad as carried the same social results.

THE PRIMARY DUTY OF ENGLAND

But because a general rising was neither possible nor probable, the heavy responsibility of England was not thereby diminished. It was for her to do the utmost to assist India to her self-realisation, she must publicly declare that she was in India for the single purpose of helping India to attain complete self-government: and must shape her policy to that end. In the meantime, all who had studied the matter would agree with Mr. Fielding Hall that the present bureaucratic government of India must be reformed root and branch. But, curiously enough, Mr. Hall was against throwing open the higher positions in the Indian Civil Service to Indians: and the race-arrogance of the Europeans was assigned by him as the obstacle. Leaving that aside, there was education to be pushed among the masses of the people. But it must be done wisely and well. The defects of education as they knew it in England must be avoided, and nothing but the virtues copied: so that it might be made a lever for self-government. There should be as much district, local, and municipal government as possible. The provincial councils should be thoroughly reconstituted, and the Viceroy's Legislative Council made properly representative of the real interests of the people. The tendency now on all hands was to keep India bound hand and foot to the care of Anglo-Indian officialism.

The objection was always raised that Indians were unfit for self-government. It was as old as the hills, and done duty in every civilised country as the one stock argument of the quidnunces who stood out against any change or against the surrender of social and political privileges. There was, of course, millions of Indians who were unfit in the ordinary sense of the party politician, but they could be matched by thousands in England in town and country.

After all, the poor had to live like everyone else, and had, therefore, the human right to order their own lives, even though they might make mistakes. However this might be, there were enough educated Indians now to justify the experiment of much more extended local self-government if only the authorities would consent to it. England must seek her strength not in dominance but in kindly help.

Mr. S. H. SWINNY

HOME RULE FOR INDIA

To secure good administration was one thing, but good government could never be a substitute for government by the people themselves.—Sir HENRY CAMPBELL-BANNERMAN at Stirling, November 23, 1905.

For a long time all proposals to introduce reforms into India, to associate the people more closely with the government of the country, and to give them more power in the administration of their own public affairs, have been met by the cry that such measures would impair that efficiency in administration for which our rule was famous. Now it may be at once admitted that efficiency and self-government are sometimes at variance, that modern democratic constitutions are not always favourable to the choice of the best rulers, and that in the past the Indian Civil Service has been fruitful in skilful administrators. Yet these considerations are very far from deciding the question at issue.

A NECESSARY CONDITION OF EFFICIENCY

One necessary condition of efficiency is a certain harmony between rulers and ruled. Without that the ability of administrators, instead of being exerted for the advancement of the community, will be expended in attempts at obstinate repression or ungracious conciliation. In such a position the party spirit which is held up to our abhorrence by the opponents of popular government appears in its most dangerous shape, and rulers and people enter the lists as contending factions. The government is under the temptation to use the public resources as a means of silencing the public voice, and the people are prone to oppose the most ordinary acts of administration as designs of the enemy. In the end, even the administration of justice becomes tainted in the public estimation. The authorities are suspected of using the law to accomplish ends which are none the less factious because the party involved consists of officials and their hangers-on; and their opponents in return cease to lend any active support, even if they do not show an open hostility, to the proceedings of the officers of justice.

THE LESSON OF THE BENGAL PARTITION

That this is no fancy picture, but a description of what has actually happened, may be proved from the history of many nations, and, not least, from the history of Ireland, the country to which Sir Henry Campbell-Bannerman was referring when he made use of the words quoted at the head of this article. Nor is India without a recent example of the same condition in its earlier stages. The partition of Bengal has been defended as necessary to efficiency. Could the most inefficient Government have produced in so short a time so many evils as this unfortunate measure produced—so much ill-will, suspicion, and disorder, so great a disturbance to trade, so complete a revolution in the feelings of the people towards their rulers? The measure was carried through in defiance of public opinion, and when it was believed that any such intention had been abandoned. It naturally provoked opposition, which was met, as it usually is, by repression. Can it be pretended, even from the Government point of view, and taking efficiency alone into account, that the two provinces were better administered, that the public peace was better preserved, trade more flourishing, the rulers more respected, and the public mind more tranquil than in the days before the partition? If not, how can it be said that that measure promoted efficiency? Could there be a stronger instance of how necessary it is for efficiency itself that government should be carried on with the active co-operation and approval of the governed?

POPULAR CONTROL

The attempt, therefore, to discriminate between efficiency and popular control is idle. In some form or other the second is necessary to the first. This is not to say that popular control can only be exercised in accordance with Western democratic theories, or that in India all considerations of previous history and social structure must be disregarded. Home Rule in that country means a Government observant of, and guided by, Indian public opinion, and administered by men in whom Indians have confidence, whether formally elected or not. It means a government all the positions in which are freely open to Indians, and in which, therefore, Indians must gradually obtain a preponderance—for strangers are not like permanently to remain in possession of authority, unless they are given some artificial advantage. It means, as Mr. Gokhale so eloquently set forth in his Presidential Address at the National Congress of 1905, a Government which has as its goal an India as much the mistress in her own house as are the Oversea Dominions.

This may be brought about in many ways. But the test which should be applied is that which Sir Henry Campbell-Bannerman has recommended for Ireland :—

> 'If he were asked for advice by an ardent Irish Nationalist he would say that his desire was to see the effective management of Irish affairs in the hands of a representative Irish authority and he further said that, if he were the Irish Nationalist, he would take it in any way that he could get it. If an instalment of representative control were offered to Ireland, or any administrative improvement, he would advise the Nationalists thankfully to accept it, provided it was consistent and led up to the larger policy. To secure good administration was one thing, but good government could never be a substitute for government by the people themselves.'

This is, indeed, the true test—does the measure proposed tend in the direction of Home Rule or away from it? Does it make the transition easier or more difficult? And it will be well for the Indian people to judge all political measures, not by their democratic professions or their popular appearance, but by this simple criterion.

Some conditions are no doubt necessary for the advent of Home Rule. India is becoming a nation; and thus the first condition is fulfilled. The autonomy of the various provinces under the present system of government would make it easy to satisfy the second —the care for local interests. But besides these conditions which directly concern India, there are others which relate to the state of public opinion in Great Britain. It is certain that the English mind has a rooted objection to sudden revolutions, and that it can only be brought to acquiesce in great changes if they are the result of a gradual approach, in which each stage is tried on its merits before the next is attempted. It will thus be seen that in the course of the attainment of Indian Home Rule each step in the process will be viewed from different standpoints in India and in England.

THE ATTITUDE OF ENGLISH OPINION

Indian public opinion will be chiefly concerned with the ultimate tendency of the measure, while the English will be swayed by the practical necessities of the immediate situation. It will also be necessary as a condition precedent to any great advance towards Home Rule to satisfy English public opinion as to the capacity for moderation or determined opposition as the particular occasion may require. To the theorician this may seem illogical, since the greater the inferiority of one nation to another, the greater is the distance between them, and therefore the less fitted is the superior to understand, to sympathise with, and to rule the inferior. But the English have never been logicians. Even when all these conditions are fufilled it is doubtful whether an extension of self-government in India will come about as a result of cold reason and the logic of events, or whether it will need an outburst of popular enthusiasm in England as well as in India in order to overcome the opposition of classes interested in the maintenance of the present order.

But it is the manifest duty of the Liberal Party to smooth the way for the great transformation. They are the professed advocates of popular self-government. They are the enemies of bureaucracy, of pride of race, and of the rule of force. If, in the day of their power, they refuse to listen to the claims of India, they will be false to their principles, they will lose a splendid occasion for doing honour alike to themselves and to their country. If they fail to seize the opportunity, they will forfeit the confidence of all those who have trusted in their professions, and they will prepare that reaction against Liberal principles which always follows the adoption of illiberal measures by the leaders of the Liberal Party. If India is governed despotically and without reference to the opinion of the people, it cannot fail to revive and strengthen those theories of government at home which have had so baneful an effect in Ireland. Those who desire freedom in Ireland and in England must not neglect it in India.—*India*.

H. E. LORD CHELMSFORD

H. E. the Viceroy in the course of his opening speech in the Imperial Legislative Council on the 5th September, 1917 *said :—*

I now turn to the constitutional reforms. At the very first Executive Council which I held as Viceroy and Governor-General I propounded two questions to my Council : (1) What is the goal of British rule in India (2) what are the steps on the road to that goal. We came to the conclusion, which I trust most Hon. Members will agree was inevitable, that the endowment of British India as an integral part of the British Empire with Self-Government, was the goal of British rule, and his Majesty's Government have now put forward in precise terms their policy, which I may say that we as the Government of India regard in substance as practically undistinguishable from that which we put forward. With regard to the second question, after careful and detailed examination of the ground, we arrived at the decision that there were three roads along which an advance should be made towards the goal. The first road was the domain of Local Self-Government, the village, the rural board, and the towns or municipal council. The domain of urban and rural self-government, is the great training ground from which political progress and a sense of responsibility have taken their start, and we felt that the time had come to quicken the advance to accelerate the rate of progress, and thus to stimulate the sense of responsibility in the average citizen and to enlarge his experience. The second road, in our opinion, lay in the domain of the more responsible employment of Indians under Government. We felt that it was essential to the progress towards the goal, that Indians should be admitted in steadily increasing proportion to the higher grades of the various services and departments, and to more responsible posts in the administration generally. It is, I think obvious, that this is a most important line of advance. If we are to get real progress it is vital that India should have an increasing number of men versed not only in the details of every day administration, but in the whole art of Government. I doubt whether there is likely to be any one who will cavil at the general conclusions at which we arrived as to these two roads of advance, but agreement must not blind us to their instruction than the liberty to make mistakes. The first and foremost principle which was enunciated in Lord Ripon's Self-Government resolution of May 1882, and was subsequently emphasised by Lord Morley and Lord Crewe in their despatches of 27th November, 1908, and 11th July, 1913, respectively, was that the object of Local Self-Government is to train the people in the management of their own local affairs and that political education of this sort must take precedence of mere considerations of departmental efficiency. We are in complete accord with that principle hence our advocacy of an advance along the first road. Equally we realise the paramount importance of training in administration which would be derived from an advance along the second road. There is nothing like administrative experience to sober the judgment and bring about an appreciation of the practical difficulties which exist in the realm of administration and it is from this source that we may look forward in the future to an element of experienced and tried material for the Legislative Assemblies.

LEGISLATIVE COUNCILS

We came now to our third road, which lay in the domain of the Legislative Councils. As Hon. Members will readily appreciate, there is no subject on which much difference of opinion exists and with regard to which greater need is required for careful investigation and sober decision. I may say frankly that we, as the Government of India, recognise fully that advance must be made on this road simultaneously with the advances on the other two and His Majesty's Government in connection with the goal which they have outlined in their announcement have decided that substantial steps in the direction of the goal they define should be taken as soon as possible. Some criticism has been directed against the Government of India on the score that we have not disclosed the policy outlined in our despatch. I must remind Hon. Members that decision on such a question rests not with the Government of India but with the authorities at Home. Moreover, on the larger question of a declaration of policy, in view of its unique importance I steadfastly refused in the face of much adverse criticism to anticipate by any statement of my own, the decision of His Majesty's Government, who alone could make a final and authoritative statement and I was careful to warn Hon. Members in my opening speech to them last February, of the likelihood of delay owing to the grave pre-occupations of the Cabinet at Home.

Mr. JUSTICE ABDUR RAHIM

In the course of his judgment in the New India case, Mr. Justice Abdur Rahim said:—

" The learned Advocate-General very rightly told us under instructions from the Government that they did not object to advocacy of any Home Rule propaganda; and in fact it is difficult to see how any such movement can be regarded as illegal *per se.* It lies entirely with the Sovereign, that is, in the compendious phrase of Dr. Dicey, the King in Parliament, to establish any Government he chooses for India or any other part of the British Empire. There can be nothing wrong, therefore, in a subject of the Crown urging the desirability of a change in the machinery of Government in India. Changes in the constitution of Government do take place from time to time with the consent or sanction of the Sovereign. In certain stages of society, reforms in the constitution of the Government are a biological and political necessity. To say that such questions are not open to public discussion, supposing that the law is not violated by the manner and the methods adopted in such discussion, would be opposed to all sound maxims of constitutional law. The principle which bears on the subject has been expressed in the following terms which have met with the approval of some of the most distinguished text writers:—' An intention is not seditious if the object is to show that the King has been misled or mistaken in his measures or to point out errors in the Government or constitution with a view to their reformation or to excite the subjects to attempt by lawful means the alteration of any matter in Church or State or to point out with a view to their removal matters which are producing or have a tendency to produce feeling of hatred or ill-will between classes of the subjetcs."

SIR WILLIAM WEDDERBURN

It is a remarkable document, breathing a spirit of reasoned loyalty to the British Empire, with a hearty desire to promote "an advance in the ideals of the Government all over the civilised world."

This manifesto of Indian aspirations recognises ungrudgingly the benefits of a British connexion: "The people of India have good reasons to be grateful to England for the great progress in her material resources and the widening of her intellectual and political outlook under British rule, and for the steady, if slow, advance in her national life, commencing with her Charter Act of India of 1833." Further, India cordially appreciates the advance made in recent years by the Morley-Minto reforms, which, especially as regards the Executive and Legislative Councils, gave the Indians a certain voice in the management of their own affairs. The time now seems to have come for a further development on similar lines.

Up to the reforms of 1909, the members of the Executive Councils were all Europeans, the majority being officials belonging to the permanent Civil Service; and the Morley-Minto reforms promoted Imperial solidarity in no small degree, when they mitigated this racial monopoly, and admitted into "the inner counsels of the Indian Empire." Indians of such character and attainments as Sir S. P. Sinha, Sir Ali Imam, and Sir Sankaran Nair. As regards the Legislative Councils, the object of the reforms was to extend the elective system, and obtain for the administration the benefit of independent Indian opinion, allowing to the wearer an opportunity of saying where the shoe pinches him.

What is now the position? India has borne her part in the great world-struggle, and now looks forward to a happier future: "Expectations have been raised and hopes held out that, after the war, the problems of Indian administration will be looked at from a new angle of vision." We hope and believe that these expectations will not be disappointed. Leading British statesmen have declared their desire to satisfy reasonable Indian aspirations; and it is most opportune that a body of trusted leaders representing united India (three of the signatories are ex-Presidents of the Indian National Congress, and three are ex-Presidents of the Moslem League) should have placed before the Viceroy a statement showing in clear terms the reforms which in their judgment are essential for the welfare of India and of the Empire: "We feel," they say, "that we should avail ourselves of this opportunity to respectfully offer to Government our humble suggestions as to the lines on which these reforms should proceed."

Accordingly, as regards the Executive Councils, Imperial and Provincial, they recommend that half the members should be Indians; and that the European members should be men trained and educated in the public life of England. As regards the Legislative

Councils, they propose that in all cases there should be a majority of elected members, the Viceroy and Governors retaining their power of veto. Further, it is suggested that the elected representatives of the people should have a voice in the selection of the Indian members of the Executive Councils.

These are some of the leading proposals tending to produce that atmosphere of sympathy desired by the King-Emperor. But, apart from constitutional reforms, there exists at the present moment a crucial matter, connected with the military situation, which demands special attention from well-wishers of the British Empire, because it intimately affects the sentiments of the Indian people, and is derogatory to their sense of national self-respect. A humiliating sense of racial differentiation is produced by the Arms Act, applied to Indians, but not to Europeans and Anglo-Indians, by the disqualification of Indians as volunteers, and by their exclusion from the commissioned ranks of the Army. With pathos these representative members of the Viceroy's Council set forth the demoralising effect of such restrictions on the civil population of India, and especially on the younger generation; and they urge that the Government should remove these "irritating disabilities as regards the possession of arms and a military career, which indicate want of confidence in the people, and place them in a position of inferiority and helplessness."

India is a lover of peace, but she possesses almost unlimited man-power, and her desire is to have her hands unbound, and, as a good comrade, to stand by England in securing victory for "the cause of justice and humanity in the international relations of the world."

In this connection the following extracts from the Report of the British Congress Committee for the year 1915-1916 may be read with interest:—

The essential principle of self-government was declared by Lord Hardinge, when he indicated the safe path of Indian reforms, founded on provincial autonomy, with a persistent, if gradual, transfer of authority from the official body to the representatives of the people. This, we trust, will be the direction in which Parliament will proceed. But in order that the Viceroy may be in a position to carry out the orders of the Home Government, it is absolutely necessary that his hands should be strengthened. At present the Viceroy is not master in his own household, the existing practice giving to the permanent officials an exceptional position of authority in his Executive Council. The constitution of that Council is determined by the India Act of 1861 (24 and 25 Victoria, c. 67,) clause 3, providing that three out of five ordinary members of that Council are to be persons who have been at least ten years in the service of the Crown in India; and this provision has been interpreted for the sole benefit of the Covenanted Civil Service; so that the Viceroy's 'Cabinet' is unduly dominated by a group of permanent officials, who enter the Executive Council automatically, imbued with the spirit of the great centralised departments, over which they have been accustomed to preside. Under this system a Viceroy, fresh from England and unfamiliar with the routine of Indian administration, is not in a position to give effect to the policy prescribed for him by Parliament and the Crown.

The remedy is a simple one; for the time has come to amend clause 3 of the India Act of 1861, by providing that the Viceroy, with the approval of the Secretary of State, shall have power to nominate the members of his own Executive Council from among men, British and Indian, of ripe experience in public affairs, their term of office ending with that of the Viceroy. Such amendent will only be an extension of the beneficial practice which, for the last eighty years, have given to India the services of such men of mark as Lord Macaulay, Mr. James Wilson, Sir Charles Trevelyan, Sir Sumner Maine, Lord Hobhouse, Sir Courtenay Ilbert, and Sir Guy Wilson. In more recent times the solidarity of the Empire has been strengthened by the addition of distinguished Indians Sir S. P. Sinha, Sir Ali Imam, and Sir Sankaran Nair. It appears that this reform is a condition, precedent to all other reforms. The principle involved is one that has been accepted by all civilised Governments. In England, especially, it has been the settled rule that a member of the permanent Civil Service must be content to close his official career as the trusted and authoritative head of his department without aspiring to political governance. The task of a

British Premier would be an impossible one if he was not free to choose the members of his Cabinet from among his political supporters, and was compelled to accept as his colleagues the permanent chiefs of the administrative departments.—(*The Nation* 1916).

BABU ARABINDO GHOSE

"Our ideal is that of Swaraj, * * * * * * * * * We claim the right of every nation to live by its own energies, according to its own nature and ideals. We reject the claim of aliens to force upon us a civilisation inferior to our own or to keep us out of our inheritance on the untenable ground of a superior fitness. While admitting the strains and defects which long subjection has induced upon our native capacity and energy, we are conscious of that capacity and energy reviving in us. We point to the unexampled national vigour which has preserved the people of this country through centuries of calamity and defeat, to the great actions of our forefathers continued even to the other day, to the many men of intellect and character such as no other nation in a subject capacity has been able to produce. . . . We have brains, we have courage, we have an infinite and various national capacity. All we need is a field and an opportunity. Our ideal of Swaraj involves no hatred of any other nation nor of the administration which is now established by law in this country. We find a bureaucratic administration, we wish to make it democratic; we find an alien government, we wish to make it indeginous; we find a foreign control, we wish to render it Indian. They lie who say that this aspiration necessitates hatred and violence. Our ideal of patriotism proceeds on the basis of love and brotherhood, and it looks beyond the unity of the nation, and envisages the ultimate unity of mankind. The strength of our position is moral, not material. . . . The whole of the moral strength of the country is with us: Justice is with us; the law of God, which is higher than any human, justifies our action. Youth is for us, the future is ours.—(*Karmayogin*).

Mr. V. P. MADHAVA RAO, C.I.E.

(Retired Dewan of Mysore, Travancore, and Baroda).

The fortunes of India are inextricably bound up with those of England, and, whatever the shortcomings of England may be, it is only through her that India can hope to become a self-governing nation. Anything therefore, that may weaken England's power cannot but tell on the well-being and prosperity of India. It is, on the other hand, to England's own interest as an Imperial Power to do everything to strengthen India's position so that she may become a self-supporting and self-reliant nation within the Empire.

I think England fully realises that the time has arrived for giving India self-government, but her difficulty appears to be whether India can safely be raised to the position of a self-governing country. The case of the Colonies is simple. They are kindred nations who are offshoots of the parent stock and the question with them is one of bringing them into closer union with the central Government and has practically been solved. But the case with India is different. Her populations belong to an alien race and a different civilisation. And the British nation, who, in the ultimate resort are the arbiters of the destinies of the Indian people, have not troubled themselves to understand Indian problems and have left the government of the country in the hands of her experts. Some catastrophe like the Mutiny and, in a milder form the Indian unrest of 1905, rouses her attention and on these occasions, through her national assembly, the Houses of Parliament. Some action is taken to redress India's grievances and improve her Government. In the present World-War, however, England appears to have been much impressed by the spectacle of a whole nation, from prince to peasant, rallying to her side and placing their resources and services unreservedly at her disposal. In the exuberance of her feelings of gratitude India was assured of her title to self-rule being recognised and to her being lifted from a position of dependency to that of partnership in the Imperial scheme. The enthusiasm, however, would appear to have cooled down somewhat latterly and the visit to India of the Editor of the *Round Table* and the *Common wealth of Nations* is not calculated to inspire confidence in the minds of the people of India as to much being done to change the character of her rule. He is supposed to represent the Lord Milner-school of thought, which, in regard to the so-called subject-races, has greater faith in the efficacy of strong, and according to their lights good government than self-government. The Government will still be bureaucratic in spirit although there may be an increase in the representative element in it and in the appointments in Government service open to the sons of the soil. But this will not meet the present requirements of India. What India needs, and is ripe for, is

Government of the people, by the people and the full recognition of the principle that there should be " no taxation without representation."

This is a matter of no mere sentiment or aspiration, due to borrowing fine phrases from the politics of the West without understanding their meaning. It is a positive necessity for the well-being of India and for the integrity of the Empire. There is no question that the bureaucracy has outlived its usefulness, and while unwilling to part with power, is unable to adapt itself to the changed conditions in India. The India of to-day is not the India of five years ago and since the war, the change is working even more rapidly than in the previous three years. The retired Governors and officials who generally shape opinion at Home on Indian questions are woefully behind the times and shout shibboleths like "vakil raj," " babu politicians," " Martial races," " unwarlike communities," " ignorant masses " and " self-seeking educated classes," which have long since been exploded. India has passed the stage of being governed on the old lines by highly trained Englishmen sent out to administer the country. So long as government was confined to policing the country, dispensing justice, collecting taxes, and promoting to large extent the material and moral welfare of the people, it was simple enough, and no agency could have done it better than the Civil Service, which has earned the gratitude of the people and the admiration of the whole world. But if India is to become a self-supporting and self-reliant nation, something more is wanted than these elements of good government. The British Government, however sympathetic and however well-intentioned it may be, cannot, from the nature of the case, undertake this task with any chance of success. The work will have to be taken up by indigenous agency, by statesmen and philosphers like Stein, Fichte and others in Germany in the beginning of the last century, or the patriots who piloted the passage of Japan from the old order into the new. The only measure of economic and social reconstruction introduced by the British Government is the co-operative credit system in Lord Curzon's Viceroyalty. Beyond this, the Government have not done much to strengthen the economic position of the people or train them in habits of self-help and self-reliance.

. . . .

It is the fashion to attribute the spontaneous rally of India to the side of England, when war was declared, to the good Government which had conciliated and secured the loyalty and devotion of the masses to the British nation. This is at best a half truth and I do not think I am exaggerating when I say that this was due mainly to the influence of the much maligned and much misunderstood intellectuals of India who alone were in a position to judge the good work England had done and what it would mean to India if Germany won in the present war. It is the educated classes that gave the lead. Of course it is well-known that a great deal of this unhesitating action is due to the emphatic and courageous way in which Lord

Hardinge had indentified himself with the national cause. I will not here attempt to show how untenable is the position, so often assumed, that the civilians are the protectors of the masses and the Indian publicists are fighting for their own aggrandisement. Masses and classes are, however, idea and phrases borrowed from the West and are utterly inapplicable to the conditions in India.

How the English rulers in India have not out-grown the ideas of Government which may have answered in the earlier years of British rule but are quite inapplicable to modern conditions may be gathered from the attitude of the spokesmen of the Indian Government in the discussions in connection with the Consolidation Acts and from the Despatch sent by the Government of India on the proposals of the Decentralisation Commission to bring schemes for revision settlements before the Legislative Councils if it were a national Government, even of the Russian type, it will be quick to respond to stimuli from without. The exigencies of self-preservation and strengthening her power of resistance has led the Russian Government to adopt compulsory education and give a voice to the representatives of the people in the Duma in deciding the policies of the State, even as the war was going on. All this will point to the necessity of increasing the representative character of Indian rule and consulting the people more generally and trusting them to a larger extent than has been the case hitherto.

The heart of India is sound at the core and Congresses

and Leagues and leaders like Mr. Tilak and Mrs. Besant require, at this crisis in India's fortunes, more freedom of speech and publicity for their utterances rather than discouragement, or repression. The people have to be educated on the one hand and on the other opinion has to be focussed on what measures should be adopted for giving India self-government within the Empire. I can, in the light of the recent speech of Lord Carmichael, understand how difficult must be the position of rulers when confronted with what they believe to be a widespread conspiracy to subvert British rule; but even in regard to such a state of things I would venture to suggest that the best course to adopt is to summon the well-disposed sections of the community to his aid and take counsel with them. However this may be, in regard to the reorganization of the Government of India, the proposals should not have gone to England without being subjected to discussion in India, both in the different Legislative Councils and in the Press. It is discussion alone that will enable Government to decide what constitution is best for each Province and for the Federal Government. The way in which the proposals have been sent to England, without even the Imperial Legislative Council being consulted, shows that the old bureaucratic spirit still rules in India.—("*Madras Mail.*")

Mr. J. RAMSAY MACDONALD, M. P.

When the war broke upon Europe, India was in a state of considerable political unsettlement. Anarchism was troublesome, and was aggravated by the way in which the authorities were handling it. Centres of disaffection and revolutionary propaganda had been established in Europe and America, and without doubt large numbers of romantic, educated young men were being allured by the fire, and were beginning to play with it. Political dacoities were prevalent in some districts, especially in Bengal; students were showing by college strikes and disturbances, not only how serious was the antagonism between them and authority, but how unsettled the mind of young India was becoming and what emotions were possessing it.

This propaganda was confined to a few, and its chief significance was the trouble it gave, and the bad influence it had on the minds of the authorities. It was, however, an indication that something was going wrong. An antagonism was being engendered which was manifesting itself in sporadic flashes of lightning, and an uncomfortable feeling that a storm might be coming began to be prevalent.

In the field of legitimate politics great changes were also evident, and a new constitutional movement far more insistent and definite than that which had hitherto existed, and also far more powerfully supported, was showing itself. The first generation of Congress champions were dead or were old, and a new body of men were taking their place. At first there was antagonism between the two, and the Congress was split and enfeebled. But the looms of Time weave incessantly, and the old generation had to accept the new propaganda. The Surat split was healed; the Mahomedan and Hindu nationalist found a common political language and a common political platform; the demand for Home Rule was taken up; the old Congress programme asking for this change and that, was merged in a general claim for self-government. A new spirit had entered the nationalist movement, and Indian politics were undergoing a transformation similar to that which came over Irish politics when Mr. Parnell first took the helm. Hitherto, Indian pride was concerned with India's treatment in her own household; now, India was beginning to claim a treatment which would give her a worthy status in the world.

Then the war came, and the interests it created swept every other to one side for the time being. No one who had the least accurate knowledge of India doubted what it would do. It would be proud to fight in a European war side by side with European troops; to take a share in Imperial defence was an honour which appealed not only to warriors but to nationalists; it was the great opportunity which India wanted. So India went to war with pride and enthusiasm. There was general satisfaction. At home we talked of turning over a new leaf. India had revealed herself to us. But by and by came a change. India's enthusiasm was not encouraged; her recruits were not accepted; her ambulance corps was disbanded; the administration became timorous. Then ensued an awkward time of suspicion and uncertainty. The Indian Press had broken out into raptures about what India was doing for the Empire, and had already begun to count upon reward in the form of greater political liberty; presently it began to doubt whether it was to get its reward, and blamed the Government for fainting in its good intentions. India felt a tremor of hesitation in the British hand she was grasping.

Into the midst of this suspicion and uncertainty the Mesopotamia Report fell, and instantly the system of Indian Government was struck as by a bomb. Whatever else this Report may have done, it has killed the Indian bureaucracy. It did to the prestige of the Government what the anarchists with their picric acid tried to do to the bodies of the governors. For it must be remembered that the failures revealed were far less those of individuals than those of a method of Government. There were individual failures undoubtedly, and there was bad administration. But the evil action of the individual was a dramatic illustration of the bad system itself. The circumstance and the individual were one and the same as in a Greek tragedy.

The relations between the India Office and Delhi, and between the Viceroy and his Council, the system of Indian military finance, the position of the Finance

Member in the Indian mechanism of administration, above all, the rigid mentality of a Government controlled by a Civil Service, and not responsible to public opinion either in this country or in India, came toppling down when that horrible tale of inefficiency, of delay, of lack of foresight, of feebleness, and of suffering was told to the world.

The question now is, how are we to repair the ruin? What are we to put in its place? If we have any concern for the peace and prosperity of India and for the reputation of the Empire, we shall approach the problem with courage, seeking not to patch up and restore, but to build anew from the foundations in accordance with modern requirements.

A phase of Indian administration has come to an end. We have governed and we have educated. We have opened doors cautiously and allowed the Indian to enter the inner shrines of our administration; we have given him a measure of self-government and some representative authority; we have taught him the philosophy of Western liberty. But we have never loosened our grip upon him; we have never trusted him fully; we have imposed galling conditions upon his liberties; we have not succeeded in making him feel that we believed in him. Hitherto, the liberties we have granted to him have been those given to a subject people, and he has known it. We have not given him power. The Morley reforms were less the beginning of a new epoch than the ending of an old one—the last concession of an old order still in authority, to a new order growing up in the womb of a nation and which had inevitably to be brought to birth.

It is a long time ago since the Directors of the East India Company devised a system of administration which put India under the control of their clerks and which made India an asset of a trading corporation; it is a long time ago since the Government at home saw that it had to impose responsible political obligations upon such a trading concern by subjecting it to Whitehall control. But that *regime* has never passed away. To this day it survives modified in its features, but characterised by its essential distribution of authority and its peculiar mechanism of government.

The viceroy with his Council of Civil Servants (in the main) is the heir to the Company's Presidents, acting with a Council of the senior merchants. In the evolution of the office, it has never departed from its original type. The Secretary of State is still the President of the Board of Control advised by experts, but not subject to Parliament as other Secretaries of State are. The expenses of the India Office in London are still borne by Indian revenues as though it was an adjunct to a business concern which was being made to bear the cost of its management. Indian military finance, in spite of the grant from the Imperial Exchequer, is the finance of a military service which belongs not to an Empire but to a company which has to meet shareholders, and which engages in wars to defend and extend its factories and its revenues. No one who has studied the features of Indian administration with close care, can fail to see how those of government by a Chartered Trading Company survive in them as those of an ancestor are found in a living generation. Scratch the Indian bureaucracy and you find the John Company.

But the declared intention of the Government has always been clear. We have been governing and educating India in order to free India. We have withheld from her none of that knowledge or thought, the fruit of which is a demand for self-government. We have been pursuing a policy which inevitably leads to a movement for Home Rule of some kind, and sooner or later the result of our policy has to be accepted by us, or met with hostility involving repression. So soon as the war is over, India will ask us, in the plainest possible language, what our intentions are, and will expect an answer also in the plainest possible language; and we ought now to be considering what our reply is to be.

There will be the old conservative councilors raising the old timorous difficulties. They will remind us that "India" means a few educated professional people whose interests are not that of the masses; that the masses are content to remain as they are; that self-government is a practical impossibility because India is too big, too diverse in population, too ignorant for a democratic experiment in Home Rule; that, in spite of the Mesopotamia Report, any diminution of British authority or weakening of the Civil Service will mean inefficiency, and mayhap corruption; that British commercial interests will not tolerate Indian political ascendancy, and so on. There may be some substance in each and all of these objections, but they still leave us faced with the difficulty that our democratic reputation is at stake, that the spread of education in India is creating a new political problem in self-govenment, that the war weakened and the Mesopotamia blunders destroyed the old *regime*. The conservative objectors must face the facts and must recognise that the problem has grown so big within the last three years that their doubts and warnings have been dwarfed into minor importance. They were obstacles for the removal of which prudence waited; they have now become risks which prudence must accept.

We can best begin by clearing our minds of the inheritance of the Company. India should no longer be regarded as a State to be governed as we govern a Crown Colony. Our fundamental axiom has been that the Indian cannot govern himself, and that has remained patent whether we put him on Legislative Councils or into a district as Collector. It is here that the great break with the past must be made. That does not mean evacuation, the disappearance of the British Army and the British official, the proclamation of Indian independence. But it means that whereas hitherto we have regarded India and Indians as subordinate not merely to our flag but our authority, henceforth we are to regard them as partners in the Empire governing themselves more and more with what assistance from us is necessary, and becoming more and more responsible for working out their own destiny. This change cannot be made in its fulness in a day or a year. The men fit to make it must be trained, the old machinery must work itself out, but beginnings should be made at once which will prove our sincerity to India and the world, and which will make further changes inevitable. A rule which John Stuart Mill laid down for compromise legislation should guide us in answering India's enquiry. "A legislator," he wrote, "is bound not to think solely of the present effects of his measures; he must consider what influence the acts he does now may have over those of his successors. Whatever changes he introduces should be a step in the direction in which a further advance is, or will hereafter be, desirable. His half measures should be so constructed as to recognise and embody the principles which, if no hindrance existed, would form the foundation of a complete measure." Whatever changes may be made in India must not consist of patches and darns, but must be the beginning of a new garment.

If that is to be our intention, we ought to begin with a complete reform of the India Office. This department should at once be made a charge, like the Colonial Office, on Imperial funds, the Secretary's Council should be abolished, and the Secretary made directly responsible to Parliament. For, so long as the Secretary's Council—composed mainly of retired Indian officials and of Indians cut off from the life of their country—exists, the Government of India will remain a bureaucracy, and the invigorating influence of Parliament and Indian opinion will have no effect upon it.

In India itself, the Viceroy's Council should cease to be a branch of the Civil Service, and should be more largely representative of the Legislative Council, whilst the Councils, both Imperial and Provincial, should have more power, but especially regarding finance. Power, however, cannot be given without responsibility. I can conceive no worse form of government for India than that which enables Councils to exercise authority, which enables them to say "No!" effectively, whilst executive offices are held by the nominees of the bureaucracy. The practice at present is that the heads of departments are chosen by the Executive and are responsible to the Executive. But legislative Councils exist which, within limits, can question them and express views upon their actions and proposals. Thus we have two rival authorities, and if, whilst retaining the Executive in its present position we add to the power of its critics, we invite the latter to act recklessly and factiously and to aim at producing deadlocks to discredit their rivals. Such a system is impossible. We shall be compelled to give the Councils more power and to increase the proportion of elected representatives upon them; we shall be compelled to allow them more influence on budgets than the mere passing of pious resolutions which the Executive may or may not take into account. But the instant we do that we have made the present position of the independent Executive absolutely untenable. We must therefore accept the fact that if we extend the authority of the Councils we must give them responsibility for their acts, which means that in some real and substantial way we must associate them with the Executive as our own House of Commons is associated with the Cabinet. In fact, in India we have to deal with a question of the same nature as that which Germany has now to face as regards her Reichstag. But there is the great difference that whereas in Germany there is the foundation of democratic election and representation, that is not available in India. How are we to get over that? The dilemma is a serious one. We have created in India the demand for self-government; that demand has now acquired a power and a reasonableness which compels us to meet it in some way or other, and we are unable to base it upon any of the electoral foundations upon which alone it rests in western countries.

To build up any system of representative government in India is to be a slow and a difficult process. But in thinking of it we should remember two important things. The first is that India ought not to be governed from a centre, but should be a federation of provinces, and the second that our conceptions of representative government are not necessarily the only ones possible.

Whatever reforms in the Council are begun, decentralisation should be kept in view. Delhi and Simla are now far too powerful. Areas like the United Provinces and the Central Provinces should be raised to the political status of Madras, Bengal and Bombay, and considerable autonomy granted to them, especially in finance, in the administration of justice, in educational work, and so on, and the central Government should concern itself with the powers which it reserves to itself and with co-ordinating, checking, and levelling up provincial legislation and administration.

Then when we turn to the question of what is to be represented, we only engage in a fruitless exploration if we try to discover a citizen whom we are to enfranchise, and a geographical constituency for which we are to compile a register of electors. It will be generations before such a thing can be thought of, and, meantime, India cannot be asked to wait. When we ask ourselves freed from our western prepossessions, what representation means in India, we discover, first of all, that India is not so much a nation of citizens as an organisation of co-operating social functions with certain institutions like colleges, professional schools, and universities which are centres of civic and political opinion, and which approach to the character of western constituencies and afford opportunities for the ordinary western election. Opinion and interests are organised, beginning with rudimentary simplicity in the village, and becoming more complex in districts, provinces, and the whole State. As a matter of fact, we find in India already a complete system of government ranging from the village panchayets to the Viceroy's Council, and it is this which we must strengthen and develop by an infusion or representative authority. Politics in India are not so differentiated from social organisation as they are here. Along this line, and with this difference in view, we should plan our system of self-government. The village, the District Board, the Co-operative Society, and such organisations, should be built into the fabric of Indian representation. The lower and more subordinate bodies should be represented on those above them with wider and more complex powers. When complete, this fabric will not be uniform as it is here; but its complexity will conform to Indian vastness and Indian social structure, and it will be representative.

As to the representatives themselves, many are already available. India has her men of political experience and ability enjoying the confidence of large groups and communities, and though they may as yet be confined rather much to the classes of landowners and lawyers, everyone who knows them must admit that their outlook is, on the whole, a civic one, and that their political aims and ambitions are based upon thoughts of their municipality, their province, and their country, growing up around them is a class of manufacturers and men engaged in commerce and industry, and these, when the interests and honours of public life are presented to them, will appear on public bodies. But the field from which to draw public men is even richer than that, for societies like the Servants of India and the various Social Reform groups are training men of public devotion second to none of those who in this country serve their nation in singleness of heart. Every year innumerable conferences on education, the out-caste, technology and commerce, agriculture, and social work, meet, and each represents some living organisation inspired by some active men. From these men the native states are drawing, more and more liberally, Diwans and other officers and councillors, and British India should do the same.

The real impediment in the way of generous change is the deepseated and almost irremovable conviction held by the ruling classes that we, and we alone, can rule India. We alone have the necessary force; we alone have the necessary efficiency. So completely has this sense of superiority of the governing people taken possession of Anglo-Indian minds that it has come to be regarded as an expression of racial differences. It is really nothing of the kind. Racialism is a cloak used to cover a multitude of prejudices. But when the two races meet on terms of political equality, as they do here at home and in Indian native states, this prejudice is not so apparent. Moreover, it is observed in every community in the world that when section is differentiated off to govern, the rest, it develops precisely the prejudices, the aloofness, and the claims which in India are attributed to racial distinctions. So, we had better admit that the gulf which separates Indians from the British in India is not a difference of race, but that of governed and governors. And we justify ourselves by our efficiency. But, admitting the claim in order that we may go to the heart of the argument, efficiency is not the end of government. Efficiency belongs to the mechanical and material aspects of a state, and if into the ends of government enter any consideration of liberty and self-expression, a high efficiency may have to be sacrificed and a lower one substituted in order to reach the further goal. I know that in numerous secret documents there are records of how unsatisfactory Indian officials have been; I know that in the privacy of secretariats tales are told of Indian failures in many departments and responsibilities. I have never been very much impressed by these. You cannot proclaim by every attitude, and during every hour of the day, that a man is inferior, and find in the end that you are wrong. Your proclamations secure their own truth. Whatever we have taught the Indian it has not been self-reliance, courage, force of character. So I am willing to believe these reports if I am compelled to do so, but I reject emphatically the conclusion drawn from them. If we were to continue to rule India as we are now doing for a hundred decades, these tales would not diminish but increase with time. Moreover, when we go into details, we find that only at a few points—important may be, but yet few—is there any risk. The judiciary will not suffer, as from top to bottom it is already predominatingly Indian. All the subordinate services are now Indian. The local administrative bodies are Indian, though most of them are under the tutelage of a District officer. Indians occupy positions of great responsibility in the Imperial Civil Service, and everyone admits that more openings must be made for them there, and more departments handed over to their control. The Indians on the Legislative Councils are men of influence and ability, and their speeches show no mean grasp of affairs. They vary, as legislators in every country vary. Upon both the Secretary of State's and the Viceroy's Councils the Indian members are quite as good as the average British members. The political sagacity and backbone shown by the Indian leaders during the South African trouble left nothing to be desired. Indeed, when the whole facts and experiences are marshalled and examined, the case for the doleful prophecies of failure if India were started on the road to self-government and to full partnership in the Empire is found to rest on very slender evidence, whereas the grounds for confidence are firm and wide. A great part of the fears that are valid arise from the existing method and spirit of government.

We shall be wise if we honestly recognise the facts and admit that a break with the past has become inevitable; that we have done all we can *for* India, and that the further help we can give to her and her people must be rendered in co-operation *with* them. (*Contemporary Review* : *September*, 1917.)

H. E. LORD HARDINGE

The maintenance of British Rule in India depends on the ultimate supremacy of the Governor-General-in Council, and the Indian Councils Act of 1909 itself bears testimony to the impossibility of allowing matters of vital concern to be decided by a majority of non-official votes in the Imperial Legislative Council. Nevertheless, it is certain that in the course of time the just demands of Indians for a larger share in the Government of the country will have to be satisfied, and the question will be how this devolution of power can be conceded without impairing the supreme authority of Governor-General-in-Council. The only possible solution of difficulty would appear to be gradually to give the Provinces a large measure of self-government, until at last India would consist of a number of administrations autonomous in all provincial affairs, with the Government of India above them all and possessing power to interfere in case of misgovernment, but ordinarily restricting their functions to matters of Imperial concern. In order that this consummation may be attained, it is essential that the Supreme Government should not be associated with any particular Provincial Government. The removal of the Government of India from Calcutta is, therefore, a measure which will, in our opinion, materially facilitate the growth of local self-government on sound and safe lines. It is generally recognised that the Capital of a great central Government should be separate and independent and effect has been given to this principle in the United States, Canada and Australia.

APPENDIX A

The Aims of the Indian National Congress as expressed by the 31 *Presidents of the Indian National Congress from* 1885 *to* 1916.

MR. W. C. BONNERJEE (Bombay, 1885).

Never has so important and comprehensive an assemblage occurred within historical times on the soil of India. . . . In meeting to discuss, in an orderly and peaceable manner, questions affecting our well-being, we are following the only course by which the constitution of England enables us to represent our views to the ruling authority. . . . Our desire to be governed according to the ideas of government prevalent in Europe is in no way imcompatible with our thorough loyalty to the British Government. All we ask is that the basis of the government shall be widened and that the people shall have their proper and legitimate share in it.

MR. DADABHAI NAOROJI (Calcutta, 1886).

The assemblage of such a Congress is an event of the utmost importance in the Indian history. . . . Although the British Government has done much, there is still a great deal more to be done if their noble work is to be fitly completed. They say this themselves; they show a desire to do what more may be required, and it is for us to ask for whatsoever, after due deliberation, we think that we ought to have. . . . We should therefore persevere, having confidence in the conscience of England, and resting assured that the English nation will grudge no sacrifice to prove the sincerity of their desire to do whatever is just and right.

MR. JUSTICE BUDRUDIN TYABJI (Madras, 1887).

The Congress represents not any one class or interest, but all classes and all interests of the almost innumerable different communities that constitute the people of India.

MR. GEORGE YULE (Allahabad, 1888).

No rational mind can believe that the present system can go on for ever, that it is the last will and dying testament of Providence regarding India.

SIR WILLIAM WEDDERBURN (Bombay, 1889).

The movement stands for unmitigated good in its origin, its objects, and its methods. As regards its historical origin, it is the natural and healthy fruit of the higher education and free institutions granted to the people of India. Its practical objects are to revive the national life and the material prosperity of the country. Its methods are open and constitutional, and based solely upon India's reliance on British justice and love of fair play.

SIR PHEROZESHAH MEHTA (Calcutta, 1890).

The loyalty, the moderation, the propriety and the constitutional and national character of our mission are now established beyond doubt. . . . It is the glory of the Congress that the educated and enlightened people of the country seek to repay the debt of gratitude which they owe for the priceless gift of education, by pleading and pleading temperately, for timely and provident statesmanship.

RAI BAHADUR P. ANANDA CHARLU (Nagpur, 1891).

Within the short period of seven years we have accomplished the great and palpable fact that the Hindu and Mahomedan populations of this country, long divided by parochial differences and kept apart and estranged from one another by sectional and sectarian jealousies, have at last recognised one another as members of a single brotherhood. This is a magnificent product of the Congress as a mighty nationaliser.

MR. W. C. BONNERJEE (Allahabad, 1892)

There can be no doubt that the Congress movement has been a success and a conspicuous success. . . . All that we wish by this movement is to ask that without any strain on the connexion which exists between Great Britain and this country, such measures may be adopted by the ruling authorities that the grievances under which we labour may be removed, and that we may hereafter have the same facilities of national life that exist in Great Britain itself.

MR. DADABHAI NAOROJI, M. P. (Lahore, 1893).

Were we enemies of British rule, our best course would be, not to cry out, but remain silent, and let the mischief take its course till it ends in disaster, as it must. But we do not want that disaster, and we therefore cry out, both for our own sake and for the sake of the rulers. . . . Our country is India ; our nationality is Indian.

MR. ALFRED WEBB, M. P. (Madras, 1894)

The ends you have in view are similar to those of politicians in other quarters of the globe. The difficulties before you are, however, greater. All the greater necessity that a deaf ear should be turned to doctrines of despair.

MR. SURENDRANATH BANERJEA (Poona, 1895)

I will claim this for the Congress that it has not taken up a single question which it has not brought within the range of practical politics, or which it has not brought nearer to solution. . . . The West owes a heavy debt to the East. We look forward to the day when that debt will be repaid, not only by the moral regeneration but by the political enfranchisement of our people.

MR. RAHIMTULLA M. SAYANI (Calcutta, 1896)

The Congress is the first rich harvest of what has been sown long before by wise and beneficent British statesmen in the shape of schools and colleges. The Congress is the visible embodiment of a new education and a new awakening such as the country has not seen for some centuries before the strong impact of Western civilisation on Eastern thought.

SIR C. SANKARAN NAIR (Amraoti, 1897)

We are more concerned with the progress of our country in the future than with the benefits we have already derived from British rule. On the race question no concession is possible. No compromise can be accepted so far as it lies in us. We must insist on perfect equality. Inequality means race inferiority, national abasement.

MR. ANANDA MOHAN BOSE (Madras, 1898)

The Indian National Congress has been described, and rightly described, as the noblest achievement of British rule in India. . . . We have succeeded in bringing together and knitting in bonds of loving regard, of mutual esteem, and fraternal co-operation, representatives from every part of this vast country, infusing national life, strengthening the ties of common citizenship, kindling the fire of loyal and patriotic service. . . . With truer knowledge and keener sympathy many things will assume a different aspect, and our rulers will see things with new eyes. For, indeed, love and sympathy work miracles in the political, no less than in the moral or spiritual world.

MR. ROMESH C. DUTT (Lucknow, 1899)

If you had been inspired by hostile feelings against British rule in India, you would have worked in the dark and not come forward from all parts of India, year after year, to place your views openly and loyally before the ruling power. Educated India has practically identified itself with British rule, seeks to perpetuate British rule, is loyal to British rule, because it is by a continuance of British rule that educated India seeks to secure that large measure of self-government and that position among the modern nations of the earth which it is our aim and endeavour to secure.

SIR NARAYAN CHANDAVARKAR (Lahore, 1900)

We have arrived at the stage when the Congress has it in its power to make its usefulness felt by carrying on its work on its old accustomed constitutional lines, by helping the Government with facts, with information, with practical suggestions, which will strengthen its hands, and enable it to pursue a policy of large and liberal measures and give up the tendency to drift in administration. This is the duty before us.

MR. D. E. WACHA (Calcutta, 1901)

So far, we are not asking for the impossible. The impossible will be asked only when, as Mr. Lowell says, the reasonable and the practicable is denied. For it is only when the possible is made difficult that people fancy the impossible to be easy.

MR. SURENDRANATH BANERJEA (Ahmedabad, 1902)

We have no higher aspiration than this, that we should be admitted into the great confederacy of self-governing States of which England is the august mother. . . We are already sufficiently loyal, sufficiently attached to the British connexion. But we are anxious for the permanence of British rule, for our permanent incorporation into the great confederacy of the British Empire.

MR. LALMOHAN GHOSE (Madras, 1903)

For our part, we prefer to climb to the belief that the English people are not barbarous conquerors, but that they are champions of liberty whose divine mission it is to rekindle the torch of genius in this ancient land of civilisation and to raise us once more to a position in some degree worthy of the greatness of our past history.

SIR HENRY COTTON (Bombay, 1904)

The ideal of an Indian patriot is the establishment of a federation of free and separate States—the United States of India—placed on a fraternal footing with the self-governing Colonies, each with its own local autonomy, cemented together under the ægis of Great Britain.

MR. G. K. GOKHALE (Benares, 1905)

The minds of the people have been familiarised with the idea of a United India working for her salvation;

a national public opinion has been created; close bonds of sympathy now knit together the different provinces; caste and creed separations hamper less and less the pursuit of common aims; the dignity of a consciousness of national existence has spread over the whole land.

MR. DADABHAI NAOROJI (Calcutta, 1906)

Agitate; agitate means information. Inform; inform the Indian people what their rights are, and why and how they should obtain them, and inform the British people of the rights of the Indian people and why they should grant them. Be united, persevere, and achieve self-government.

SIR RASH BEHARI GHOSE (Madras, 1908)

We do not know what the future destiny of India may be. But of this I am assured that on our genuine co-operation with the British Government depends our future progress and the development of a fuller social and political life. Of this, also, I am assured that the future of the country is now in a large measure in our own hands. . . . Our co-operation will impart to the administration an efficiency which a foreign bureaucracy with the best intentions can never hope to attain.

PANDIT MADAN MOHAN MALAVIYA (Lahore, 1909)

I should like to know if there exists another organisation throughout the length and breadth of this vast Empire which has set nobler objects before itself to achieve. The objects of the Congress are large and comprehensive enough to afford occupation to the most varied inclination in the minds of our people.

SIR WILLIAM WEDDERBURN (Allahabad, 1910)

Our watchwords must be "Hope"—"Conciliation"—"United Effort." . . . The one weapon that is used effectively against Indian reformers by those opposed to India's aspirations is to be found in the charge that the great Hindu and Mahomedan communities are opposed to each other, that Indians are hopelessly divided among themselves, and thereby show themselves unfit for self-government. I ask you to show to the world that this charge is unfounded, and that Indians are prepared to go forward shoulder to shoulder in their march towards a happier future.

PANDIT BISHAN NARAYAN DAR (Calcutta, 1911)

The ideal of self-government within the Empire has come to be cherished by some of the best men of our generation, and with the co-operation of Englishmen we hope to realise it. For it must be borne in mind that the destinies of India and England are now linked together, and that in order to succeed in our political struggles it is indispensable that the sympathies of the English people shall be enlisted on our side. But above all we must instruct and organise our own public opinion.

RAO BAHADUR R. N. MUDHOLKAR (Bankipur, 1912)

The basic principles of the Congress, on the lines of which its work has been carried on for the past twenty-seven years, constitute a goal which, while it is the only one possible and attainable, is also elevating and inspiring. British rule has brought about conditions which make a united India and an Indian nation possible. . . . British subjects, we claim the full rights of British citizenship. Members of a world-wide Empire, we demand to be placed on a footing of equality with the people of the most advanced part of it. That is our goal. And we aim at attaining it by constitutional procedure and peaceful methods.

NAWAB SYED MAHOMED (Karachi, 1913).

The Congress has from its very inception set before itself the ideal of a united Indian nationality, and has consistently advocated the cause of the Indian people as a whole without being influenced by party or sectarian considerations. The changes which India has witnessed since the organisation came into existence are immense, and the Congress may well take credit for bringing about not a few of them. . . . . We are entering upon a new phase but there are still many questions requiring settlement which can be dealt with only by an organisation such as ours.

MR. BHUPENDRANATH BASU (Madras, 1914)

The two extremes—the one of separation, the other of subordination—are equally impossible. The ideal that must be pursued, and which the Congress has set before itself, is that of co-ordination and comradeship, of joint partnership on equal terms. I do not say that it must materialise to-day, but I do say that every step which we take, or ask the Government to take, must point in that direction. . . . . From the very extent of India and the diversity of her population, she must have a system of government modelled on the lines of the Commonwealth of Australia, or the United States of America, modified according to Indian conditions and presided over by a representative of the Sovereign. In this constitution all will find a place, the Englishman as well as the Indian, the prince as well as the peasant, and all communities, by a judicious combination of the methods of election and selection.

SIR S. P. SINHA (Bombay, 1915)

It must be obvious to all sincere and impartial judges that no mandate, either of the Government or of the Congress, would be able to still the throbbing pain in the soul of awakening India unless the ideal held up by the Congress and accepted by the Government commended itself first to the heart and then to the head. The only satisfactory form of Government to which India can aspire cannot be anything short of "government of the people, for the people, and by the people." . . We will continue our labours until really free institutions are established for the whole of the country—not by any sudden or revolutionary change, but by gradual evolution and cautious progress.

MR. AMBIKA CHARAN MAZUMDAR (Lucknow, 1916)

Although the first Indian National Congress passed no resolution directly bearing on the question, the notification under which it was called into existence clearly stated that one of the objects of the future assembly was "indirectly to form the germ of an Indian Parliament which, if properly conducted, will constitute in a few years an unanswerable reply to the assertion that India is still wholly unfit for any form of representative institution." A generation has passed away, but a generation has risen whose sole and whole-hearted demand is nothing short of self-government as the sovereign remedy for the present unsatisfactory situation. . . . As loyal subjects of His Majesty, we of the Congress deem it our duty to tell all whom it may concern not to treat the Indian problem after the war as lightly as some irresponsible and mischievous critics are evidently disposed to do.

APPENDIX B

Representative views and declarations as to the duty of Liberalism and the absolute necessity of self-government for progress and prosperity.

THE RT. HON.
SIR HENRY CAMPBELL-BANNERMAN

There is one thing in which I will yield to none of them namely, in my devotion to the Liberal Party and my faithful adherence to Liberal principles. . . . We are members of the party of progress and action and movement, and not the party of mere resistance and delay. (THE REFORM CLUB, 6*th February*, 1899).

The Liberal Party was described by its great Leader as a great instrument of progress. It is a great instrument for progress, and the question is how are we best to use that great instrument? (HOUSE OF COMMONS, 16*th February*, 1899).

The views and opinions which I have set before you are those of a Liberal. They are the opinions which have been traditions in that Party. We seek the good of the people through the people and by trusting the people. We wish to destroy privilege or monopoly whether of class or sect or person when it is hurtful to the people. And whether in internal constitution or in external policy, we hold that it is not power, nor glory, nor wealth that exalteth a nation, but righteousness, justice and freedom. It is for you to say whether you are with us or against us.

I do not confound territorial extent with strength, nor do I see that the glory or success of the Empire is increased by beating down our neighbours. (ELECTION ADDRESS, 21*st September*, 1900).

The British power cannot there and elsewhere rest securely unless it rests upon the willing consent of a sympathetic and contented people. (OXFORD, 2*nd March*, 1901).

It is only by the consent of the governed that the British Nation can govern. (PLYMOUTH, 19*th November*, 1901).

What are these principles and facts? The virtues, the efficacy, the justice of self-government. That is one Liberal principle. The appreciation and encouragement of National sentiment. That is another Liberal principle. The recognition of the popular will constitutionally expressed through the people's representatives. That is another Liberal principle. That may do for principles. (LEICESTER, 19*th February*, 1902).

We, Liberals are accustomed to freedom of thought and action. Freedom is the breath of our life . . . . . It possesses in two of its most sacred dogmas, the only solution of the chief problems which confront our country in Imperial Policy and in regard to our domestic needs. . . . It is the universal doctrine of government by assent—government with the consent of the governed . . . . Why there is but one cardinal condition again of Liberal principle—that of direct popular control by those concerned Now these are two of the beacons by which Liberal policy should be guided. (NATIONAL LIBERAL CLUB, 5*th March*, 1902).

The principles of the Party [Liberal]—not any news

fangled principles, but the old ones which were as good to-day and as much required as they were two or three hundred years ago—were the only principles which could lead to the happiness of the people and to the development of the power and prosperity of the community. (SKIPTON, 10*th December*, 1902).

If it can be shown that poverty, whether it be material poverty, or poverty of physique and of energy, is associated with economic conditions, which though supported by the laws of the country are nevertheless contrary to economic laws and to public policy, the State can intervene without fear of doing harm. (NEWPORT, 30*th November*, 1903).

What is the Liberal Policy? . . . We stand for liberty. Our policy is the policy of freedom. It is the policy of freedom in all things that affect the life of the people, freedom of conscience . . . . freedom from class ascendency. . . . (NORWICH, 26*th October*, 1904).

John Bull had many weak points no doubt, but he had one good point above all others—that he liked that which was straightforward and open and candid, and honest and above-board both in language and in action. (NATIONAL LIBERAL CLUB, 1*st June* 1905).

Now I say if there is any man who is a true John Bull in respect of straightforwardness, etc., Sir Henry Campbell Bannerman is one.

Our principles . . . and one of these principles, let me tell you, is that the interests of persons, classes and sections must yield to the general interests of the community. (PORTSMOUTH, 16*th November*, 1906).

Good government could never be a substitute for government by the people themselves. (STIRLING, *23rd November*, 1905).

Ladies and gentlemen, so much for peace, so much for economy—two cardinal Liberal principles. But here is another—self-government and popular control: and we believe in that principle, not only on grounds of justice and on the grounds of effective administration, but on this other ground—that it exercises a wholesome influence on the character of the people who enjoy the privilege. (ALBERT HALL, *21st December*, 1905).

Sir, in all these subjects on which I have been touching, what is the aim to be kept in view, what is the star which we ought to keep our eyes upon to see that we are moving in the right direction? It is that we should promote the welfare and happiness and interests not of any particular class or section of the community but of the nation at large. That is the work of true patriotism, these are the foundations upon which a solid empire may be built. (ALBERT HALL, *15th December*, 1905).

The new Government had, he verily believed, the public conscience, the public sense of right, the public love of equity. With these they would win. (LIVERPOOL, *9th January*, 1906).

The present Government would set themselves to apply the old Liberal principles to Legislation and administration, the principles of freedom, of equal treatment of all sections of the community in civil and ecclesiastical affairs. They will include the principle of self-government, the idea that people knew best about their own affairs and would give up the old idea that there should be some-superior people in the country who were to tell their neighbours what was good for them. (STIRLING BURGHS.—CULROSS, 12*th January*, 1906).

The policy and spirit which would govern the action of the present government would be based on justice and liberty, not on privilege and monopoly. (GLASGOW, 15*th January*, 1906).

And the third is the belief that in Ireland as in every-other country throughout the King's dominions self-government is the best and safest and healthiest basis on which a community can rest. (INVERNESS, 18*th January*, 1906).

We, lovers of our country, lovers of our constitution, lovers of our public traditions and lovers of plain dealing ....I am proud and glad and relieved to see a revival of the old political spirit.........the spirit which has made Liberalism a moral force, a force making for justice sustained by a belief in mankind, and anxious to better the condition of our common life.........It was a great uprising against a doctrine, a habit of thought and a practice in public life, a method of government abhorent to the conscience and heart of the nation. (NATIONAL LIBERAL CLUB, 14*th February*, 1906).

THE RT. HON. JOHN MORLEY

Imperialism by all means if it means mercy, if it means humanity, if it means justice, but if it means your own demoralization, if it means lowering your own standard of civilization and humanity, then in the name of all you hold precious beware of it and resist it. (SYDNEY, 25*th May*, 1899).

When he [Mr. Gladstone] died Lord Salisbury said of him that he was a great Christian. Yes, and I would add that he was not a Christian for nothing. I think he must often have used to himself the language of Wordsworth, "Earth is sick and heaven is weary of the swollen words that States and Kingdoms utter when they talk of truth and justice". He, at all events, in face of all the demands of practical politics, did his best to bring those considerations of truth and justice into the minds and hearts of his countrymen.........But I do say that Mr. Gladstone, when he saw the nations going on a wrong path, saw high in the heavens that flash of the uplifted sword and the gleam of the arm of the Avenging Angel. (MANCHESTER–UNVEILING OF STATUE, *10th October*, 1901).

It is this policy of passing measures for Ireland without reference to the Irish themselves that is responsible for most of the mischief and misgovernment from which Ireland has so long suffered.........From observation of Irish Government, from experience of Irish Government, from responsibility of Irish Government, I say to you, gentlemen, face to face, it is a bad government it is a government which no nation, no set of people can be expected to endure in peace, and it is a government which we in our conscience ought to do our very best, when the time comes, when opportunity presents itself to put right as we have put so many other evils in our own system of government right.

With how much more force do these words apply to India! (MANCHESTER, *12th March*, 1902).

We are going to have I suppose—well we may have a proposal to suspend the constitution of Cape Colony. Just picture the scene in the House of Commons. The motion is made to protest against the suspension of Parliamentary Institutions in the Cape Colony. We then all get up, and we all make eloquent, passionate, argumentative speeches in favour of the right of the Colonies to govern themselves. The next day Mr. Redmond makes a motion in favour of giving self-government in one shape or another to Ireland. We then all pick out a new set of arguments. What was on Monday unanswerable on Tuesday becomes not worth mentioning. What was on Monday a sacred principle of self-government becomes on Tuesday mere moonshine and claptrap. That is a comedy in which I at least do not propose to take part. The Boers are to have self-government in order to make them loyal. The Irish are not to have it because they are disloyal. (EDINBURGH, *7th June*, 1902).

What a true picture of the way in which India is treated !

We are citizens, common citizens of a grand country ; we are the heirs of a noble tradition; we believe that human progress can only be won by human effort—and that effort, I hope, all of us in our different degrees, ages and situations will pursue with determination, with un-selfishness and with a resolute directness and simplicity that must in the end win a crowning victory. (NATIONAL LIBERAL FEDERATION ANNUAL MEETING. *13th May*, 1901).

He was for liberty wherever they could get it.

* * * * *

He looked forward to a vigorous, progessive, pacific, rational policy. The new Government, he hoped, would realise that courage in large politics was the true common sense, and he looked forward to the true progressive movement.

*   *   *   *   *

Last Session the whole Liberal Party in the House of Commons voted in favour of Mr. Redmond's Amendment, which stated that the present system of government in Ireland was in opposition to the will of the Irish People, and gave them no voice in the management of their affairs, was extravagantly costly and did not enjoy the confidence of any section of the population, was productive of universal discontent and unrest, and had been proved to be incapable of satisfactorily promoting the material and intellectual progress of the people.

Surely then it was incredible that a Party which supported an indictment so damning should have no policy for dealing with such a state of affairs. . . . . .

He would recall the fact that Sir Henry Campbell-Bannerman, the Leader of the Liberal Party, who had stuck to his guns, and had saved his party, said, speaking on that very amendment.

What was the principle at the root of the policy? It was the right of the Irish people to the management of their own domestic affairs. The successive plans by which this was to be given to them failed to satisfy the country; but the principle of self-government, the principle of an elective element that shall be the governing element in Irish affairs still remains. (FORFAR, *20th October*, 1905).

But whatever the schemes and wisdom of a statesman might be, he should know that all the glittering adventures of imperial pride were vain and empty, were delusive and guilty, if he did not constantly have before him the aim of mitigating the lot of the great masses of men, women and children who were always very near to hunger and nakedness. (WALTHAMSTOW, *20th November*, 1916).

THE RT. HON. H. H. ASQUITH

The Liberal Party is—as it always has been--the standing enemy of unjustified privileges and of unequal laws............The spirit of Liberalism is a strong and a vital factor—is as strong and as vital as it ever was—in moulding the conceptions and the ideals of the British people. (KILMARNOCK, *5th October*, 1897).

No one in this country—no British Liberal at any rate—can contemplate with satisfaction a system under which numbers of our own countrymen are denied some of those civil and political rights which we are accustomed to regard as the necessary equipment of a civilized social community. (LEVEN, *2nd Sepember*, 1899).

We call ourselves Liberals. We are proud of the name. We are prepared to maintain our title to it against all comers . . . . . . But how do we stand? What has been in days gone by the essence of the Liberal creed and the spirit of Liberal work? I think I may say, and you will agree with me, that for the first sixty or seventy years of the present century, the chief mission of Liberalism was the mission of emancipation. It waged war with religious disabilities that offended the conscience and blocked the road to talent . . . . . . more important than either it was the Liberalism of that time which laid the foundations of Democratic Government, in a society which had never been swept and levelled by the tornado of revolution. . . .

. . . If we look beyond these shores to the Greater Britain of which we have become Trustees, I think we see there again equally clear ground for the application of old principles to new problems. We are proud of the British Empire. There is no distinction on that point between one party in the State and the other. But empire is a blessing or a curse according to the spirit in which its responsibilities are approached and handled. . . . .

According to what I believe to be the liberal conception of Empire, it is something vastly greater and higher than this. There are—I belive I am speaking your sense as well as my own—in the judgment of us Liberals two tests of a standing or falling empire. We ask, in the first place, does it in all its parts make the standard not merely of material life, but of all that goes to enrich civilization and humanity higher and more deeply founded, more securely safeguarded. We ask next, does its unity arise not from the compulsory acquisition of subject races, but from the conscious and willing co-operation of living and self-determining members? Does it rest not upon the predominance, artificial and superficial, of race or class, but upon the loyal affection of free communities built upon the basis of equal rights? (EDINBURGH, *10th January* 1900).

I pause here a little. We, Indians also had the good fortune in sharing in the glorious work of the Liberal statesman of the thirties of the last century. We also had our emancipation by the Act of 1833. What a glorious and truly noble and liberal work was that at that time! I have already touched upon that subject. Had that Act been honourably, loyally and sincerely carried out what a glorious empire would by this time the British Empire have become, and how truly and nobly would the two tests laid down above have been fulfilled! The present grand revival of Liberalism, with its irresistible power, is just the opportune moment to accomplish, by a bold effort, the redemption of the past failure of duty, conscience, humanity and honour.

Liberty and justice, the touchstone of the Empire and its external arrangements. . . . . In these methods lay the only hope for the future honour of our Empire. (OXFORD, 24*th February*, 1894).

Liberty was the best antidote or medicine for discontents and disloyalty. (TAYPORT, 4*th Sepember*, 1900).

It is the work of statesmanship in this country to make the Empire worth living in, as well as worth dying for. In the long run every society is judged and every society survives according to the material and moral minium which it prescribes to its members. (HOTEL CECIL, 19*th July*, 1901).

You should aim from the very beginning at such a progressive development in self-government as will in time ripen into the full autonomy of Australia or Canada. That policy ought to commend itself not only to the Liberal Party but to the whole country. (HANLEY, 14*th January*, 1902).

The great experience of Canada, where, by the granting of free institutions, races which seventy years ago were flying at one another's throats were now sitting down side by side in harmony and contentment. That will be the case in India. (ST. LEONARDS, 14*th March*, 1902).

Mr. Asquith proceeded to set forth the Liberal ideal.

This, he said, implied self-government and self-development in fiscal as in all other matters. An excellent example was to be found in the history of Canada, where internal dissensions and external revolt against the Empire had been quelled by self government. So that the French and British portions of the population had worked out an ideal for themselves resulting in prosperity. (MORLEY, *21st February*, 1906).

If they gave the new Liberal Government a strong strenuous, independent working majority, they would find many directions, in which arrears had to be made up, reactionary steps retraced, and lost ground recovered, they would do what they could both to set right the past and to give the country a new and vigorous start for the future. (ST. MONANS, *13th January*, 1906).

In all this there was a lesson which ought to be taken to heart, namely, that in English politics it was the straightforward, the direct, the plain policy which in the long run paid. (HENLEY, *18th January*, 1906).

This country, by carrying out the great Liberal principle of confidence in the people and allowing them to manage their own affairs, would have our imperial unity on the broadest, soundest and most stable foundation. It was in this spirit that the new Government hoped to attack other problems of legislation and administration which lay before them. (EAST FIFE, *20th January*, 1906).

I conclude these declarations by two more of one who, though dead, is still living in our hearts and minds, and whom Mr. Morley himself has given his immortality in this world.

Mr. Gladstone says :—It has been providentially

alloted to this favoured isle, that it should show to all the world how freedom and authority, is their due and wise developments, not only may co-exist, in the same body, but may, instead of impairing, sustain and strengthen one another. I am deeply convinced that among us all systems, whether religious or political, which rest on a principle of absolutism, must of necessity be not indeed tyrannical, but feeble and ineffective systems, and that methodically to enlist the members of a community, with due regard to their several capacities in the performance of public duties, is the way to make that community powerful and healthful, to give a firm seat to its rulers, and to engender a warm and intelligent devotion to those beneath their sway. (DAILY NEWS, *5th May*, 1905).

The following is one of Mr. Gladstone's latest utterances on the occasion of one of the greatest achievements of his life—Home Rule for Ireland ? He said:—

It is the predominance of that moral force for which I heartily pray in the deliberations of this House and the conduct of our whole Public Policy. . . . There can be no more melancholy, and in the last result no more degrading spectacle upon earth than the spectacle of oppression or of wrong in whatever form inflicted by the deliberate act of a nation upon another nation. . . . .

But on the other hand there can be no nobler spectacle we think is now dawning upon us, the spectacle of a nation deliberately set on the removal of injustice, deliberately determined to break—not through terror and not in haste but under the sole influence of duty and honour—determined to break with whatever remains still existing of an evil tradition, and determined in that way at once to pay a debt of justice and to consult by a bold, wise and good act its own interest and its own honour.

THE RIGHT HON. R. B. HALDANE.

It was their duty to try to govern the Irish people in a sense which was more akin to their ideas and less entirely subordinate to our own . . . . . they recognised it was a duty binding upon them by every obligation of honour and policy that they should strive to bring the administration of Ireland in harmony with the minds of her people and should endeavour by every means to convert the people of this country to a juster view of their obligations to that unhappy land and to a fuller recognition of their title to admin ister those things that were their own (NORTH BERWICK, *23rd January*, 1906).

Now these sentiments and principles apply with manifold force to India to whom the British people are bound to give self-government, not only by rights of births as British citizens, but also by a "duty binding upon them [the British people] by every obligation of honour and policy" by the most solemn pledges given several times before God and the world.

The breath to the nostrils of the Imperial Organisation was FREEDOM. (DARLETON, *24th January*, 1906).

I make no comments on these declarations, as being the statesmen's own, nobody can more realise their full scope, significance and application to India than themselves.

All these declarations apply with manifold force to India under the peculiar circumstances of a foreign draining domination under which she is suffering—a circumstance, which in its very nature cannot but be evil.

LORD ROBERTS

Our greatest strength must ever rest on the firm base of a united and contented India.

SIR CHARLES ELLIOT

I do not hesitate to say that half the agricultural population do not know from one year's end to another what it is to have a full meal.

LORD MACAULAY

We are free, we are civilized, to little purpose, if we grudge to any portion of the human race an equal measure of freedom and civilization. 1833.

SISTER NIVEDITA

. . . Political freedom is the birthright of every nation ; and even a bad and inefficient swadesi government is much better than the most angelic government by absente rulers and their irresponsible servants.

ABRAHAM LINCOLN

The doctrine of Self-Government is right—absolutely and internally right. . . . When the white man governs himself, that is Self-Government, but when he governs himself and also governs another man, that is more than Self-Government—that is Despotism.

MR. COWLEY

The liberty of a people consists in being governed by laws which they have made for themselves, under whatever form it be of Government. The liberty of a private man, in being master of his own time and actions as far as may consist with the laws of God and of his country

MR. W. T. STEAD

I am more deeply impressed than ever I was with the immense influence which might be wielded in the future history of the world by Britain and India acting together. Such co-operation must be, of course based upon the recognition of the right of India to be treated as a free and equal partner and not as a dependent of the Empire.

SIR FRANCIS MACLEAN

He had heared great deal recently, since coming to India of sedition, and measures in connection with it; but it seemed to him the only rational way of putting down sedition was by sympathy, boundless sympathy, with the people in their needs and their sufferings, and with their legitimate hopes and aspirations.

THE DUKE OF DEVONSHIRE

It is not wise to educate the people of India, to introduce among them your civilization and your progress and your literature, and at the same time to tell them that they shall never have any chance of taking any part or share in the administration of the affairs of their country, except by getting rid in the first instance of their European rulers.

LORD LAWRENCE

The people of India are capable of administering their own affairs, and the municipal feeling is deep-rooted in them. The village communities, each of which is a little republic, are the most abiding of Indian institutions. Holding the position we do in India, every view of duty and policy should induce us to leave as much as possible of the business of the country to be done by the people.

MARQUESS OF SALISBURY

No system of Government can be permanently safe where there is a feeling of inferiority or of mortification affecting the relations between the governing and the governed. There is nothing I would more earnestly wish to impress upon all who leave this country for the purpose of governing India that that if they choose to be so, they are the only enemies England has to fear. They are the persons who can, if they will, deal a blow of the deadliest character at the future rule of England.

MR. LOWELL THE REFINED AMERICAN SCHOLAR AND STATESMAN

It is only by the instigation of the wrongs of men that what are called the rights of men become turbulent and dangerous. It is then only that the syllogise unveil come truths. It is not the insurrection of ignorance that are dangerous, but the revolts of intelligence. It is only when the reasonable and the practical are denied that men demand the unreasonable and impracticable; only when the possible is made difficult that they fancy the impossible to be easy.

DR. RASH BEHARY GHOSE

All we ask is that our country should take her rightful place among the nations under the ægis of England. We want in reality, and not in mere name, to be sons of the Empire. Our ambition is to draw closer to England and to be absorbed in that greater Britain in which we have now no place. The ideal after which we are striving is antonomy within the Empire and not absolute independency.

THE RT. HON. LLOYD GEORGE

There are times in history when this world spins so leisurely along its destined course that it seems for centuries to be at a stand-still. There are also times when it rushes along a giddy pace covering the track of centuries in a year. These are such times. Six weeks ago Russia was an autocracy. She is now one of the most advanced democracies in the world. (American Luncheon Club, London).

CHARLES BRADLAUGH

We don't want to rule India by the sword. We want to put before the people of India a future in which, if they will be patient, as they have been, they may climb, slowly it may be, but surely, to the fullest right of self-government. . . . If we are to rule these 250 millions of people at all, we must rule them not in the way in which we have gone to their country and taken possession of it but in the way in which we should like to be ruled if it had been their people who had come and taken possession of our country. I regret that it should be needful, before an audience speaking the tongue which pretends to be identified with the traditions of liberty, to make such an appeal; but it is needful.

SIR S. SUBRAMANIA IYER, K.C.I.E., LL.D.

If the will of a handful of resolute men in South Africa, exerted without overt acts of violence or injury, has enabled them successfully to resist gigantic tyranny and wrong, by compelling an unwilling public opinion, as it were throughout the civilised world, to cast its vote in favour of the oppressed passive resisters, what cannot the will of hundreds of millions of our people accomplish by its own sheer force, without the least resort to any militancy if organised and turned towards the attainment of our legitimate national aims and aspirations.'

SIR W. W. HUNTER

I cannot believe that a people numbering one sixth of the whole inhabitants of the globe and whose aspirations have been nourished from their earliest youth on the strong food of English liberty, can be permanently denied a voice in the Government of their country. I do not believe that races * * * into whom we have instilled the maxim of "no taxation without representation" as a fundamental right of a people, can be permanently excluded from a share in the management of their finances.

DR. RAJENDRA LAL MITRA

Diverse we are in origin, in religion, in language, and in our manners and customs, but we are not the less members of the same nation. We live in the same country, we were subjects of the same sovereign, and our good and evil depends entirely on the state of the Government and the laws passed, in this country, whatever is beneficial to the Hindus is equally beneficial to the Muhamandans and whatever is injurious to the Hindus is equally injurious to the followers of Muhamad. Nations are not made of sects but if tribes bound together by the same political bond and therefore we constitute one nation.

SIR HENRY COTTON

Let us accustom ourselves to the conception which the realisation of a national spirit in India involves. The present form of British administration cannot survive the fulfilment of those national tendencies which the British Government itself has brought into existence. . . many years must elapse before we can expect the consummation of a reconstructive policy. But it is a policy we should always keep before our eyes. Indian patriots look back on their past with a sense of pride and they know that India will again take her own rank among the nations of the East. They are striving for the attainment of this ideal which however it may be delayed or marred in execution, is sure in the west.

HON. G. K. GOKHALE

I recognise no limits to my aspiration for our Motherland. I want our people to be in their own country what other people are in theirs. I want our men and women, without distinction of caste or creed, to have opportunities to grow to the full height of their stature, unhampered by cramping and unnatural restrictions. I want India to take her proper place among the great nations of the world, politically, industrially, in religion, in literature, in science and in arts. I want all this and feel at the same time that the whole of this aspiration can, in its essence and its reality, be realised within this Empire.—Speech at Allahabad, 4th February, 1907.

MARQUESS OF HASTINGS

A time, not very remote, will arrive when England will, on sound principles of policy, wish to relinquish the domination which she has gradually and unintentionally assumed over this country India and from which she cannot at present recede. In that hour it would be the proudest boast and most delightful reflection that she had used her sovereign towards enlightening her temporary subjects, so as to enable the native communities to walk alone in the paths of justice, and to maintain with probity towards their benefactors that commercial intercourse in which we should then find a solid interest. (*17th May*, 1816).

LORD MACAULAY

Are we to keep the people of India ignorant in order that we may keep them submissive ? or do we think that we can give them knowledge without awakening ambition ? Or do we mean to awaken ambition and to provide it with no legitimate vent? Who will answer any of these questions in the affirmative? Yet one of them must be answered in the affirmative by every person who maintains that we ought permanently to exclude the native from high office. I have no fears. The path of duty is plain before us: and it is also the path of wisdom of National prosperity, of national honor.

MR. JOHN BRIGHT

I believe that it is our duty not only to govern India well now for our sakes and to satisfy your own conscience but so to arrange its Government and so to administer it that we should look forward to the time when India will have to take up her own Government and administer it in her own fashion. I say he is no statesman he is no man actuated with a high moral sense with regard to our great and terrible moral responsibility. Who is not willing thus to look a head and thus to prepare for circumstances which may come sooner than we think, and sooner any of us hope for, but which must come at some not very distant date. (*Manchester*, *11th December*, 1877).

SIR H. J. S. COTTON

The ryots cry aloud for bread and we have given them a volume of new laws to comfort them. The statute book grows exceedingly. From an object of wonder it has become an object of suspicion and distrust.

DR. H. S. GOUR, L.L.B.

Without Self-Government it is impossible for India to utilise its vast unlimited material and moral resources to the full extent India wants to play her part honourably in the Empire.

MR. BERNARD SHAW

All demonstrations of the virtues of a foreign bureaucracy, " though often conclusive, are as useless as demonstrations of the superiority of artificial teeth, glass eyes, silver wind-pipes and patent wooden legs to the natural products."

LORD MAYO

I admit the comparative poverty of this country (India) as compared with many other countries of the same magnitude and importance, and I am convinced of the impolicy and injustice of imposing burdens upon this people which may be called either crushing or oppressive.

LORD CURZON

Powerful empires existed and flourished in India while the Englishmen were still wandering painted in the woods. India has left a deeper mark upon the history, the philosophy and the religion of mankind than any other territorial unit in the universe.

SIR WILLIAM HUNTER

Forty millions of the people of India habitually go through life on insufficient food. The Indian Congress has outlived the early period of misrepresentation, it has shown that it belongs to no single section of the population. Indian political reformers have, if they only know it, an opportunity such as seldom happened in the history of Nations.

MR. ALFRED WEBB, M. P.

There is no possibility of turning back. Once imbue nations with aspirations for progress and enlightenment and they must go forwards towards liberty.

For fifty years the Anglo-Indian Government has been urging you to educate yourselves, to imbibe principles of constitutional liberty, to obliterate old divisions, to break down caste prejudices, to rise to the level of British citizenship, and unite for the good of a common country.

SIR JAGADISH CHUNDER BOSE

What are our duties to our country? These are essentially to win honor for it and also win for it security and peace. As regards winning honor for our country it is true that while India has offered from the earliest times welcome and hospitality to all peoples and Nationalities, her children have been subjected to intolerable humiliation in other countries even under the flag of our king. There is no question of the fundamental duty of every Indian to stand up and uphold the honor of his country and strive for the removal of wrong.

MR. WILFRIDS BLUNT

I rejoice to learn from them that the All-India Moslem League has now adopted as its settled programme to act in cordial concert with the progressive Hindu and other communities in India in the patriotic work of obtaining at our hands some measure of Home Rule. This is a new departure of the very highest significance, and I trust that its full meaning will be understood at the India Office. Until it is brought home to the official understanding that the old system of administration through an alien bureaucracy is out of date, nothing will even begin to be accomplished in the direction of progressive liberty.

SIR GEORGE CHESNEY

The lame and halting defence made by the Secretary of State of the high handed action of the Government he represented the ignominous position exhibited by the Government of India forced to carry out a measure against their obvious wishes and sense of duty, from an episode in our relations towards that country, indispensible nature of which may be measured by the indignation felt and expressed among all classes in India, Indians and Englishmen alike, so barefaced a declaration of the desire to rule India in British interests against the wishes and interests of its people and its Government can hardly fail to lead to injurious consequences.

MR. G. SUBRAMANIA IYER

Who are they that say the people of India are not fit for swaraj ? The English people say so, those who profit by Indian's subjection say so. But it is an old cry. It was raised against the middle class in England, it was raised against the mechanics of the great towns ; it was raised against the country rustic, it is now being raised against women, and in every case it was raised and is raised by the people in possession who did not and do not want to lose their power. Foreign observers with a sufficient insight into the social conditions of the country do not think that our variety of castes and creeds is an obstacle to the growth of Nationality.

SIR JOHN MALCOLM

We are not warranted by the History of India, nor indeed by that of any other nation in the world, in reckoning upon the possibility of preserving an Empire of such a magnitude by a system which excludes, as ours does, the natives from every station of high rank and honorable ambition. * * * If we do not use the knowledge which we impart, it will be employed against us. * * * If these plans are not associated with the creation of duties that will employ the minds which we enlighten, we shall only prepare elements that will hasten the destruction of our Empire. The moral evil to us does not thus stand alone. It carries with it, its Nemisis, the seeds of the destruction of the Empire itself.

MR. HERBERT BURROWS

I attach no importance to the theory of "fitness for self-government." England should make a public declaration to the world that she was in India, not for her own advantage but for the good of India herself, and that at the earliest possible moment—to be decided by friendly and peaceful consultation with the best representatives of Indian thought—she would withdraw her government from the country, while helping in the interval by every means in her power the self-development of India. These were the fundamental principles which should apply equally to Ireland and to India, and to every part of the Empire—free self-government and development as free and equal partners in a federation of free States.—*July* 2, 1916.

Mr. ZANGWILL

Mr. Israel Zangwill, said he was in favour of self-government for all races, including even such a low race as women. (Laughter.) He had always held the opinion that the English blundered into India as they blundered into most things, and the best they could wish for her now was not to blunder out of India, but by a long, careful, diplomatic and statesmanlike process so to govern India as to make the people of that country wish to remain an integral portion of our empire in exactly the same way as Canada and South Africa. He hoped that before long India would be granted the fullest measure of self-government. Lord Hardinge was a strong man, but unlike most strong men he could appreciate what was in other men's minds as well as his own.

Dr. RUTHERFORD

Dr. Rutherford expressed a hope that the people of India would at no distant date get self-government and Home Rule, and that the English people would be made to feel that they had never succeeded in their mission in the world until India did govern herself. The Indians, by the grand stand they were making in South Africa, were, showing that they had the courage of their convictions and the sooner both Briton and Boer gave justice, liberty, and equal rights to Indian subjects in South Africa, the sooner would they get that credit which such action alone could entitle them to. He desired to wish their hosts God speed in their work. The growing solidarity between Hindus and Moslems was one of the greatest achievements of the time.

PROCLAMATION OF QUEEN VICTORIA

When by the blessings of Providence internal tranquility shall be restored it is our earnest desire to stimulate..............and to administer its government for the benefit of all our subjects resident therein. In their prosperity will be our strength, in their contentment our security and in their gratitude our best reward......... Queen Victoria's Reply to Jubilee address of the Bombay Municipal Corporation.

Addition is made to the Proclamation issued on the occasion of my assumption of the direct government of India as the Charter of Liberties of the Princes and Peoples of India. It has always been and will be continued to be my earnest desire that the principles of that Proclamation should be unswearingly maintained.

DR. RABINDRANATH TAGORE

Where the mind is without fear and the head is held high;
Where knowledge is free;
Where the world has not been broken up into fragments by narrow domestic walls;
Where words come out from the depth of truth;
Where tireless striving stretches its arms towards perfection;
Where the clear stream of reason has not lost its way into the dreary desert sand of dead habit;
Where the mind is led forward by Thee into ever-widening thought and action—
Into that heaven of freedom, my father, let my country awake.

BABU AUROBINDO GHOSE

Have you got a real faith ? Or is it merely a political aspiration ? Is it merely a larger kind of selfishness ? Or is it merely that you wish to be free to oppress others as you are being oppressed ? Do you hold your political creed from a higher source ? Is it God that is born in you ? Have you realised that you are merely the instruments of God, that your bodies are not your own ? You are merely instruments of God. For the work of the Almighty. Have you realised that ? If you have realised that then you are true Nationalists, then alone will you be able to restore this great Nation. Then there will be a blessing on our work and this great Nation will rise again and become once more what it was in the days of its spiritual greatness. You are the instruments of God to save the light, to save the spirit of India from lasting obscuration and abasement.

PANDIT MOTILAL NEHRU

Our position has been clearly stated in the representation made by the joint conference of the National Congress and the Moslen League held at Bombay. That representation embodies our answer to the policy of repression in a dignified and emphatic manner. It makes it clear that the newly awakened spirit is not to be suppressed by the Defence of India Act or the Press Act. It asks for the complete reversal of the policy of repression and the immediate release of the interned patriots. While demanding the Congress-moslem League scheme of reforms be given effect to after the close of the war, it invites the Government to publish its own proposals for public discussion. It insists on an authoritative pronouncement pledging the Government to a policy of making India a self-governing member of the British Empire, being made at an early date. We ask for no more and will be satisfied with no less.

DR. ANANDA K. COOMARASWAMY

We feel it then our duty to realise our unity and national self-consciousness in concrete form as much for the advantage of others as of ourselves ; and this without any feeling of bitterness or exclusiveness towards other races, though perhaps for a time such feelings may be inevitable. And to show what spirit moves us we have such a statement of belief in the unity of the Indian people, as the credo of Shiv Narayen; and the beautiful national song, called "Bande Mataram" (Hail! Motherland") which expresses the aims and the power of the unawakened Indian National....,.......Their words are not the hysterical utterance of a people uncertain of their unity or doubtful of their future. They express the Indian recognition of the Motherland, their quiet but profound assurance of her greatness and their consciousness of the high calling which is hers. They voice the hope of an Indian Nation, which shall not be disappointed.

MR. B. G. TILAK

The mere shifting of the centre of power and authority from one official to another is not in my opinion, calculated to restore the feelings of cordiality between officers and people prevailing in earlier days. English education has created new aspiration and ideals amongst the people and so long as these national aspirations remain unsatisfied, it is useless, to expect that the hiatus between the officers and the people could be removed by any scheme of decentralisation whatever its other effects may be. It is no remedy, not even palliative against the evil complained of, nor was it ever put forward by the people or their leaders. The fluctuating wave of decentralisation may infuse more or less life in the individual members of the bureaucracy, but it cannot remove the growing estrangement between the rulers and the ruled, unless and until the people are allowed more and more effective voice in the management of their own affairs in an ever expansive spirit of wise liberalism and wide sympathy aiming at raising India to the level of the governing country.

MR. ANDREW CARNEGIE

That there is a strong and growing desire on the part of educated Indians ultimately to govern their own country goes without saying. They would not be educated if this aspiration did not arise within them. Education makes rebels against invaders. Material benefits conferred by them, however great, count for little against the spirit of national independence. . . . British history cannot be read and understood without inspiring within the studious reader under military control an invincible desire to govern his own country.

If India be properly guided, no violent revolution need be feared. The movement towards independence would be orderly and slow, although irresistible. . . . The true policy of Britain is to say some day to India, as she said to Canada and Australia, that if she ever feels the time has arrived when she must establish government for herself, so be it. It is because this had been said to the British self-governing colonies that they remain loyal colonies to-day. Proclaim coercion and the part of America will soon be played by them again. When India is told this, the effect will be as it has been with the colonies—to bind her closer and to keep her longer than otherwise within the Empire.

BABU ANANDA MOHAN BOSE

It is *because* we are friends to British Rule it is *because* all our highest hopes for the future and not our hopes only but the hopes of generations to come are indissolubly bound up with the *continuance* of that rule, with the strengthening and lecturing of that rule, with the removal of all and every cause which may tend to the weakening of that rule and there are such causes in operation that we speak out, and point the impolicy, the unwisdom, yea, the danger of the recent course of administrative and legislative proceedings. It is because of this feeling that we are trying to the best of our power alas, so limited to induce the authorities, and the great body of justice loving and generous minded Englishmen, both here and in England to withdraw from that course and find the path of safety, of honor of mutual advantage and the truest and most abiding glory, in going forward in fearless confidence, trusting the people, extending the bounds of freedom, not forgoing new features but gradually removing those that exist not taking away but adding to the rights of the people helping on the cause of India's regeneration with the passionate longing and the loving ardour that come from consciousness of a duty and a solemn responsibility from on high.

SIR HENRY COTTON

Autonomy is the keynote of England's true relations with her great Colonies. It is the keynote also of India's destiny. It is more than this—it is the destiny of the world. The tendency of Empire in the civilised world is in the direction of compact lautonomous States, which are federated together, and attached by common motives and self-interest to a central Power. . . . It was the dream of John Bright and he indulged in no mystic prophecy when he foresaw that India would fulfil her ultimate destinies by a process of evolution, out of which she would emerge, not through force or violence as an independent state, or torn from Great Britain, or abandoned to England's enemies, but as a federated portion of the dominion of the Great British Empire. The ideal of the Indian patriot is the establishment of a federation of free and separate States, the United States of India, placed on a fraternal footing with the self-governing Colonies, and with its own local autonomy cemented together under the ægis of Great Britain.

MR. CHARLES ROBERTS

It was clear that India claimed to be not a mere dependant of, but a partner in, the Empire, and her partnership with us in spirit and on the battlefields could not but alter the angle from which we should all henceforward look at the problems of the Government of India. (Cheers.) He might call the attention of the House of Commons to one possible illustration of this change in the point of view. It must be a source of pride and satisfaction to India that she had sent the first of the great contingents from the Over-Seas Dominions into the European theatre of War, and that one of her brave soldiers, if the newspaper statements were correct, had been recommended for the coveted distinction of the Victoria Cross.—*Speech in the House of Commons as Under Secretary for India.*

APPENDIX C

THE SELF-GOVERNMENT RESOLUTIONS OF THE NATIONAL CONGRESS AND THE ALL INDIA MOSLEM LEAGUE

1. That having regard to the fact that the great communities of India are the inheritors of ancient civilisations and have shown great capacity for Government and administration and to the progress in education and public spirit made by them during a century of British rule and further having regard to the fact that the present system of Government does not satisfy the legitimate aspirations of the people and has become unsuited to the existing conditions and requirements, the Congress is of opinion that the time has come when His Majesty the King-Emperor should be pleased to issue a proclamation announcing that it is the aim and intention of British policy to confer self-government on India at an early date; that this Congress demands that a definite step should be taken towards self-Government by granting the reforms contained in the scheme prepared by the All-India Congress Committee in concert with the Reform Committee appointed by the All-India Moslem League; that in the construction of the Empire, India shall be lifted from the position of a Dependency to that of an equal partner in the Empire with the self-Governing Dominions.

2. All India Muslim League, while adopting the scheme of reforms prepared by the Reform Committee of the League and approved by its Council, submits it in conjunction with the Indian National Congress to Government for its introduction after the War as a first necessary step towards the establishment of complete Self-Government in India.

APPENDIX D

THE CONGRESS AND THE MOSLEM LEAGUE'S SCHEME OF POST-WAR REFORMS

I. *Provincial Legislative Councils*

1. Provincial Legislative Councils shall consist of four-fifths elected and of one-fifth nominated members.

2. Their strength shall be not less than 125 members in the major provinces, and from 50 to 75 in the minor provinces.

3. The members of Councils should be elected directly by people on as broad a franchise as possible.

4. Adequate provision should be made for representation of important minorities by election, and that the Mahomedans should be represented through special electorates on the Provincial Legislative Councils.

Provided that Mahomedans shall not participate in any of the other elections to the Legislative Councils.

5. The head of the Provincial Government should not be the President of the Legislative Council but the Council should have the right of electing its President.

6. The right of asking supplementary questions should not be restricted to the member putting the original question, but should be allowed to be exercised by any other member.

7. (*a*) Except customs, post, telegraph, mint, salt opium, railways, army and navy, and tributes from Indian states, all other sources of revenue should be provincial.

(*b*) There should be no divided heads of revenue. The Government of India should be provided with fixed contributions from the Provincial Governments, such fixed contributions being liable to revision where extraordinary and unforeseen contingencies render such revision necessary.

(*c*) The Provincial Council should have full authority to deal with all matters affecting the internal administration of the province, including the power to raise loans, to impose and alter taxation, and to vote on the Budget. All items of expenditure, all proposals concerning ways and means for raising the necessary revenue should be embodied in Bills and submitted to the Provincial Council for adoption.

(*d*) Resolutions on all matters within the perview of the Provincial Government should be allowed for discussion in accordance with rules made in that behalf by the Council itself.

(*e*) A resolution passed by the Legislative Council shall be binding on the Executive Government, unless vetoed by the Governor in Council, provided however that if the resolution is again passed by the Council after an interval of not less than one year, it must be given effect to.

(*f*) A motion for adjournment may be brought forward for the discussion of a definite matter of urgent public importance if supported by not less than one eighth of the members present.

8. Any special meeting of the Council may be summoned on a requisition by not less than one-eighth of the members.

9. A Bill, other than a money Bill, may be introduced

in Council in accordance with the rules made in that behalf by the Council itself, and the consent of the Government should not be required therefor.

10. All Bills passed by Provincial Legislature shall have to receive the assent of the Governor before they become law, but may be vetoed by the Governor-General.

11. The term of office of the members shall be five years.

II. Provincial Governments

1. The head of every Provincial Government shall be a Governor who shall not ordinarily belong to the Indian Civil Service or any of the permanent services.

2. There shall be in every province an Executive Council which, with the Governor, shall constitute the Executive Government of the Province.

3. Members of the Indian Civil Service shall not ordinarily be appointed to the Executive Councils.

4. Not less than one half of the members of Executive Council shall consist of Indians to be elected by the elected members of the Provincial Legislative Council.

5. The term of office of the members shall be five years.

III. Imperial Legislative Council

1. The strength of the Imperial Legislative Council shall be 150.

2. Four-fifths of the members shall be elected.

3. The Franchise for the Imperial Legislative Council should be widened as far as possible on the lines of the Mahomedan electorates and the elected members of the Provincial Legislative Councils should also form an electorate for the return of Members to the Imperial Legislative Council.

4. The President of the Council shall be elected by the Council itself.

5. The right of asking supplementary questions shall not be restricted to the member putting the original question but should be allowed to be exercised by any other member.

6. Any special meeting of the Council may be summoned on a requisition by not less than one-eigth of the members.

7. A Bill, other than a Money Bill, may be introduced in Council in accordance with rules made in that behalf by the Council itself, and the consent of the Executive Goverument should not be required therefor.

8. All Bills passed by the Council shall have to receive the assent of the Governor-General before they become law.

9. All financial proposals relating to sources of income and items of expenditure shall be embodied in Bills. Every such Bill and the Budget as a whole shall be submitted for the vote of the Imperial Legislative Council.

10. The term of office of members shall be five years.

11. The matters mentioned hereinbelow shall be exclusively under the control of the Imperial Legislative council:—

(*a*) Matters in regard to which uniform legislation for the whole of India is desirable.

(*b*) Provincial legislation in so far as it may affect inter-provincial fiscal relations.

(*c*) Questions affecting purely Imperial Revenue excepting tributes from Indian states.

(*d*) Questions affecting purely Imperial expenditure, except that no resolution of the Imperial Legislative

Council shall be binding on the Governor-General in Council in respect of Military Charges for the defence of the country.

(*e*) The right of revising Indian tariffs and customs-duties, of imposing, altering, or removing any tax or cess, modifying the existing system of currency and banking, and granting any aids or bounties to any or all deserving and nascent industries of the country.

(*f*) Resolutions on all matters relating to the administration of the country as a whole.

12. A resolution passed by the Legislative Council should be binding on the Executive Government, unless vetoed by the Governor-General in Council: provided, however, that if the Resolution is again passed by the Council after an interval of not less than one year, it must be given effect to.

13. A motion for adjournment may be brought forward for the discussion of a definite matter of urgent public importance, if supported by not less than one-eighth of the members present.

14. The Crown may exercise its power of veto in regard to a Bill passed by a Provincial Legislative Council or by the Imperial Legislative Council within twelve months from the date on which it is passed, and the Bill shall cease to have effect as from the date on which the fact of such veto is made known to the Legislative Council concerned.

15. The Imperial Legislative Council shall have no power to interfere with the Government of India's direction of the military affairs and the foreign political relations of

India, including declaration of war, the making of peace and the entering into treaties.

IV. The Government of India

1. The Governor-General of India will be the head of the Government of India.

2. He will have an Executive Council, half of whom shall be Indians.

3. The Indian members should be elected by the elected members of the Imperial Legislative Council.

4. Members of the Indian Civil Service shall not ordinarily be appointed to the executive council of the Governor-General.

5. The power of making all appointments in the Imperial Civil Services shall vest in the Government of India as constituted under this scheme, and subject to any laws that may be made by the Imperial Legislative Council.

6. The Government of India shall not ordinarily interfere in the local affairs of a province, and powers not specially given to a Provincial Government shall be deemed to be vested in the former. The authority of the Government of India will ordinarily be limited to general supervision and superintendence over the Provincial Governments.

7. In legislative and administrative matters, the Government of India, as constituted under this scheme, shall, as far as possible, be independent of the Secretary of State.

8. A system of independent audit of the accounts of the Government of India should be instituted.

V. The Secretary of State in Council

1. The Council of the Secretary of State for India should be abolished.

2. The salary of the Secretary of State should be placed on the British estimates.

3. The Secretary of State should, as far as possible, occupy the same position in relation to the Government of India as the Secretary of State for the Colonies in relation to the Governments of the Self-Governing Dominions.

4. The Secretary of State for India should be assisted by two permanent under secretaries, one of whom should always be an Indian.

VI. Military and other Matters of Policy

1. The military and naval services of His Majesty both in their commissioned and non-commissioned ranks, should be thrown open to Indians and adequate provision should be made for their selection, training and instruction in India.

2. Indians should be allowed to enlist as Volunteers.

3. Indians should be placed on a footing of equality in respect of status and rights of citizenship with other subjects of His Majesty the King throughout the Empire.

4. The executive officers in India shall have no judicial powers entrusted to them and the judiciary in every province shall be placed under the highest Court of that Province.

N. B.—As regards communal representation in Legislative Councils, the following percentages have been agreed upon.

Mahomedan representation for the Punjab 50 per cent.; Bengal 40 per cent.; Bombay $33\frac{1}{2}$ per cent.; United

Provinces 30 per cent ; Central Provinces 15 per cent. ; Madras 15 per cent. It has also been agreed to, that if in any province two thirds of a community be against any measure or Bill, it should be dropped by both communities.

APPENDIX E

REFORMS AFTER THE WAR

THE NON-OFFICIAL MEMORANDUM

Submitted by the 19 *elected members of the Imperial Legislative Council*

There is no doubt that the termination of the War will see a great advance in the ideals of Government all over the civilised world, and especially in the British Empire, which entered into the struggle in defence of the liberties of weak and small nationalities, and is pouring forth its richest blood and treasure in upholding the cause of justice and humanity. In the international relations of the world India has borne her part in this struggle, and cannot remain unaffected by the new spirit of change for a better state of things. Expectaticns have been raised in this country, and hopes have been held out that, after the War, the problems of Indian administration will be looked at from a new angle of vision.

UNCOMPLETED WORK

The people of India have good reason to be grateful to England for the great progress in her material resources and the widening of her intellectual and political outlook by the British Rule and for the steadiest, if slow, advance. Commencing with the Charter Act of India of 1833 up to 1909, the Government of India was conducted by a bureaucracy almost entirely non-Indian in its composition.

and not responsible to the people of India. The reforms of 1909, for the first time, introduced an Indian element in the direction of affairs in the administration of India. This element was of a very limited character. The Indian people accepted it as an indication on the part of the Government of a desire to admit Indians into the inner counsels of the Indian Empire.

So far as the Legislative Councils are concerned, the number of non-officials was merely enlarged with increased facilities for debate and interpellation. The Supreme Legislative Council retained an absolute official majority, and in the Provincial Legislative Councils, where a non-official majority was allowed, such a majority included nominated members and European representatives. In the measures, largely affecting the people whether of legislation or taxation, an European would naturally support the Government and the nominated members, being nominees of the Government, would be inclined to take the same side. Past experience has shown that this has actually happened on various occasions. The non-official majorities, therefore, in the Provincial Councils have proved largely illusory, and give no real power to the representatives of the people. The Legislative Councils, whether Supreme or Provincial, are at present nothing but advisory bodies without any power of effective control over the Government Imperial or Provincial. The people or their representatives are practically as little associated with the real government of the country as they were before the reforms, except for the introduction of Indian Members in the Executive Council where again the nomination rests entirely with the Government, the people having no voice in the selection of Indian members.

The object which the Government had in view in introducing the reforms of 1909 was, as expressed by the Prime Minister in his speech in the House of Commons on the second reading of the Indian Council Bill on the 1st April of 1909, that it was most desirable in circumstances to give to the people of India the feeling that these Legislative Councils are not mere automate, the wires of which were pulled by the official hierarchy. This object, it is submitted has not been attained.

OTHER DISABILITIES

Apart from the question of the constitution of the Legislative and Executive Councils, the people labour under certain grave disabilities, which not only prevent the utilisation but also lead to the wastage of what is best in them, and are positively derogatory to their sense of national self-respect. The Arms Act which excludes from its operation Europeans and Anglo-Indians, and applies only to the pure natives of the country, the disqualifications of Indians for forming or joining Volunteer Corps and their exclusion from the commissioned ranks of the army are disabilities which are looked upon with an irritation and sense of racial differentiation. It would be bad enough, if these were mere disabilities. The restrictions and prohibitions regarding the possession and use of arms have tended to emasculate the civil population in India and expose them to serious danger. The position of Indians in India is practically this that they have no real part or share in the direction of the government of the country and are placed under very great and galling disabilities from which the other members of the British Empire are exempt, and which have reduced them to a state of utter helplessness. The existence moreover of the system of Indentured Emigration gives to the British Colonies and the outside world the impression that Indians, as a whole, are no better than indentured coolies, who are looked upon as very little, if at all, above the slave. The present state of things makes the Indians feel that, though theoretically they are equal subjects of the King, they hold a very inferior position in the British Empire. Other Asiatic races also hold the same, if not a worse, view about India and her status in the Empire. Humiliating as this position of inferiority is to the Indian mind, it is almost unbearable to the youth of India, whose outlook is broadened by education and travel in foreign parts where they come in contact with other free races.

In the face of these grievances and disabilities, what has sustained the people is the hope and faith inspired by promises and assurances of fair and equal treatment which have been held out from time to time by our Sovereigns and British statesmen of high standing. In the crisis we are now going through, the Indian people have sunk domestic differences between themselves and the Government and have faithfully and loyally stood by the Empire. The Indian soldiers were eager to go to Battle fields of Europe not as mercenary troops but as free citizens of the British Empire which requires their services, and her civilian population was animated by one desire, namely to stand by England in the hour of her need. Peace and tranquillity reigned throughout India when she was practically denuded of British and Indian troops. The Prime Minister of England, while rousing the sentiments of the English people in regard to India's part in this great

War, spoke of Indians as "the joint and equal custodians of one common interest and future."

WHAT IS WANTED

India does not claim any reward for her loyalty, but she has a right to expect that the want of confidence on the part of the Government, to which she not unnaturally ascribes her present state, should now be a thing of the past, and that she should no longer occupy a position of subordination, but one of comradeship. This would assure the Indian people that England is ready and willing to help them to attain Self-Government under the aegis of the British Crown, and thus discharge the noble mission which she has undertaken, and to which she has so often given voluntary expression through her rulers and statesmen. What is wanted is not merely good government or efficient administration, but government that is acceptable to the people, because it is responsible to them. This is what India understands, would constitute the changed angle of vision.

If, after the termination of the War, the position of India practically remains what it was before, and there is no material change, it will undoubtedly cause bitter disappointment and great discontent in the country and the beneficent efforts of participation in common danger, overcome by common effort, will soon disappear, leaving no record behind save the painful memory of unrealised expectations. We feel sure that the Government is also alive to the situation, and has contemplated measures of reform in the administration of the country. We feel that we should avail ourselves of this opportunity to respectfully offer to the Government our humble suggestions as to the lines on which these reforms should proceed. They must in our opinion, go to the root of the matter. They must give to the people real and effective participation in the government of the country and also remove those irritating disabilities as regards the possession of arms and a military career, which indicate a want of confidence in the people and place them in a position of inferiority and helplessness. Under the first head, we would take the liberty to suggest the following measures for consideration and adoption :—

(1) In all the Executive Councils Provincial and Imperial, half the number of members should be Indians. The European element in the Executive Councils should, as far as possible, be nominated from the ranks of men trained and educated in the public life of England so that India may have the benefit of a wider outlook and larger experience of the outside world. It is not absolutely essential that the members of the Executive Councils, Indians or Europeans should have experience of actual administration, for, as in the case of the ministers in England, the assistance of the permanent officials of the department is always available to them. As regards Indians, we venture to say that sufficient number of qualified Indians, who can worthily fill the office of members of the Executive Councils and hold portfolios, is always available. Our short experience in this direction has shown how Indians like Sir S. P. Sinha, Sir Syed Ali Imam, the late Mr. Krishnaswamy Iyer, Sir Shamsul Huda and Sir Sankaran Nair have maintained the high level in the discharge of their duties. Moreover, it is well known that the Native States where Indians have

opportunities have produced renowned administrators like Sir Salar Jung, Sir T. Madhava Rao, Sir Seshadri Iyer, Dewan Bahadur Raghunatha Rao, not to mention the present administrators in the various Native States of India. The Statutory obligation now existing that three of the members of the Supreme Executive Council shall be selected from the public services in India. and similar provisions with regard to Provincial Councils, should be removed. The elected representatives of the people should have a voice in the selection of the Indian members of the Executive Councils and for the purpose a principle of election should be adopted.

(2) All the Legislative Councils in India should have a substantial majority of elected representatives. We feel sure that they will safeguard the interests of the masses and the agricultural population, with whom they are in closer touch than a European officer however sympathetic, can possibly be. The proceedings of the various Legislative Councils and the Indian National Congress and the Muslim League bear ample testimony to the solicitude of the educated Indians for the welfare of the masses and their acquaintance with their wants and wishes. The franchise should be broadened and extended directly to the people, Mahomadans or Hindus wherever they are in a minority, being given proper and adequate representations having regard to their numerical strength and position.

(3) The total number of the members of the Supreme Council should not be less than 150 and of the Provincial Councils not less than 100 for the major provinces and not less than 60 to 70 for the minor provinces.

(4) The budget should be passed in the shape of money bills, fiscal autonomy being conceded to India.

(5) The Imperial Legislative Council should have power to legislate on all matters and to discuss and pass resolutions relating to all matters of Indian administration, and the Provincial Councils should have similar powers with regard to provincial administration, save and except that the direction of military affairs, of foreign relations declarations of war, the making of peace and the entering into treaties other than commercial should be vested in the Government of India. As a safeguard the Governor-General-in-Council, as the case may be should have the right of veto, but subject to certain conditions and limitations.

(6) The Council of the Secretary of State should be abolished. The Secretary of State should, as far as possible hold in relation to the Government of India, a position similar to that which the Secretary of State for the Colonies holds in relation to the Colonies. The Secretary of State should be assisted by two permanent Under Secretaries, one of whom should be an Indian. The salaries of the Secretary and the Under Secretaries should be placed on the British Estimates.

(7) In any scheme of Imperial Federation, India should be given, through her chosen representatives, a place similar to that of the Self-Governing Dominions.

(8) The Provincial Governments should be made autonomous as stated in the Government of India's despatch of the 25th August, 1911.

(9) The United Provinces, as well as the other major provinces, should have a Governor brought from the United Kingdom with an Executive Council.

(10) A full measure of local Self-Government should be immediately granted.

(11) The right to carry arms should be granted to Indians on the same condition as to Europeans.

(12) Indians should be allowed to enlist as volunteers and units of a territorial army to be established in India.

(13) Commissions in the army should be given to the Indian youths under conditions similar to those applicable to Europeans.

SIGNATORIES

Maharaja Manindra Chandra Nandi of Kasimbazar, Mr. D. E. Wacha, Mr. Bhupendranath Basu, Mr. Vishnu Dutta Shukul, Pandit Madan Mohan Malaviya, Mr. K. V. Rangaswamy Iyanger, Mr. Mazhar ul Haque, Mr. V. S. Srinivasa Sastri, Dr. Tej Bahadur Sapru, Mr. Ibrahim Rahimtullah, Mr. B. Narasimeswara Sarma, Mr. Mir Asad Ali, Mr. Kamini Kumar Chanda, Mr. Krishna Sahay, Mr. R. N. Bharja Deo of Kanika, Mr. M. B. Dadabhoy, Mr. Sita Nath Roy, Mr. Mahomed Ali Mahomed and Mr. M. A. Jinnah.

APPENDIX F

REPORT OF THE BRITISH COMMITTEE FOR 1915-1916.

The following report of the year 1915-1916 *has been issued by the British Committee of the Indian National Congress:—*

This year has essentially been one of anxious preparation. Both in India and in England, it has been fully recognised that, after the war, India should receive her due share of self-government, and should take, within the British Empire, a place worthy of her ancient civilisation and the high ideals of her people. Accordingly, during this year steady preparation has been carried on by Congress workers both in India and in England, so that, when peace is assured proposals may be placed before Parliament for such constitutional reforms as will satisfy the Indian people, and be in conformity with British principles of freedom and progress.

From the nature of things, this work of preparation is necessarily carried on partly in India and partly in England. It is for India herself to mature a scheme of reform suited to her special requirements; it is in England, as the seat of power, that arrangements have to be made for the due hearing of her case. Congress workers, in the East and in the West, have been diligent in the performance of this double duty.

WORK IN INDIA

First, as regards work in India. By Resolution XIX of the last Congress, under the heading of "Self-government," the All-India Congress Committee was authorised to frame a scheme of reform, having regard to the principles embodied in the Resolution; and, further, it was authorised to confer with a Committee of the All-India Moslem League, and to take such further measures as may be necessary. The action accords with the advice of Sir S. P. Sinha, the President of the Congress who pointed out that for the general welfare, we need "a reasoned ideal of India's future, such as will satisfy the aspirations and ambitions of the rising generation of India, and at the same time will meet with the approval of those to whom India's destinies are committed." The representatives of the Congress and the Moslem League have met in conference as contemplated by Resolution XIX, and the final result of their deliberation is now awaited. There can be no doubt that the representations of a united India will receive from the British people the attention demanded by its importance for the welfare of the Empire.

Steps having thus been taken in India to formulate the wishes of the Indian people, we have to consider the action required from friends in England. At the proper time, when peace is within sight, it is proposed that the Indian scheme of reform shall be brought to England by a deputation of the most trusted Indian leaders; and the practical question is, how should this deputation proceed, so that the case may be brought effectively before the Home Government, the Imperial Parliament, and the British public, with a view to a settlement beneficial alike to India and the world?

ACTION IN ENGLAND

Naturally the first approach will be made to the Home Government. In the Government as now constituted, both the great parties in the State are united; and, fortunately, even before the Coalition, the leaders on both sides pledged themselves, by declarations in Parliament, to a generous policy to India, promising her a worthy place in our free Empire, as a partner, and not as a dependant. Mr. Charles Roberts gave this assurance, speaking for the Secretary of State, and Mr. H. W. Forster was authorised by Mr. Bonar Law to say how closely the opposition associated itself with the sentiments expressed on behalf of the Government. Further-more, the King-Emperor has repeatedly insisted on sympathy as the keynote in dealing with Indian aspirations. There is, therefore, every reason to expect that India's representations will be received by His Majesty's Government with careful and sympathetic attention, and that the Secretary of State for India will receive the Deputation in friendly conference, so that there may be a free interchange of views, having for its object to meet the reasonable wishes of all concerned. Proceeding on these lines, the way seems open for the Government, in consultation with India's representatives, to prepare and place before Parliament proposals for such constitutional reforms as will satisfy the Indian people, and be in conformity with British principles of freedom and progress.

From the above considerations there seems reason to hope that a satisfactory scheme of reform may be framed by agreement. At the same time we must not shut our eyes to the fact that the Government may not see its way to grant all that the Indian representatives consider essential. Doubtless offers will be made, but in the Indian view these may not be sufficient. What under the circumstances, is the wise course to pursue ? How can it best be arranged to secure what the Government is willing to give, and at the same time to provide means of progressive improvement in the future ? The suggestion is that, if the Government proposals do not come up to India's expectations as formulated in the scheme brought by the Deputation, the Government offer should be considered, with a view to acceptance as an instalment, the points of difference being reserved for submission to Parliament, on the report of a Parliamentary Committee, with a view to further legislation.

It will be for India's representatives to consider whether they should not ask for a revival by statute of the periodical Parliamentary enquiries which, up to 1858, originated all the most notable improvements in the condition of India. The recent action of the Joint-Committee of both the Houses, in dealing with the India Consolidation Bill on sound judicial lines, must give India confidence that such Parliamentary Committees will give a fair hearing to Indian claims, so that, from time to time, progress may be made in constituting India a free and prosperous partner in the British Empire.

THE ESSENTIAL PRINCIPLE

The essential principle of self-government was declared by Lord Hardinge, when he indicated the safe path of Indian reforms, founded on Provincial autonomy, with a persistent, if gradual, transfer of authority from the official body to the representatives of the people. This, we trust, will be the direction in which Parliament will proceed. But in order that the Viceroy may be in a position to carry out the orders of the Home Government, it is absolutely necessary that his hands should be strengthened. At present the Viceroy is not master in his own household, the existing practice, giving to the permanent officials an exceptional position of authority in his Executive Council. The constitution of that Council is determined by the India Act of 1861 (24 and 25 Victoria, c. 67), clause 3 providing that three out of five ordinary members of that Council are to be persons who have been at least ten years in the service in India of the Crown; and this provision has been interpreted for the sole benefit of the Covenanted Civil Service; so that the Viceroy's "Cabinet" is unduly dominated by a group of permanent officials, who enter the Executive Council automatically, imbued with the spirit of the great centralised departments, over which they have been accustomed to preside. Under this system a Viceroy, fresh from England, and unfamilar with the routine of Indian administration, is not in a position to give effect to the policy prescribed for him by Parliament and the Crown.

The remedy is a simple one; for the time has come to amend clause 3 of the India Act of 1861, by providing that the Viceroy, with the approval of the Secretary of State shall have power to nominate the members of his own Executive Council from among men, British Indian, of ripe experience in public affairs, their term of office ending with that of the Viceroy. Such amendment will only be an extension of the beneficial practice which, for the last eighty years, has given to India the services of such men of mark as Lord Macaulay, Mr. James Wilson, Sir Charles Trevelyan, Sir Sumner Maine, Lord Hobhouse, Sir Courtenay Ilbert, and Sir Guy Wilson. In more recent times the solidarity of the Empire has been strengthened by the addition of distinguished Indians ; Sir S.P. Sinha, Sir Ali Imam, and Sir Sankaran Nair. It appears that this reform is a condition precedent to all other reforms. The principle involved is one that has been accepted by all civilised Governments. In England especially, it has been the settled rule that a member of the permanent Civil Service must be content to close his official career as the trusted and authoritative head of his department, without aspiring to political governance. The task of a British Premier would be an impossible one if he was not free to choose the members of his Cabinet from among his political supporters, and was compelled to accept as his colleagues the permanent chiefs of the administrative departments. (*India*).

APPENDIX G

THE IMPERIAL WAR CONFERENCE

A number of resolutions passed by the Imperial War Conference have been published in the Press. Among them are the following:—

THE REPRESENTATION OF INDIA

That the Imperial War Conference desires to place on record its view that the resolution of the Imperial Conference of April 20, 1907, should be modified to permit of India being fully represented at all future Imperial Conferences, and that the necessary steps should be taken to secure the assent of the various Governments in order that the next Imperial Conference may be summoned and constituted accordingly.

INDIA AND THE DOMINIONS

That the Imperial War Conference, having examined the memorandum on the position Indians in the self-governing Dominions presented by the Indian representatives to the Conference, accepts the principle of reciprocity of treatment between India and the Dominions, and recommends the memorandum to the favourable consideration of the Governments concerned.

IMPERIAL DEFENCE

That the Admiralty be requested to work out immediately at the conclusion of the war what they consider the most effective scheme of naval defence for the Empire for the consideration of the several Governments summoned to this conference, with such recommendations as the Admiralty consider necessary in that respect for the Empire's future security.

That this Conference, in view of the experience of the present war, calls attention to the importance of developing an adequate capacity of production of naval and military material, munitions, and supplies in all important parts of the Empire (including the countries bordering on the Pacific and Indian Oceans), where such facilities do not presently exist, and affirms the importance of close co-operation between India, the Dominions and the United Kingdom with this object in view.

That this Conference, recognising the importance of assimilating as far as possible the military stores and equipment of the Imperial Forces throughout the Empire, recommends that an expert Committee, representative of the military authorities of the United Kingdom, the Dominions, and India, be appointed as early as possible to consider the various patterns in use with a view to selecting standard patterns for general adoption, as far as the special circumstances of each country admit.

This Conference is of opinion that it is desirable that the ordinance personnel of the military organisations of the Empire should, as far as possible, be trained on the same methods and according to the same principles and that to secure this end selected officers of the ordinance service from all parts of the Empire should be attached for adequate periods to the Imperial Ordinance Department.

CONSTITUTIONAL REFORM

The Imperial War Conference is of opinion that the readjustment of the constitutional relations of the component parts of the Empire is too important and intricate a subject to be dealt with during the war, and that it should form the subject of a special Imperial Conference to be summoned as soon as possible after the cessation of hostilities.

It deems it its duty, however, to place on record its view that any just readjustment, while thoroughly preserving all existing powers of self-government and complete control of domestic affairs, should be based upon a full recognition of the Dominions as autonomous nations of an Imperial Commonwealth, and of India as an important portion of the same, should recognise the right of the Dominions and India to an adequate share in foreign policy and in foreign relations, and should provide effective arrangements for continuous consultation in all important matters of common Imperial concern, and for such necessary concerted action, founded on consultation, as the several Governments may determine.

TRADE AND COMMERCE

The time has arrived when all possible encouragement should be given to the development of Imperial resources, and especially to making the Empire independent of other countries in respect of food supplies, raw materials, and essential industries. With these objects in view, this Conference express itself in favour of :—(1) The principle that each part of the Empire, having regard to the interests of our Allies, shall give specially favourable treatment and facilities to the produce and manufactures of other parts of the Empire. (2) Arrangements by which intending emigrants from the United Kingdom may be induced to settle in countries under the British flag.

FOOD SUPPLY AND MANUFACTURES

Having regard to the experience obtained in the present war, this Conference records its opinion that the safety of the Empire and the necessary development of its component parts require prompt and attentive consideration, as well as concerted action, with regard to the following matters :—(1) The production of an adequate food supply and arrangements for its transportation when and where required, under any conditions that may reasonably be anticipated. (2) The control of natural resources available within the Empire, especially those that are of an essential character for necessary national purposes, whether in peace or in war. (3) The economical utilisation of such natural resources through processes of manufacture carried on within the Empire.

The Conference commends to the consideration of the Governments summoned thereto the enactment of such legislation as may assist this purpose.

MINERAL RESOURCES

That it is desirable to establish in London an Imperial Mineral Resources Bureau, upon which should be represented Great Britain, the Dominions, India, and other parts of the Empire. The bureau should be charged with the duties of collection of information from the appropriate departments of the Governments concerned and other sources regarding the mineral resources and the metal requirements of the Empire, and of advising from time to time what action, if any may appear desirable to enable such resources to be developed and made available to meet the metal requirements of the Empire.

That the Conference recommends that His Majesty's Government should, while having due regard to existing institutions, take immediate action for the purpose of establishing such a bureau, and should as soon as possible submit a scheme for the consideration of the other Governments summoned to the Conference.

TRADE COMMISSIONERS FOR THE EMPIRE

That the Imperial War Conference welcomes the proposed increase of the Board of Trade service of Trade Commissioners and its extension throughout the British Empire in accordance with the recommendations of the Dominions Royal Commission and recommends that the Governments concerned should co-operate so as to make that service as useful as possible to the Empire as a whole, especially for the promotion of inter-Imperial trade.

NATURALISATION

The Conference recognise the desirability and importance of securing uniformity of policy and action throughout the Empire with regard to naturalisation.

THE DOUBLE INCOME TAX

The present system of Double Income Taxation within the Empire calls for review in relation :—(1) To firms in the United Kingdom doing business with the overseas

Dominions, India, and the Colonies; (2) To private individuals resident in the United Kingdom who have capital invested elsewhere in the Empire, or who depend upon remittances from elsewhere within the Empire; and (3) To its influence on the investment of capital in the United Kingdom, the Dominions, and India, and to the effect of any change on the position of British capital invested abroad. The Conference, therefore, urges that this matter should be taken in hand immediately after the conclusion of the war, and that an amendment of the law should be made which will remedy the present unsatisfactory position.

It is resolved that the proposals set forth in the memorandum submitted by the Home office be commended to the consideration of the respective Government summoned to the Conference.

The members of the Conference representing India and the Overseas Dominions desire before they separate to convey to the Secretary of State for the Colonies their earnest and sincere appreciation of his labours in preparing for, and presiding over, the Conference.

They desire also to put on record their deep sense of gratitude for the many courtesies which they have received from the Prime Minister and the other Members of His Majesty's Government, as well as for the generous hospitality which has been extended to them by the Government and the people of United Kingdom.

APPENDIX H

INDIA, TO-DAY AND TO-MORROW

Mr. S. K. Ratcliffe writes:—

We stand upon the threshold of momentous changes in India. The Government as proclaimed it, and what is even more significant, official India is accepting the logic of events. In political thought, no less than in practice, the war is overturning the world; and the completeness of the revolution is nowhere more strikingly illustrated than in the field of Imperial Government. The war had not been going on for half a year when the most thorough going stand patters in our midst were repeating as a common place that peace would bring with it a new Imperial Commonwealth in which India would be, no longer a dependant, but a partner.

To those whose contact with India goes back over a decade or more this is one of the startling, the most hopeful, facts of the world situation. One recalls, for example, the Curzonian regime, with its resonant insistant upon administrative rigour, its confident assumption that India must not, and would not be subject to constitutional change. The India of Lord Curzon's conception called, not for political reform, but for executive mastery, and when the hand of the master was withdrawn the hierarchy looked for the enjoyment of its reinforced authority under less exigent viceregal direction.

MORLEY, THE LIBERATOR

The epoch of movements dates, in India as elsewhere, from the great election of 1906. Mr. John Morley went to the India office, and his Councils Act came as the fitting second stage in that scheme of Imperial statemanship which made a brilliant beginning with Campbell-Bannerman's constitution for South Africa. It may be said that the Morely reforms were small in content; and so, regarded from our standpoint to-day, they were. But no Liberal of lower power and prestige could have carried them in 1909, when desperate anarchic outrages were furnishing the Lords and the bureaucracy with an effective argument against concession. Lord Morley's splendid service to India and the Empire can be stated in a sentence. He broke the hard ring of bureaucratic privilege; established the principle of direct election, and of non-official majorities in the Indian legislatures; appointed the first Indian Cabinet Ministers at Simla and the first Indian councillors in Whitehall, while, moreover he carried the whole discussion of Indian affairs into a fresh atmosphere of fine and generous debate.

True, the bureaucracy was to some extent successful in whittling down the reforms. Indian official regulations reduced the influence of the new bodies, and Anglo-India generally said to the party of reform: "Now you have got your councils, be satisfied; show what you can do with them, and above all, help us to stamp out your revolutionaries, and don't ask for anything more." The hope of official India, manifestly, was that the changes would suffice for at least a generation, that in a word, Lord Morley in Indian history could be "Finality John," precisely as Lord John Russell was made to stand in the England of the first reform Act. Without the war that hope must have proved foolish; in 1914 it melted swiftly away.

RESPONSIBLE PARTNERSHIP

During the past three months one statement of liberal policy after another has revealed the Governments' purpose. Both Mr. Montagu and his Under Secretary (Lord Islington) have spoken, and the Viceroy, addressing the Legislative Council in August sketched in broad outline the proposals upon which the Home and Indian Governments are working, in advance of the Secretary of State's visit, Lord Chelmsford indicated three lines of advance:

1. Liberal constitution of the legislative councils, with greatly extended powers of control.
2. Increased opportunity for qualified Indians in the higher posts of the administration.
3. Decentralisation and local Self-Government, with elective village and urban councils as the basis of system of provincial Autonomy.

The one essential principle to be established is responsibility. The one blunder that would imperil the scheme is the refusal, for any reason or through any fear, of an adequate measure of responsibility to Indian representatives and legislative bodies. Here is, of course, an almost irresistible temptation to an all-powerful Government having behind it an unbroken tradition of authority. There is something to be said for autocracy; there is as the English-speaking world believes, everything to be said, when a certain stage have been reached, for self-Government. But the system for which there is nothing at all to be said is a system possessing the appearance of autonomy with none of its reality.

SELF-GOVERNMENT

Now the main and governing fact of the problem as Mr. Asquith used to say, is that in the Imperial Commonwealth of to-morrow there must be room for a self-governing and responsible India. This is the place which the greatness of India involves, which the extraordinary loyalty of India has earned. The wheel, as everyone who follows the Indian Press can see, has come full circle. There has been nothing like the consensus with which to-day the organs of Anglo-Indian or semi-official opinion, such as the powerful "Times of India," declaring that the immediate goal of all parties is a self-governing India in the Empire standing before the world as a great confederation of democratic peoples.

But, needless to say, there survives still a party of irreconcilables, who are now becoming extremely local in a section of the Anglo-Indian Press. They are unhappily, setting out to "crab" the Secretary of State's visit, and they are using the release of Mrs. Besant as the occasion of an attack upon the policy of advance and reconciliation. They will fail, for democratic England is with the Government in its new purposes; but Mr. Montagu and the Viceroy must be fortified to meet them.

The opportunity calls for a splendid decision and a fine gesture and one is convinced that, after the experience of these years the authorities of Delhi understand this as fully as it is understood in London and throughout England. If the war has taught us anything, said that brilliant and beloved soldier-professor, Tom Kettle, killed a year ago on the Somme, it has taught us that the great thing must be done in a great way. That is true in the affairs of all peoples. It is supremely true in relation to Britain and India.—(*Daily News*).

INDEX.

E

Q

R